Linguistic Justice at the International Criminal Tribunal for the Former Yugoslavia

"This book is about the first tribunal of its kind to be established since the tribunals that tried the war criminals of World War Two. It has broad implications for both academics and practitioners in the humanities and social sciences in a wide range of fields extending beyond law and language to every area of human relations. Dr Fidahić has addressed both legal and linguistic fields, and, at the same time, has done an admirable job summarizing complex historical and practical issues. He has used his first-hand experiences and academic training to produce a work of important insight into the workings of the United Nations and the need to learn from these insights."
—Victor A. Friedman
Andrew W. Mellon Distinguished Service Professor Emeritus in the Humanities, University of Chicago; Honorary Associate, La Trobe University, Australia

"This is a meticulous, comprehensive study, a real eye-opener on how dysfunctional the UN is. A vast bureaucratic apparatus failed to provide appropriate interpretation and translation services for witnesses and victims of ethnic atrocity crimes. Nor has it promoted reconciliation between Serbs, Croats, and Bosnians. The book explains how judicial practice can be undermined. Besmir Fidahić has performed a service that the UN should learn from."
—Robert Phillipson
Professor, Copenhagen Business School, Denmark

"For international (criminal) lawyers, the work and jurisprudence of the ICTY is indispensable. While the ICTY's decisions and related primary and secondary sources are accessible via mostly English and French texts, those legal researchers with a desire for a deeper understanding of the original testimony in proper context, inevitably encounter various linguistic barriers. Besmir Fidahić's book provides the solution. The book is first and foremost a resource: it is a compilation of materials (including primary sources) made more accessible by the author. This is not yet another book on the ICTY, its cases and institutional and political background, but rather concerns an aspect that is very inaccessible for most international criminal lawyers and others interested in the work of the ICTY. The author should thus be commended for the terse and very clear explanation of the sometimes dry and inaccessible primary data and sources. Fidahić's book is required reading for all international (criminal) lawyers interested in a proper understanding of the legal, cultural and historical legacies of the ICTY; legacies that can only be appreciated with the help of a proper understanding of the role of language and translation at the ICTY."
—Gerhard Kemp
Professor of International and Transnational Criminal Justice, University of Derby, UK

Linguistic Justice at the International Criminal Tribunal for the Former Yugoslavia

By

Besmir Fidahić

Cambridge
Scholars
Publishing

Linguistic Justice at the International Criminal Tribunal
for the Former Yugoslavia

By Besmir Fidahić

This book first published 2021

Cambridge Scholars Publishing

Lady Stephenson Library, Newcastle upon Tyne, NE6 2PA, UK

British Library Cataloguing in Publication Data
A catalogue record for this book is available from the British Library

ISBN (10): 1-5275-6155-0
ISBN (13): 978-1-5275-6155-7

My first engagement with the ICTY was early in 1996 when the mass graves containing the bodies of Srebrenica men and boys were discovered. I was working at the mass graves sites, interpreting for the spokesperson. I felt a strong connection with the Srebrenica cause from the very beginning of my engagement at the ICTY and have stayed with the ICTY Srebrenica Team ever since, mainly because of their inspiring legal and investigatory leadership. No matter what other investigation team I was assigned to, I made sure to make time whenever the ICTY Srebrenica Team needed me.

In the late 2010s, I was called by the ICTY Srebrenica Team to interpret for the drivers who had taken the Srebrenica men and boys to the execution site and who were now appearing as witnesses for the prosecution. One of the drivers said he took a liking to a small boy aged about 13-14. He took him aside and put him on the front seat with him in the truck. "Together" they transported many other Srebrenica men and boys from detention locations to the execution site where they were all killed. Their journey lasted all day and all night and consisted of about 10-12 different rounds. They passed the time by talking and singing together. The driver described this boy as beautiful, happy, engaging, and chatty.

Once the transports and executions were completed, the driver found the boy sleeping on the front seat. He sneaked off and got into contact with the Main Staff Office of the Army of Republika Srpska Drina Corps. There he woke up the Army of Republika Srpska Drina Corps Duty Officer, a Major. This Duty Officer got into a car and drove to the location of the driver's truck. He pulled the sleeping boy out and shot him dead in the bushes. He then returned to the headquarters. The driver said he didn't know what else to do.

I am dedicating this book to the children of all those in Bosnia and Herzegovina who "didn't know what else to do."

TABLE OF CONTENTS

List of Tables

LIST OF APPENDICES

NOTE ON TOPIC AND SOURCES

This study only has time, space, and patience to dedicate to the effects of Serbian nationalism in B&H. It does not have ample time, space, or patience to delve into the minutest details of the many conflicts between the Croatians and the Serbians throughout the First and Second Yugoslavias.

As to documentary sources, I used the UN Official Document System. Unfortunately, it proved imperfect. When I was checking links, at the end of the project, I discovered the links to documents from the system had expired. Apparently, as UN authorities explained, one must have a username and password to prevent such expiry and one cannot get a username and password unless one is a UN staff member on a fulltime contract. I went back and rewrote the footnotes linking to documents on the Official Document System to include the searchable symbol (for example, A/RES/71), thus enabling researchers to find the referenced documents on their own. The same goes for vacancies: they no longer exist at UN sites, so I linked them to a third party, UNJobs.org, a Bhutan-based association that pioneered the aggregation of vacancy announcements from multiple UN System organizations in 2000.

As to the ICTY sources, I used the official site of the ICTY Court Records and the official ICTY site. This proved enabling because it prevented me from unintentionally discussing classified documents I remembered from my work. Unfortunately, the ICTY videos were posted in such a botched way that it impacted the entire visual presentation of my study: those that could have been uploaded as a single file have been broken down into at least two and at most nine different video segments (*Popović et al.*, trial judgment, 01:26:12) regardless of their duration. Links to these videos could not have been left in the original form because they would have significantly added to the length of the entire study as some of them were two or three lines long. I had to resort to shortening them. This proved a success: my study looks much cleaner and neater, and it is much shorter than if I posted the original links. However, when I was checking links before submitting a final version of my book to the publisher, I discovered most of these shortened links do not work, either. This is the reason why all the ICTY Court Records sources have the ERN number after them; the reader can make a username on that site and check them. The links to other ICTY documents and videos are linked to the individual page where the accused to which they refer is first mentioned: "ICTY, Cases, *Trial name*, T. transcript page/Name and year of the document: link."

Discussion of the ICTY and its language-related rules and regulations and the case law, UN rules and regulations relating to language staff, and ICTY language arrangements and services was informed both by Annual Reports (ARs) produced by the UN and the ICTY, and inspection reports made by the UN System's Joint Inspection Unit (JIU), the UN Office of Internal Oversight Services (UN OIOS), and the UN Board of Auditors (UN BoA). The ICTY ARs could not have been used alone to give a realistic picture of the ICTY and its language services. However, financial and audit reports are straightforward because they mostly deal with the organizational and financial realities of the organization concerned and are geared toward straightening out that organization's shortcomings.

Finally, my colleagues from the ICTY and the International Association of Conference Translators (AITC) have been consulted for their understanding of practices and experiences in translation, interpreting, and transcription, and overall UN policies and practices relating to language professionals across the UN System. These discussions were conducted over email, were semi-structured, and followed the basic principles of qualitative research where a problem was discussed from the perspectives of practitioners whom it involved. Permissions to quote were obtained from all participants in the research (on file with the author). It is hoped that these three groups – internal, external, and freelancer sources – will provide a balanced, holistic analysis of the ICTY's language services.

The UN does not sing "Kumbaya" in all its languages looking up to the skies with a faint smile on its face all day long. The UN is the most important organization in the world and has a final say on everything that goes internationally on the planet Earth and in the entire known universe. We are all a part of human family and this is why it is important to involve as many people in the UN's work as possible. We have a duty to react to the UN's work results so that the UN can receive feedback, fix, if needed, and, ultimately, deliver its services properly and in time to its audiences. Otherwise, the UN will turn into an out-of-tune, self-singing, and audienceless "Kumbaya" singer *cum* silent and powerless collector of world unhappiness and misery. So, I thank you for reading and informing yourself about the following small snippet of the UN's work, kind reader. I hate to put you on the spot, but some things you will read here happened because you did not react. But, now that you have been informed, as French would say: *á toi*!

INTRODUCTION

MAY WE HAVE THE APPEARANCES, PLEASE

This book is a result of years of research and 25 years of practical experience as a legal translator, interpreter, and editor in the conflict-, post-conflict-, humanitarian-, development-, and international criminal tribunals'-context. It deals with the delivery of linguistic justice at the International Tribunal for the Prosecution of Persons Responsible for Serious Violations of International Humanitarian Law Committed in the Territory of the Former Yugoslavia since 1991 – commonly known as the International Criminal Tribunal for the Former Yugoslavia (ICTY). The ICTY was an *ad hoc* tribunal established for specific purposes by the United Nations (UN) Security Council Resolution 827 on 25 May 1993 as an impermanent UN body to prosecute perpetrators of serious crimes committed during the wars in the former Yugoslavia which were waged in Croatia, Bosnia and Herzegovina (B&H), and Kosovo between 1991 and 1999. The ICTY was the first international criminal tribunal to emerge after the closure of the International Military Tribunal at Nuremberg (IMT) in 1946 and the International Military Tribunal for the Far East at Tokyo (IMTFE) in 1948.

The UN presents the main venue where the prevention of war and protection of human rights are discussed and is the only institution that can set up an international criminal tribunal with limited or universal jurisdiction. The ICTY was established under the auspices of the UN and falls under the Subsidiary Organs of the UN Security Council. However, the UN mission, management, powers, and programs are plagued by a set of problems revolving around the absence of clear leadership, the flux created by the power of veto in the hands of the UN Security Council permanent members, and the lack of clear mandates governing the work performed by UN entities which makes it plausible to question how adapted the UN administration was for such a task as establishing an international criminal tribunal.

Heads of states, politicians, former staff, and the media have never stopped criticizing UN efficiency when it comes to maintaining international peace and security, hinting at flaws in its internal structure and a sheer pointlessness to its existence. As to scholars, Weiss word-played on the self-appointed UN's attributes and likened the UN membership structure and its bureaucracy to a feudal kingdom and dysfunctional family. Weiss reminds the UN is the state-centric organization and sees continuity in the relationship between the UN System organizations and the world policies. Weiss criticizes UN administration for its bureaucracy and the lack of central authority with the power to make decisions on organizational mandates and resource allocation. He warns that all this leads to a situation in which many UN entities have overlapping goals and compete against each other for patronage, putting more emphasis on protecting their turf than service delivery to their audiences.[1]

In response to criticism, the UN engages in series of reforms. But it seems the mainstream ignores the fact that the UN administration has been involved in active reforms since its inception in 1946. The most recent – Kofi Annan's 1998 staff reforms – turned the UN into a self-protective bureaucratic machine run by managers. Annan's reforms centralized all actions in the UN around a single manager with subordinate managers merely providing some checks and balances.[2] Unfortunately, this approach to management could be described as the main contributor to the creation of a self-protective managerial environment where top managers refrain from acting against their subordinate managers because misconduct of their subordinates implies their own misconduct. Warah documented just a few of the many post-1998 Annan reforms sex scandals, corruption scandals, and kickback scandals, as well as the poor protection of the whistleblowers who revealed them.[3]

Amidst all this, five permanent members of the UN Security Council have a free run of the UN and the world. Indeed, the 255 vetoes (14 by China, 16 by France, 29 by the UK, 81 by the USA, and

---

[1] Weiss, Thomas G. (2012), What's wrong with the UN and how to fix it. Polity Press: Cambridge.
[2] UN, Secretary-Generals' Bulletin: Building the future (ST/SGB/1998/6) (1998).
[3] Warah, Rasna (2016), UNsilenced: unmasking the United Nations' culture of cover-ups, corruption and impunity. AuthorHouse: UK.

115 by the USSR/Russia) passed by the UN Security Council permanent members between 1946 and 2020 affected the functioning of the world in many ways.[4] They stretched the limits of language, starting to describe the pressing problems that countries and their peoples were facing as mere "questions" and "situations", but offering no solutions or answers. The UN's verbosity turned all those "questions" and "situations" into veritable political buzzwords for every generation from 1946 onwards: the 1946 Spanish question, the 1947 Greek question, the 1954, 1956, 1963, 1964, 1966, 1976, 1980, 2001, 2002, 2003, 2004, 2006, 2011 Palestinian question, the 1974, 1977, 1981, 1986, 1987, 1988 South Africa question, the 1982 Falkland Islands question, the 1980 Iran hostages question, the 1963, 1970, 1971, 1972, 1973 Southern Rhodesia question, the 1957, 1962, 1971 India-Pakistan question, the 1974 Cyprus "situation" – where two NATO Allies, Greece and Turkey – fought each other, etc.

Once tabled, all these "questions" and "situations" put international peace and security and international human rights in a state of flux where one permanent member of the UN Security Council would rise to take charge of the issue and others would criticize. Eventually, after a lot of back and forth, all permanent members of the UN Security Council would join the efforts of the veto-issuing country and reach a collective understanding on the issue with the emphasis on what works best for their own countries, dependent territories, and dominions. After major media outlets announced that the "breakout of the Third World War has been prevented," humanity would let out a deep sigh of relief. In the meantime, the situation in the country over which the permanent members of the UN Security Council disagreed in the first place would remain largely unchanged.

Enter the ICTY in 1993, right after the end of the Cold War and in the afterglow of Western triumphalism.

There had been pressure for the establishment of a permanent international criminal tribunal, one that could investigate and judge all equally, for such a long time that, once something remotely resembling it was set up, the international community either did not know what to make of it or they found

[4] UN, Security Council veto list: https://bit.ly/2xC8jNo.

solace in parroting the similar arguments that prevented the establishment of an international criminal tribunal right after the IMT and IMTFE closed their doors. The media in the five permanent members of the UN Security Council described the ICTY as an innovative method of intervention in government affairs or an unlucky project incapable of solving an armed conflict. Some claimed that the blending of international courts, judges, and legal systems had never worked before and that there was a lack of international cooperation with the ICTY, some considered it the impossible new Nuremberg, some hoped it would finally put a stop to inhumane acts and widespread massacres, and some saw the establishment of the ICTY as a new milestone in international criminal justice, hailing it as an unprecedented move.

The UN administration may have been ill adapted for the task of establishing an international criminal tribunal, but the ICTY staff was not. The ICTY was the first of its kind: an international, independent, non-military tribunal. Once the first investigators, the finders and collectors of facts, went into active warfare and soon returned from the former Yugoslavia, things started moving so quickly that the fact the ICTY was established in such a short time could freely be described as a triumph of UN administration. Nevertheless, the ICTY still had some very big legal and mindset lacunae to fill.

Right after the First World War, a special tribunal foreseen by the Treaty of Versailles never materialized due to political reasons: American President Woodrow Wilson insisted that, in order to achieve the "honorable peace" with Germany, Kaiser Wilhelm II must abdicate, because his punishment would only destabilize peace further. So, Kaiser Wilhelm II only abdicated and spent the rest of his life in the Netherlands. The Allied and Associated Powers allowed Germany to prosecute a limited number of war criminals at a local Supreme Court in Leipzig. The Commission on the Responsibilities of the Authors of War and on Enforcement of Penalties which was established at the Preliminary Peace Conference at Paris in 1919 as an investigative body identified 895 individuals believed to have committed war crimes, but only 12 military officers were convicted, and the maximum sentence imposed was three years. These 12 military officers were cheered by the crowds attending the courtroom trials and outside the courtrooms and instead of being recognized and punished as war criminals were celebrated as national heroes and martyrs to foreign oppression.[5]

The Treaty of Sèvres, Article 143 authorized the first great ethnic cleansing of the twentieth-century in the shape of a population exchange between Turkey and Greece in 1923. The Treaty – imposed by the Allies of the First World War on the Ottoman Empire – also provided for Turkey's surrender of persons accused of having committed acts contrary to the laws and customs of war. However, the Allies changed their minds due to the political considerations. The Ottoman Empire ceased to exist, with the new national hero Mustafa Kemal Atatürk toppling the sultan and the sultanate, thereby establishing a brand-new country. Whereas the most notorious leaders (Enver Pasha, Talaat Pasha, and Djemal Pasha) fled to Germany and were never tried, several Istanbul-based leaders, including many regional leaders, were tried between 1919 and 1920. The momentum fell apart as the Greeks invaded Turkey and the nationalists took over, ending these trials.[6] Each of the three Pashas was killed by exiled Armenians while abroad.

The denazification process which the Allies started after the Second World War cannot be said to have been comprehensive or to have extended uniformly outside post-Nazi Germany. In France, for example, some domestic Nazi collaborators were left intact until the then French President Chirac purged them in 1995.[7] The US government is said to have attracted Nazi scientists to come to the USA and work on weapons development programs.[8] In the former Yugoslavia, the winning troops rounded up escaping Nazi remnants and domestic Nazi collaborators when they failed to surrender to the Allies in the border town Bleiburg and executed them *en masse* while escorting them back into the country. Those who remained in the country were encouraged to defect by a declaration of amnesty issued before the Bleiburg events and, once they did, they simply

---

[5] Bassiouni, Cherif (1994), Former Yugoslavia: Investigating Violations of International Humanitarian Law and Establishing an International Criminal Tribunal. Fordham International Law Journal, 18/4, p. 1194.

[6] Dadrian, Vahakn and Akçam, Taner (2012), Judgment at Istanbul: the Armenian genocide trials. Berghahn Books: New York.

[7] Carrier, Peter (2006), Holocaust monuments and national memory cultures in France and Germany since 1989. Berghahn Books: New York.

[8] NPR book reviews (2014), The secret operation to bring Nazi scientists to America: https://bit.ly/2RMGAjR.

put on the uniforms of the victorious Yugoslav People's Army. These and similar examples of disproportionality in the prosecution of Second World War crimes include the fact that suspected events and individuals on the side of the Allies were never even investigated.

The IMT and IMTFE trials unequivocally established that the gravest international crimes and crimes against peace would not go unpunished, that celebrating war criminals would no longer be acceptable, that human rights were inalienable, and that states' claims about the violation of their sovereignty and prerogatives had limits. The ICTY continued a tradition whereby the celebration of war criminals is objectionable and international crimes are not to be allowed go unpunished. The biggest achievement of this collaboration is the rejection of impunity. The legal successes of the ICTY paved the way for the establishment of many other international criminal tribunals, such as: the International Tribunal for the Prosecution of Persons Responsible for Genocide and Other Serious Violations of International Humanitarian Law Committed in the Territory of Rwanda and Rwandan Citizens Responsible for Genocide and Other Such Violations Committed in the Territory of Neighboring States, between 1 January 1994 and 31 December 1994 (ICTR), the Special Court for Sierra Leone (SCSL), the Extraordinary Chambers in the Courts of Cambodia (ECCC), the Special Tribunal for Lebanon (STL), and, most importantly, the first permanent international criminal tribunal, the International Criminal Court (ICC), which, after having been established in 2002, saw the beginning of its first trial in 2009. The ICTY was and remains the most successful of all. The ICTY closed its doors on 31 December 2017.

Substantially, the ICTY dealt with ethnic crimes committed with a cruelty unseen in Europe since the Nazis. Operationally, most ICTY cases adjudicated on crimes committed against Bosnian Muslims by the Serb(ian)s and/or Croat(ian)s in B&H. The official site of the ICTY, Cases lists 114 individuals who stood trial before this institution: 74 of them stood trials for crimes committed against Bosnian Muslims in B&H. Of these 114, 77 have been released, 18 have died, and 19 are still serving their sentence.[9] Unfortunately, most of those 77 who have been released have

[9] ICTY, Cases: https://bit.ly/2xBEH2E.

merely continued with their philosophies of hate, picking up right where they stopped before their arrest.

The Trial Chamber acquitted Vojislav Šešelj of three counts of crimes against humanity and six counts of violations of the laws or customs of war. On his release, Šešelj declared: "I exposed all sham testimonies and uncovered all fake documents [...] I escaped without punishment, but, in hindsight, I should have received at least a short sentence, so that the internal and external enemies of the Serbs would not be as furious."[10]

"There are still many innocent people in [the UN Detention Unit]," said Zoran Kupreškić. "A part of me is still there with Drago Josipović and the others. Please, continue to pray for all the innocent people to be released," said Mirjan Kupreškić. "We cannot forget our Serb friends who were brave enough to go there. They defended me," said Vlatko Kupreškić, a B&H Croat.[11]

After his early release, Dario Kordić exclaimed: "This is a victory for the Croat people. But this victory will not be complete until the last Croat hero from The Hague, from all the prisons in Croatia, Bosnia, Sweden, and Serbia touches the ground of our Croatian homeland."[12]

Continuing with the theme of homeland, Momčilo Krajišnik had this to say: "It is very important to preserve one's country, as a poet Petar Kočić once said: *Without a country, all is nothing*."[13]

After having been released early, Duško Tadić, the concentration camp warden, said: "I never stepped into the Omarska detention camp. I left Kozarac before the conflict. I was informed, by the Serb Army, that Kozarac was about to be bombed and I left."[14]

The executor of Srebrenica boys and men, Ljubomir Borovčanin said: "Once the defense reacted when it became obvious that witnesses were not credible, that they manipulated the facts, or

---

[10] Statement on release, Vojislav Šešelj: https://bit.ly/2K94H8a.
[11] Statement on release, Zoran Kupreškić, Mirjan Kupreškić, and Vlatko Kupreškić: https://bit.ly/3abF94U.
[12] Statement on release, Dario Kordić: https://bit.ly/2z3Mbf3.
[13] Statement on release, Momčilo Krajišnik: https://bit.ly/3anbBBC.
[14] Statement on release, Duško Tadić: https://bit.ly/2xqGXd7.

simply lied, the Chambers waited to respond until the end of the trial. Even when it was obvious that one was lying, one was not discredited right then and there."[15]

After what was seen as a heartfelt confession in court, Biljana Plavšić had this to say after having been released: "I sacrificed myself. I have done nothing wrong. I pleaded guilty to crimes against humanity, so I could make a deal on other charges. If I hadn't, the trial would have lasted three, three and-a-half years. Considering my age that wasn't an option."[16]

And, finally, after hearing his sentence, in the aftermath of Muslim fundamentalist attacks in Paris and Brussels in 2015, Radovan Karadžić, the chief executor of Serb crimes in B&H, switched premises on everyone one last time and exclaimed: "Even after Paris and Brussels, Europe still cannot see who we had to combat?"[17]

What went wrong?[18]

Legal professionals who worked at the Office of the Prosecutor (OTP) at the ICTY wrote the pages of the nascent international criminal law and moved mountains in the fields of impunity, rape, enslavement, etc. Their colleagues from defense put up a fair fight and fought them tooth and nail at every corner like lions although with inferior resources, staff numbers, and time constraints. The facts about crimes as found by the ICTY OTP and defense investigators, argued by these parties to the proceedings, corroborated by the victims and witnesses they called and by the documents they tendered, enabled the ICTY judges to establish undeniable legal truths about the events in the former Yugoslavia.

In order for this whole process to be complete, somebody needed to package all the ICTY legal truths in a timely, user

---

[15] Statement on release, Ljubomir Borovčanin: https://bit.ly/3biO4mp.
[16] Statement on release, Biljana Plavšić: https://bit.ly/3cnL6NC.
[17] Statement on release, Radovan Karadžić: https://bit.ly/3ev81bK.
[18] From the formal legal point, it was only in 2019 that the International Residual Mechanism for Criminal Tribunals, the legal successor to the ICTY, issued what could be called a gag order barring the released from discussing his case, contacting the victims, or being harmful to the public. ICTY, Cases, *Čorić*, Decision on motions related to Valentin Čorić's request for variation of early release conditions: https://bit.ly/2wZGfDo.

friendly, and comprehensive manner to the audiences in the former Yugoslavia in a language and manner they understood. As to them, the audiences in the former Yugoslavia had a job to engage in critical thinking, with an ultimate goal of, if not preventing the history from repeating itself, then at least refraining from the denialism which is rampant even 25 years after the war ended. And that job was supposed to be done by the representatives of the UN administration at the ICTY: the ICTY Registry. It was their job to make sure linguistic justice was served, as well.

The very concept of linguistic justice is not originally mine. Although the concept was around since Herder in one way or another, the term was coined by van Parijs who proposed the first normative theory of linguistic justice that rests on two normative pillars: an argument for English as a global *lingua franca*, and an argument that each language group be entitled to a policy of official multilingualism within its territory.[19]

I am also not the first scholar to discuss the concept of linguistic justice in the realm of international law. Mowbray brought the concept in and concluded there is no generally accepted theory explaining prevailing intuitions in terms of linguistic justice or a set of normative guidelines for realizing and institutionalizing linguistic justice in the realm of international law.[20]

I am the first scholar to discuss the concept of linguistic justice in the realm of international criminal law. I took it upon myself both to set some normative guidelines for the delivery of linguistic justice and to set the criteria for translation, interpretation, and transcription at international criminal tribunals. I am very much in a position to do that both owing to my education in languages and the law and, of course, my professional career spent entirely in the UN.

All international agreements and treaties on communication with defendants during criminal proceedings deem linguistic justice has been served if s/he has been communicated with in "his/her language". The same overarching criterion in the examination of

---

[19] Van Parijs, Phillipe (2011), Linguistic justice for Europe and for the world. Oxford University Press: Oxford.

[20] Mowbray, Jacqueline (2012), Linguistic justice: international law and language policy. Oxford University Press: Oxford.

linguistic justice has been used for this study, as well, as I go on to explain what this formula entails in the context where language is the tool in conflict.

The main purpose of language is communication and as soon as one enters an international criminal tribunal, one discovers that there are strict rules about communication revolving around the languages that may be used to address the court, when one can talk and write, what one can talk and write about, how long one can talk and write, to whom and how one can talk and write, and to what end. This entails examining the following lines of communication at judicial institutions:

- First line: the situation country towards the working institution
- Second line: the working institution towards the parties to the proceedings
- Third line: the working institution towards the language services providers
- Fourth line: the working institution towards the situation country.

Linguistically speaking, the ICTY legal professionals had big shoes to fill to prosecute speech atrocity crimes like their predecessors at IMT or, at least, to alert to the devastating effects of philosophy of hate against Bosnian Muslims which led to ethnic crimes and genocide. In that, they relied on the ICTY and its language services provider, the Conference and Language Services Section (CLSS). The CLSS, the main subject of this research, had to fulfil their legal obligations under ICTY laws to deliver specific documents in translation, and in time to enable proper defense. The CLSS also had to fulfill their legal obligation under ICTY laws to inform all ICTY language policies and other recruitment- and service delivery-related lacunae. Seeing that the UN had standing language services, that legal and language professionals had worked together since Hammurabi, and that they had colleagues working in police investigation contexts all over the world and in every language imaginable, the CLSS had their work cut out for them.

In Chapter 1, I am going to present a very brief history of language quarrels in the former Yugoslavia and point to a series of examples where language, and underlying ethnic and national identity, was used as a tool for a conflict. Then I am going to test whether linguistic justice has been served along the first line of communication with the judicial institution: the situation country towards the working institution. I will do this by examining whether the ICTY and the CLSS, the ICTY language services provider, were aware the language spoken in the former Yugoslavia was vested with ethnic and national affiliations and used as a tool in the conflict.

In Chapter 2, I am reviewing ICTY language laws, language-related case law, and procedural linguistic equality of arms between the ICTY prosecution and defense. Then I am going to examine whether linguistic justice has been served along the second line of communication with the judicial institution: the working institution towards the parties to the proceedings. I will do this by cataloguing the lacunae in the language laws and examining whether the CLSS, the ICTY language services provider, informed any language-related laws or took stock of ICTY language-related case law. As an example, I am introducing the concept of procedural linguistic equality of arms between the parties to the proceedings and testing whether it was served.

In Chapter 3, I am reviewing the history, the recruitment, the professional criteria and standards, and the training of all ICTY language professionals. Then I am going to test whether linguistic justice has been served along the third line of communication with the judicial institution: the working institution towards the language service providers. I will do this by examining the position in which the CLSS has put the ICTY language professionals within the realm of international criminal law and the ICTY laws.

In Chapter 4, I am examining whether linguistic justice has been served along the fourth line of communication with the judicial institution: the working institution towards the situation country. Did the ICTY deliver language services? I will show in practice first overall outputs in translation and interpretation as well as overall ethnicity- and nationality-based language service delivery. Then I will analyze the permanent court record: translation of evidence, exhibits, and court documents; court interpreting; and court transcripts.

Finally, I am concluding in the last chapter.

I am an insider to the UN and the ICTY practices, so most situations and documents you read in this book come from my practice, unless otherwise stated. As to the situations, I must say right at the beginning, genuinely hoping you have already bought the book, that the kind reader will not read any stories where names are dropped. The client is the king, even if a suspected or convicted war criminal.

My topic of research seems simple and easy enough, you say. Delivering translation on time is not that hard, you say. Tell us now, did the UN, the ICTY Registry, and the ICTY CLSS deliver, you ask? Well, there is much more to provision of language services at an international criminal tribunal adjudicating on ethnically motivated war crimes than submitting a translated document. And all those other things are exactly what my book is about. Let us imagine a Bosnian Muslim lady who came to seek justice from the ICTY after being gangraped by Croatian or Serbian soldiers who, as was the practice, kept her in the rape camp until abortion was no longer possible. She took a deep breath before embarking on this immense task, put on her headphones, looked at the panel of judges smiling at her, and heard the judges address her in the language of her rapists through interpreters. That is how the UN, the ICTY Registry, and the ICTY CLSS deliver its language services to victims. And there is more.

The first tenet of the international criminal law established in one of the IMT judgments is "these international crimes have not been committed by abstract entities." This book aims to set the second tenet of the international criminal law to say: "these international crimes have not been committed *against* abstract entities" but living creatures who cannot wait decades to be served with actual cashable justice or the bodies of their loved ones to finally put to rest. Until that happens, this is a book that will keep on screaming: *timeo Danaos et dona ferentes*.

CHAPTER 1

MAY THE LOCAL CONTEXT TAKE THE STAND, PLEASE

Language has always been used as a basis for discrimination. In the best-case scenario, the majority makes fun of those who do not properly speak the language. The Old Testament, Judges 12:6, also tells a story about the word "shibboleth" which was used as a password by the Israelites because their enemies could not pronounce it: 42,000 Ephraimites were killed because they said "sibboleth," instead.

Speaking the language of the majority of the country has always been important. Albanian language, for example, has a word for a Romany who speaks Albanian and a word for a Romany who does not. And then, if there are several majorities in the country, the so-called cultural elites, the language they speak becomes but a political nominal concoction, like the former Serbo-Croatian.

It is considered that ethnic groups are identifiable by – and discriminated against on account of – a common language, culture, spirit, history, and geography. In Omarska concentration camp, active in the Serb-held part of B&H between approximately May and August 1992, a guard came up to a group of Muslim prisoners sitting on a bench eating and casually told them to enjoy their meal. One of these Muslim prisoners automatically answered *bujrum*. This is a Bosnian word meaning *come join us*, a loan word from Ottoman Turkish used widely throughout the former Yugoslavia, but associated with Muslims. The guard took him up from the bench, ordered him to stand up against the wall, raise three fingers – the symbol of Serbian Orthodoxy – and stretch out his legs. He then beat him for about five to ten minutes.[21]

---

[21] ICTY, Cases, *Kvočka et al.*, T. 4501-4502 (31 August 2000): https://bit.ly/2Vt3tdi.

In Chapter 1, I am going to present a very brief history of language quarrels in the former Yugoslavia and point to a series of examples where language, and underlying ethnic and national identity, was used as a tool for a conflict. Then I am going to test whether linguistic justice has been served along the first line of communication with the judicial institution: the situation country towards the working institution. I will examine whether the ICTY, the international criminal tribunal adjudicating on ethnic crimes committed in the former Yugoslavia, and its language services, by extension, were aware the language spoken in the former Yugoslavia was vested with ethnic and national affiliations and used as a tool in the conflict.

1.1. Pre-Yugoslavian B&H

In medieval times, Europe was divided between the Catholic and the Orthodox churches. The line of demarcation between these two churches ran along the river Drina on the eastern border of Bosnia and was established, albeit for a different purpose at the time, by the Roman Emperor Theodosius when he divided the Roman Empire into the East and the West in 395.

Until it fell to the Ottomans, Bosnia was surrounded by the Hungarian Empire and its tributaries on the north and failing Serbian states on the east. Both wanted its territory. The medieval times in the whole of Europe were times of religious fanaticism, so belonging to the proper religion was a burning issue in/around Bosnia, as well. The sources of religious and, therefore, political legitimacy, were either Rome, the seat of the Pope and the Catholic church, or Constantinople, the capital of the Byzantine Empire and the seat of Orthodox church. In that climate, Bosnia decided it did not want to belong to any of the offered churches and established its own: the Bosnian Church.[22]

This was a largely unorganized church in a classical territorial sense. The members of the Bosnian Church called themselves simply "Christians" (*Krstjani*) or "Good Bosnians" (*Dobri Bošnjani*). Naturally, both the Catholic and Orthodox churches considered

[22] Fine, John V. A. (1985), The Bosnian Church: A new interpretation: A study of the Bosnian Church and its place in state and society from the 13th to the 15th centuries. East European Quarterly.

them heretics and waged several crusades against Bosnia without much success. The peoples of Bosnia of that time seem to have promised the Catholic enforcers that they would denounce their heretical ways but, once they left, the Good Bosnians seem never to have done what they had promised.[23]

Although present in the area since the mid-1300s, the Ottomans took full control of Bosnia in 1464, Herzegovina in 1482, and Serbia in 1521. Although never gaining full control over the whole of Croatia, they kept a presence in various towns and cities, mostly in Dalmatia and Slavonia. In their expansion, the Ottomans took full advantage of the weakness of Byzantium, the extreme discord between the Bosnian and Serbian gentry that led to feudal anarchy in those countries, and, more or less, the passive control by the Catholic states of that time. In 1462, the last Bosnian king, Stjepan Tomašević, the son of Stjepan Tomaš, wrote the following letter to Pope Pious II.

> I have been informed that the Turkish Emperor Mohamed [*sic*] plans to strike against me with his armies next summer and that he has already mobilized the troops and the cannons. I cannot resist such a force alone. I have already requested assistance from the Hungarians, the Venetians, and Juraj Arbanas. Now, I am requesting it from you. I am not asking for the impossible, but I would be glad if my enemies and my compatriots knew that they will not come short of your keenness. [...] Should the Bosniaks learn I won't be left alone in the war, they would become braver, and, in turn, the Turks wouldn't dare strike against my lands because the entry points are difficult, and the cities are almost unconquerable in many places, as it is. [...] Your predecessor Eugene offered a crown to my father and wanted to build churches in Bosnia. My father was reluctant because he did not want to bring the Turkish wrath on himself. He was a new Christian who has not expelled Manicheans from the Kingdom. However, I have been baptized as a child, have studied the Christian book, have firmly accepted the Christian faith, and do not share my father's fears. I wish you would send me a crown and holy bishops as a sign that you won't leave me if the war breaks out. Your crown on my head shall instill confidence in my subjects and fear in my enemies. [...] The Turks erected several forts in my kingdom and are showing themselves to the peasants as kind. They are promising freedom to each who defects. The simple mind

[23] Škegro, Ante (2005), Bilino polje: primjer jedne historiografske kontroverze in Fenomen 'krstjani' u srednjovjekovnoj Bosni i Humu. Institut za istoriju: Sarajevo; Hrvatski institut za povijest: Zagreb.

> of a peasant does not see through their deceitful ways, thinking the freedom will last forever. Should they not see me protected by your authority, once tricked, they will easily defect from me. The gentry did not remain long in the cities left by the peasants, either. [...] This letter is sent to you by Stjepan. Father of Christianity: send me advice and help [author's translation].[24]

Although Stjepan Tomašević hoped the Pope would send him troops to salvage whatever was left of Bosnia, the Pope just sent him a crown. Indeed, this symbolically put him in the ranks of Catholic countries that deserved help with defense against the Ottomans, but the Catholic armies never came to his rescue. Having caught him for the second time and having trounced his resistance, the Ottomans killed the last Bosnian king, Stjepan Tomašević, in 1463. His forced conversions and the related violence took its toll: the local populace, fed up with all sorts of Catholic, Orthodox, and royal persecutions, under the strong influence of Ottoman spies present in the country, offered little, if any, resistance to the Ottomans, giving rise to the popular expression "Bosnia was subdued in a whispering campaign" (*Bosna je šapatom pala*). The Ottomans and Islam became a force to be reckoned with. Bosnia remained at the border between the two worlds.

The medieval B&H populations, like all Slavic speakers, wrote in the Glagolitic script (*glagoljica*), which was invented specifically for translating the Scriptures and other religious works into Slavic. The language itself is now known as Old Church Slavonic. In the Orthodox Slavic-speaking world, Glagolitic script was replaced by the Cyrillic script, which was based on Greek and named for St Cyril, but probably invented by St Naum in Ohrid.[25]

In Bosnia, a variant of chancery Cyrillic developed into the Bosnian Cyrillic script, known as *Bosančica*. Although based on the Cyrillic that developed originally to the south of Bosnia, *Bosančica* became a distinct form of Cyrillic. The *Bosančica* script was used in various trading agreements Bosnian rulers concluded with surrounding countries, in religious texts, in other written documents, and on the medieval Bosnian Church tombstones called *Stećak*, the

---

[24] Klaić, Vjekoslav (1899), Povijest Hrvata. Knjižara Lav Hartmana (Kugli i Deutsch): Zagreb.

[25] Lunt, Horace (1974), Old Church Slavonic grammar. Mouton: The Hague.

contemporary unofficial symbol of the country. The *Bosančica* script remained in use among selected B&H elites, especially Franciscans, and women until the 1980s and it is experiencing a popular revival.[26]

The Ottomans, who were on their way to toppling the Hungarian Empire, were exhausted by the Bosnian campaign. They felt grateful that they did not have to employ much military force to conquer Bosnia and that they had found troops willing to fight their wars.[27]

Unlike other conquerors, the Ottomans did not care whether their religion, Islam, spread with their expansion or not. Their ultimate goal was to build a kingdom bigger than that of Genghis Khan, their military idol. The Ottomans were very different from other conquerors throughout history in that they relied greatly on local leadership, not on the sword and fire. The Ottoman Sultan was the absolute owner of the land his troops conquered and could give conquered lands to whomever he pleased. The Ottoman Sultan did something completely unprecedented and gave the land to local people who proved to be loyal to him, regardless of the recipients' religion. Those possessions were called *timar*; the *timar* system changed over time and declined, but ownership of the land by local notables continued until the mid-nineteenth century. Advocates of Ottoman rule and their proxy rulers, the new *timar* owners, were both Christians and Muslims.

After a lengthy period of military victories, it can be argued that the Ottomans started having their own worries following the second unsuccessful siege of Vienna (1683) and the subsequent territorial losses and wars with Austria-Hungary and, later, Russia. These Ottoman troubles became known as the "Eastern question" – or the question as to which European Great Power would get most of the Ottoman lands once the Empire collapsed under political and economic instability. This "question" became a pressing issue for Europeans throughout the late-eighteenth and the nineteenth centuries.

---

[26] Hadžijahić, Muhamed (1985), Građa o posljednjim ostacima bosančice u nas. Anali Gazi Husrev-begove biblioteke, Sarajevo.
[27] Imber, Colin (2002), The Ottoman Empire, 1300-1650: the structure of power. Palgrave Macmillan: London.

In addition to external pressures, the Ottoman Empire was shaking under a series of uprisings and internal liberation movements. The European powers at that time claimed to be concerned about the peoples living under Ottoman rule, most specifically the Christians. As a consequence, the weakening Ottoman Empire was forced to concede to many European requests designed to protect non-Muslims in the Ottoman Empire.

After the end of the Russo-Turkish War (1768-1774), the Russians received a right of protectorate over the Orthodox population in the Ottoman Empire. On the other hand, the Sultan also received a right of religious jurisdiction over Muslims who came under non-Muslim authority as a *khalif*, the ruler of all Muslims. The segmentation of society in Bosnia had begun.

In addition to remaining on the border between the two major religions, B&H was also frequently a border region of the Ottoman Empire, which continually expanded and retreated in the Balkans. People in the countries beyond B&H which the Ottomans conquered accepted Islam at the same pace and for the same reasons as others. Once the contemporary Ottoman tax registers recording the local populace by religion were discovered in the 1950s, it became clear that the process of the acceptance of Islam by local populations was a process that lasted for about 250 years and that it was simultaneous to the process of conversion to Catholicism and Orthodoxy.[28]

Once the Ottomans retreated, those new Muslims were converted, killed, or forced to withdraw into B&H and other areas of the Ottoman Empire. Local Christians, those who returned to the freshly liberated territories, or those who gained autonomy or independence from the Ottomans, called local Muslims *poturs*. These *poturs* would be called "first-generation Muslims" using the contemporary politically correct terminology. The Christians truly despised the *poturs* and had no reservations about committing their disgust to paper.[29]

---

[28] Imamović, Mustafa (2014), Historija države i prava Bosne i Hercegovine. University Press: Sarajevo.

[29] Mirko Žeželj was one of the most prolific authors of didactical books for primary school children. His "Prošlost u slikama" (The past in images) history textbook, teaches that the Montenegrins were the first to get rid of

The Romantic *cum* nationalist discourse of the eighteenth century onwards considers the former members of the Bosnian Church and others who accepted Islam as renegades, actively advocating for their inclusion in the ranks of either the Croatian or the Serbian populace by means of conversion. The alternative was expulsion or annihilation. An epitome of the philosophy of hate, the first book to get banned after the beginning of the war against B&H, was the poem "The mountain wreath" (*Gorski vijenac*) written by the Montenegrin prince-bishop Petar Petrović Njegoš (1813-1851) in 1846. Given that nineteenth-century Montenegro was a loose and semi-independent confederation of warring tribes, the primary purpose of "The mountain wreath" was to unify these tribes into a functioning state against the common enemy, namely Muslims and non-Serb Christians, under the leadership of prince-bishop Petar Petrović Njegoš. But, here, I am concerned with language.

"The mountain wreath" describes a pseudo-historical event that took place at the end of the seventeenth century where Montenegrins engaged in the "extermination of *poturs*" (*istraga poturica*).[30] Essentially, it is a story about how Montenegrins killed *en masse* every living Turk (umbrella term for Muslims), convert to Islam (*potur*), Latin (Catholic), and Arbanas (Albanian-speaking Catholics) living in Montenegro at that time. Selection for the killings was made according to the religion as a way of determining who was a "Turk" and a "Latin." This poem considers ethnic violence justifiable and necessary because "[o]ur struggle won't come to an end until we or the Turks are exterminated." The perpetrators were motivated to killing because "[m]ay God strike you, loathsome degenerates, why do we need the Turk's faith among us?"

This xenophobic description of "others" also contains overpowering tones of Orthodox religious fundamentalism. Although a work of fiction, it is disturbing because of the day that had been chosen for the killings: the Serb Orthodox Christmas. In that vein, this work is unsettling because Njegoš openly claims that

---

the Ottomans. "They began their struggle for liberation by the extermination of *poturs* in the beginning of the XVIIIth century. *Poturs* were traitors who converted to Islam and served the Turks." Žeželj, Mirko (1967), Prošlost u slikama. Školska Knjiga: Zagreb.

[30] Petrović, Petar II Njegoš (2012), The mountain wreath. Nova knjiga: Beograd.

religious holidays, Christmas here, are appropriate for mass killings, asking: "Is today not a festive occasion on which you have gathered Montenegrins to cleanse our land of loathsome infidels?" The description of the aftermath of the alleged operation is equally disturbing: "We put under our sharp sabers all those who did not want to be baptized by us."[31]

However, all this was considered an expression of patriotism by the powers that started ruling over the territory of the former Yugoslavia once the Ottomans left B&H in 1878. "The mountain wreath" was on the obligatory elementary, secondary, and university-level reading lists throughout the former Yugoslavia until the wars. Students were obliged to memorize certain sections and encouraged to draw lessons from it. But there was knowledge that messages sent by literary oeuvres of this kind were wrong.

In the 1980s, Bosnian award-winning poetess, translator, and academic, Mubera Mujagić suggested "The mountain wreath" be expunged from the academic reading lists because its language and philosophies were offensive to Muslims and created active animosity towards them, suggesting appropriate literary replacements. She was banned from public life, all associations, and died in poverty.[32]

---

[31] Unfortunately, killing non-Serbs during religious and national holidays turned into a rather recognizable pattern, if not tradition. For example, Gavrilo Princip assassinated Archduke Franz Ferdinand of Austria on the Serb Orthodox holiday, St Vidus Day *(Vidovdan)*, 28 June 1914. St Vidus is traditionally celebrated as the Memorial Day to Prince Lazar and the Serbian Holy Martyrs who fell defending Serbia from the Ottomans during Kosovo Polje battle in 1389 where Serbian principalities lost their independence to the Ottomans. The Serb paramilitaries and loyalist troops of the Yugoslav People's Army charged against B&H cities closest to the river Drina bordering with Serbia, Bijeljina, Zvornik, Vlasenica, and Brčko, on the Muslim religious holiday, Ramadan Eid, 4 April 1992. The Second Markale Shelling resulting in 118 victims (43 dead, 75 injured) occurred on 28 August 1995 right after the truce coinciding with another great Serb Orthodox religious holiday, Dormition of the Mother of God (the death of Virgin Mary, *Velika Gospojina*), traditionally commemorating the end of 14-day fast period. The Shelling of Tuzla City Center resulting in 311 victims (71 dead, 240 injured) fell on 25 May 1995 celebrating Tito's birthday which was universally celebrated in the former Yugoslavia as a Youth Day (*Dan mladosti*).

[32] Faktor.ba (2016), Podsjećanje na stradanje pjesnikinje Mubere Mujagić: Profesorica kojoj su dohakali Njegoš i Ivan Mažuranić:

"The mountain wreath" would be mentioned at the ICTY in *Mrkšić* and *Popović* in passing, *Simić,* and *Karadžić*. The defense in *Simić* had started the questioning of a prosecution witness about the merits of the poem, but never seemed to have finished the questioning or countering the thesis advanced by the witness that the poem was, indeed, calling for genocide. In that sense, this questioning did not lead to any intellectual culmination on the issue of incitement to genocide and "The mountain wreath."[33]

In his closing argument, Karadžić pointed out that "the Prosecution portrays the Serbs as vagabonds, who are sticking a thorn into a healthy leg in peacetime", offering that "when I quote Njegoš's verses, if you were to put them all in one pot, a broth could not be blended together" to conclude that the prosecution "should have made an effort to get [my quoting of Njegoš] interpreted properly, rather than dragging Njegoš through court."[34]

The reason why Njegoš was mentioned in *Karadžić* in the first place was because Karadžić's own defense witnesses mentioned Karadžić often quoted the following line from "The mountain wreath" to his closest associates: "A timid chief has no business ruling."[35] When it appeared from the Prosecution's questioning of those defense witnesses that Karadžić would quote "The mountain wreath" and that particular line before making autocratic and heavy-handed decisions in the context of ethnic cleansing and genocide, Karadžić and his defense suggested that the whole poem should be admitted as evidence. "The mountain wreath" is not mentioned in the *Karadžić* Trial Judgment.

Linguistically, the nineteenth-century Herderian ideology of celebrating the relationship between language and nation found very fertile ground in the former Yugoslavia. This was heavily explored by language activists Vuk Karadžić (1787-1864), a Serbian, and Ljudevit Gaj (1809-1872), a Croatian. These two were nineteenth-century polymaths for whom language was at the center of their concern.

---

https://bit.ly/3b7Uxkf.

33 ICTY, Cases, *Simić et al.*, T. 1197-1198 (13 September 2001): https://bit.ly/2XGmmvM.

34 ICTY, Cases, *Karadžić*, T. 47846 (1 October 2014): https://bit.ly/3emv88r.

35 ICTY, Cases, *Karadžić*, T. 46877-46890 (12 February 2014).

Hajdarpašić explains Vuk himself was born in an *ijekavian*-speaking part of Serbia and considered Serbian was spoken in the purest and most correct way in *Herzegovina* and in *Bosnia*. He recognized Bosnian Muslims as members of the South Slavic national community under the condition that they would eventually "realize and admit that they were not Turks, but Serbs." Vuk collected contemporary folk songs from the territory of Serbia, B&H, Montenegro, and Dalmatia, with special attention to Herzegovina, which he called the "land of the people." He discovered that these popular "heroic songs" are in the same language and concluded that all those people living in the territory of Serbia, B&H, Montenegro, and Dalmatia of that time must have been Serbs. This faulty parallelism led him to conclude "[They are] all Serbs everywhere" (*Srbi svi i svuda*).

Hajdarpašić explains that Vuk articulated a broadly assimilationist stance that insisted on the primacy of language, not religion, as *the* national marker. In regard to the rather large Bosnian Muslim population, Vuk insisted that these "Turks" were in fact "Serbs" because they spoke "Serbian," and spoke it "most purely" and "beautifully" at that. In reality, what Vuk discovered wherever he went was the *ijekavian* or *ikavian* version of the *štokavian* dialect. Hajdarpašić pointed to a rather curious fact omitted both in domestic and English-language studies: Vuk never visited or traveled through Bosnia or Herzegovina.[36]

Eventually, two representatives of the nineteenth-century Serbians, five representatives of the nineteenth-century Croatians, and one nineteenth-century Slovene met up in Vienna in 1850 to agree on a common literary language for the future country of South Slavs. They agreed that the new common language should be the *ijekavian* version of the *štokavian* dialect. They identified various dialects of, essentially, the same language, basing the names of those dialects on the words meaning "what", namely *štokavian* (*šta/što*?), *kajkavian* (*kaj*?), and *čakavian* (*ča*?). They also identified various dialects within *štokavian* based on the reflex of Common Slavic *ē (*jat*), namely *ikavian* (*mliko*, milk), *ijekavian* (*mlijeko*), and *ekavian* (*mleko*).

---

[36] Hajdarpašić, Edin (2015), Whose Bosnia? Nationalism and political imagination in the Balkans 1840-1914. Cornell University Press: Ithaca and London.

Territorial distribution of these pronunciations and dialects did not correspond to any clear-cut physical or other borders or, for the most part, potential national identities — especially in the case of *štokavian*. *Štokavian* was present in all of Serbia, most of B&H, all of Montenegro, and much of Croatia, and *čakavian* and *kajkavian* in parts of Croatia. *Ikavian* was pronounced in parts of B&H and Croatia, *ijekavian* in most of B&H, much of Croatia, all of Montenegro, and parts of Serbia, and *ekavian* in most of Serbia and some small parts of Croatia. To a certain degree, these nineteenth-century linguists and language activists were willing to ignore all these differences, but the problem that they faced then, and that we face still, was how to name what is essentially the same language. They named it to correspond to their own newly found identities, calling it "Serbian" in Serbia and "Croatian" in Croatia.

As to B&H, Serbian and Croatian language activists *cum* political activists and political activists *cum* language activists and artists of the Romantic revolutions onwards engaged in a series of campaigns. These appropriated, mystified, and, ultimately, misunderstood B&H and its peoples to the point that it could be understood from Hajdarpašić's study into these issues that they created their own "B&Hisms," fashioned after contemporary theories that Said would later label "Orientalism."

Although aware of these Croatian and Serbian expansionist trends, it seems the peoples of B&H did not feel like they had to refute systematically, extensively, and constantly something which, to them, was self-evident: that discussions about the common language in what became Yugoslavia ignored B&H's unique identity and language. Their annoyance could be best portrayed by the following excerpt from Fra Antun Knežević's rebuttal published in 1870 in "Bosanski prijatelj" (Bosnian Friend), the oldest B&H magazine for culture and language:

> Some of our neighbors are enraged that we proudly rejoice in our ancient name, language, and customs, and that we wouldn't embrace their labels for nationality and language for the life of us. These attacks are launched against us in concerted action by our neighbors whom we shall call Jovo [typical Serbian name] and Ivo [typical Croatian name], for better understanding. Still, each of them asks something different of us, because they cannot - for the life of them - agree between themselves. Friend Jovo tells us to take his label, whereas friend Ivo says: "*Jok* [Ottoman Turkish for "Nope"], Bosniak, you are mine and you have to embrace my label."

> Pull us here, pull us there, without any input from us. Our friends wish to break us apart claiming love, but they are motivated by their own endless quarrels; if we were not already aware of it all since long ago, we would find ourselves caught marveling at their wonders. But, as things stand, we ask our friends of letters and pen: why are you fighting for our sake when you know very well that the Bosniak is proud of the language and the name that is his own, faithfully holding to traditions and memories of his grandparents, from antiquity. The celebrated *tarih* [Ottoman Turkish for "history"] of our beloved fatherland reminds us of those times when our local nobility clearly and openly expressed their nationality, calling themselves a proud and a heroic name Bosniak every chance they got. Looking at many a document penned by the local writers from the past centuries who unfailingly mention our correct national name Bosniak we find that to be the reason why we, their grateful and true descendants, call ourselves by the glorious name Bosniak. And from that we cannot and dare not depart; we shall keep this name loyally and at all times. We are proud that it is precisely our language of our fatherland that is taken as the basis for the literary language of our neighbors the Serbs and the Croats. Renowned linguists Vuk Karadžić, Daničić, and Ljudevit Gaj, too, passed on our beautiful language to the literatures of both said nations, calling it as they pleased, one "Serbian" and the other "Croatian", failing to mention us anywhere. We certainly have a right to rejoice that our friends Ivo and Jovo use our language in their literatures, but that is the least they should recognize. We cannot understand why they want the label that they stuck on our language at their will and without our permission imposed on us no matter what, forbidding us to name our language of our people in our own home. It is as if someone else would try to name your own child. We do not condone such treatment and such a tendency and we shall not make *kail* [Ottoman Turkish for "to consent"]. Well done to both our friends, Serb and Croat alike. We do not despise their peoples, we do not hold any grudges, we will never deny that we are of the Yugoslav tribe, but we only want to show clearly to everyone that we are, firstly, Bosniaks of illustrious lineage. We shall always be Bosniaks like our great-grandparents who have been and nothing else. Therefore, take a good look around, our brothers residing and living in B&H for many centuries, still wishing you were Serbs or Croats. May you study this and think hard about it [author's translation].[37]

Expansionism, sweeping statements, and monopolism did not stop at language. Politically, Ilija Garašanin (1812-1874) could be

---

[37] Knežević, fra Antun (2012) Bosanski prijatelj. Duh Bosne, Svezak 07, Br. 1, Januar. https://bit.ly/2VtiNq5.

described as the first Serbian politician with articulated political plans. His "Načertanije" (The Draft) from 1844 offered a political program and platform for the newly semi-independent (autonomous) Principality of Serbia at that time. The idea of Yugoslavia, the country that would unify all Southern Slavs, was nascent. However, Garašanin had a different idea. He started his exposé with an affirmation that "the bustle and the welter among the Slavs has already begun and shall, indeed, never cease," warning that "the facts and foundations of such a background command the Serbian contemporary politics to un-limit itself from its present boundaries and to nestle all the Serbian peoples around it, instead."

Garašanin considered Serbia to be very well entitled to nestle all the Serbian peoples around it because "both the same origins and the single language indicate a continuity and a great future [of the new Serbian state in the south]." He believed the process of nestling thus implied would be completely painless because "the Serbian peoples are so good that anything can be achieved with us as long as it is reasonable." After the successful completion of this unification, "we, the Serbs, will face the world as true descendants of our great forefathers who did not do anything novel, but rather continued our ancestry." Garašanin concluded Serbia must endeavor to rebuild and resurrect a great new Serbian state on the old and good foundations of the ancient Serbian Empire.[38]

At the level of language of political philosophy, "Načertanije" is full of words, expressions, and mentalities that still dominate contemporary Serb(ian) discourse, including the way the Serbs and Serbians see themselves in isolation, together, and in relation to others:

- Rich and illustrious Serb history (*bogata i slavna srpska istorija*)
- [Serbia has a] holy historical right (*[Srbija ima] sveto pravo istoričesko*)
- [Serbs are] true patriots (*[Srbi su] prave patrijote*)
- Let this be a sign and a warning for Serbia and let Serbia not forget that (*neka ovo za Srbiju bude znak i opomena i neka ona ne zaboravi*)

---

[38] Garašanin, Ilija (1844), Načertanije. Institut za istraživanje genocida, Univerzitet u Sarajevu: Sarajevo. https://bit.ly/3b9GSJc.

- [Serbia is] the only one that can (*[Srbija] jedina može*)
- [Serbia has an] obligation to incessantly (*[Srbija je] dužna [da] neprestano*)
- [Serbia is a] natural patron (*[Srbija je] prirodna pokroviteljica*)
- [Serbia is an] unwilling tool (*[Srbija je] bezvoljno orudije*), etc.

Judah clarifies that "Načertanije" was, until 1906, a secret document, but it was the guiding light of foreign policy until at least 1914, if not until the founding of the Kingdom of the Serbs, Croats, and Slovenes in 1918, later renamed Yugoslavia.[39]

Indeed, in practical terms, none of this political philosophy remained at the level of platitudes: Serbia started a war with Bulgaria in 1885 and 1913 to assimilate freshly "liberated" territories from the Ottomans (parts of what became Serbia and Macedonia, respectively). The annexation of countries or regions bordering on Serbia, such as B&H, Croatia, Montenegro, Kosovo, and Macedonia was successful because these territories were incorporated into a single state with Serbia after 1918, for the most part, against their will, except Croatia. Montenegro lost its independence and subjugated its national and ecclesiastical identity to the Serbian one. Macedonia, which was known as Old Serbia, was annexed in 1913 and was subjected to policies of intense Serbianization in terms of politics, language, and identity.[40] These policies were not particularly successful. Rather, they created deep resentments between the ethnicities living there. Bosnian identity was likened to that of Ottoman Turks throughout the region.

"Načertanije" will be mentioned at the ICTY in the context of *Milošević* and *Šešelj*. Milošević argued that looking for the roots of Serbian nationalism in "Načertanije" is methodologically incorrect because "historians never consider[ed] it to be a great Serbian program [but] [...], rather, a Yugoslav program whose objective it was to create a great Yugoslav state."[41] However, neither the word Yugoslavia nor any of its derivatives have been explicitly or implicitly mentioned in "Načertanije" in a way that would even

---

[39] Judah, Tim (1997), The Serbs: The Sweet and Rotten Smell of History. Daedalus, 126.

[40] The Serbian Gazette LXXX/257 (1913), Decision to enact the following provisions of the Constitution of the Kingdom of Serbia of 5 June 1903 in the annexed Old Serbia.

[41] ICTY, Cases, *Milošević*, T. 24867-24910 (24 July 2003): https://bit.ly/2V8d9uB.

remotely suggest that "Načertanije" was a pan-Yugoslav project. As a word and a concept, "Yugoslavia" was in use since the late eighteenth century and there was no impediment for Garašanin to use it or refer to it, especially in the "secret" document, if he wanted to do so. Instead, he geared "Načertanije" very straightforwardly and narrowly in the direction of the creation of "the new Serbian state in the South" (*nova srbska država na jugu*).

Šešelj did not deny any of the commonly accepted claims about "Načertanije," but advanced arguments that it was not "the first" political platform for the unification of all Serbian lands, attempting to discredit an expert witness because he had not read the entire oeuvre on the issue.[42] "Načertanije" was not mentioned at all in the *Šešelj* Trial Judgment.

Alerted by the rise of nationalism in the territory that would become Yugoslavia with the aim of unifying all South Slavs in a single country, the Austro-Hungarian Empire took issue with the poor agrarian situation in B&H as a proxy solution for the non-creation of a large Slavic country in that territory. In 1840, the Ottomans allowed an Austro-Hungarian protectorate over Bosnian Catholics. A new series of uprisings started in B&H with the aim of abolishing the existing agrarian system and creating a freehold peasantry. Newly independent Serbia and Montenegro, joined by Austria and Russia, took an active part in caring about what happened to B&H, and, very soon, the uprising in B&H turned into a struggle between these four countries on whether to divide B&H or to unify it with Serbia and Montenegro.[43]

On 4 July 1878, in the wake of a Russo-Turkish war, six countries on the one side, and the Ottoman Empire on the other, met to decide the fate of B&H, Bulgaria, Serbia, and Montenegro in Berlin. Bulgaria, Serbia, and Montenegro gained independence from the Ottoman Empire and the Berlin Treaty gave a mandate to the Austro-Hungarian Empire to occupy B&H.[44] The Ottomans agreed to this.

---

[42] ICTY, Cases, *Šešelj*, T. 3149-3155 (5 February 2008): https://bit.ly/2zooRir.

[43] Imamović, Mustafa (2014), Historija države i prava Bosne i Hercegovine. University Press: Sarajevo.

[44] Treaty of Berlin (1878).

The official language of B&H under the Austro-Hungarians was called *Landessprache* (*zemaljski jezik*, language of the Land), later to be renamed *Bosnische Sprache* (*bosanski jezik*, Bosnian language). The peoples of B&H were collectively called "Bosniaks" and the Austro-Hungarians divided them into Muslims, Catholics, and Orthodox.[45] Benjamin Kallay became the Austro-Hungarian governor of B&H. Kallay's politics in B&H were designed to strengthen B&H specificity and nationality under the inter-confessional 'Bosniakhood', i.e. whoever lived in B&H should be called Bosniak, regardless of that person's religion.

Croatian and Serbian circles were outraged: they had been ignoring Bosniaks and, ostensibly, did not know what to do with them, other than try to assimilate them into their ranks. They were scandalized by the favorable treatment B&H received from the Austro-Hungarian authorities. Croatians had already been in the Austro-Hungarian Empire for some time, but Austro-Hungarian authorities did not promote Croatian uniqueness and Croatian unity. On the contrary, the Croats had been subjected to a policy of Magyarization (making the populace more Hungarian-like) after 1848.[46] On the other hand, Serbian foreign policy-makers wondered what to do with Muslims and how to accept that they were a majority anywhere or at least a factor with which to be reckoned. These sentiments were justified by annoyance with the name "Bosnian". On the insistence of certain Serbian circles, in explanation of the name "Bosnian", Kallay said "the name 'Bosnian' was not invented, even less imported. [It] is the name of this Land and it was adopted as such by [the] government."

The Austro-Hungarian government issued several further orders regulating the language in schools as: Bosnian, language of the Land (Croatian or Serbian), Bosnian language of the Land (*bosanski zemaljski jezik*), and Bosnian or Serbo-Croatian language of the Land (*bosanski ili srpskohrvatski zemaljski jezik*) with equal representations in Cyrillic and Latin script. In 1884, a government commission started the project of writing the grammar of the Bosnian language with single phonetic rules which was, finally, published in 1890, and applied in official documents and education.

---

[45] Joint Ministry of Finance, Decree 6687 (1880), Arhiv Bosne i Hercegovine: Sarajevo.

[46] Kamusella, Tomasz (2009), The politics of language and nationalism in modern Central Europe. Palgrave Macmillan: London.

After Kallay's death in 1903, Stephan Burian von Rajecz became the new governor and protector of B&H. On 4 October 1907, von Rajecz delivered an order purging "the name Bosnian hitherto used for the language of the Land [...] entirely from official traffic and documents of the government, offices, and institutes of the Land, including administration of the land registry, and [replacing it] by the name Serbo-Croatian language as an official language of the Land without any exception."[47] B&H was annexed to Austro-Hungary on 6 October 1908.

This put an end to the Austro-Hungarian sponsored policy of "Bosniakhood". The Government of the Land issued a separate decision on 29 November 1907 allowing the Bosnian Muslims to call their language Bosnian in their institutions. Bosnian Muslims wanted the equal use of *Arebica*, alongside the Latin and Cyrillic scripts, on the road signs and administration, because *Arebica* was the only source of literacy for most of them. In addition, *Arebica* was the script used by the Muslim religious institutions, magazines, and in about 500,000 different books.[48] But the wish to use *Arebica* was not granted, making most Muslims throughout the former Yugoslavia functionally illiterate. Coupled with the fact that they lacked a national leader and that their private lands were being "nationalized," Bosnian Muslims ended up utterly disempowered. The term "Bosnian" or "Bosniak" as a designation of a citizen of B&H started being used only to denote Bosnian Muslims.

In 1912, the Government of the Land started the revision of Serbo-Croatian orthography and delivered a Law on the official language and the language to be used in schools in B&H, establishing Serbo-Croatian as the official language and the equality of Cyrillic and Latin script. When the First World War started in 1914, the Government of the Land issued an order that communication with the main government (Austria-Hungary) was to be done in German or Hungarian, whereas communication with the Government of the Land was to be done in Serbo-Croatian: should the respondent address the government in Cyrillic, he should receive an answer in Cyrillic, otherwise Latin script would be used.

---

[47] Joint Ministry of Finance, Decree 168539 (1907), Arhiv Bosne i Hercegovine: Sarajevo.

[48] Rizvić, Muhsin (1996), Bosna i Bošnjaci: jezik i pismo. KDB Preporod: Sarajevo.

In 1915, the Government of the Land issued an order banning the use of Cyrillic script except within the Serbian Orthodox church.[49]

1.2. B&H in Yugoslavia

On 1 December 1918, the Kingdom of the Serbs, Croats, and Slovenes, the first Yugoslavia, was created. The then ruling ideology was based on the idea of national unitarism and did not recognize any nations in the Constitution (1921), but only three "tribes," the Serbs, the Croats, and the Slovenes, as parts of "a single Yugoslav people" along with minorities of "a different race and language." The official language was just a political nominal concoction: Serbo-Croatian-Slovene. The minorities of "a different race and language" were to be "accorded elementary education in their mother tongue according to rules to be set by a separate law."[50]

The 1929 Kingdom of the Serbs, Croats, and Slovenes Law on people's schools did not set these minority rights as a matter of principle, but as an issue to be resolved from case to case.[51] Implementation of this Law greatly depended on international relations between the Kingdom and the home countries of these minorities of "a different race and language." Elementary schools for minorities were reserved for German, Hungarian, and Romanian minorities.

Bosnian Muslims, or rather members of the Islamic religious community of the Kingdom of Yugoslavia, were not considered to be members of the three original "tribes" that constituted Yugoslavia, but nor were they seen as minorities of "a different race and language," either.[52]

On 2 September 1929, the king delivered the Orthographic Instructions for all elementary, high, and professional schools to regulate the two ways of writing, *ijekavian* and *ekavian*, because

---

[49] Šipka, Milan (1999), Standardni jezik u Bosni i Hercegovini u dokumentima jezičke politike. Open Society Institute: Budapest.
[50] Constitution of the Kingdom of the Serbs, Croats, and Slovenes (1921), Articles 1, 3 and 16.
[51] The Kingdom of Yugoslavia, Official Gazette CXIX/289 (1929), The Law on People's Schools.
[52] The Kingdom of Yugoslavia, Official Gazette LXIII/167 (1930), Constitution of the Islamic Religious Community of the Kingdom of Yugoslavia.

"often it happens that the teachers do not know which way of writing is better or which way of writing to practice", establishing the principle that "two ways of writing should be avoided as much as possible." Teachers practicing in areas with two ways of writing were instructed to opt for one or the other.[53] This meant that the authorities in the country were instructed to choose either the Serbian or the Croatian version which, effectively, killed the overlapping areas and created sharp boundaries.

After the assassination of a deputy in the Parliament, in 1929, King Aleksandar Karađorđević abolished the 1921 Constitution and the Parliament and started a dictatorship. The king delivered a new Constitution and brought a series of new laws changing the name of the country to "the Kingdom of Yugoslavia" and establishing new administrative borders in the country based on the names of the major rivers.[54] This was the first time in history that B&H found itself anywhere but inside its historical borders, as it was divided between the provinces (*banovinas*) of Drina (seat in Sarajevo), Vrbas (seat in Banja Luka), Primorje (Littoral) (seat in Split), and Zeta (seat in Cetinje), two of which were outside B&H.

Effectively, this unhappy marriage between the Serbs, the Croats, and the Slovenes in the first Yugoslavia, and the ensuing Serbian dictatorship, forced the opposition, communists, and separatists into illegality. The king was killed by a Macedonian separatist on 9 November 1934. The former deputy leader of the Croatian Pure Party of Rights and the future leader of the Croatian Nazi puppet state, the Independent State of Croatia, Ante Pavelić, went abroad and started organizing his *Ustaša* troops.[55]

The passive-aggressive conflict between the Serbs and the Croats, which was characteristic of the First Yugoslavia, culminated in the most violent way during the Second World War. Contributions to studies on the banality of evil are plentiful in the Nazi occupation of the former Yugoslavia. The Independent State of Croatia and

---

53 The Kingdom of the Serbs, the Croats and the Slovenes, Official Gazette LXXXI/204 (1929), Orthographic Instructions for all elementary, high, and professional schools.

54 The Kingdom of Yugoslavia, Official Gazette LXVI/207 (1931), Constitution of the Kingdom of Yugoslavia.

55 Čulinović, Ferdo (1961), Jugoslavija između dva rata. Jugoslavenska akademija znanosti i umjetnosti: Zagreb.

Nazi collaborators in Serbia each established concentration camps for local internal enemies who included the "enemies of the state" and "undesirables," such as Jews, Romas, Bolsheviks, homosexuals, degenerate artists, etc. The Nazi Croatians immediately began adopting a series of racist laws similar to those in other Nazi countries and were the only non-German Nazis allowed to run their own concentration camps.[56] Serbian extremists engaged in a macabre *en masse* extermination of their own people who had defected to the communists. They also joined the Nazis in reprisals for the killing of Nazi troops (100 Serbs for one killed Wehrmacht soldier and 50 Serbs for one wounded). Finally, the Serbs found themselves the major targets of the *Ustaša* policies in the Independent State of Croatia and the Muslims found themselves the major targets of *Četnik* raids in B&H.

Under the occupation, the Nazis partitioned the territory of Serbia and reduced it to the territory of central Serbia, northern Kosovo, and Banat, which were part of the administration and authority of local *Volksdeutsche*. The presence of a large number of Serb(ian) collaborators, the *Četniks*, cost the Yugoslavian royal family international support. The *Četniks* started out as royalist opponents to the Nazis, but some of them then started collaborating with the Nazis against the Partisans. The defection of these troops to the Nazis cost the royalists the support of the international community, which recognized the communist leader Josip Broz Tito and his partisan troops as the legal representative of the Yugoslavian peoples, not the King Petar II Karađorđević, who went abroad at the beginning of the war, or his royalist troops who stayed behind.

The *Četnik* troops were led by General Draža Mihajlović, who was executed after the Second World War after having been convicted of treason and war crimes by the Yugoslav authorities. The Republic of Serbia's Law on Rehabilitation came into force on 13 December 2011.[57] This Law regulates the rehabilitation and legal consequences of rehabilitation of persons who have been executed, arrested, or deprived of their other rights due to their political, religious, ethnic, or ideological beliefs and affiliations. Subject to this Law are persons residing in and outside of the Republic of Serbia

---

[56] Dedijer, Vladimir (1987), Vatikan i Jasenovac: dokumenti. Izdavačka radna organizacija Rad: Beograd.

[57] Republic of Serbia, Official Gazette of the Republic of Serbia 92/2011 (2011), Law on Rehabilitation.

with citizenship or residence in the Republic of Serbia at the time of the alleged offense.[58] Mihajlović was rehabilitated on 14 May 2015. The first hearing on the second request for rehabilitation of the Prime Minister of Nazi-occupied Serbia, Milan Nedić, was held in December 2015.

Scholars are increasingly using the term "Nazifascism" to describe the unique kind of Nazism and Fascism in Nazi Croatia during the Second World War.[59] Croatian extremists established a state under Nazi auspices incorporating large parts of present-day Croatia, all of B&H, and small parts of Serbia and they called it the Independent State of Croatia. Since some parts of the then-Croatia were annexed by Italy and Hungary, B&H formed the major part of this puppet state until Italy's capitulation in 1943 when Dalmatia was incorporated into the Independent State of Croatia. B&H Muslims found themselves inside a Nazi Croatia that proclaimed them to be Aryans, i.e. Croat Muslims, and divided the territory of B&H into six counties whose names were taken from the early feudal times of B&H. The Nazi Croatian authorities instructed the media to use these new-old names of counties when referring to B&H as much as possible.[60]

After he was recognized by the Allies as a military partner and ally in 1943, Josip Broz Tito became the only legitimate representative of Yugoslavia and its peoples. The country – named the Democratic Republic of Yugoslavia – was recognized by the international community in 1945. The political cadres of Tito's partisan troops were organized into committees whose representatives got together several times between 1942 and 1945 to set up an interim government. They formed the Presidency of the Anti-Fascist Council for the National Liberation of Yugoslavia which later became the Presidency of Yugoslavia. This committee recognized six Yugoslavian republics, including B&H, decided Yugoslavia would be a federal state that would "ensure full equality of Serbs, Croats, Slovenes, Macedonians, and Montenegrins, i.e. the peoples of Serbia, Croatia, Slovenia, Macedonia, Montenegro, and B&H."

---

58 Republic of Serbia, Higher Court in Belgrade, About rehabilitation.

59 Blažević, Robert and Alijagić, Amina (2010), Antižidovsko i rasno zakonodavstvo u Fašističkoj Italiji, Nacističkoj Njemačkoj i Ustaškoj NDH. Zbornik Pravnog fakulteta: Zagreb.

60 Imamović, Mustafa (2014), Historija države i prava Bosne i Hercegovine. University Press: Sarajevo.

Their decisions were published in Serbian, Croatian, Slovenian, and Macedonian.

The highest body of this committee in B&H was set up as the State Anti-Fascist Council for the National Liberation of B&H which later became the People's Assembly of the Republic of B&H. In its "Declaration on the rights of citizens [of B&H]," this B&H committee named Muslims, Serbs, and Croats as citizens of B&H, declaring that it was the wish of these citizens of B&H that B&H be neither Serb, Croat, or Muslim, but of the Serbs, of the Croats, and of the Muslims.[61] The official language of Yugoslavia remained a political nominal concoction: Serbo-Croatian.

And, once the Second World War ended, the peoples of Yugoslavia gave the idea of a single state of Southern Slavs another chance, albeit under a nondemocratic government.

The 1946 Constitution of the People's Republic of B&H declared that national minorities have the right to use their own language and that court proceedings shall be held in the Serbian or Croatian language.

The 1963 Constitution of the People's Republic of B&H declared that the peoples of Yugoslavia and certain minorities have the right to education in their own language, the minorities have the right to use their own language, all B&H laws and other official documents shall be delivered in Serbo-Croatian and, although court proceedings shall be held in Serbo-Croatian, the minorities can use their own language.

The 1974 Constitution of the People's Republic of B&H declared the official language Serbo-Croatian/Croato-Serbian of *ijekavian* pronunciation and the equality of Latin and Cyrillic script, the equality of languages and scripts of all peoples and minorities in that the minorities have the right to education in their own language, all have been given the right to use their own language in the courts, and should territorial defense units (the lowest form of defense units at the local level) be composed of minority members, those minorities will have the right to use their own language in command and training.

---

[61] Šipka, Milan (1999), Standardni jezik u Bosni i Hercegovini u dokumentima jezičke politike. Open Society Institute: Budapest.

Serbo-Croatian was one of the three official languages at the federal level in the former Yugoslavia, alongside Macedonian and Slovenian – standard languages that are completely separate from Serbo-Croatian to the point where these speakers often cannot understand one another. The reunified language, Serbo-Croatian, as a national language of the Serbs, the Croats, and the Montenegrins, has two linguistic variants, the Western – i.e. Croatian (*ijekavian*) – and the Eastern – i.e. Serbian (*ekavian*). These variants and the equality of Cyrillic and Latin script were affirmed in the Novi Sad Agreement of 1954.

This means that Serbo-Croatian, with its two linguistic variants, served as a politically correct *lingua franca* in communication among the peoples of the former Yugoslavia. It also means that B&H remained unmentioned in language-related laws during the Second Yugoslavia.

Bosnian identity remained likened to that of Ottoman Turks. Isaković gives a very interesting political evolution of the word "aždaha" (dragon), which has a Turkish origin. This is how this word has been recorded in the "Dictionary of the Serbo-Croatian language" by the author Aleksandar Belić:

- aždaha (aždaja) in 1923
- aždaha=aždaja in 1934
- aždaja=aždaha in 1950
- aždaha, no see *aždaja*, in 1960.[62]

Some contemporary B&H linguists blame the trend of general undecidedness among the Bosniak population that was also reflected in the language,[63] others point out that the B&H populations, especially the Muslims, had no reason to agree to the existing linguistic and literary agreements between Croatians and Serbians, and a random Slovene or two, because they were not included in the agreement and its conclusions had no bearing on them. However, not inviting the peoples of B&H to get involved in literary agreements led to a lack of recognition of the Bosnian language, the un-naming of the Bosnian nation, and thus to the

---

[62] Isaković, Alija (2001), Vid bosanskog jezika. Anali Gazi Husrev-begove biblioteke XIX-XX, Sarajevo.

[63] Kasumović, Ahmet (2001), Bosanskohercegovački muslimani i njihov jezik. Anali Gazi Husrev-begove biblioteke XIX-XX, Sarajevo.

entire "Bosnian Muslims issue," by inference.[64]

Language and identity-related troubles restarted outside B&H when the passive-aggressive conflict between the Serbs and the Croats resurfaced in the former Yugoslavia. The first two volumes of the unified Serbo-Croatian/Croato-Serbian dictionary by the cultural-scientific institutions Matica Srpska and Matica Hrvatska were published in 1967 in accordance with point 5 of the 1954 Novi Sad Agreement.[65] Croatian intellectuals denounced the dictionary and Matica Hrvatska withdrew from the project.

That same year, a group of Croatian authors and academics issued a "Declaration on the name and position of the Croatian literary language," complaining about the dominance of the Serbian language and calling for a larger representation of the Croatian language at the state level. In 1971, Dalibor Brozović wrote "Ten theses on the Croatian language," declaring Croatian to be a separate language.

A group of Serbian writers responded with a "Proposal for consideration" offering the annulment of the conclusions of the Vienna and Novi Sad literary agreements, the abolition of the name Serbo-Croatian/Croato-Serbian, and calling for the equality of all Yugoslavian languages and scripts. Their proposal was considered to be a chauvinistic match to the "Declaration on the name and position of the Croatian literary language."

Whereas all these proposals may seem benign in today's context, Tito's Yugoslavia was a country governed by the concept of brotherhood and unity (*bratstvo i jedinstvo*) where any separatism or any form of national movement that could be interpreted as separatist was unacceptable. These Croatian and Serbian authors did not suffer any legal consequences. As a matter of fact, Brozović continued advancing professionally and became a full member of the Yugoslavian Academy of Sciences and Arts in the 1980s.

---

[64] Isaković, Alija (2001), Vid bosanskog jezika. Anali Gazi Husrev-begove biblioteke XIX-XX, Sarajevo.

[65] Some argument could be made about these two institutions being the Serbian and the Croatian equivalent of the language institutes, such as British Council, Alliance Française, Instituto Cervantes, Goethe Institut, etc. which are established to promote these cultures and languages in the country and abroad. There was no Bosnian equivalent to these institutions.

Besides, the whole discussion brought the issue back to B&H, the proverbial name of the language spoken there, directly infringing on the rights of the peoples of B&H. The B&H politicians described these two documents as not only an expression of the nationalistic and chauvinistic attitudes of their signatories, but also an open attempt at political diversion against the brotherhood and unity, the equality, and the socialist patriotism of the peoples of Yugoslavia. They urged the Serbs, the Croats, and the Muslims to fortify the brotherhood and unity as a guarantee of their socialist progress. The University of Sarajevo professors reacted along the same lines.

The Central Committee of the League of Communists of B&H issued another series of conclusions on 15 March 1968: the peoples of B&H – Serbs, Croats, and Muslims – can freely and equally use both variants of the Serbo-Croatian or Croato-Serbian language. The Symposium on language tolerance was held between 23 and 25 April 1970 in Sarajevo to conclude that the name of the official language in B&H shall be Serbocroatian-Croatoserbian, both scripts shall be in equal use, and education in schools shall be delivered in the *ijekavian* dialect. The next decisions of the League of Communists affirmed all the earlier language policies and called for "mothering autochthonous literary, linguistic, and cultural values that are the commonwealth of all peoples in B&H, bridging their cultures i.e. insisting on all that connects and brings us together", and establishing that literary and linguistic expression in B&H "cannot be determined by a variant." The schools were instructed to use the name Serbocroatian-Croatoserbian language and to use both scripts.[66]

The 1974 Constitution of the Socialist Federative Republic of Yugoslavia cemented all these decisions: equality of all regardless of, *inter alia*, language, freedom to affiliate with any people or minority and free use of, *inter alia*, language and script, including the freedom not to affiliate with anyone, minorities' right to use their language and script before official organs of the state and the freedom to educate in their language, guaranteed use of their own language in courts, the equality of the languages and scripts of people and minorities in the armed forces, the equality of languages and

[66] Šipka, Milan (1999), Standardni jezik u Bosni i Hercegovini u dokumentima jezičke politike. Open Society Institute: Budapest.

scripts of all peoples and minorities, guaranteed free use of language and script for all minorities, and the equal use of all official languages and scripts in communication at an international level.

As far as language in the Yugoslav People's Army is concerned – the only venue where all peoples of the former Yugoslavia came together and had to communicate due to mandatory military service and where Serbo-Croatian/Croato-Serbian was the mandatory language – the 1974 Constitution proclaimed the equality of the language and the script of peoples and minorities, stipulating that the command and military instructions in the Yugoslav People's Army shall be in one of the languages of the peoples of Yugoslavia and the languages of peoples and minorities in its parts.[67]

However, all the commands, most laws, and the rules and regulations in the Yugoslav People's Army remained, in fact, in the Serbian language. Although the 1974 Constitution and the Rules of Service of the Yugoslav People's Army define the language in the Yugoslav People's Army as Serbocroatian, former serving officers of the Yugoslav People's Army interviewed for the purposes of this study agree on the following: although not committed to paper in the form of a written rule, all official commands were given in *ekavian* because most officers and noncommissioned officers spoke that dialect as they were either Serbs or from Serbia. The others – non-Serbs and non-Serbians – merely conformed to this use of language.[68]

When Tito died in 1980, a popular uprising of Albanians in Kosovo began in 1981 and resulted in the imposition of martial law, the first since the end of the Second World War. The whole country was suffering from a severe economic crisis.

The Draft Memorandum of the Serbian Academy of Arts and Sciences (SANU) was written between 1985 and 1986. This was yet another "secret" document which somehow leaked out and got

---

[67] Constitution of the SFRY (1974).

[68] The following Prosecution Brief from *Blagojević* Trial Judgment cites more than 10 different Rules of Service of the Yugoslav People's Army published between 1970s and 1990 in various republics of the former Yugoslavia. Most were originally written in the Serbian *ekavian* dialect, regardless of the location of the publication. ICTY, Prosecution Brief in *Blagojević*: https://bit.ly/2RxTsu4.

published in the Serbian daily tabloid "Večernje Novosti" on 24 and 25 September 1986. It has been generally accepted that this was a political program of the "Serbian intelligentsia" that was authored by the Serbian writer/historian/politician Dobrica Ćosić – who later became the President of the rump Yugoslavia – and 14 members of the SANU. The SANU Memorandum consists of two parts: an overview of the state of politics and the economy and an overview of the condition of the Serbian peoples across the former Yugoslavia.[69]

The SANU Memorandum is very hard to describe in clear academic terms in parts where it addressed the state of the economy and politics because it is both for and against modernity, for and against political change, for and against social equality, and for and against a liberal market economy in a series of buzzwords that are still the *leitmotif* of the Serb(ian) self-image:

- The difficult position of the Serbian peoples (*težak položaj srpskog naroda*)
- Official politics failing to admit the real causes of conflict (*zvanična politika izbegava da prizna prave uzroke*)
- Anti-historical routes to progress (*antiistorijski putevi razvoja*)
- The awareness of the people (*svest ljudi*)
- Unjustified violence (*neopravdano nasilje*)
- Gradual and unwilling recognition (*postupno i nevoljno priznanje*)
- Insurmountable obstacles in conflict of interest (*nesavladive prepreke u sukobima interesa*)
- Backstage games (*zakulisne igre*)
- Unanimous decision-making (*jednoglasno odlučivanje*)
- Separatism and nationalism (*separatizam i nacionalizam*)
- Ideological oneness (*idejno jedinstvo*)
- The means of repression (*sredstva represije*)
- Moral crisis (*moralna kriza*)
- Ideological crisis (*ideološka kriza*)
- Pressures by the Great Powers (*pritisak velikih sila*), etc.

The drafters very clearly propagate Serbia's liberation from all the roles that Yugoslavia, allegedly, imposed on it: the role of a feeder, moral compass, and beacon of liberty for the whole country.

---

69 Various authors (1986), Draft Memorandum of the Serbian Academy of Arts and Sciences. Serbian Academy of Arts and Sciences. https://bit.ly/2xweuT9.

Soon, the SANU Memorandum turns to the position of Serbs in the former Yugoslavia. Here, it very clearly defines the future battlefields in B&H, Croatia, and Kosovo in a series of buzzwords that are still the *leitmotif* of the Serb(ian) contemporary explanations of the conflict:

- Genocide in Kosovo (*genocid na Kosovu*)
- The stability of Yugoslavia (*stabilnost čitave Jugoslavije*)
- The dismembering of Yugoslavia (*razbijanje Jugoslavije*)
- The Serbian peoples have an historically implanted feeling of guilt (*srpski narod ima istorijski usađen osećaj krivice*)
- The vital interests of the Serbian people (*vitalni interesi srpskog naroda*)
- The oppressing and the oppressed nation (*ugnjetavačka i ugnjetena nacija*)
- A referendum of the Serbian people (*referendum srpskog naroda*)
- The traditional discrimination of Serbia (*tradicionalna diskriminacija Srbije*)
- The historic moment (*istorijski trenutak*)
- The Serbs are the most populous nation (*Srbi najbrojnija nacija*)
- Separatist tendencies (*separatističke tendencije*)
- The complexity of unsolved problems (*splet nerešenih odnosa*)
- Only Serbia does not have its own state (*jedino Srbija nema svoju državu*)
- The Ballist rebellion of 1944 (*balistička pobuna*)[70]
- The physical, political, legal, and cultural genocide of the Serb population (*fizički, politički, pravni, kulturni genocid nad srpskim stanovništvom*)
- The darkest times of the Turkish impaling of people (*najmračnija vremena turskog nabijanja na kolac*)
- The historical home country (*matična zemlja svog istorijskog postojanja*)
- Ottoman paramilitaries (*bašibozuk*)
- Violence and physical, moral, and psychological terror (*zulum i fizički, moralni i psihološki teror*)
- The fate of Kosovo remains the life issue of the entire Serbian people (*sudbina Kosova ostaje životno pitanje čitavog srpskog naroda*)
- Achievements paid in blood (*krvlju stečene tekovine*)

---

[70] The *Balli kombëtare* "national front" was the Albanian analogue of the Serbian *Četniks*. They were royalist-nationalists who ended up collaborating with the Nazis against the Partisans under Enver Hoxha. They were especially strong in northern Albania and Kosovo, most of which was annexed by Albania during the Second World War.

- The disintegration of the Serbian people (*dezintegracija srpskog naroda*)
- The Serbian language is being pushed out and Cyrillic is gradually being lost (*srpski jezik se potiskuje, a ćirilsko pismo postepeno gubi*)
- Ancestral hearths (*vekovna ognjišta*)
- Fateful task and the obligation of history (*sudbonosni zadatak i nalog istorije*), etc.

The main message of the second part is completely unsubstantiated owing to a complete lack of factual examples. Whereas it is strikingly clear that the SANU Memorandum calls for Serb dominance in the former Yugoslavia in almost all segments of life, it remains unexplained why that should be the case. Given that the SANU Memorandum was written by 14 leading Serbian contemporary intellectuals, some of whom were serious scholars in their respective fields, scientists whose work reposes on empirical data, if the wars had not happened the way they did, the SANU Memorandum could have been written off as analytical fiction.

The SANU Memorandum was mentioned at the ICTY in the context of *Aleksovski*, *Prlić*, *Mrkšić*, *Milošević*, *Brđanin*, *Kordić*, *Dokmanović*, *Mucić*, and *Šešelj*. In *Aleksovski*, a prosecution witness explained the basics of the SANU Memorandum,[71] but the defense in *Dokmanović* took issue with the apparent official non-existence of the SANU Memorandum, given that it leaked out in draft form. The prosecution responded they would be happy calling this document "a draft."[72]

In *Milošević*, a defense witness, one of the authors of the SANU Memorandum, stated that the SANU Memorandum was a forecast of what might happen given the crisis unless certain steps and measures were taken to deal with it.[73] Such an answer seems to confirm in short that the events that followed the publication of the SANU Memorandum, namely the attack of the Republic of Serbia on other republics of the former Yugoslavia under the pretext of the economic, social, and ethnic stagnation of Serbia and the Serbs, was based on entirely wrong beliefs.

---

[71] ICTY, Cases, *Aleksovski*, T. 772-790 (25 February 1998): https://bit.ly/3a6zc9l.
[72] ICTY, Cases, *Dokmanović*, T. 263 (21 January 1998): https://bit.ly/3b8CqdR.
[73] ICTY, Cases, *Milošević*, T. 34736-34737 (17 December 2004).

Serbocroatian/Croatoserbian with a specific literary and linguistic expression which "cannot be determined by a variant" served as an umbrella language in B&H. Although acknowledging that the language spoken in B&H "cannot be determined by a variant," i.e. it is not just a version of the Serbian or the Croatian language, B&H was the only area throughout Yugoslavia where the Serbo-Croatian language ideology was consistently applied. For example, the B&H daily newspaper "Oslobođenje" would one day publish in Latin and another in Cyrillic script. Primary school students would learn one script the first year and the second script the second year of elementary school, and, according to some decisions discussed earlier, they were obliged to take notes and exams intermittently in Latin and in Cyrillic script throughout their education. Readers throughout the former Yugoslavia marveled at the wonders of the Serbo-Croatian literary expression of B&H writers Meša Selimović and Ivo Andrić.

On the level of identity, Yugoslav Muslims were still not recognized as a people (*narod*), but as a *narodnost* (nationality) which is a communist term for minorities. The 1963 SFRY Constitution uses the term *nacionalna manjina* (national minority), the 1974 SFRY Constitution uses the term *narodnost*. Up to 1974, Muslims could declare themselves in Yugoslavian Censuses as Muslims-Serbs, Muslims-Croats, Muslims-undeclared, or Yugoslavs, i.e. being a segment of a *narodi*, but not as a *narod* (people) in their own right. Although having gained the right to call themselves Muslims in the 1960s, they could freely declare themselves as Muslims, the *narod,* from 1974 onwards in public documents, when needed. However, almost a century of cultural, identity, and political appropriation and/or distortion of what is theirs took a toll on how Muslims viewed themselves and how others viewed them. Some joke that Krleža, who sneered at the "Croatian culture and Serbian heroism" should have also sneered at Bosnian self-hate – a byproduct of a Yugoslavian indoctrination.

Due to all legal restrictions on expressions of national and religious identity in the former pre-1974 Yugoslavia, one of the most persistent Serb(ian) *canards* is that Meša Selimović, a Muslim from B&H, used to declare himself as a Serb. Serbian nationalists often declared then and now that Meša Selimović's "Death and the Dervish" is the "greatest Serbian novel of the twentieth-century." B&H writer Alija Isaković rebutted this, saying "Isn't it a little bit strange that the greatest Serbian novel of the twentieth-century begins with 'In the name of Allah, the Most Gracious, the most Merciful'?" However, the nationalists remained unfazed. Obviously, appropriation of all that is of B&H and faulty parallelisms that started during the Romantic revolutions resumed in the former Yugoslavia but under different affiliations: Meša Selimović is a Serb brother and rightfully ours because we live in brotherhood and unity.

Meša Selimović is mentioned at the ICTY in the context of *Šešelj*, *Karadžić*, *Milošević*, and *Župljanin*. Šešelj, testifying in *Milošević*, best summarized the broadness of the appropriation of all non-Serbs to Serbs when testifying that the top Muslim and Catholic minds that ever existed were, in fact, Serbs, it was just that they did not know it. According to Šešelj, Selimović made sure to declare himself as a Serb in his last will and testament because he knew that after his death somebody would try to claim otherwise, so he put it in writing that he was not a member of an invented nation, i.e. a Muslim.[74]

The same argument about unconscious Serbs among non-Serbs has been used by Karadžić who even claimed that there was a poll of the greatest Serbs of all time that was made up mostly of non-Serbs or people who did not contribute to Serb causes.[75] In a different session, Karadžić concluded "but we are proud of the fact that some of the most creative individuals of the Muslim faith preserved their Serb roots."[76]

The prosecution saw no relevance in his arguments and did not take up the issue, not even to clarify the facts of the alleged poll or the "Serbian nature" of any of the individuals mentioned. This obscured several other problems with this argument: what are the actual contributions to the Serb(ian) cause made by Serbs, such as Mehmet-Paša Sokolović, Nikola Tesla, and Prince Lazar, and what bearing does it have on the 1992-1995 ethnic cleansing and genocide of the B&H Muslims?

For example, the *Župljanin* defense mentioned that the Army of Republika Srpska (VRS) Commander Lisica, an ethnic

[74] ICTY, Cases, *Milošević*, T. 43467 (31 August 2005).
[75] ICTY, Cases, *Karadžić*, T. 3678-3679 (10 June 2010).
[76] ICTY, Cases, *Karadžić*, T. 22609 (9 December 2011).

Serb, christened a mixed unit composed of volunteer Muslims and Croats "Combat Group Meša Selimović."[77] A witness clarified that it was "not customary at the time" to make such a unit, but those volunteer Muslims and Croats wanted to form such a unit of their own volition and it is of their own volition that they asked Commander Lisica to be its godfather. It is worth noting that none of those volunteer Muslims and Croats were called to testify to confirm or deny such claims or to confirm or deny whether they were actually volunteers, as Muslims and Croats who stayed in Republika Srpska during the war were often taken to the front lines against their will, both to dig trenches and to serve as human shields in front of the advancing B&H Army troops.

Although an ethnic Croat from B&H, Ivo Andrić is said to have declared that he was a Serb, too. Andrić was a member of the literary elite throughout his life in the First and the Second Yugoslavia, having been a political activist and diplomat who served in Germany, the Vatican, Graz, Trieste, Madrid, Brussels, etc. Andrić was a Yugoslavian Ambassador to Germany but was allowed to return to Nazi-occupied Yugoslavia in 1941 where he spent the rest of the Second World War writing "The bridge on the Drina," among other works.[78]

"The bridge on the Drina" is a work of fiction situated in sixteenth-century Ottoman B&H and revolving around the alleged circumstances of building an actual bridge over the river Drina which included a grisly description of the impalement of a local man by the Ottomans and a description of Serb men, women, and children being mutilated on the bridge and thrown into the Drina river by the Ottomans.

As to its language, "The bridge on the Drina" is an example how to create otherness. It directly juxtaposes the members of two ethnicities living together in the same community in that in one and the same sentence or in a related paragraph it makes a sharp distinction between the members of the two religions and their characters, intentions, and motivations:

---

[77] ICTY, Cases, *Stanišić and Župljanin*, T. 19675-19676 (15 April 2011): https://bit.ly/2V5HCte.
[78] Andrić, Ivo (2004), The bridge on the Drina. Bosanska riječ: Sarajevo.

- Serbian lands vs. the vizier's authority (*srpske zemlje – vezirova vlast*)
- Serbian children vs. Turkish children (*srpska deca – turska deca*)
- Radislav, a Serbian hero vs. one of [the vizier's] men, smart and skillful who bribed Radislav's aide and got information out of him (*Radisav, srpski junak - neki od [vezirovih] ljudi, mudar i vešt [koji je] podmitio i ispitao momka Radisavljevog*)
- There were both Turks and Serbs in the town who claimed to have heard the sound of Karađorđe's cannons (but with diametrically opposed feeling, of course) [because] one often thinks to have heard what one fears or what one hopes for (*bilo je u kasabi i Turaka i Srba koji su tvrdili da su svojim ušima čuli tutanj "Karađorđevog topa". (Naravno, sa potpuno oprečnim osećanjima.) [J]er čovek često misli da čuje ono čega se boji ili čemu se nada*)
- A [Serbian] old man tied up vs. a Turkish commander getting ready to go downtown and miss watching him getting executed (*[srpski] starac vezan [a] turski komandir se spremao da ode u varoš i ne gleda njegovo pogubljenje*)
- Turkish homes vs. Serbian homes (*i turske i srpske kuće*)
- The Serbian language vs. the Turkish language (*i na srpskom i na turskom jeziku*), etc.

Particularly odious is the frequency by which Andrić juxtaposes Serb children vs. Muslim/Turkish children (who have not been baptized, *koja nisu uopšte krštavana*), almost on every second or third page, suggesting that they can never live together because they are divided by religion.

The tone of "The bridge on the Drina" is one of authority although Andrić recounts legends about fairies and other supernatural forces in at least two thirds of the book. This tone could even be said to be cunning because Andrić identifies himself with legends, using expressions such as "as we will shortly see" as if he was relating historical facts all along. In one of those legends it becomes apparent that Andrić also considered Bosnia as one of the "Serbian lands." According to Andrić, the building of the actual bridge was commissioned by a former Serb, Mehmet-Paša Sokolović. The bridge was erected by a great Serbian builder Rade *Neimar* (construction worker, Ottoman Turkish) who built all those beautiful and eternal Serbian buildings with the assistance of Serb workers. Rade *Neimar* encountered problems and, in order to neutralize the spells of a Ship Fairy who did not appreciate the bridge being built, the Ottomans had two Serb children entombed in the central pillars.[79]

The only historical fact here is that the bridge was, indeed, commissioned by a former Serb, Mehmet-Paša Sokolović, who, just like many Ottoman officials and Janissaries, was recruited through the *Devşirme* process (collection of Christian and non-Christian boys between the ages of 8 and 18 to military and diplomatic training in the Ottoman administration). But just like many *Devşirme* boys, Mehmet-Paša Sokolović did not return home as soon as he could. He stayed in Ottoman employ and spent his entire political and military career enforcing Ottoman policies and Ottoman military aims. The bridge itself was built by the great *Mimar* Sinan (architect, Ottoman Turkish) under Suleiman the Magnificent's administration. Culturally, the Ottomans were undeniably superstitious, but it is highly improbable that they would be moved to anything before the threat of a quintessential Slavic deity, such as a fairy. The pillars of the bridge have been destroyed several times throughout history and there were no bones found in any of their foundations. The legend of human sacrifice by inhumation during the construction of a significant object occurs in the folklores of many peoples, not only in the Balkans, but from North Africa to India. Finally, it is most likely that freehold peasants constructed the bridge, rather than Serbs only. Today, the term Andrićism in B&H stands for poetic stories of heavy-handed and needless crimes based on semi-truths and blindly believed without any critical analysis.

Ivo Andrić dictated trends and topics of writing after re-finding himself in the Second Yugoslavia, experimenting with his new-found Yugoslavianism by explicitly or implicitly blaming "the Turks" for everything that ever went wrong in the territory of the former Yugoslavia. The educated took notice and the uneducated listened carefully. When the educated failed to refute some of these historical inaccuracies or call Ivo Andrić and other insufficiently informed writers-historians-philosophers *cum* political activists to account, the uneducated took Ivo Andrić's shoddy research as undeniable truth and started taking revenge against "the Turks" the first time they had a chance. However, when the uneducated started their revenge in the 1990s, the Turks had been long gone from the former Yugoslavia. What they found was a local Muslim population

[79] Rizvić, Muhsin (1995), Bosanski muslimani u Andrićevom svijetu. Ljiljan: Sarajevo.

living on their own turf. Ivo Andrić's writings in the Nobel Prize Award winning "The bridge on the Drina," in particular, gave rise to numerous incidents of destruction and killings during the war in B&H: the uneducated took the fiction for facts and persecuted them worse in Višegrad than was described in Andrić's novel.

The Milan Lukić and Sredoje Lukić trial was about two ethnic Serbs and cousins from Višegrad who formed a paramilitary group called the "Avengers" in Višegrad and then went on a spree killing local Muslims and Muslims in Serbia well into the end of the 1990s.[80] *Lukić* has been very interesting because the factual evidence sounded like it came off the pages of Ivo Andrić's books, albeit with switched roles: the Serbs were clearly the perpetrators.

Five centuries after the bridge over the Drina had been erected, Witness VG21 testified in *Lukić* to crimes such as mutilation and the hurling of Muslims down the Višegrad bridge having been committed by the Serbs in 1992:

> A. The bodies that we retrieved from the Drina Lake were in varying stages of decomposition. Some were whole, intact, some were without heads, without clothing, others were with clothing; younger people, older people, and even children. [...] We retrieved bodies which had parts of noses cut off, ears, women with their breasts cut off, then legs tied, naked, both arms slung through the breasts and decomposing. It's indescribable. Some were killed with knives, sledge hammers. I don't know what to say. There were killings of all kind. But in the beginning, bodies mostly arrived that were with a nose cut off, ear cut off, hit with a hammer or a knife. There were few killed with firearms during the first few days.

Five centuries after the bridge over the Drina had been erected, Witness VG21 testified in *Lukić* to the crucifixion of Muslims in Višegrad by the Serbs in 1992.[81]

The killings in Višegrad amounted to extermination. Milan Lukić and his associates ushered 70 elderly men, women, and children into a house and set them on fire. The Lukić cousins followed this *modus operandi* on two occasions, once in Bikavac, and the other time in Pionirska Street in Višegrad, burning alive a total number of 140 victims.

---

[80] ICTY, Cases, *Lukić*: https://bit.ly/2VvYmJa.

[81] ICTY, Cases, *Lukić*, T. 923 (24 September 2001).

In her expert report for *Lukić* on changes in the ethnic composition in the municipality of Višegrad between 1991 and 1997, Tabeau concluded that although the prewar ethnic structure of Višegrad had two main ethnic groups, Muslims (63.5%) and Serbs (31.8%), the post-war ethnic structure of Višegrad was dominated by Serbs (95.9%).[82]

Lukić was also related to *Karadžić*, *Krajišnik*, *Milošević*, *Plavšić*, *Stanišić,* and *Vasiljević*. When asked whether he was trying to justify the burning of 70 people alive as a provocation, Milošević answered that it was important to understand Ivo Andrić, "who is a writer, and the only Yugoslav Nobel prizewinner, a Serb, [because he and his oeuvre] fall [...] within the context of the war in B&H."[83]

1.3. The war against B&H

As soon as they got a chance to declare who they really were, once Yugoslavia was about to collapse, the B&H populations did not hesitate to do that. According to the 1991 B&H Census which, *inter alia*, asked respondents to declare their language, the peoples of B&H described their language in the following terms:[84]

• Bosnian	1,631,991	37.2853%
• Serbo-Croatian	1,160,962	26.5239%
• Serbian	824,871	18.8454%
• Croatian	588,099	13.4360%
• Croato-Serbian	61,165	1.3974%
• Yugoslavian	11,575	0.2644%
• Serbo-Croatian and Croato-Serbian	4,117	0.0941%
• Muslim	2,545	0.0581%
• Islamic	451	0.0103%
• Serbo-Croatian and Croato-Serbian	427	0.0098%
• Montenegrin	266	0.0061%

[82] Tabeau, Ewa (ed.) (2009), Conflict in numbers: casualties of the 1990s wars in the Former Yugoslavia (1991–1999). Helsinki Committee for Human Rights in Serbia: Belgrade.

[83] ICTY, Cases, *Milošević*, T. 25607 (29 August 2003).

[84] Republic of B&H, Institute for Statistics of the Republic of B&H, Statistical Bulletin 233, The 1991 Census of population, households, dwellings and agricultural lands, Ethnic characteristics of the population, The 1991 results on the level of the Republic and on the municipal level, Sarajevo, October 1993.

• Orthodox	232	0.0053%
• Bosnian Serbo-Croatian	190	0.0043%
• Bosnian Croatian	148	0.0034%
• Croatian Bosnian	120	0.0027%
• Bosnian Muslim	104	0.0024%
• Bosnian Serbian	89	0.0020%
• Herzegobosnian-Croato-Serbian	73	0.0017%
• Serbo-Croatian-Croato-Serbian-Bosnian	36	0.0008%
• Bosnian Yugoslavian	19	0.0004%
• Bosnian Croato-Serbian	15	0.0003%
• Roma Bosnian	8	0.0002%
• Croato-Bosnian-Serbian	4	0.0001%
• Unknown	41,743	0.9537%

There are two major categories of language-related responses in the 1991 B&H Census: language as determined by religion and language as determined by national identity.

Language as a determinant of religion includes the following answers: the Muslim language, the Islamic language, the Orthodox language, and the Bosnian Muslim language; this notion of language was supported by 0.0761% of citizens of B&H.

Language as a determinant of national identity can be broken down into two further groups: a group including a B&H identity and a group excluding a B&H identity. The group including a B&H identity includes answers such as: Bosnian, Bosnian Serb, Herzegovinian Bosnian Croato-Serbian, Serbo-Croatian-Croato-Serbian-Bosnian, Bosnian Yugoslavian, Bosnian Croato-Serbian, Roma Bosnian, Croato-Bosnian-Serbian, Bosnian Serbo-Croatian, Bosnian Croatian, Croatian Bosnian. This notion of language was supported by 37.3008% of citizens of B&H. The group excluding B&H identity could be broken down into separate Croatian and Serbian groups, and a common Serbo-Croatian or Yugoslavian group. The separate Croatian and Serbian group included: Serbian, Croatian, and Montenegrin; this notion of language was supported by 32.2875% of the citizens of B&H. Common Serbo-Croatian or Yugoslavian groups included: Serbo-Croatian, Croato-Serbian, Yugoslavian, Serbo-Croatian and Croato-Serbian, and Croato-Serbian and Serbo-Croatian; this notion of language was supported by 28.2896% of B&H citizens.

In other words, the 1991 B&H Census on the subject of language showed that 37.3008% of citizens of B&H stated that they spoke a B&H affiliated language, 32.2875% of citizens of B&H stated that they spoke a Serbia and Croatia affiliated language, and that 28.2896% of citizens of B&H stated that they spoke a Yugoslavia affiliated language. Not even 1% of the peoples of B&H affiliated their language with religion, which is in keeping with their ancestral disdain of organized religion.

B&H declared independence from Yugoslavia on 1 March 1992 and became a member state of the UN in May 1992. The Serb minority declared their own internationally unrecognized state in B&H and called it Republika Srpska. The Croat minority also declared their own internationally unrecognized state in B&H and called it Herceg-Bosna. Herceg-Bosna later "united" with B&H Government-held territory in what is today called the B&H Federation.

On 14 March 1993, the B&H Government delivered a Constitution establishing that the citizens of B&H are Serb, Croats, Muslims, and members of other peoples, and that the Serbocroatian-Croatoserbian language of *ijekavian* pronunciation and both scripts are in official and equal use. Muslim intellectuals reacted, requesting the change of the name of the official language into "Bosnian, Croatian, and the Serbian language of *ijekavian* pronunciation." On 1 September 1993, the B&H Government delivered a Law Decree on the name of the language in official use in B&H during the state of war, declaring that the "Republic of B&H recognizes the official use of the standard literary language of *ijekavian* pronunciation of its constitutional peoples called either Bosnian, Serbian, or Croatian. Both scripts, Latin and Cyrillic, shall be equal." On 21 July 1994, the Government of the B&H Federation declared Croats and Bosniaks the constituent peoples and Croatian and Bosnian languages written in Latin script as official languages.

The Constitution of Republika Srpska delivered on 28 February 1992, declared that the official language was Serbian with *ijekavian* pronunciation written by Cyrillic script. After the war, on 8 July 1996, the President of Republika Srpska delivered a Law on the official language and script establishing Serbian with *ekavian* pronunciation written with Cyrillic script as the official language. The public in the Republika Srpska reacted, blaming the government for "making us abandon the *ijekavian* script of Petar

Kočić and Branko Ćopić [B&H writers of ethnic Serb origin] to the Croats and the Muslims." The Republika Srpska's government motion was not approved. Indeed, all of B&H remained either *ijekavian* or *ikavian* as it always was.[85]

Post-war B&H, i.e. the B&H Federation and the Republika Srpska, circumvented the issue of the name of the language, declaring the languages of the Bosniak people, of the Serb people, and of the Croat people as official languages. The latest Constitution of Republika Srpska and the Constitution of the B&H Federation establish Bosniaks, Serbs, and Croats as constitutional peoples, the languages of the Bosniak people, of the Serb people, and of the Croatian peoples as official languages with equal use of Latin and Cyrillic script, equality of all regardless of, *inter alia*, language, the right to use their own language and script to all in general and in communications with the State, prohibition of discrimination on the basis of, *inter alia*, language, prohibition of abolition of citizenship on the basis of, *inter alia*, language, language as one of the vital interests of the constitutional peoples, and the 1992 UN Declaration on the Rights of Persons Belonging to National or Ethnic, Religious and Linguistic Minorities and the European Charter for Regional or Minority Languages as instruments for the protection of human rights with the legal effects of constitutional provisions.[86]

Despite all this, language and identity wars in the former Yugoslavia are going on uninterrupted.[87]

---

[85] Šipka, Milan (1999), Standardni jezik u Bosni i Hercegovini u dokumentima jezičke politike. Open Society Institute: Budapest.
[86] Constitution of the FB&H (1994). Constitution of the Republika Srpska (2005).
[87] Apart from making references to Montenegro, whose national language is Montenegrin, in Part I.1. on Script, the Orthography of the Serbian language from 2010 published in the Republic of Serbia makes a series of statements that are not normally expected in books of this type and seem to continue to feed into the nationalist discourse: "In order of importance, the Cyrillic script is the primary and the elementary Serbian script. Since the 1970s, the Cyrillic script has been neglected, marginalized, and abandoned, suppressed from the official and public use, and suffered artistic stagnation. In Serbian traditions, the Cyrillic script has an indisputable symbolic function. Therefore, favoring the use of the Cyrillic script in official, public, educational, and cultural activities is justified. The latest

1.4. Linguistic justice: the situation country towards the working institution

I am now in a position to test whether linguistic justice has been served along the first line of communication: the situation country towards the working institution. Was the ICTY, the international criminal tribunal adjudicating on ethnic crimes committed in the former Yugoslavia, and its language services, by extension, aware the language spoken in the former Yugoslavia was vested with ethnic and national affiliations and used as a tool in the conflict?

The ICTY was established under the auspices of the UN and falls under the Subsidiary Organs of the UN Security Council. The ICTY Registry is the voice of UN Administration in the ICTY. It is comprised of Immediate Office of the Registrar, Division of Judicial Support Services, Chambers Legal Support Section, and the Administration Section.[88] The CLSS, the ICTY language services provider, falls under the Registry. The CLSS was in charge of addressing the situation country through translation, interpreting, and transcription. Their job was to know all the ins and outs of

---

cultural, historical, and political development of the Cyrillic script is in primary connection with the existence of almost one century of Serbian-Croatian linguistic community (or 70 years of common state). This led to the production of a rich Serbian heritage written or printed in the Latin script (of course, parts of that heritage date from an earlier period). It also catered to the contemporary exigences of culture, science, and communication, which is dominated by Latin script-based cultures. However, this facilitated the writing of the Serbian language in the Latin script and turned it into our daily practice. Such coexistence of two scripts is rare, although, for our consideration, the only acceptable sequence of learning and use of those scripts would be Cyrillic first and then the Latin script. At any rate, this use cannot be considered detrimental to Serbian culture unless Cyrillic script becomes existentially threatened." [Author's translation] In Part II.6. on *Ekavian* and *Ijekavian* Pronunciation it is established that the Serbian standard (literary) language has two equal ways of speaking and writing: *ekavian* and *ijekavian*. In reference to the discussions on the word *aždaja*, Part III.15.g. on Sound changes and relationships, Consonant *h*, reads the following: "The sound *h* is consistently replaced by sound *j* in following words: aždaja, proja, promaja, jendek (the variants with *h*, such as aždaha, etc., are only pronounced by the Muslims." Pešikan, Mitar, Jerković, Jovan, Pižurica, Mato (2010), Pravopis srpskoga jezika (izmenjeno i dopunjeno izdanje). Matica Srpska: Novi Sad.

[88] ICTY, About, Tribunal, Organizational chart: https://bit.ly/2wDMpc1.

ethnic conflict in the former Yugoslavia anchored in language and to inform all the subsequent language-related legal and practical arrangements.

Before I start, I must make two disclaimers: the first one about the philosophy of hate, which is the basis for the commission of the so-called speech atrocity crimes (genocide, crimes against humanity, war crimes). The speech atrocity crimes have not been prosecuted by the ICTY and have been seldom prosecuted by the subsequently established international criminal tribunals. The ICTR tried individuals for hate speech, as it recognized the importance of words and other verbal and semiotic messages in the time of conflict and brought to justice the main media leaders for their role in crimes committed in Rwanda.[89] However, the ICTY did not try to tackle the main source of hatred in the former Yugoslavia, Radio and Television of Serbia, because it cannot try organizations. At the same time, there was no process similar to denazification or lustration in the former Yugoslavia, either. Finally, the ICTY did not charge any individual for speech atrocity crimes. This means that nobody ever tackled the philosophy of hate behind the crimes in the former Yugoslavia.

In his study on speech and atrocity crimes, Gordon reminds that speech and atrocity are constant companions on the battlefield where armed actors seek to kill one another. Drawing on the fact that atrocity speech that results in genocide and crimes against humanity has been criminalized, Gordon proposes that advocacy to commit war crimes should be criminalized, too, and proposes seven elements as a test for determining whether hate speech constitutes incitement. Gordon also discusses how speech atrocity crimes could have been prosecuted in *Kupreškić, Kordić, Šešelj, Brđanin, Tadić,* etc.[90]

All the works of fiction discussed here and their underlying philosophy of hate set the stage for ethnic cleansing and genocide in B&H. They shaped the mentality of the entire people, peddling the quasi-knowledge that B&H and Yugoslavian Muslims were aliens who were threatening the non-Muslims to the point that they needed to be exterminated. The ICTY trials uncovered a great deal

---

[89] ICTR, Cases, *Nahimana et al.*: https://bit.ly/2XzT1Dx.

[90] Gordon, Gregory S. (2017), Speech atrocity crimes: foundation, fragmentation, fruition. Oxford University Press: Oxford, p. 17.

of evidence about the citizens of B&H being persecuted during the war on B&H only because they were speaking the Bosnian language and displaying their B&H identity,[91] standard cultural persecution in the Serbian concentration camps,[92] and non-uniform differences between the peoples which continued to be used as a basis for the persecution and murder of B&H Muslims.[93] The literary oeuvres discussed here are still hailed as beacons of humanism and nation building and are taught in Serbian and Serbia-affiliated schools in the former Yugoslavia.

The second disclaimer is about multilingualism in the UN because some benefit of the doubt must be given to the whole concept of provision of language services at the ICTY. The overall UN Administration did not make the ICTY CLSS's job easy at all and it could be argued they set them up to fail from the beginning.

The UN has six official languages, namely Arabic, Chinese, English, French, Russian, and Spanish. The UN Department for General Assembly and Conference Management (DGACM) is the main body that recruits UN language professionals who can accommodate language services in these combinations only. The UN DGACM language professionals service only the principle organs of UN in offices in Addis Ababa, Bangkok, Beirut, Geneva, Nairobi, New York, Santiago, and Vienna. Such provision of language services is done through the policies of multilingualism. These were around since 1946, but came to the fore again in the 1990s. Multilingualism is continuously sold as a UN value and refers to the use, in fairness and parity, to official and working UN languages.[94]

However, UN policies on multilingualism are an extremely damaging and dangerous UN-wide trend completely divorced from linguistic realities. They simply do not work at international criminal tribunals that have much different concrete priorities. As

---

[91] ICTY, Cases, *Vasiljević*, T. 3617-3618 (30 November 2011): https://bit.ly/3b9CZEe; *Stakić*, T. 15-21 (9 May 2002); *Kvočka*, T. 271-272 (23 March 2004), T. 1732-1733 (9 May 2000).
[92] ICTY, Cases, *Kvočka*, T. 5158 (11 September 2000).
[93] ICTY, Cases, *Krnojelac*, T. 2737-2738 (1 February 2001): https://bit.ly/2RCPksS.
[94] UN, JIU, Multilingualism in the UN System organizations: status of implementation (JIU/REP/2011/4) (2011).

to the ICTY, this means that once the ICTY proclaimed English and French as working languages, they precluded the former Yugoslav public who needed to see and hear the atrocities of wars fought in the territory of the former Yugoslavia from doing that in their own language. The former Yugoslavian audiences had a job to read and watch the ICTY trials to start eliminating the causes that led to the situation in the first place, to start gaining critical perspectives on the issues discussed by the parties to the proceedings, and to start neutralizing all causes perpetuating the situation in the present. However, the UN Administration conditioned the ICTY Registry who conditioned the CLSS not to communicate with the former Yugoslavian audiences in their language or any other language but English and French. The ICTY put the priorities on creation of the court record in English and French. This makes the war crimes tribunal *for* the former Yugoslavia an oxymoron because the UN did not communicate *with* the former Yugoslavia. Rather, it communicated with itself.

The ICTY CLSS did have a full and free run of the entirety of internal language-related policies. This is obvious because the ICTY CLSS management took an initiative to change the ubiquitous name of the language spoken in the former Yugoslavia again at the ICTY. In 1995, in anticipation of an issue about the name of the language used and underlying problems of comprehension, the CLSS consulted with two linguistic experts, Morton Benson and Wayles Browne, arguably the best general linguist with former Serbo-Croatian as his specialty. They stated that the varieties of Serbo-Croatian were mutually intelligible to all citizens of the former Yugoslavia, that the differences between Serbian and Croatian were small, and that there was no valid reason to justify the refusal of Serbo-Croatian interpreting.[95] Moreover, when asked for an opinion on the differences between Bosnian, Croatian, and Serbian, Browne stated the following:

> Not all speakers from Serbia are aware of all the terminology used in Croatia, and not all speakers from Croatia are aware of all the terminology used in Serbian, so that a conversation about a technical field such as chemistry may require clarification of particular terms. People schooled in [B&H] were exposed to both sets of everyday vocabulary and terminology. Therefore, one should

95 ICTY, Cases, *Mucić et al.*, Order on Zdravko Mucić's oral request for Serbo-Croatian interpreting (1997): https://bit.ly/3civnPX.

> not expect difficulties in understanding when a Bosnian and a person from Croatia or Serbia are speaking.[96]

Following the assessment of independent experts that people schooled in B&H were exposed to both sets of everyday vocabulary and terminology, it would be assumed that B&H language professionals were well represented among the ICTY CLSS managerial and staff ranks, as well. The official site of the ICTY, Cases lists 114 individuals who stood trials before this institution: 74 of them stood trials for crimes committed against Bosnian Muslims in B&H. Indeed, this would make sense operationally as the bulk of the victims and the perpetrators are from B&H where the population speaks the Bosnian language or, rather, does not speak Croatian as spoken in Croatia or Serbian as spoken in Serbia and where speaking those variants constitutes a very clear political statement.

In itself, this raises an issue related to language staff: should language staff recruitment at an international criminal tribunal adjudicating on ethnic crimes be based on nationality and/or ethnicity? Should language professionals of the nationality/ethnicity of the former attacking forces be precluded from working with victims and witnesses of the nationality/ethnicity of the victims? Should they have access to documents considered classified or secret in the countries of the former attacking forces?

The ICTY CLSS circumvented all these critical issues by inventing a B/C/S. This is a practical abbreviation that stands for Bosnian/Croatian/Serbian or, as the CLSS claimed, the language formerly known as Serbo-Croatian. But Serbo-Croatian was just a name, not an actual language which people spoke and the renaming of the former Serbo-Croatian into the neutrally perceived B/C/S did not preclude the defendants, the region, or the victims and witnesses from actually hearing the language. The first Chief of the CLSS, Draženović-Carrieri, who stayed in that position, to the author's best knowledge, from the establishment of the ICTY until about 2000, blamed the ICTY core laws:

---

96 Draženović-Carrieri, Maja (2002), B/C/S - A practical approach. Lexicography and language policy in South-Slavic languages after 1989. Verlag Otto Sagner: Munich.

> If we were to follow strictly the wording of the [ICTY Statute and Rules of Procedure and Evidence], all translation, including that of the witness statements, should automatically be done into the language of the accused. However, the real situation in the courtroom makes the choice of the target language somewhat more complex. This became evident with the first trial ever held at the Tribunal, which was against an accused from Bosnia. During his initial appearance, when the accused is called upon to enter a plea of guilty or not guilty on each count of the indictment, he stated that he spoke Serbian. However, he spoke in exactly the same way as most of the witnesses or victims who were bringing charges against him, who were of different ethnic backgrounds. They were all claiming to speak Bosnian and used, as did the accused, [*ijekavian*]. The [CLSS] was faced with a dilemma both in interpreting and in translation of how to proceed during the trial.[97]

However, evidence points that there was no place for such dilemmas. That very much insisted upon name of the language of the accused by the ICTY Registry CLSS had absolutely no place in the Court in practice.

The initial appearance of the accused in the court is regulated in the ICTY Rules of Procedure and Evidence, Rule 62(A)(ii) and follows a very simple and strict speech topology: the presiding judge introduces him/herself, asks for appearances, satisfies him/herself that the rights of the accused stemming from the ICTY Statute and Rules of Procedure and Evidence are respected and, should the accused want, instructs the Registrar to read the indictment. The presiding judge would ask the accused to state their full name, date of birth, place of residence, and occupation. He or she would then ask the counsel to introduce themselves, declare whether the client read or was read the indictment in a language which s/he understands, and, finally, say whether s/he understood the charges. Then the presiding judge would turn to the accused asking whether s/he is satisfied with his/her counsel, whether s/he read the indictment in a language which s/he understands, and whether s/he understood the charges.

There was *a priori* awareness and knowledge on the part of ICTY judges that the name of the language was vested with ethnic and national affiliations. The judges did not make a single mention of Bosnian, Croatian, Serbian, Serbo-Croatian, Croato-Serbian,

---

[97] Ibid.

Serbo-Croatian, Croato-Serbian, or B/C/S, only "a language which [you] understand" when referring to defendants' language. As a matter of fact, my research confirmed the ICTY judges mentioned the name of the language only and exclusively when referring to the document (*Blaškić*, T. 12901, 13715; *Dokmanović*, T. 35, 51, 52; *Dukić*, T. 45; *Karadžić*, T. 5142, 6193, 40093; *Tolimir*, T. 12480; *Župljanin and Stanišić*, T. 17, 22152, etc.). I also found two examples where the judges advised Serbian speaking defense counsels that it was better to switch back to speaking Serbian if they did not know the right words in English (*Perišić*, T. 8956 and *Pavković*, T. 209).

There was *a priori* awareness and knowledge on the part of ICTY management that victims and witnesses' language also had to be taken into consideration when translating and interpreting. The 1994 ICTY Annual Report (AR) acknowledges throughout that the judges are very much aware that there may be considerable reluctance on the part of witnesses to appear before the Tribunal to testify because the principal witness against the perpetrator of a crime will be the victim, that the crimes involving the civilian population were committed on, *inter alia*, ethnic grounds, and that the judges have never allowed themselves to lose sight of the fact that victims and witnesses have rights worthy of protection.[98] In other words, the judges clearly stated that the UN languages-centric, defendant-centric, and interpreter-centric approach to language services alone are inappropriate for the context of an international criminal tribunal adjudicating on ethnic crimes.

There was *a priori* knowledge on the part of CLSS managers that victims and witnesses' language also had to be taken into consideration when translating and interpreting.

> Interpreters who were working with witnesses had to be handpicked not only as to their professional skills, but also with regard to their ethnic background and the language they spoke. In general, fact witnesses require special care during the trial and it is provided to them by the [ICTY'S Victims and Witnesses Unit]. Those who are specially fragile might be upset to hear a language they identify with the aggressor. Therefore, the wrong assignment of an interpreter could easily cause suspicion or mistrust or could even result in witnesses refusing to testify. Given the sensitivity of the matter, it

[98] UN, Report of the ICTY (A/49/342) (1994).

> was decided to avoid risking such extreme reactions from witnesses who, back in 1995, could become very emotional or suspicious when hearing Serbian [*ekavian*]. The choice opted was to man the "B/C/S" interpreting booth during the Prosecution case with interpreters who spoke *either* Croatian or Bosnian, i.e. [*ijekavian*].[99]

Although singling out Serbian *ekavian*, Draženović-Carrieri has forgotten to mention Croatian *ijekavian*. This forgetfulness is somewhat strange as most of the ICTY trials during her tenure tried Croat(ian) perpetrators on B&H soil and B&H victims and witnesses testifying against them would have felt equally uncomfortable hearing the Croatian language (see Appendices 3 and 4).

Finally, in addition to awareness and knowledge among the ICTY management and the CLSS management, including the clear instructions of the judges about linguistic variants, there was *a priori* knowledge on the part of interpreters that victims and witnesses' language also had to be taken into consideration during the recruitment of translators and interpreters. Croatian interpreters interviewed for the purposes of this study stated that there was an unofficial policy in the CLSS to speak "the old version" of the Croatian language. They were unable to define the "old version" of the Croatian language except to say it corresponded to language in which words readily associated with the Croatian language (names of months, for example) would be replaced with corresponding terms in the Bosnian language. The very fact that Croatian-speaking interpreters deviated from the standard Croatian language using Bosnian language terminology shows that they were aware of their public and acutely aware of the fact they were interpreting into the language of the aggressor. These interpreters also pointed out that implementation of such an unofficial policy depended on an individual interpreter and that there were some who stuck to the unadjusted version of the Croatian language throughout.[100] CLSS Croatian language interpreters, at least,

---

99 Draženović-Carrieri, Maja (2002), B/C/S - A practical approach. Lexicography and language policy in South-Slavic languages after 1989. Verlag Otto Sagner: Munich.

100 Not all testifying witnesses had time to comment on the interpreting while testifying, but this one was unhappy and "want[ed] the names of the months to be interpreted in a dialect he understands better. Third and fourth month." ICTY, Cases, *Kupreškić et al.*, T. 7288 (25 February 1999): https://bit.ly/2xr3c2k.

remembered that language was always a political statement in the former Yugoslavia and unofficially worked to minimize the effects of such a political statement made by the ICTY as an institution.

ICTY management, CLSS management, and the judges were aware the language spoken in the former Yugoslavia was vested with ethnic and national affiliations and used as a tool in the conflict. The language experts confirmed it. The problem is that the ICTY Registry did not hire appropriate language service managers to act on any of it in practice.

Since the speech atrocity crimes and underlying philosophy of hate have never been prosecuted by the ICTY, it is on the basis of my research that I strongly recommend that the parties appearing before international criminal tribunals, especially those adjudicating on ethnic crimes, before the beginning of the trial make a habit of submitting to judges an independent brief authored by an interdisciplinary group of academics on the historical development of ethnic aspects of the conflict, including the philosophy of hate anchored in language or literature, as an introduction to the case.

It is on the basis of my research that I strongly recommend a departure from the UN's policies of multilingualism at international criminal tribunals. The official languages of international criminal tribunals must be limited to a minimum to provide for the least expensive, the most effective, and the most practical translation, interpreting, and transcription combination: English into the language of the situation country and vice versa. Should the international criminal tribunal adjudicate on crimes that occurred in a bi- or multilingual country, both or all relevant languages must be made official.

It is on the basis of my research that I strongly recommend that in addition to making official the language of the situation country, the rules and regulations of international criminal tribunals adjudicating on ethnic crimes must also include the different language variants spoken in the situation country when these variants are invested with ethnic and/or political significance because they reflect on the provision of language services to defendants, defense attorneys from the situation country, victims and witnesses, and posterity. Moreover, when the dialect/language of victims differs significantly from the standard language, these differences must be taken into account and accommodated.

CHAPTER 2

MAY THE LEGAL INSTITUTION TAKE THE STAND, PLEASE

Situation countries often seem to be overlooked by international criminal justice authorities when it comes to all the intricacies related to local cultures, customs, languages, etc. Unfortunately, the situation countries and professionals who do not speak the language of the judicial institution are sometimes ignored in the laws, even though those laws may pertain to them the most. Such was the case at the ICTY.

The ICTY Statute (ICTY-S) was modelled after the IMT Charter (IMT-C).[101] The ICTY President Meron stated that the ICTY-S was "drafted quickly," but added that the ICTY judges have been entrusted with the authority to write their own Rules of Procedure and Evidence (RPE) which, according to him, has largely proven a success, although there have been many revisions. Even so, the large number of revisions to the RPE reflect one of the main advantages of having judges do the rule-writing: the ability to quickly take into account lessons learned from concrete experiences in the courtroom.[102] Indeed, the self-explanatory Procedure for the Proposal, Consideration of and Publication of Amendments to the [RPE] of the [ICTY] was first delivered in 1998, and revised in 2001 and 2002, stipulating that the Rules Committee shall consider all proposals for amendment of the Rules forwarded to it by the President, a Judge of the International Tribunal or other body.[103] This included the ICTY language services, the CLSS.

---

[101] Gordon, Gregory S. (2017), Speech atrocity crimes: foundation, fragmentation, fruition. Oxford University Press: Oxford.

[102] Meron, Theodore (2011), The making of international criminal justice, a view from the bench: selected speeches. Oxford University Press: Oxford.

[103] ICTY, Procedure for the Proposal, Consideration of and Publication of Amendments to the [RPE] of the International Tribunal (2002).

In Chapter 2, I am reviewing normative procedural due process language-related rights, obligations, and requirements in the ICTY laws, language-related case law, and procedural linguistic equality of arms between the ICTY prosecution and defense. Then I am going to examine whether the linguistic justice has been served along the second line of communication with the judicial institution: the working institution towards the parties to the proceedings. This is done by cataloguing the lacunae in the language laws and examining whether the CLSS, the ICTY language services provider, informed any language-related laws or took stock of ICTY language-related case law.

2.1. Normative procedural due process language-related rights, obligations, and requirements in the ICTY laws

Bassiouni teaches that procedural due process includes guarantees that ensure that defendants have every reasonable opportunity to make a full and free defense including, *inter alia*, the right to have all proceedings conducted in or translated into his own language.[104] Accordingly, normative language-related rights, obligations, and requirements on the parties to the proceedings fall under the procedural due process.

The IMT-C and the IMT Rules of Procedure (IMT RoP) imposed several normative procedural due process language-related rights, obligations, and requirements on all parties to the proceedings. The IMT-C established that the official documents and court proceedings shall be held in English, French, Russian, the language of the defendant, and, if it is in the interests of justice and public opinion, in the language of the country where the IMT is sitting, without proclaiming any official languages.[105] In practice, the IMT operated in the first three languages only.

The IMT-C also established that the preliminary examination and trial of the defendant shall be conducted in, or translated into, a language which the defendant understands.[106] The IMT RoP extended

---

104 Bassiouni, Cherif (2011), Crimes against humanity: historical evolution and contemporary application. Cambridge University Press: Cambridge.
105 IMT-C, Article 25.
106 IMT-C, Article 16(c).

this principle further to German and the language of the document.[107] The IMT-C established that the defendant has a right to translation of the indictment and accompanying documents into a language which s/he understands.[108] The IMT RoP extended this further to include the right to a translation of IMT-C, the statement of defendants' right to defense, amendments or additions to the indictment, and evidence for the defense.[109] The IMT RoP established that the General Secretary of the IMT Secretariat should appoint, *inter alia*, interpreters.[110] However, IMT RoP also explicitly orders that of all persons participating in the proceedings, only the witnesses are obliged to pledge an oath.[111] The IMT rules and regulations do not provide the text of the oath. The IMT-C and RoP do not explicitly mention the right to an interpreter because the interpreting was "revamped" for the purposes of these trials (see below).

The IMTFE Charter (IMTFE-C) and the IMTFE RoP describe the defendant as the "accused" and English and the language of the accused as the official languages.[112] The accused has all the language rights described in the IMT-C and IMT RoP without any significant departures. The only significant difference between the two is procedural in that the Supreme Commander for the Allied Powers appoints, *inter alia*, interpreters.[113] The Japanese language has been explicitly mentioned in the context of translation of records, exhibits and documents, and in the context of the forms of oath and affirmation.[114]

The IMTFE set a precedent by obliging interpreters to pledge an oath and affirmation to the accuracy of their interpreting.[115] The difference between an oath and an affirmation is that an oath is widely considered to be a religious pledge whereas an affirmation is secular. Bassiouni reminds us that the 1907 Hague Convention establishing the "laws of humanity" which served as a basis for

---

107 IMT RoP, Rule 9(b).
108 IMT-C, Article 16(a).
109 IMT RoP, Rules 2(a), 3 and 4(e).
110 IMT RoP, Rule 8.
111 IMT RoP, Rules 6.
112 IMTFE-C, Article 9(b).
113 IMTFE RoP, Rule 3(b)(1).
114 IMTFE RoP, Rule 6(a) and 8.
115 IMTFE RoP, Rule 8(b).

prosecuting crimes at the IMT and the IMTFE was a Western European exercise which reflected Western European Christian values, as they emerged from the natural law of doctrine and practices of these Christian states, as well as whatever they absorbed from the pre-Christian Greco-Roman civilizations and borrowed from Islamic civilization. So, the distinction the IMTFE made between the oath and an affirmation was no longer Christian-centric.[116] This was an important contribution to the fairness of trials by the IMTFE, bearing in mind that Japan is a non-Christian country.

The IMT set a precedent by revamping the existing mode of interpreting, consecutive interpreting, into simultaneous interpretation. Both the defendants and interpreters felt that simultaneous interpretation played a key role as one of the requirements for a fair trial. Gaiba reports that Herman Göring took most advantage of the new system of simultaneous interpretation, although he is reported to have said "This system is very efficient, but it will also shorten my life." So, he learned very quickly how to "play the system" of simultaneous interpretation and turned his examination by the prosecution completely to his advantage. Since he spoke English, Göring did not have to listen to the interpretation to the extent that he depended solely on it. Instead, he used the time during the prosecutor's discourse to think of the most appropriate answers and to scrutinize the translation of the evidence being presented, thus avoiding all factual and linguistic pitfalls and turning the tables on the prosecution. No matter how counter-productive for the actual realm of justice this might be, that is exactly what prosecutors and defense who speak several languages that are used in international criminal tribunals actually do, as well. Another accused sentenced to death, Otto Ohlendorff, the Head of Intelligence and Security inside Nazi Germany, wrote the interpreters a letter to thank them for giving him a chance to understand and be understood in the court.[117]

As the fields of international criminal law and international human rights developed after 1946, so did the normative procedural due process language-related rights, obligations, and requirements

---

[116] Bassiouni, Cherif (2011), Crimes against humanity: historical evolution and contemporary application. Cambridge University Press: Cambridge.
[117] Gaiba, Francesca (1998), The origins of simultaneous interpreting: the Nuremberg trial. University of Ottawa Press: Ottawa.

on parties in the proceedings held before international criminal tribunals. As the nature of international criminal law is oriented toward the criminal responsibility of an individual, these rights are individual-centric.

The Universal Declaration of Human Rights (UDHR) and the International Covenant on Civil and Political Rights (ICCPR) provide a legal basis for assurance of the right to a fair trial to defendants, which is the father right to the use of an interpreter. The UDHR from 1948 is very important because it abolished discrimination, at least nominally, and enabled the expansion of procedural due process recognized by international law, which is an essential principle for all dealings with systems of justice at the national and international level.[118]

The ICCPR further elaborated on the concept of normative procedural due process recognized by international law. It limited the rights of the States Parties to the Covenant in times of emergencies in that they cannot take measures derogating from their obligations which are inconsistent with their other obligations under international law involving discrimination solely on the ground of race, color, sex, language, religion, or social origin. In addition, the ICCPR forbids discrimination on the basis of language, *inter alia*, against children, all persons appearing before the law, and ethnic, religious, or linguistic minorities. The ICCPR expanded on the rights of defendants before courts giving them the right to be informed promptly and in detail in a language which they understand of the nature and cause of the charge against them; and to have the free assistance of an interpreter if they cannot understand or speak the language used in court.[119]

This is the first time in history that international law acknowledged defendants' language and guaranteed defendants the right to an interpreter. This may also be seen as a tacit acknowledgment that the language of a judicial institution is a language of power and that assuring that both the defendant and the representatives of the judicial institution communicate in the same language naturally or through an interpreter establishes an equal footing in communication.

---

118 UN, Universal Declaration of Human Rights (1948).
119 UN, International Covenant on Civil and Political Rights (1966).

Although the mountains were moved in the field of the normative procedural due process rights to language, translation, and interpretation, once the ICTY entered the field, things stopped being innovative and turned much more cut-and-pasty.

The ICTY-S recognizes the following organs as part of their structure: Chambers (consisting of Trial Chambers and Appeals Chambers), Prosecutor, and Registry (servicing both the Chambers and the Prosecutor).[120]

As to the ICTY, the ICTY-S does not set the **official languages** of the institution.[121]

The ICTY RPE explicitly sets English and French as the **working languages**.[122] Although mentioned twice in the ICTY RPE, "official languages" have nowhere been clearly set in this document.[123] The ICTY RPE combines "other persons appearing before the Tribunal, other than as counsel," giving those persons the right to use their own language.[124] The ICTY RPE also ushers the concept of the "native language of the suspect or accused" into the field of international criminal law without any further definition.[125]

The ICTY RPE also establishes that the RPE text shall be equally authentic where the version which is more consonant with the spirit of the ICTY-S and of the RPE shall prevail in cases of disputes between different language versions.[126]

Obviously, the lawmakers set two UN languages as the working languages of the legal institution and completely ignored the language of the situation country in line with the UN policies of multilingualism.

As to the **judges**, the ICTY RPE provides a definition of permanent judges and *ad litem* judges. There were a total of 78 judges who adjudicated crimes at the ICTY: 43 permanent judges

[120] ICTY-S Article 11.
[121] ICTY-S, Article 33: English and French.
[122] ICTY RPE Rule 3(A).
[123] ICTY RPE Rules 47(G) and 55(C).
[124] ICTY RPE Rule 3(C).
[125] ICTY RPE Rule 44(B).
[126] ICTY RPE Rule 7: English and French.

and 35 *ad litem* judges.[127]

Table 1. Tenure of the ICTY permanent judges and *ad litem* judges

Judge	Years of tenure	1	2	3	4	5	6	7	8	9	10	12	13	14	17
Permanent		1	6	8	9	4	2	4	4	1	0	1	1	1	1
Ad litem		5	6	12	3	3	1	3	1	0	1	0	0	0	0

The ICTY-S does not explicitly mention any normative procedural due process language-related rights, obligations, and requirements on the judges.

Normative procedural due process language-related rights, obligations, and requirements placed on the ICTY judges in the RPE are explicit in that the defense counsel who does not speak any of the working languages or the language of the accused may apply to the Presiding Judge of a Chamber for leave to use a language other than the language of the accused.[128] These aspects are also explicit in the context of the initial appearance of the accused where the Trial Chamber or the Judge shall read or have the indictment read to the accused in a language the accused understands, satisfying himself that the accused understands the indictment.[129]

The ICTY RPE also provides that "other persons appearing before the [ICTY], other than as counsel" have the right to use their own language; obviously, this may include judges, as well. The ICTY RPE states that permission to use one's own language is to be sought from the judges, which might be taken to mean that the ICTY judges must speak and understand at least one of the ICTY official or working languages.[130]

The most important prerequisite for the effective functioning of judges in the context of an international criminal tribunal is that judges can communicate with each other during deliberations. Gaiba reports that IMT judges spoke their own languages throughout (English, French, Russian), but had their own interpreters assisting

127 ICTY, Former judges: https://bit.ly/2VsVpsT.
128 ICTY RPE 3(D).
129 ICTY RPE 62(A)(ii).
130 ICTY RPE 3(D).

them when they wanted to communicate with each other inside and outside the courtroom and during deliberations on sentencing. These interpreters would move in with the judges and could not communicate with the rest of the world during deliberations on sentencing. Gaiba also reports that interpreting for judges was more difficult than interpreting in the courtroom because it was impossible to impose the same discipline on the judges as on the speakers in the courtroom.[131] In practice, although first language speakers of different languages (Chinese, Dutch, English, French, Maltese, Turkish, etc.), the ICTY judges functioned in French and/or English and there has never been a case where they used any other language but these two in their official capacity. As a matter of fact, those who spoke both English and French would, indeed, use both English and French wherever possible, as per UN policies on multilingualism.

The ICTY RPE establishes that the **Registrar** shall make all arrangements for translation and interpreting into and from working languages.[132] This means the Registrar is in charge of language services. The ICTY RPE extends this to documents filed in a language other than one of the working languages of the Tribunal.[133]

The Registrar also must be satisfied that qualified counsel representing a suspect or accused has written and oral proficiency in one of the two working languages of the ICTY but can also waive this requirement at the request of the suspect or accused and where the interests of justice require this.[134] The ICTY RPE does not define written or oral proficiency and does not elucidate on the means of checking a person's written or oral proficiency in one of the two working languages of the Tribunal.

The obligation on the Registrar from the ICTY RPE to make all arrangements for translation and interpreting into and from working languages[135] has been repeated in specific examples of the indictment,[136] the execution of arrest warrants,[137] and the person or

---

131 Gaiba, Francesca (1998), The origins of simultaneous interpreting: the Nuremberg trial. University of Ottawa Press: Ottawa.
132 ICTY RPE Rule 3(E).
133 ICTY RPE Rule 3(F).
134 ICTY RPE Rule 44(A)(ii) and 44(B).
135 ICTY RPE Rule 3(E).
136 ICTY RPE Rule 47(G).
137 ICTY RPE Rule 55(C).

authorities cautioning the accused of his rights when arrested if the accused does not understand either of the official languages of these tribunals and if the language understood by the accused is known to the Registrar.[138] The ICTY RPE adds that these do not apply if at the time of arrest the accused is served with, or with a translation of, the indictment and the statement of rights of the accused in a language that the accused understands and is able to read.[139]

The ICTY-S is not explicit about the normative procedural due process language-related rights, obligations, and requirements of the **Prosecutor**. It authorizes the prosecutor to conduct investigations and question suspects, victims, and witnesses giving such suspects, victims, and witnesses the right to *translation and interpretation*.[140]

The ICTY RPE gives suspects certain language-related rights when being questioned by the prosecutor in that the suspect has the right to be informed of his rights in a language they understand and the right to have the free assistance of an interpreter should they not understand or speak the language used for questioning.[141] The ICTY RPE also obliges the prosecutor to inform the suspect in a language the suspect understands that the interview is being video or audio recorded.[142]

The ICTY RPE establishes certain language-related obligations of the prosecutor toward the defense in that the prosecutor must make available to the accused in a language they understand: copies of the supporting material which accompanied the indictment when confirmation was sought, all prior statements obtained by the prosecutor from the accused, copies of the statements of all witnesses whom the prosecutor intends to call to testify at trial, copies of all transcripts and written statements, and copies of the statements of additional prosecution witnesses, which shall be made available to the defense once a decision is made to call those witnesses.[143]

---

138 ICTY RPE Rule 55(E).
139 ICTY RPE Rule 55(F).
140 ICTY-S Articles 18(1), 18(2) and 18(3).
141 ICTY RPE Rule 42(A) and 42(A)(ii).
142 ICTY RPE Rule 43.
143 ICTY RPE Rule 66(A)(i) and 66(A)(ii).

All these documents – delivered in the language of the defendant – represent the court sanctioned translation load at the ICTY.

Although the ICTY-S does not recognize the **Defense** as a constituent part, that did not stop the ICTY from explicitly mentioning normative procedural due process language-related rights, obligations, and requirements on the defense and imposing the Defense Code of Conduct.[144]

The ICTY RPE states that defense counsels must have written or oral proficiency in one of the two ICTY working languages, speak the native language of the accused or suspect, or, on application for leave, use a language different from the language of the accused or suspect or the working languages.[145]

Should defense counsel speak only the native language of the accused or suspect, it is required that the counsel or accused undertake to meet all translations and interpretation costs not usually met by the ICTY and undertake not to request any extensions of time as a result of the fact that he does not speak one of the working languages.[146]

Neither the ICTY-S nor the ICTY RPE elaborate on "translation and interpretation costs not usually met by the Tribunal," how to establish "the native language of the accused," or provide a definition of "a native language."

The ICTY RPE provides that the defense is given a copy of the judgment and the Judges' opinions in the language of the accused or the language in which they were delivered.[147]

Defendants appearing before the ICTY are called both suspects and accused. Although an *ad hoc* tribunal with specific temporal and territorial jurisdiction, the ICTY-S does not define the notion of a **suspect**. When it comes to the normative procedural due process language-related rights, obligations, and requirements

---

144 ICTY, Documents, Miscellaneous: Code of Professional Conduct for Defense Counsel Appearing Before the International Tribunal (2009).
145 ICTY RPE Rule 44(A)(ii), 44(B) and 3(D).
146 ICTY RPE Rule 44(B).
147 ICTY RPE Rule 98*ter* (D).

of the suspects, the ICTY-S entitles the suspect to necessary translation into and from a language he speaks and understands when questioned.[148]

When it comes to the normative procedural due process language-related rights, obligations, and requirements of the **accused**, the ICTY-S gives the accused the right to be informed of the nature and the cause of charges against him in the language he understands and the right to an interpreter if he cannot understand or speak the language used at the ICTY.[149]

The accused have general language-related rights, obligations, and requirements during pre-trial proceedings, in the context of arrest and warrants, at initial appearance, and at publication of a verdict and the judges' opinions as elaborated in the ICTY RPE which gives the accused the right to use "his or her own language."[150]

At the pre-trial proceedings, the ICTY RPE gives the accused the right to a translation of the indictment, when confirmed, if the accused does not understand either of the official languages of these tribunals and if the language understood is known to the Registrar, who will serve the indictment and certified copies of the indictment.[151]

When arrested, the ICTY RPE gives the accused the right to a translation of the warrant of arrest and a statement of the rights of the accused.[152] The accused also has the right to be read the indictment and the statement of the rights of the accused, unless these are already translated as per the ICTY RPE.[153] The accused also has the right to be cautioned that he has the right to remain silent, and that any statement he makes shall be recorded and may be used in evidence in a language he understands.[154]

---

148 ICTY-S Article 18(3).
149 ICTY-S Article 21(4)(a) and 21(4)(f).
150 ICTY Rule 3(B).
151 ICTY RPE Rule 47(G).
152 ICTY RPE Rule 55(C).
153 ICTY RPE Rule 55(E).
154 ICTY RPE Rule 55(D).

When taken into custody, the ICTY RPE gives the accused the right to be informed of the charges against him and of the fact that he is being transferred to the Tribunal in a language he understands, including the right to be read the indictment and the statement of the rights of the accused in a language he understands and to be cautioned in the language he understands, unless these documents are already translated.[155]

During the initial appearance of the accused, the accused has the right to read or have the indictment read in a language he understands.[156]

At the end of the proceedings, the accused also has the right to a copy of the judgment and of the Judges' opinions in a language which he understands and in the original language.[157]

As to the **victims and witnesses**, the ICTY-S gives the prosecutor the right to *question victims and witnesses*[158] and gives the accused the right to *examine or have the witnesses examined.*[159]

The ICTY RPE does not explicitly mention any victims and witnesses' language-related rights, obligations, and requirements, grouping them together with "(any) (other) persons appearing before the Tribunal, other than as counsel" with the right to use "their own language."[160]

2.2. ICTY language- and language professionals-related case law

Language and identity-related conflicts moved to The Hague with the ICTY defendants and their defenses to support the denial of each other's unique language, identity, and culture by claiming to misunderstand the languages used for interpreting and translation and wanting the written communication to be conducted in Cyrillic script. As expected, perhaps, defendants of Serb origin before the ICTY were the loudest in their claims not to understand the other

155 ICTY RPE Rule 59*bis*(B) and 59*bis*(C).
156 ICTY RPE Rule 62(A)(ii).
157 ICTY RPE Rule 68*ter*(D).
158 ICTY-S Article 18(2).
159 ICTY-S, Article 21(4)(e).
160 ICTY RPE Rule 3(C).

two versions of the former Serbo-Croatian, Bosnian, and Croatian, putting on a constant show about their language, identity, religion, and history.

Paradoxically, most ICTY defendants originated from B&H, where they spent most, if not their entire lives. The official site of the ICTY, Cases lists 114 individuals who stood trial before this institution: 86 of them were born, raised, and spent their entire professional lives in B&H.

However, with regard to Serbian nationalism, that did not stop B&H Serbs from trying very hard to switch from their native Bosnian language of *ijekavian* pronunciation to Serbian *ekavian*. This particularly applies to Messrs. Župljanin,[161] Mladić,[162] and Karadžić,[163] whose determination to speak *ekavian* seems to be associated with their political affiliations and loyalties and can be said to constitute a clear political statement. What brings their linguistic political statement to the realms of absurdist drama is that their speech pattern is a mishmash of the Bosnian language intonation, sentence structure, and expression in both the Bosnian, *ijekavian*, and the Serbian, *ekavian*, dialect and that, bizarrely, in the same sentence. In that sense, mixing *ekavian* and *ijekavian* or Bosnian *ijekavian* with Croatian *ijekavian* should send a message that the Court is dealing with a person with a non-linguistic agenda. It is unfortunate that this point was not explored by the OTP, either.

Although denial of the other's culture, language, and identity is the core of nationalist discourse, the major requirement in all legal processes is fairness to and a presumption of the innocence of the defendant, who can be seen as the most protected person in any trial. The court must ensure that the fundamental rights of a defendant in a criminal case are protected throughout that person's trial.

---

[161] ICTY, Cases, *Župljanin and Stanišić*, T. 21-22 (9 June 2009): *zahtjev* (request, *ijekavian*), *razriješimo* (resolve, *ijekavian*), *rešimo* (resolve, *ekavian*), *razrešimo* (resolve, *ekavian*).

[162] ICTY, Cases, *Mladić*: *Ja bih želio* (I want, *ijekavian*), *stariji čovek* (elderly man, *ekavian*), *mesec dana* (one month, *ekavian*): https://bit.ly/2ybPeBy.

[163] ICTY, Cases, *Karadžić*: *cenim* (I think/would have thought, *ekavian*), *Tužilaštvo* (Office of the Prosecutor, Bosnian), etc. It is worth noting that Karadžić was born in Montenegro (Montenegrin, *ijekavian*) and that he spent most of his life in B&H either in prison or in high public offices.

As stated before, in 1995, in anticipation of an issue about the name of the language used and underlying problems of comprehension, the CLSS consulted with two linguistic experts, Wayles Browne and Morton Benson, who stated, *inter alia*, that the varieties of Serbo-Croatian were mutually intelligible to all citizens of the former Yugoslavia, that the differences between Serbian and Croatian were small, and that there was no valid reason to justify the refusal of Serbo-Croatian interpreting.[164]

In 1996, the issue of alleged miscomprehension of language used for translation and interpretation came up as a legal issue for the first time during the testimony of a rather unwilling witness. After having exhausted all of the options not to testify, a witness complained that he did not understand the language used for interpretation. It is only in *Mucić* where the Trial Chambers actually delivered a decision on the issue when Mucić's defense orally applied for interpretation of the trial proceedings into Croatian for the benefit of the accused, instead of Serbian. However, there were two problems with this decision. The first is in the wording "the refusal of Serbo-Croatian interpretation" because the issue was not interpretation into Serbo-Croatian, but into Serbian. The second is that this decision does not mention the citizenship of the defendant (B&H) or the Bosnian language: it only decided on differences between Serbian and Croatian.

Clearly, given the discussion in Chapter 1, B&H and its citizens were again disadvantaged. The third and the most important problem is that this decision is very limited: it is unacceptable for someone claiming to be a speaker of Croatian to not understand interpretation by a Serbian interpreter. Therefore, the defense of miscomprehension concerning all other languages and interpretative combinations seemed an excellent one. Naturally, other defendants picked up on that.

The defense in *Delalić*, a Bosnian Muslim, requested that all transcripts and other documents be provided in Bosnian. They argued that the application was based on the right of an accused to use his own language in order to ensure equal treatment as a party to the proceedings and that the requirement that counsel address the ICTY in one of its working languages presents a restriction on

---

[164] ICTY, Cases, *Mucić et al.*, Order on Zdravko Mucić's oral request for Serbo-Croatian interpreting (1997).

the right of the accused to choose his own counsel. As to the restriction, the Court reiterated that the ICTY did provide a facility for counsel to speak the language of the accused during the proceedings, in addition to the two working languages, concluding there was no restriction on this right. The Prosecution and Chambers agreed that certain documents must be provided in the language of the accused but contended that both the ICTY-S and the ICTY RPE required *all* documents to be submitted in the language of the accused. It is noteworthy that this request was not a request to un-recognize or block the use of all other languages, but a legitimate request to the Court to provide the official court transcripts in the language of the accused. The Trial Chamber partially obliged.[165]

In 1997, the defense filed a motion about an alleged omission or incompleteness in the record of the proceedings of an interpreted interview, claiming that the interpreter was a witness or potential witness as to whether there was in fact such an omission or gap and as to what in fact occurred at that time. This defense motion was mainly based on ICTY RPE Rule 54, stating that a Judge or a Trial Chamber may issue such orders, summonses, subpoenas, warrants, and transfer orders *as may be necessary* which, obviously, includes language staff. When considering the issue, the Trial Chamber defined an interpreter as "one who interprets from either an official or unofficial language of the [ICTY] into the official languages of the [ICTY] and *vice versa* in judicial proceedings or proceedings related thereto." As to the status and duty of interpreters, the Trial Chamber clarified that the interpreter is not one of the parties to the proceedings, but an officer of the ICTY, and when providing interpreting before the Trial Chamber, an officer of the Trial Chamber. As such, the interpreter has the status of an impartial third party in the furtherance of the administration of justice. The Trial Chamber also pointed out that an interpreter is in a unique position as his or her services are available to both parties. Although relied on to constitute the record of all proceedings, an interpreter is not responsible for its authentication and is not required to keep a record of the proceedings s/he interprets or translates. The function of the interpreter is merely to pass on to the Trial Chamber, for the benefit of the parties or to the parties directly,

---

165 ICTY, Cases, *Mucić et al.*, Decision on Defense application for forwarding the documents in the language of the accused (1996).

whatever is said during the proceedings. S/he is merely the means through which the parties and the Trial Chamber are made to understand each other and to follow the proceedings.

The Trial Chamber tested whether there was a legal duty on the interpreter to make a record of the interpreting between the parties; whether there is any other way of obtaining the evidence sought other than through the testimony of the interpreter; and whether the determination of the issue should depend entirely on the evidence to be given by the interpreter. The Trial Chamber decided that judicial functionaries such as clerks or registrars of courts should be protected from matters arising from their official duties. The Trial Chamber stated that interpreters make a declaration under ICTY RPE Rule 76 to ensure the maintenance of the position of impartiality owed to the parties, which is an essential prerequisite of the interpreter's function and emphasizes the independence of the interpreter from either party in the proceedings and the confidentiality of the subject matter interpreted. The Trial Chamber also decided that it is undesirable, invidious, and not to be encouraged to compel an interpreter into the arena of conflict on behalf of either party to the proceedings for the determination of an issue arising from such proceedings: an interpreter cannot be relied on to testify on the fleeting words of his/her interpretation in the proceedings between the parties. It is also an important consideration in the administration of justice to insulate the interpreter or other functionaries of the ICTY from constant apprehension of the possibility of being personally involved in the arena of conflict, on either side, in respect of matters arising from the discharge of their duties. On both these grounds, the interest of justice frowns on any of the parties being able to call an interpreter as a witness.[166]

In September 1997, the defense argued, *inter alia*, that evidence obtained from the accused or having belonged to him had been excluded, claiming that the statements of the accused were taken under improper conditions in that at the outset, the interpreter was instructed "not to interpret every single word especially when we are talking about background matters." As a

---

[166] ICTY, Cases, *Mucić et al.*, Decision on the motion ex parte by the defence of Zdravko Mucić concerning the issue of subpoena to an interpreter (1997).

result, the defense claimed that the accused was not informed of each word which was part of the questions being asked and the statement does not contain each word of his answer. The prosecution argued that the interpreting of the interview was complete and correct. The defense counsel, who speaks both English and Bosnian, was present throughout the interviews and could have raised objections about inaccurate translations there and then. The interview was recorded in full and thus any questions or issues disputed can be resolved by a review of the question and answer in the accused's language, i.e. the issue ought to have been raised before. The Trial Chamber denied the motion for exclusion.[167]

In 1999, the prosecution submitted a motion on a "sensitive issue of whether an employee of the International Committee of the Red Cross (ICRC) may be called as a witness." The prosecution described the witness as an eye-witness who, as a former ICRC interpreter, accompanied ICRC staff on visits to places of detention and during exchanges of civilians supervised by the ICRC. This witness contacted the OTP, was interviewed about facts that came to his knowledge by virtue of his employment and was willing to give evidence before the ICTY. The prosecution wished to call the witness, stating that his testimony was important to prove the guilt of the accused. However, although concurring on the facts, the parties could not agree on the consequences that flow from the ICRC's status as an international legal personality and its mandate as conferred on it by the international community. The Trial Chambers decided that evidence from the former ICRC employee should not be given due to confidentiality interests barring the Trial Chamber from admitting the information, and a difference in the tasks, functions, and mandates of these organizations: the ICRC's activities are "preventive," while the ICTY is empowered to prosecute breaches of international humanitarian law once they have occurred.[168]

In 2000, the parties could not agree on a statement of a deceased witness. The prosecution wanted to introduce the statement of a witness taken by an OTP investigator, but since the

---

[167] ICTY, Cases, *Mucić et al.*, Decision on motion of Esad Landžo pursuant to Rule 73 (1997).

[168] ICTY, *Simić et al.*, Ex parte confidential: Decision on the Prosecution motion under Rule 73 for a ruling concerning the testimony of a witness (1999): https://bit.ly/2XGmmvM.

witness had died, the prosecution contended that it was in the interests of justice to admit his statement into evidence. The Trial Chamber first declined, but after hearing further arguments from the parties, the Trial Chamber decided to admit the statement. The Trial Chamber held that Rule 89(C) gave it discretion to admit the statement, and that the fact that the statement had not been subjected to cross-examination and was not made under oath were factors that affected the weight to be given to the *statement*, and not its *admissibility*. The Trial Chamber noted that, pursuant to the European Court of Human Rights jurisprudence cited by the parties, "it would not be possible to convict the accused on the basis of this statement alone if that evidence was uncorroborated" without violating his fundamental rights. The Defense argued that the statement was erroneous in several respects: the OTP investigator admitted that she did not speak Croatian, the language of the witness, and relied on the interpreter's account of what he was saying. Although witness statements can be taken through an interpreter, this particular statement was unusual as it was not taken in formal circumstances: the witness statement was written in English by the OTP investigator, whose native language was Dutch, and was then translated back into Croatian for the witness to sign it. Trial Chambers found that these multiple translations in an informal setting create a much greater potential for inaccuracy than is the case when both the declarant and the witness speak the same language or when the original statement is given in court with a professional, double-checked simultaneous translation. The Appeals Chamber found the statement so lacking in *reliability* that it should have been excluded as without probative value under Rule 89(C).[169]

In 2002, the prosecution sought to introduce in evidence a newspaper article written by a journalist (1) who conducted the interview with the accused through the interpreting services of a second journalist. The accused responded that the second journalist had been hostile to him and that what was written in journalist 1's article did not correspond to his words. The prosecution argued further that the position between the two journalists was effectively no different from "an investigator seeing a witness and taking a statement through an interpreter," and that this was a matter that should depend on the weight of journalist 1's article and his

[169] ICTY, Cases, *Kordić and Čerkez*, Decision on appeal regarding statement of a deceased witness (2000): https://bit.ly/2XyXoAb.

testimony, rather than on their admissibility. Moreover, the prosecution reminded the court that "statements made through interpreters are routinely admitted by the Trial Chamber without requiring the interpreter to testify." However, journalist 1 made the entire issue about himself, claiming: "I am willing to speak with [ICTY] investigators but I hesitate as a journalist to testify before the court. I would prefer that my statement and article stand for themselves. However, if that were not possible I would be willing to testify that the quotes accredited to [the accused] are true and accurate." The Trial Chamber dismissed the motion.[170]

In 2003, Šešelj surrendered to the ICTY, where he gained the status of a self-representing defendant. Šešelj's sole job, as such, was to defend himself against all allegations made by the prosecution. Šešelj almost immediately turned against the interpreters during his initial appearance, insisting that the ICTY find an interpreter who could speak the Serbian language well and complaining that he did not understand Croatian words that were being used in the interpreting. Obviously, the name of the language played no role in translational and interpretational practice. A reasonable foundation for claiming one does not understand the language is just that: an evidence of complete or partial miscomprehension of that language. It is clear the person does not speak the language he claims not to speak, because he does not understand that language. Šešelj claimed not to have understood the interpreter speaking Croatian, but then provided the Serbian version of disputed words himself (*tačka, hotimice, hapšenje* for *točka, hotimično, uhićenje* (point, random, arrest)).[171] As to translators, Šešelj insisted that "every document, each and every document, must be translated into the Serbian language; otherwise it is unacceptable to this Tribunal."[172] However, except for making a show that it was important that he exercised his rights to use his own language during the preparation of his defense, Šešelj never really made any substantive language-related point relevant to his overall argument.

In 2004, realizing that no one was buying his argument, Šešelj took his ICTY-given rights to translation and interpreting into

---

[170] ICTY, Cases, *Brđanin*, Decision on motion to set aside confidential subpoena to give evidence (2002): https://bit.ly/3b9NozM.
[171] ICTY, Cases, *Šešelj*, T. 57-59, 76 (25 March 2003).
[172] ICTY, Cases, *Šešelj*, T. 98-99 (3 July 2003).

the realm of the bizarre. ICTY RPE Rule 65*bis*(i) on status conferences calls the parties to organize exchanges between them to ensure expeditious preparation for trial where the OTP, in this case, surrenders to the defense all documents they plan to use to prove their claims in trial. However, Šešelj, a PhD, stated that he did not want the OTP to submit documents in an "electronic form, on diskettes" but rather on paper, because a "document on paper is a basic document."[173] He continued asking for documents to be submitted in paper form, stating that submitting documents in electronic form is "the same as if you decided that I had to stand on my head in the courtroom,"[174] exclaiming "I do not use a computer. I do not use this form. I'm never going to use a computer."[175] After having waited two years to receive disclosure documents, including statements of all protected and open court witnesses on paper, Šešelj bound them all together, manipulated pictures of the judges or prosecutors by giving them horns or other animal-like features, wrote derogatory titles on the cover, called the whole thing a book, and published it in Serbia.[176]

In 2004, the defense submitted a motion that the prosecution should cease proofing witnesses with immediate effect, or allow representatives of the defense to be present during proofing or provide the defense with a video or audio recording of the proofing sessions. The Trial Chamber described proofing as "a meeting held between a party to the proceedings and a witness, usually shortly before the witness is to testify in court, the purpose of which is to prepare and familiarize the witness with courtroom

---

[173] ICTY, Cases, *Šešelj*, T. 237 (14 June 2004).
[174] ICTY, Cases, *Šešelj*, T. 675 (3 November 2006).
[175] ICTY, Cases, *Šešelj*, T. 1065-1066 (2 May 2007).
[176] Some titles include: "Plucked Turkey from The Hague: Christine Dahl," featuring a plucked turkey with Ms. Dahl's head on the cover (Ms. Dahl was a Senior Trial Attorney in his case), "Bristling Scottish Piece of Shit: Iain Bonomy" (Judge Bonomy was one of the judges on his case), "Wrinkled Kangaroo's Ball: Kevin Parker" (Judge Parker was one of the judges on his case), "South Korean Mite O-Gon Kwon" (Judge Kwon was one of the judges on his case), "Dumbass from Manitoba: Bruce MacFarlane" featuring Mr. MacFarlane with donkey ears on the cover (MacFarlane was a Prosecution's Senior Trial Attorney in his case), "We Resume Plucking Turkeys from The Hague" featuring four plucked turkeys with the heads of Ms. Dahl, Mr. MacFarlane, Ms. Del Ponte and Mr. MacFarlane's unidentified female assistant on the cover.

procedures and to review the witness's evidence." The proofing is done through the assistance of an interpreter. The Trial Chamber concluded that proofing is beneficial to witnesses coping with the stress and cultural differences. The Trial Chamber noted as particularly relevant the cultural differences encountered by most witnesses when brought to The Hague and required to give a detailed account of stressful events, which occurred a long time ago, in a formal setting, and doing so in response to structured, precise questions, translated into a different language. Such factors also demand time in preparing a witness to cope adequately with the stress of these proceedings. These matters, in the Chamber's view, were properly in the realm of proofing and were not to be left to the different form of support provided by the ICTY Victims and Witnesses Unit.[177]

In 2005, the defense submitted a motion requesting the Trial Chamber not to admit the record of the interview of the accused taken by OTP investigators and tendered by the prosecution arguing, *inter alia*, that the statement had not been taken according to the ICTY RPE Rules: an interpreter was present during the interviews, but the prosecution did not keep notes of the interview in its records and the interviews were not audio or video recorded. The prosecution submitted that the statement was taken with the assistance of a competent UN interpreter, with good knowledge of military terms, who read the statement, as written by the investigator, to the accused before he signed it, and argued that there was no strict requirement to keep records of any notes on the investigator, nor a requirement to keep a list of questions. The Trial Chamber found that the ICTY RPE Rule 43 on recording interviews of suspects was not applied, the accused had not chosen to waive his right to remain silent during trial, and that the admission of the disputed statement would infringe on his right to a fair trial.[178]

In 2007, Šešelj's efforts seemed to have opened avenues for other accused to experiment with, seemingly using the same tactics. Tolimir, another self-representing defendant who would routinely bless all in the courtroom with a sign of cross at the beginning of

---

[177] ICTY, Cases, *Limaj et al.*, Decision on the Defense motion on Prosecution practice of "proofing" witnesses (2004): https://bit.ly/3elhIJF.
[178] ICTY, Cases, *Halilović*, Decision on motion for exclusion of statement of accused (2005): https://bit.ly/2XyYJ8D.

each and every trial session,[179] another PhD, and another Bosnian speaker who mixed the two linguistic variants when speaking, made similar claims to Šešelj's during his initial appearance, asking for all the documents for his review to be provided to him in Cyrillic script and that the written communication with the Court should be conducted in Cyrillic. B&H born and raised Tolimir provided no coherent argumentation for such a request. He pointed out that "language is a basic characteristic of mankind, which enables complex social life and all aspects of that life" and stressed that "it is with great effort that I would be able to read a document in Serbian but written in a Latin script." The Presiding Judge retorted: "I'm taking from your submission that you do, in fact, read and understand the Latin script; however, it is more difficult for you to read in the Latin script than in the Cyrillic script. That's the way I'm going to summarize what you've said on that particular point. But you do read and understand it." Tolimir's request was dismissed.[180]

In July 2008, Šešelj made a number of submissions relating to the quality of interpreting. This prompted the Trial Chambers to clarify that interpreting, unlike translation, deals with fleeting messages in real time where synthesizing and editing are not only legitimate interpreting techniques, but make interpreting possible. The Trial Chambers offered the view that the quality and precision of interpreting depended on the intelligibility of the speaker, the speed of the delivery, and the practice of pauses between questions and answers – factors that also could greatly reduce the quality and legibility of the transcript. The Trial Chambers also reflected that interpreting into French is liaison interpreting (meaning that what has been said in B/C/S is first interpreted into English and then from English into French) which multiplies all the difficulties and increases the risk of errors. The Trial Chambers reminded the court that official verification of the transcript is always at the disposal of the parties. The Trial Chambers rejected all Šešelj's other claims that interpreting errors were intentional and that the interpreters were unprofessional and ignorant of the substance. The Trial Chambers referred Šešelj to the CLSS for all further issues on translation and interpreting.[181]

---

[179] ICTY, Cases, *Tolimir*, T. 4-18 (25 February 2010): https://bit.ly/3bkrzxi.
[180] ICTY, Cases, *Tolimir*, T. 62-70 (14 September 2007).
[181] ICTY, Cases, *Šešelj*, Decision on defendant's motions concerning the quality of interpreting (2008).

In September 2008, Karadžić filed a motion that all materials in his case, including transcripts, should be submitted in Serbian and in Cyrillic script. The Court informed him that court session transcripts were not available in B/C/S, but that the audio tapes of the court sessions could be made available in B/C/S for his perusal. Karadžić appealed, claiming that listening to the audio tapes was unacceptable because the process of listening would be too onerous and would impede his preparation of his defense. He repeated the request and reiterated that he needed all materials, including transcripts, to be delivered to him in the Serbian language and in the Cyrillic script. The Deputy Registrar responded, reminding him that delivery of audio tapes in B/C/S was consistent both with CLSS translation policy and ICTY jurisprudence. The prosecution responded, reminding him that the request had no support in ICTY-S, ICTY RPE, jurisprudence, or practice, adding that similar requests had been routinely denied by the Court and that the accused did not provide any reasonable justification for such a request. The Chamber started a discussion on the issue by relating that the accused stated he did not deny understanding the English language, but that his knowledge of English was insufficient to "understand legal matters." The Chamber noted that there was evidence that the accused did have broad understanding of English, as he was trained in the USA and has published in English. The Chamber noted that "B/C/S" was the proper qualification of languages used in parts of the former Yugoslavia. As to "all materials," the Chamber reiterated that materials referred to in Rule 66(A), Rule 66(A)(i), and Rule 66(A)(ii), namely disclosure documents, material supporting the indictment and witness statements, including all transcripts disclosed pursuant to Rule 66 should be transcribed into a language the accused understands, rather than provided to him in audio format. The Court remarked that this decision, however, did not affect documents that are beyond the scope of Rule 66. Moreover, in court, the accused received real-time audio interpretation and there was no reason that he should receive transcripts on the top of that. The accused was free to use existing translation and interpretation facilities, to find a counsel who spoke his language, and to be assigned a Language Assistant. As to the Cyrillic script, the accused only argued a preference, which was insufficient justification for departing from standard practice.[182]

---

[182] ICTY, Cases, *Karadžić*, Decision on the Accused's request that all

In March 2009, the prosecution in *Karadžić* filed a motion seeking a determination that the accused understood English for the purposes of ICTY-S and ICTY RPE. The accused was a self-representing accused, had two legal associates and one investigator who were paid by the Registry as per standing rules, and several *pro bono* advisers and interns. In that regard, the prosecution requested the revision of the Chamber's decision that "all transcripts disclosed pursuant to Rule 66 should be transcribed into a language the Accused understands, rather than provided to him in audio format" arguing it was inconsistent with ICTY case law and "practically infeasible as transcription into B/C/S would require significant expenditure of time and resources." The accused responded by saying he had no formal training in English, the prosecution had only managed to show that he resided in the USA more than 30 years previously, and that he conversed in English "from time to time 14 to 17 years ago." Therefore, the prosecution had not shown that he had a sufficient understanding of English in 2009 and that, from 1996 through 2008, he almost never spoke English. His communication with his associates did not equate to a sufficient understanding of the language for the purposes of his trial. The accused stated that his associates' draft pleadings and correspondence on his behalf in English was simply evidence of the delegation of tasks within his defense team. The accused also claimed that he was unfamiliar with English legal terms and, therefore, could not confidently handle legal matters in English: he had a far better understanding of legal terms in Serbian than in English and that was just common sense. After a lengthy reflection on English-speaking defense team members, the history of the accused's education, and his use of English in public, the Court found that the accused "is capable of conversing and understanding the English language, even in the context of a complex criminal trial" as witnessed by his conversations with his legal representatives and his signature on the English documents submitted to the Court. The Court granted the motion and notified the prosecution and the Registry that "English is a language that the Accused understands for the purposes of the Rules and the Statute, and in particular, for the purposes of the Chamber's Decisions of 25 September and 25 November."[183]

---

materials, including transcripts, be disclosed to him in Serbian and Cyrillic script (2008).

183 ICTY, Cases, *Karadžić*, Decision on Prosecution motion seeking

In July 2009, the prosecution sought the admission into evidence of a witness's written statement pursuant to Rule 92*quater* on unavailable persons because the witness was presumed dead. The defense objected, claiming that the witness's evidence was never subjected to cross-examination, was not taken under oath, and was therefore not reliable. The defense objected to the language in which the witness interview was conducted, the statement recorded, and the witness's ability to speak and understand English. The Trial Chamber found that, while the absence of an interpreter may be a relevant factor, in those circumstances the Chamber was not satisfied that the absence of an interpreter rendered the statement inadmissible. By his signature recorded on each page and the witness acknowledgment, the witness indicated that he spoke and understood English. The Chamber granted the motion and the statement was admitted to evidence.[184]

In November 2009, the prosecution argued for the reliability of the information given in the witness statement and proposed the following language-related factors that guaranteed that reliability of the witness statement: 1) the presence during the interview of duly qualified interpreters appointed by the Registry; [...] 3) the Statement was read back to the witness in the presence of a duly qualified interpreter appointed by the Registry; [...] 5) the witness signed the Statement and indicated that it was true and correct to the best of his knowledge and that it had been read over to him in his own language; and 6) the interpreter and the investigators also signed the Statement [...].The Trial Chamber confirmed that the statement was made with the assistance of an interpreter duly qualified and approved by the Registry of the Tribunal. Consequently, the Trial Chamber considered that the disputed statement met sufficient indicia of reliability.[185]

In 2013, the prosecution submitted a motion to admit into evidence three ICTY witness statements of Witness RM-012 under ICTY RPE Rule 92*quater* on unavailable persons, alleging that

---

determination that the Accused understands English for the purposes of the [ICTY-S] and [ICTY-RPE] (2009).

184 ICTY, Cases, *Đorđević*, Decision on Prosecution's renewed motion for admission of evidence of [witness] pursuant to Rule 92*quater* (2009): https://bit.ly/3a9E9hM.

185 ICTY, Cases, *Šešelj*, Decision on motion for admission of [witness] testimony pursuant to Rule 92*quater* (2009).

Witness RM-012 was unavailable because his mental condition rendered him objectively unable to testify due to the diagnosis of Alzheimer's disease. The defense objected, stating it considered the evidence in the statements to be unreliable, submitting, *inter alia*, that none of the statements were taken under oath or subjected to cross-examination, but instead only taken through interpreters. The Chamber noted that, with regard to the reliability of the statements, they were neither given under oath nor had been subjected to cross-examination, but they were signed by Witness RM-012 with an accompanying acknowledgment that they were true to the best of his recollection and taken with the assistance of a duly qualified interpreter approved by the ICTY Registry.[186]

In 2013, the defense counsel submitted the view that "translation issues" may have led a doctor to draw incorrect conclusions on the health of the accused. The Appeals Chamber noted the examination of the accused required interpreting from/into English and B/C/S and that the examining doctor was alert to the associated risks involved, namely that simultaneous interpreting is actually unwanted in an examination situation such as this, as it gives the examining physician insufficient opportunity to evaluate the answers given on questioning. The doctor's report did not indicate any difficulty with interpreting during the two-and-a-half-hour examination. On the contrary, his report contained many detailed and comprehensible quotes from the accused. The Chamber decided that the argument of counsel was based on nothing more than speculation as he failed to substantiate any allegations.[187]

2.3. Procedural linguistic equality of arms between the ICTY prosecution and defense

The defendant is the person at the center of all investigative and lawyerly activities at any court. Defendants are the first translation and interpreting clients at international criminal tribunals. Not all language professionals encounter defendants, but all their activities revolve around them. Defendants cannot determine their own legal

---

186 ICTY, Cases, *Mladić*, Decision on Prosecution Rule 92quater motion (2013).

187 ICTY, Cases, *Popović et al.*, Public redacted version of 30 November 2012 decision on request to terminate appellate proceedings in relation to Milan Gvero (2013): https://bit.ly/2xjN4zW.

position in an appropriate manner without translation and interpreting into their language. So, it is of the utmost importance that defendants can exercise their language rights. The question that will be discussed now is whether the defense counsel, representing the defendant, is at a disadvantage due to a violation of the defendant's language rights. It should be established whether the finances, resources, facilities, and other material conditions put the defense at a linguistic disadvantage and constitute procedural inequality with an effect on the fair trial of the accused.

I will discuss this examining equality of arms, one of the principles used to determine whether a trial is fair. And, since my focus is on languages, I will introduce a new concept into the study of equality of arms: procedural linguistic equality of arms.

The general principle of equality of arms has not been explicitly incorporated into most international criminal tribunals' statutes or international treaties: the European Convention on Human Rights and Freedoms (ECHR), UDHR, ICCPR, ICTY-S, etc. only suggest the equality of arms under the right to a fair trial.[188] All these provisions under the umbrella of the right to a fair trial require that the defendant is informed promptly of the charges against him, has adequate time and facilities to prepare his defense, can access and comment on evidence against him, and has the right to secure the attendance and examination of witnesses on his behalf under the same conditions as witnesses against him. Procedural equality implies that both parties have the same procedural rights before, during, and after the trial without any of them being at the disadvantage. The procedural linguistic equality of arms implies translation, interpreting, and transcription: the defendant must not be at a disadvantage if he does not speak the languages of the court.

Before I continue, I must make a reminder of the "popular" background. The defense complains that, in practice, there is no equality of arms between them and the prosecution for a host of reasons: the prosecution forms part of the Court itself, does not have an *a priori* stigma of blameworthiness, has more and better resources, has a larger team of investigators, trial attorneys, and legal advisers, and a much larger overall support system. The latter refers to the various professional associations and civil society

[188] European Convention on Human Rights and Freedoms Article 6, UDHR Article 10, ICCPR Article 14, ICTY-S Article 21.

organizations lobbying for the prosecution. Whereas the entire world seems to support the prosecution, those associations and organizations supporting defense are rare and, at times, could be described as denialist, at best.[189] It is beyond the scope of this study to determine the effects of such discourse on defense efforts. Suffice it to say that the main role of defense-supporting organizations should revolve around shedding light on the proverbial "other side of the coin."

Indeed, defense is *a priori* much more successful locally than the English/French-speaking Court. This is because the location and motivation of that "other side of the coin" are in the situation country, which means that B/C/S speaking defense can get faster to the situation country than the English/French-speaking court officials, who then have to either compete with B/C/S speaking defense to provide novel information or engage in damage control clarifying the defense's ambiguous and other statements. Would this mean the English/French-speaking Court's efforts in the situation country are *a priori* a lost cause? No, it just means they have to put serious efforts into addressing the situation country in the language and the way they understand through appropriate outreach activities and a big picture legal and factual analysis of their work results. I have made comments on the ICTY Outreach Program services as it pertained to the present study elsewhere.

There is also communication between legal professionals, namely those of the Court and those from the region who only speak B/C/S. The ICTY Defense Manual acknowledges that one of the major barriers to regional information sharing is linguistic in nature. While there have been efforts by multiple organizations to translate documents into B/C/S, the most relevant jurisprudential and other materials are only published in French and English and untranslated.[190] Ultimately, this is problematic because not many counsels from the former Yugoslavia understand these two languages sufficiently well for use in legal matters.

The Criminal Defense Section (OKO) and its relevant procedural rules were proposed by the Registry of the B&H Court

---

189 Council for Defense of Radovan Karadžić: https://bit.ly/3clS99p and Defending Milošević! Defending Serbia!: https://bit.ly/3aa6cxm to name just two.

190 ICTY, Press, Publications: ADC-ICTY Developed Practices: Manual of International Criminal Defense (2011), UNICRI Publisher.

and adopted by the B&H Court on 30 June 2005. One solution to the issue of uninformedness that the OKO proposed was the publication and dissemination of a regional magazine on international crimes: the OKO War Crimes Reporter. This magazine is published four times a year in English and B/C/S. It has law reports of decisions from courts in B&H, Serbia, Montenegro, and Croatia. It is designed to be a regular source of up-to-date case law interpreting war crimes codes in the former Yugoslavia.[191] Obviously, the defense started a targeted information campaign informing the regional public about defense activities in their own language.

As to the facilities at their disposal, the defense interviewed for the purposes of this study divide their time at the ICTY into: pre-Electronic Disclosure System (EDS) phase and post-EDS phase. The EDS is the system of electronic disclosure of documents which was introduced at the ICTY in 2004. The EDS allows for electronic disclosure of exculpatory and other relevant documents by the prosecution to the defense and it removes the reciprocal obligation of disclosure by the defense to the prosecution when seeking access to certain classes of material held by the prosecution.

Defense teams had offices at and outside the ICTY; they worked from those offices and, naturally, from home. At the ICTY, the defense had at their disposal five premises. If there were 161 individuals indicted by the ICTY, as claimed in ICTY Infographics, that also means there were 161 defense teams in total. One of the premises given to defense at the ICTY was a room with a computer linked to all databases with relevant evidentiary materials. During the pre-EDS era, the defense received one computer containing a Judicial Database. This implied that the defense support staff, a hybrid professional combining the roles of case manager, translator, interpreter, researcher, and legal assistant in one person, would have to go to the room with the computer, when that computer was free, search for documents, and, since search results could not be saved electronically, print out all the relevant documents to go through them later manually. Apart from that, the defense did not have access to the ICTY Intranet and it was only in about 2006 when the defense received ICTY email addresses.

---

[191] B&H Court Criminal Defense Section, OKO Reporter: https://bit.ly/2VrjKiS.

Naturally, this was an immense waste of time and paper, leading to very long working hours because the entire working day revolved around the availability of that one computer. *Šljivančanin* seems to have been the first trial functioning through the e-court system. According to the ICTY 2004 AR, the height of ICTY activities was in 2004 when three Trial Chambers ran six trials simultaneously and the Appeals Chamber dealt with 17 interlocutory appeals, four appeals from judgment, and one request for review.[192] All these activities coincided with the EDS teething troubles.

As to the mechanics of their involvement with their client, two defense counsels are usually assigned to each accused at the ICTY: one from the same region as the accused and trained in the Civil Law tradition who speaks the same language as the accused, and an attorney trained in the Common Law system. Authors of the Defense Manual claim that this maximized the team's ability to absorb and function within the mixed legal system at the ICTY and generally obviated the need to employ a translator for meetings with the accused. However, it is unclear whether these two counsels interpreted for each other or whether the Common Law defense counsel spoke B/C/S.

The Defense Manual states that this distribution of counsels was not required and was not done in every case: there are successful teams comprised of two lawyers from the region and successful teams comprised of two lawyers who are not from the region. Each lead counsel appointed to a case is free to create the kind of legal team which best fits the circumstances of his client's case.

As to the training, the Registry provides some limited training for the defense right before the scheduled beginning of a trial regarding essential technology used in court during the trial and appeal and on administrative issues including, *inter alia*, the translation of documents. In preparation for the trial, the defense must always be in communication with the prosecution and request that they fulfill their obligation of, *inter alia*, translation of evidentiary documents.[193]

---

192 UN, Report of the ICTY (A/59/215) (2004).

193 ICTY, Press, Publications: ADC-ICTY Developed Practices: Manual of International Criminal Defense (2011), UNICRI Publisher.

As to finances, the Registry determines whether an accused is indigent, administers payment to the accused's defense team and has financial investigators to ensure that the legal aid system functions effectively. The Registry is responsible for ensuring that defense counsels are provided with help and assistance with issues such as resources, translators, and the assignment of defense staff. All aspects of representation, except for necessary travel and daily subsistence allowances (DSA), are covered by a lump sum, including interpreting and translation costs. The lump sum includes all interpreting costs and costs of translation of documents other than those documents to be adduced as evidence (translated by the ICTY CLSS and OTP Language Assistants) and other than interpreting and translation costs incurred pursuant to the ICTY-S which may be invoiced separately up to a maximum of €1,000 per month.[194] These provisions are repeated verbatim in the ICTY's Trial Legal Aid Policy for the defense.[195]

In other words, the defendant and his defense team will not have to settle the costs of translation and interpreting sanctioned by the ICTY-S and ICTY RPE Rules 66(A)(i) and 66(A)(ii). This leaves out settling payment for translation and interpretation costs related to the defense evidence. To remind, the ICTY-S and ICTY RPE do not contain a single word about defense evidence, except that the Registrar may admit a counsel who speaks the native language of the suspect or accused, but that such counsel or accused must undertake to meet all translation and interpretation costs not usually met by the Tribunal and must undertake not to request any extensions of time as a result of the fact that he does not speak one of the working languages. Furthermore, such person can be assigned only as co-counsel in accordance with ICTY-S Article 16(D). According to the Annex to the Directive on Assignment of Defense Counsel, co-counsel is paid a flat rate of around €80 an hour, just like a novice lawyer with up to nine years of professional experience.[196]

---

194 ICTY, Documents, Defense: Defense Counsel: Pre-Trial Legal Aid Policy (2006).

195 ICTY, Documents, Defense: Defense Counsel: Trial Legal Aid Policy (2009).

196 ICTY, Documents, Defense: Directive on the assignment of defense counsel (undated), Appendix I.

How founded were all these provisions in reality? The crimes in the former Yugoslavia happened in the former Yugoslavia. It would not be strange to assume *a priori* that legal professionals from the former Yugoslavia are in the best position to understand, defend, and prosecute crimes committed in their own backyard. Obviously, the ICTY imposed restrictions on the employment of such legal professionals, requiring them to be professionally functional in English or French and allowing those who could function professionally only in B/C/S to practice at their own linguistic, financial, and time-related detriment.

Again, defense is not a part of ICTY, but the ICTY went above and beyond the mere requirement that local professionals of the defense must be professionally functional in English or French: the ICTY did not allow them to see any benefit from being fully functional in these, for defense counsels from the former Yugoslavia, completely unimportant languages.

In order to be professionally certified and allowed to practice before the ICTY, the ICTY requires members of the defense team whose native language is not English or French to submit a certificate from a language institute or other evidence of proficiency in English or French. The Registrar may also require such applicants to demonstrate their language ability by means of a language proficiency test.[197] Language Proficiency Tests are used at the UN System to check the knowledge of UN languages.[198] This test consists of a written and an oral part: the written part consists of writing a thematic essay followed by a grammar and language use test and the oral test consists of a conversation with the examiner. Once the candidate passes the Language Proficiency Test, he starts receiving a language allowance in addition to his salary.[199] However, the defense teams who passed this test did not receive a language allowance.

How many defense counsels appearing before the ICTY spoke only the language of their client? The official site of the ICTY, Cases lists 114 individuals who stood trial before this institution.

---

197 ICTY, Documents, Defense: Directive on the assignment of defense counsel (2006).

198 UN, Language Proficiency Tests (2016): https://bit.ly/2RzJo5g.

199 UN, Administrative Instruction: Language Allowance and Language Incentives (ST/AI/1999/2) (1999).

These were represented by teams of one or two lawyers. Some of these teams were B/C/S speaking, some non-B/C/S speaking, and some mixed B/C/S and English speaking as presented in Table 2 below.[200] Bobetko, Alagić, and Ražnatović died before being assigned a counsel and Milošević was self-represented, so these were not considered in this examination.

Table 2. Languages of the ICTY defense counsel teams

	Entirely B/C/S speaking	Entirely non-B/C/S speaking	Mixed B/C/S and non-B/C/S speaking
Main trial	53	15	42
Appeals	32	17	41

These numbers do not come to 111 because some accused chose not to appeal. They show that defendants prefered being defended by entirely speaking B/C/S teams in the trial stage and then switched preference to mixed B/C/S and non-B/C/S speaking defense teams in the appeals stage. These reasons will be clearer as you read further. I must remark that I find it curious that those accused of the most glaring nationalism chose not to be represented by lawyers coming from the national corpus of their own peoples, like Babić, Brđanin, Krajišnik, Plavšić, etc.

According to defense counsels interviewed for the purposes of this study, during the first ten or so years there were teams where defense counsels did not speak French or English at all or where their knowledge of those languages was insufficient for effective communication with the Court or for drafting motions. Such defense teams would overcome this obstacle by engaging a legal assistant who would write, i.e. translate, motions into/from English or French. The ICTY 2008 AR reveals that the ICTY Registry adopted a special remuneration scheme for persons assisting indigent self-represented accused and made provisions for the assignment of an investigator, a case manager, and, where

---

[200] Note that ICTY Registry, Outreach Program did not use the uniform template for Case Information Sheet: in the first, the majority version they clearly named defense counsels and in the second version they did not do so. This is the reason why I took information about defense attorney from Trial and/or Appeals Judgement in cases *Hadžić, Krstić, Popović et al., Prlić et al., Stanišić and Župljanin,* and *Šainović et al.*

necessary, a Language Assistant.[201] The engagement of Language Assistants for such purposes was closely regulated.[202]

Let us put this into context: this means that some segments of the defense, not all, got a right to budgeted language support 15 years into the existence of the ICTY, after 48 completed trials, and pending completion of 16 trials. Again, the problem here is operational reality: the defense had to translate their own documents and interpret for their own witnesses all along. The ICTY did not seem to open their purse generously, either. Finances at the disposal of defense teams for translation and interpretation costs were scant. A directive on the assignment of the defense counsel allows a gross rate of €0.068 per word for translators with three or more years of professional experience and €0.045 per word for translators with zero to three years of professional experience.[203] The UN Secretariat pays about 0.22 USD per word. As to interpretation, whereas the CLSS paid the UN approved daily rate for interpreting of about €620, regardless of the duration of the engagement, the defense paid an hourly rate of about €35. The ICTY supported defendants who were indigent to appear fair, but in doing so it indirectly gave freelancers a choice about whose request for assistance to respond to, the ICTY's or the defense team's.

The official site of the ICTY, Cases lists 114 individuals who stood trial before this institution. Table 3 below gives approximate years between the individual's initial appearance in the court and the reading of their final and binding sentence. The data from individual Case Information Sheets could not be used alone because they provide this data in trial days, not years. The following examination did not take the following individuals into consideration because their case either never got to the trial stage or was incomplete due to their passing: Alagić, Bobetko, Dokmanović, Đukić, Kovačević, Milošević, S., Ražnatović, and Talić.

---

201 UN, Report of the ICTY (A/63/210) (2008).

202 ICTY, Documents, Defense: Remuneration scheme for persons assisting indigent self-represented accused (2010).

203 ICTY, Documents, Defense: Directive on the assignment of defense counsel (undated).

Table 3. Approximate duration of trials between initial appearance of an individual and the reading of the final sentence

Years	±1	±2	±3	±4	±5	±6	±7	±8	±9	±10	±12	±13
Defendants	2	10	11	14	14	6	21	9	12	1	1	5

ICTY-S Article 21(4)(b) gives the accused the right to expeditious trial and time for preparation of a defense. To a certain extent, this also implies that victims have the right to expeditious justice, but Table 3 above shows plainly that the trials that have been heard before the ICTY have dragged on way too long. It cannot be said that expeditious justice has been served to anyone.[204]

Indeed, the 2017 Amnesty International report on wartime rape survivors in B&H quotes Bakira Hasečić of the B&H Women Victims of War Association who said "most survivors will not live long enough to see justice being done." As to the living victims of sexual violence, including their offspring that might have resulted from rape, for many victims of wartime sexual violence, the status of civilian victims of war represents a gateway to a desperately needed monthly allowance and other social benefits, including medical care and social support. Victims can apply for the status under separate, and often considerably different, laws in the Federation of B&H, Republika Srpska, or Brčko District. This system in which victims' rights and access to services are regulated by entity and cantonal laws in an unharmonized and disconnected way, rather than universally guaranteed by the state, is inherently discriminatory, with the degree of access varying widely and

[204] Given that it takes only several months to complete a trial in national jurisdictions where for cases completing in the Crown Court the average number of days from first listing at the magistrates' court to completion in the Crown Court decreased by 2 days from 196 days in 2015 to 194 days in 2016 (UK, Ministry of Justice (2017), Criminal court statistics quarterly, England and Wales, January to March 2017 https://bit.ly/3cMaUmZ) and given that judges, prosecution and defense practicing before international criminal tribunals have much less on their working plate and much more on their financial, resource, and support plate to motivate them to work harder than their colleagues from national jurisdictions (Starr, Sonia B. (2009), Ensuring Defense Counsel Competence at International Criminal Tribunals. UCLA Journal of International Law and Foreign Affairs, 14/1: 169-206), the data on the length of trials at ICTY is hard to explain, to say the least.

depending on one's place of residence. After they manage to overcome hurdles revolving around compensation claims, finding a free legal assistance, and coping with retraumatization, victims almost routinely face negative court decisions due to the recent view of the B&H Constitutional Court stating that a statute of limitation should apply to compensation claims directed against the state or the entities. Following such rulings, victims are forced to pay high court fees or face administrative seizure of their assets. Indeed, the B&H Constitutional Court's position on the statute of limitations and the inability of the authorities to implement decisions on compensation leave victims without an enforceable right to remedy, which is contrary to international law.[205]

What does this mean in practice? As to international justice, the ICTY did not have any retributive function, meaning it did not provide, arrange, or push for any compensation to victims. For victims, this meant that, on hearing the ICTY judgments, they might have been able to declare that justice had been served – but that was about all. The fact that the ICTY may have recognized them as a testifying victim has no bearing on their status in their home country whatsoever. But I am concerned with language.

It seems these protracted trials had to do with the provision of language services to the point that the main client, the ICTY President, started taking things into his own hands. The ICTY 2012 AR reported that the ICTY President focused on problems that might impact the efficiency of proceedings, such as, *inter alia*, delays in translations. In that vein, measures were taken to reform the ICTY's procedures to maximize efficiency and, in particular, to implement measures to ensure that the pace of translations would not unduly delay proceedings in that additional resources were assigned to *Prlić et al.*, *Tolimir*, and *Šešelj* to reduce previously forecast translation times by 50%.[206]

The ICTY 2014 AR reported that the ICTY President focused his efforts on completing the judicial work expeditiously, while maintaining high standards of procedural justice, including expedited translations of trial judgments, by actively managing the

---

[205] Amnesty International (2017), We need support, not pity: last chance for justice for Bosnia's wartime rape survivors. London: Amnesty International: https://bit.ly/3cRKvUT.
[206] UN, Report of the ICTY (A/67/214) (2012).

translation process. The CLSS delivered the English translation of the French trial judgment issued in the *Prlić et al.* case at the beginning of June 2014, only 13 months after the date of the original judgment.[207] The ICTY 2015 AR reported that in September 2014, the CLSS delivered the B/C/S translation of the French Trial Judgment issued in *Prlić et al.* only 16 months after the date of the original judgment.[208]

Obviously, translation issues offset the length of trials with a significant impact.

2.4. Linguistic justice: the working institution towards the parties to the proceedings

I am now in position to examine whether linguistic justice has been served along the second line of communication with the judicial institution: the working institution towards the parties to the proceedings. My research shows that the CLSS, the ICTY language services provider, cannot be said to have informed any language-related laws or to have taken stock of ICTY language-related case law through the available legal mechanisms set by and at the ICTY judges.

As to the language-related laws, the ICTY lawmakers suffered immensely to define the most basic principles revolving around the language of the defendants, calling it: his or her own language, their own language, language of the accused, language that the accused understands, language understood by the accused, language the suspect understands, the native language of the suspect or accused, language understood [by the defendant] known to the Registrar, language to be used for questioning, language that he or she understands, and language the accused understands and is able to read.

This issue mostly has to do with the clear absence of editing: a language editor, if hired, would construct the sentence in such a way as to convey the same principle in an absolutely uniform way throughout. The CLSS never had anyone with the functional title of Editor or Terminologist on their staff.

---

[207] UN, Report of the ICTY (A/69/225) (2014).
[208] UN, Report of the ICTY (A/70/226) (2015).

Instead, this lack of editing also resulted in a number of false contingencies due to the immense influence of American legal thinking, evident in formulas, such as: language understood [by the defendant] known to the Registrar and language the accused understands and is able to read, to name just two. Clearly, lawmakers resorted to a Common Law writing standard. Since Anglo-American legal professionals are deeply skeptical of abstract norms and their legal thinking is inductive, this Anglo-American-centric approach resulted in wordy and lengthy texts and formulas listing seemingly similar notions.[209] The latter is merely evidence of the fact that the international criminal law is still blending the Civil and the Common Law traditions.

As to the language-related legal lacunae, the ICTY does not make any provision for illiterate persons. There have been several illiterate persons testifying before the ICTY. However, their illiteracy had no bearing on their testimony. Such a person would sign the statement with a cross or thumb, confirm that he was illiterate before the judges and, like other witnesses, would declare whether his statement was read to him and whether he accepts it as his own. In other words, as long as an illiterate person is read back his statement, the ICTY would be satisfied that they have before them an original and untampered statement (ERN 01003532-01003537).

In addition, the lawmakers do not reflect the official position of deaf and mute persons. They should have done that because at the time when they were copying and pasting these rules and regulations, they could not have known whether there would be any deaf, mute, or illiterate persons testifying.

Moreover, the communication between the defense counsel and a defendant who does not speak his language has not been covered explicitly in the ICTY laws. However, EU Directive 2010/64/EU of the European Parliament and of the Council on the right to interpreting and translation in criminal proceedings specifically stipulates that there must be free and adequate linguistic assistance, allowing suspected or accused persons who do not speak or understand the language of the criminal proceedings fully to exercise their right of defense, thus safeguarding the

[209] Cao, D. (2007), Translating law. Multilingual Matters: Bristol.

fairness of the proceedings.[210]

As to the linguistic procedural equality of arms, it was almost nonexistent in terms of facilities, finances, and time to respond to or access documents.

The ICTY imposed restrictions on acceptable languages, accepted a counsel who did not speak those languages but downsized him to the level of co-counsel and charged him, effectively, for translation and interpretation costs. This means that a counsel X could have been a major legal mover and shaker in the former Yugoslavia, but if he did not speak English or French, he would get paid as a novice lawyer.

The ICTY supported defendants who were indigent to appear fair, but in doing so, they indirectly decided for freelancers whose request for assistance to respond to: the ICTY's or the defense's. The clients who offer such low rates as the ICTY Registry gave to the defense are called bottom feeders in the translation, interpretation, transcription, and editing industries where they are viewed as a source of amusement, not income.

As to translation, apart from financed translations (ICTY RPE Rules 66(A), 66(A)(i), and 66(A)(ii), namely disclosure documents, material supporting the indictment and witness statements), it is not the case that other documents used in trials were in the language of defendant, here B/C/S, or the language of the Court, i.e. English or French, which means they required translation.

Defense members interviewed for the purposes of this study stated that there were several large documents, including several videos, in the Srebrenica trial concerning the Dutch Battalion originally submitted in Dutch, for example. Some of those documents were translated by the OTP and some by the CLSS, but only into English. Those which were translated into B/C/S took months to receive. It seems the Netherlands Institute for War Documentation Report of several thousand pages has never been fully translated into B/C/S, so the defense team had to undertake

---

210 EU, Official Journal of the European Union L 280/1 (2010), Directive of the European Parliament and of the Council on the right to interpreting and translation in criminal proceedings.

translation of certain parts themselves. Internal UN documents used during trials have also not been routinely translated, such as various UN Protection Forces (UNPROFOR) daily reports from 37 different countries participants speaking 21 distinct languages, cables, and other internal information, unless they were meant to serve as exhibits.[211] Finally, in *Hadžihasanović* and *Delić*, the defense received some documents in Italian and Arabic, but did not have any resources for any of these languages and had to turn to the OTP for assistance.[212] Obviously, since they were not mentioned in the ICTY laws, the translation of documents other than those in English, French, or B/C/S is currently in the limbo.

But, in addition to the trial documents, there are also trial briefs that have not been covered by the ICTY language-related laws. Three types of briefs, namely pre-trial, final, and appeals brief, which could be defined as summaries of all the facts presented during trial, were also not translated for non-self-representing defendants for their perusal and had to be submitted in English or French. The most important part of the pre-trial period is a pre-trial brief. The pre-trial brief is loosely discussed under ICTY RPE Rule 65*ter* on the responsibilities of the pre-trial judge. ICTY RPE Rule 65*ter* (E) defines the types of documents that the prosecution must serve on the defendant whereas ICTY RPE Rule 65*ter* (F) defines the type of response the defense must provide “not later than three weeks before the Pre-Trial Conference.” The same goes for the final trial brief mentioned in ICTY RPE Rule 86(B), where it is said that the parties should submit the final brief “not later than five days prior to presenting a closing argument.”

In January 2001, the ICTY President established that there was a need to reduce the number of motions filed and the length of documents and, to that effect, issued a direction on the length of briefs and motions.[213] However, this direction only affected court materials which are, as a rule, delivered in English and French; the problem with trial documents did not go away. Judges made the first pick, as expected, and imposed a strict word count on the documents *they* had to deal with. As to the language, the Practice

---

[211] UN, Peacekeeping, UNPROFOR: https://bit.ly/3bafD1b.
[212] ICTY, Cases, *Delić*, Response to urgent defence motion concerning failure of prosecution to comply with Rule 68 (2008): https://bit.ly/2VqCteh.
[213] UN, Report of the ICTY (A/56/352) (2001).

direction on the length of briefs and motions stipulates the length of the pre-trial brief at 50 pages or 15,000 words and the final trial brief at 200 pages or 60,000 words in all its versions from 2001, when it was delivered the first time, 2002, and 2005.[214]

Appendix 1 contains the pre-trial, final, and appeal briefs requiring translation into/from B/C/S.[215] Appendix 1 does not contain documents from those cases that have been transferred to the ICTY's successor, the Mechanism for International Criminal Tribunals, such as *Karadžić* (pre-trial, final, appeal), *Mladić* (pre-trial), *Stanišić and Simatović* (pre-trial, final, appeal), and *Šešelj* (final brief). It also does not contain various errata, corrigendum, or supplements to the existing submission. Others have been found on the official ICTY site, Case, as submitted in 13 trials: *Đorđević* (final and appeal), *Galić* (pre-trial), *Gotovina et al.* (pre-trial, final, and appeal), *Hadžić* (pre-trial), *Lukić Milan & Lukić Sredoje* (pre-trial, final, appeal), *Milošević, D.* (appeal), *Perišić* (appeal), *Popović et al.* (pre-trial, final, appeal), *Prlić et al.* (final), *Stanišić & Župljanin* (pre-trial, final, appeal), *Strugar* (pre-trial), *Šainović et al.* (pre-trial, final, appeal), and *Tolimir* (pre-trial, final, appeal).

Linguistic justice was served in only three cases of briefs that have been translated into B/C/S (*Krajišnik, Šešelj,* and *Tolimir*) who were self-representing defendants. Obviously, briefs are not translated for other defendants, but their defense still has three, i.e. five weeks to review them although most of them exceed well over the page and word limit set by the above Practice direction as shown clearly in Appendix 1.

In response, as, perhaps, could have been expected, the ICTY site is replete with various requests for extensions of time to submit pre-trial/final/appeals brief. Appendix 2 contains the outcome of decisions on requests for time and/or word extension to submit the pre-trial, final, and appeal briefs as found on the official

---

214 ICTY, Documents, Practice directions: Practice direction on the length of briefs and motions (2001, 2002, 2005).

215 Note in Appendix 1 that the ICTY Registry, Outreach Program misnamed, misfiled, and broke down in several parts otherwise single files on the individual pages of cases concerned. They named almost every file in *Prlić et al.*, for example, "Decision." This user-unfriendly approach made the making of the Appendix 1 extremely difficult and cannot be said to make researchers' work easy at all.

ICTY site under Selected Case Documents in all cases heard before ICTY. In fact, there were 80 such requests: 17 of which have been granted partially, 20 of which have been denied, and 43 of which have been granted in full. As the reason for denial of such requests, Chambers mostly quoted that they had already extended the time for several months or words for several thousands.

The very existence of these shows the ICTY CLSS should have taken stock of repeated requests for extensions of time or word limits to inform new policies on the lengths of documents.

I have already established the accused switch preference to being represented by mixed B/C/S and non-B/C/S speaking defense teams in the appeals stage. This is most probably because the defendants do not get any translation into B/C/S, including the Defense Appeal, the Prosecutor Appeal, replies, or any other appeal motion, save for some orders and decisions of the Appeals Chambers. On the other hand, the defense must submit an appeal to judgment several months, even a year, prior to receiving the Trial Judgment translated into the language of the defendant. Any brief filed with the Appeals Chamber must contain a Book of Authorities "containing a separate compilation setting out clearly all authorities relied upon." All legal authorities, other than authorities of the ICTY and the ICTR must also be provided in "an authorized version of the authority in question, complete with an English or French translation, if the original is not in one of the languages of the International Tribunals." Any relevant exhibits and documents, when necessary, must also be translated into one of the official languages of the Tribunal.[216]

This means that the defense must invest their own money to translate parts of the trial judgment and legal authorities for their client so that the defendant can know the overall logic, conclusions, and decisions of the Trial Chambers. This also means that, once the official translation comes out, it is viewed merely as a formality. Finally, it means it is there for the use of professionals from the region, not necessarily the defendant or the defense teams.

Once the defense receives a translation of the Trial Judgment into the language of the defendant, they might receive an

216 ICTY, Press, Publications: ADC-ICTY Developed Practices: Manual of International Criminal Defense (2011), UNICRI Publisher.

additional extension of time to submit additional grounds for appeal to the Trial Judgment. However, they must argue justifiable and valid reasons why they had to wait until their client read the Trial Judgment and provide input.

The ICTY RPE and ICTY-S have been amended 52 and 9 times by 2017, respectively. None of the issues relevant to the normative procedural due process language-related rights, obligations, and requirements, language- and language-related ICTY case law, and underlying procedural linguistic equality of arms between the ICTY prosecution and the defense explained in this chapter were ever addressed in the laws and are as they appeared the first time the ICTY RPE and ICTY-S were written.

As to the repeated requests for documents in the Cyrillic script, online convertors of scripts, e.g. Latin script into Cyrillic script and vice versa, have existed since the late 1990s. All that was needed to accommodate any defendant wanting translation submitted in his script was cutting and pasting translated text into the appropriate column.[217]

As to the procedural equality of arms, it is on the basis of my research that I strongly recommend defendants' rights to translation and interpreting must be absolute: they need to be provided with the essential documents of the court record in a language they understand.

The way the selection procedure of defense attorneys is conducted affects the free choice of defense attorneys. It is on the basis of my research that I strongly recommend defense attorneys who do not speak the languages of the court and defense attorneys who do not speak the languages of defendants must be afforded exactly the same translation and interpreting rights as defendants.

As to the language-related laws, it is on the basis of my research that I strongly recommend that language services must be compelled to give their feedback to such laws and bylaws, including all related rules and regulations.

---

217 Information taken from SixPack design studio from Belgrade. I converted the first 10 pages of Ivo Andrić's "The bridge over the Drina" and can confirm their online convertor could take more: SixPack design studio: https://bit.ly/3btol7P.

CHAPTER 3

MAY THE LANGUAGE PROFESSIONALS TAKE THE STAND, PLEASE

Language professionals working in a legal context have been described in many different ways: as a phonograph, a transmission belt, a bilingual transmitter, an electric transformer, a conduit of communication, a cipher, a medium of communication, a language machine, a black box, a cultural mediator, a piece of gum on the bottom of a shoe – ignored for all practical purposes, but almost impossible to remove.[218]

Acting CLSS Chief between the second and the third management periods, Nikolić described ICTY translators and interpreters as professionals working at the same administrative level as lawyers or investigators; all have a university degree, most of them in linguistics or modern languages, and several or more years of related work experience. The revisers are native speakers of the target language. All are hard-nosed practitioners and have worked assiduously to earn the professional respect they now enjoy from judges, prosecution, and defense counsel, and from numerous other users of their services.[219] Nikolić, the recipient of the OIOS Audit Report used heavily in this chapter, confides in a different interview that the greatest challenge the ICTY management ever faced was to raise the clients' awareness about the nature of conference interpreting and, in the event of a language dispute, to defend the interpreter's legitimate choice of words and expressions without succumbing to the pressures of an adversarial courtroom.[220]

---

[218] Mulayim, Sedat and Lai, Miranda (2016). Ethics for police translators and interpreters. CRC Press: Boca Raton.
[219] Nikolić, Marijana (2005), Interpreting after the Nuremberg: international war crimes trials. Proteus 14.
[220] Pavetić, Janja (2012), Interview with Greiss lecturer Marijana Nikolić. SlavFile: Newsletter of the Slavic Languages Division.

Nevertheless, the ICTY management called "court reporters," as they are professionally known, "specialized steno typists." They were proud to announce that in the course of 1995, the courtroom was equipped with electronic facilities to support "simultaneous translation." The Defense Manuals alerted the court to the idea that if investigators or legal assistants were not familiar with the language, it was important to hire a translator. The OTP lawyers called the CLSS, "the CLSS world," probably referring to the fact that they are an entity isolated from the rest of the institution with rules of their own and little in common with the rest of the ICTY.[221] The OTP investigators would normally come over and request a translator to "type this in Serbo-Croatian" referring to a document they wanted translated. And thus they all contributed to Montaigne's maxim that *le monde n*'est *qu'une branloire pérenne.*

The reality of communication on an international level is such that underneath whatever Bourdieu had to say about the language and power, whatever Hart had to say about the language and the law, whatever Bassiouni had to say about the mechanics of the international criminal law, whatever Weiss had to say about the UN, whatever Fitchelberg had to say about international criminal and hybrid tribunals, whatever van Parijs had to say about the global linguistic justice there is a very simple but callously overlooked and often shamelessly ignored truth: nothing international can go without the involvement of language professionals. And the ICTY language professionals, their status, their rights and obligations, the mechanics behind their recruitment, and their output have been ignored, belittled, and trivialized by none other but ICTY CLSS management.

In Chapter 3, I am reviewing the history, recruitment, professional criteria and standards, and training of all ICTY language professionals. Then I am going to test whether the linguistic justice has been served along the third line of communication with the judicial institution: the working institution towards the language service providers. I am doing this by examining the position in which the CLSS has put ICTY language professionals within the realm of the international criminal law and the ICTY laws.

---

[221] ICTY, Cases, *Hadžić*, T. 48 (13 September 2012): https://bit.ly/2VhBWg3.

3.1. Legal background to the engagement of language professionals at the ICTY

UN Staff Rules,[222] UN Staff Rules and Staff Regulations,[223] and the UN Charter are the three main documents governing UN staff service, duties, obligations, privileges, etc. There are several types of UN staff: regular and temporary staff, as well as locally hired and internationally hired staff. There are also several types of contracts that UN staff sign: permanent or continuing, fixed-term, and temporary contracts.[224]

Finally, there are three main categories of staff at the UN:

- Professional (P-level) and Higher Categories: ranked between P-1 and P-5, then Principal Officer and Director category, and Under-Secretary-General and Assistant Secretary-General (the latter two form a category of their own because staff on these levels are either career UN staff or political appointees)
- Field Service Category (FS-level category): ranked between FS-1 and FS-7
- General Service and related Categories (GS-level category): ranked between GS-1 and GS-7 comprising Language Teacher Category, National Professional Officer Category, Trades and Crafts Category, Public Information Assistant Category, and Security Category.

These categories differ from each other in the type of work the staff perform, the manner of recruitment, the level of education, remuneration, and rights and obligations.[225]

The International Civil Service Commission (ICSC) is an independent expert body established by the UN General Assembly with a mandate to regulate and coordinate the conditions of service of staff in the UN System, while promoting and maintaining high

[222] UN, Staff Regulations (ST/SGB/2014/2) (2014).
[223] UN, Staff Rules and Staff Regulations (ST/SGB/2014/1) (2015).
[224] UN, Policies for Obtaining the Services of Individuals on Behalf of the Organization (ST/SGB/177) (1982).
[225] UN, Details of UN Salaries, Hazard Pay, Rental Subsidy, Mobility and Hardship Scheme, and other Allowances, Benefits: https://bit.ly/3enl7rC.

standards in the international civil service.[226] Since all posts in the P-level categories are filled by internationally recruited staff, whether or not the applicant is a resident of a duty station, internationally recruited staff are paid according to the so-called Noblemaire principle whereby staff remuneration is set by reference to the highest paid national civil servant.

Since some organizations in the UN System placed certain jobs in the P-level category while others, sometimes within the same duty station, placed the same jobs within the GS-level category, the ICSC recognized the importance of developing a methodology for distinguishing between P-level category and GS-level category work.[227] The ICSC defined work performed by the P-level category staff as "analytical, evaluative, conceptual, interpretive and/or creative and thus requir[ing] the application of the basic principles of an organized body of theoretical knowledge, such as a field of science, learning or specialized discipline." The work performed by the GS-level category staff has been described as "contribut[ing] to the execution of the programs of the organization through work that is procedural, operational and technical."[228] The ICSC also passed self-explanatory Standards of Conduct for the International Civil Service (2013) affecting all civil servants.[229]

As to the language professionals, the ICSC issued a series of standards affecting various job profiles, including Standards for Translators and Revisers (1981), which set out the duties and responsibilities of translators and revisers.[230] In theory, these standards are supposed to be adhered to by all UN System entities. In practice, they are adapted to the individual needs of each entity.

The profession of interpreting was recognized as a profession in its own right and formalized for the first time during the UN General Assembly session held on 15 November 1947, when

[226] UN, ICSC Statute and Rules of Procedure and Evidence (1987).
[227] Alexovičková, Iveta (2012), From hiring to firing: a comparative study on selected legal safeguards for the independence and impartiality of international civil servants serving in the United Nations Secretariat and in the European Commission. Wolf Legal Publishers: Nijmegen.
[228] UN, ICSC Compendium (1980).
[229] UN, ICSC Standards of Conduct for the International Civil Service (2013).
[230] UN, ICSC Standards for Translators and Revisers (1981).

simultaneous interpreting was adopted for permanent service at the UN by General Assembly Resolution 152 (II) "to be used alternatively or in conjunction with consecutive interpreting as the nature of debates may require."[231] The ICSC did not issue any similar standards of conduct for interpreters. Consecutive interpreting is also widely used at the UN.

UN System staff mobility, which also applies to language staff, presents one of the ways in which vacant posts may be filled. It comprises a broad range of possible moves, including the change of duty station. The Secretary-General can place staff wherever they are needed.[232] The idea behind staff mobility is to provide the Secretary-General with the tools needed to ensure proper operation of the UN. However, Alexovičková noticed that voluntary or mandatory mobility is not envisaged in the UN Staff Regulations, UN Staff Rules, or that it is being practiced.[233] In the 1980s and 1990s, the UN General Assembly adopted a series of resolutions calling for increased mobility of internationally recruited staff, going as far as to state that their mobility presents an "integral part" of their employment regulations.[234]

This led the Secretary-General to set out a new mobility policy where mobility was defined as the ability of staff to move within and between functions, departments, occupations, duty stations, and organizations of the UN System.[235] The Administrative Instruction on Managed Reassignment Programme stipulates the following could be understood to mean that, notwithstanding the duration of mobility trends, there has never been any *a priori* UN impediment to move trained UN Department for General Assembly and Conference Management (DGACM) language staff elsewhere.

---

[231] UN, UN General Assembly Resolution 152(II) on simultaneous interpreting (1947).

[232] UN, Staff Rules and Staff Regulations (ST/SGB/2014/1) (2015).

[233] Alexovičková, Iveta (2012), From hiring to firing: a comparative study on selected legal safeguards for the independence and impartiality of international civil servants serving in the United Nations Secretariat and in the European Commission. Wolf Legal Publishers: Nijmegen.

[234] UN, Human resources management (A/RES/49/222) (1995); UN, Human resources management (A/RES/51/226) (1996); UN, Human resources management (A/RES/53/221) (1999).

[235] UN, Human resources management reform (A/55/253) (2000), Appendix III.

On the contrary, it seems a special program was being established to sort out the details.[236]

The UN DGACM recognizes the following groups of language professionals: translators, interpreters, editors, verbatim reporters, terminologists (P-level category), and reference assistants, copy preparers, and proofreaders (GS-level category). The UN DGACM translators' and revisers' hierarchy is as follows: Associate Translator (P-2), Translator (P-3), Reviser/Self-revising translator (P-4), Senior Reviser (P-5), and Chief of Service (D-1). In non-headquarters duty stations, Senior Reviser may be the same as Chief of Section, as D-1 posts might not exist at that level. These language professionals' generic job profiles are not that different from those of their peers outside the UN.

UN DGACM language professionals are recruited through semi-regular Language Competitive Examinations (LCEs) which are mostly held in the main UN DGACM-serviced centers: Addis Ababa, Bangkok, Beirut, Geneva, Nairobi, New York, Santiago, and Vienna. In order for a candidate to apply for a job in UN DGACM, that candidate must have three UN languages. The recruitment or placement of candidates successful in LCEs for posts requiring special language skills, i.e. translators, interpreters, editors, and interpreters, is governed by several documents of which the last was amended in 2012,[237] including special conditions for such recruitment (last amended in 2003).[238] Breaking with a long tradition of pen-and-paper tests, both remote and computer-based testing were piloted in LCEs for English translators/précis-writers and for English editors held in July 2015 and they are now completely transitioning online.

---

[236] UN, Managed Reassignment Programme (ST/AI/2007/2) (2007).

[237] UN, Competitive examinations for recruitment and placement in posts requiring specific language skills in the professional category (ST/AI/1998/7) (1998). UN, Competitive examinations for recruitment and placement in posts requiring specific language skills in the professional category (ST/AI/1998/7/Amend.1) (2012).

[238] UN, Special conditions for recruitment or placement of candidates successful in a competitive examination for posts requiring special language skills (ST/AI/2000/1) (2000). UN, Special conditions for recruitment or placement of candidates successful in a competitive examination for posts requiring special language skills (ST/AI/2003/1) (2003).

There are no nationality, gender, or geographic location requirements for applying to LCEs. All that is needed is that the candidate holds at least a three-year first-level degree or equivalent qualification from a university or institution of equivalent status where one of the six UN official languages is the language of instruction or holds a university degree from a recognized school.

There are two other general documents governing translators and interpreters worldwide. The first general document governing translators and interpreters worldwide is UNESCO's Recommendation on the Legal Protection of Translators and Translations and the Practical Means to Improve the Status of Translators (1976). UNESCO's Recommendation defines the general legal position of translators, with measures designed to ensure the practical application of protection afforded to translators under international conventions and in national laws relating to copyright, social and fiscal situation of translators, and training and the working conditions of translators, including translators in developing countries.[239]

The second is the Translator's Charter (1994) by the International Federation of Translators' (FIT) which does not significantly depart from the UNESCO Recommendations. FIT's Translator's Charter sets out the general obligations, rights, and economic and social position of the translator, translators' societies, and translators' unions. It also outlines the relationship between national organizations and the FIT. It defines a translation product as the sole responsibility of the translator, stipulating the translator shall respect the legitimate interests of the user by treating as a professional secret any information which may come into his possession as a result of the translation entrusted to him because he is a secondary author.[240]

As to the mechanics of the daily work, UN-wide daily translation output seems to be a work in progress throughout the UN's existence. The contemporary UN System-wide output standards for translation were approved by the UN General Assembly in 1999:

---

239 UNESCO, Recommendation on the Legal Protection of Translators and Translations and the Practical Means to improve the Status of Translators (1976).

240 FIT, Translator's Charter (1963-1994).

- 1,650 words for translation subject to revision
- 1,815 words for self-revised translation
- 3,960 words for revision.

The length of documents for translation and editing were also reduced, with a 20-page limit (9,000 words) given for documents originating in the Secretariat and translators being engaged to draft summary records.

As to interpreting, the standard assignment is seven three-hour segments per week with at least a two-hour break between the segments. Other activities of interpreters include preparing glossaries, reading background documents, and assisting in preparing examinations for recruiting new interpreters. Time performing these tasks was not tracked.[241]

Legal translation theorist Šarčević agrees with general translation theorists that legal translation revolves around the production of an equivalent legal effect, but criticizes general translation theorists for misleading statements and a failure to recognize the proper communicative function of legal texts. Šarčević agrees that translation in a legal context is a receiver-oriented exercise, emphasizes preserving the letter of the law, sets the whole text as the basic unit of translation, and suggests that such a translation must take legal considerations into account.[242] In other words, Šarčević stresses the paramount importance of operational information contained in text subject to the scrutiny of legal professionals – translation in a legal context must be receiver-oriented.[243]

In the context of international criminal justice, these receivers include the parties to the proceedings. I explained in the Introduction that this would include: ICTY Chambers (judges), ICTY OTP (prosecutors and investigators), ICTY defense and defendants, the UN as the founding institution of the ICTY, and posterity because they were the immediate, the final, and the most important recipients of the legal truths established by the ICTY.

---

[241] UN, Improving the performance of the DGACM (A/57/289) (2002).
[242] Šarčević, Susan (1997), New approach to legal translation. Kluwer Law International.
[243] Šarčević, Susan (2000), Legal Translation and Translation Theory: a Receiver-oriented Approach. Legal Translation: History, Theory/ies, Practice.

However, the basic international laws incumbent on the judges (the 1985 UN Basic Principles on the Independence of the Judiciary,[244] the 2016 ICTY Code of Professional Conduct for the Judges of the Tribunal[245]), on the prosecution (the 1990 UN Guidelines on the Role of Prosecutors,[246] the International Prosecutors Association's 1999 Standards of Professional Responsibility and Statement of the Essential Duties and Rights of Prosecutors,[247] the 1999 ICTY Standards of Professional Conduct for Prosecution Counsel[248]), on the defense (the 2009 ICTY Code of Professional Conduct for Defense Counsel Appearing Before the International Tribunal[249]), and on the police (the 2004 UN Human Rights Standards and Practice for the Police: Expanded Pocket Book on Human Rights for the Police[250]) do not mention translators and interpreters nor any underlying duties and responsibilities these parties may have towards them, except the last one on the police which mentions interpreters in one single sentence in the context of arrests saying: "Where necessary, an interpreter shall be provided during interrogation."

As far as the ICTY laws are concerned, language-related rights, obligations, and requirements of language professionals are not explicit under ICTY laws. In ICTY-S, the involvement of translators is explicitly mentioned in the context of investigation and preparation of indictments in that the suspect has the right to translation from and into a language s/he speaks and understands and in the context of the rights of the accused in that the accused has the right to the free assistance of an interpreter if s/he cannot understand or speak the language used at the ICTY.[251]

---

[244] Basic Principles on the Independence of the Judiciary (1985).
[245] ICTY, Documents, Miscellaneous: Code of professional conduct for the judges of the Tribunal (2016): https://bit.ly/3cu7V2q.
[246] Guidelines on the Role of Prosecutors (1990).
[247] International Prosecutors Association, Standards of Professional Responsibility and Statement of the Essential Duties and Rights of Prosecutors (1999).
[248] ICTY, Documents, Miscellaneous: Standard of Professional Conduct for Prosecution Counsel (1999).
[249] ICTY, Documents, Miscellaneous: Code of Professional Conduct for Counsel Appearing Before the International Tribunal (2009).
[250] Human Rights Standards and Practice for the Police: Expanded Pocket Book on Human Rights for the Police (2004).
[251] ICTY-S Article 18(3) and 21(4)(f).

Language professionals are addressed directly only in one provision: the ICTY RPE declares that interpreters and translators must make a solemn declaration before conducting any duties that they will do it "faithfully, independently, impartially and with full respect for the duty of confidentiality."[252] This might also be taken to a definition of a language professionals' product at the ICTY that legal professionals can rely on.

The Registrar delivered the Code of Ethics for Interpreters and Translators Employed by the Tribunal (I&T Code) in 1999. The I&T Code contains rules on professional conduct (standards of conduct, professional integrity and dignity, reliability), general obligations such as confidentiality (general obligations, information sharing, lawyer-client privilege, continuation of obligations), impartiality, proficiency (competence: level of expertise), accuracy (truth and completeness, uncertainties in transmission and comprehension, clear transmission), and duties toward the profession (professional development: upgrading and professional solidarity). The I&T Code is meant to provide standards of conduct applicable to: interpreters on a fixed-term contract who interpret in simultaneous mode the proceedings held in the Tribunal's courtrooms, interpreters on a short-term contract or SSA during field-assignments, interpreters on a short-term contract, and translators on a fixed-term contract. The judges and the prosecution did not object.

The I&T Code also commands that translators and interpreters should maintain high standards of conduct as employees of the ICTY as their very functions require them to act faithfully, independently, impartially, and with full respect for the duty of confidentiality, noting their obligations regarding confidentiality do not cease after their engagements at the ICTY as they could be held accountable for any breach of such confidentiality, including, but not limited to, referral to their respective national or international professional associations.[253]

The I&T Code is a clear cut-and-paste job of the existing codes of ethics for freelance interpreters. It has been almost completely professionally refuted by the ICTY's language- and

---

[252] ICTY RPE Rule 76.

[253] ICTY, Documents, Miscellaneous: The Code of Ethics for Interpreters and Translators Employed by the Tribunal (1999).

language professionals-related case law. As the I&T Code has not been updated since its delivery in 1999, there is no sense repeating here information from Chapter 2.1.

3.2. ICTY language professionals

The ICTY and ICTY language services began when the late Cherif Bassiouni, the godfather of international criminal law, was appointed Chairman and Special Rapporteur on the Gathering and Analysis of Facts – the first fact-finding mission to start collecting testimonial evidence about atrocities in the former Yugoslavia by taking statements from victims and witnesses in B&H and Croatia.[254] This evidence was collected by an interdisciplinary team that was in charge of gathering and analyzing facts, on-site investigations and issues of law, Prijedor Project (Manjača, Keraterm, and Omarska concentration camps), the destruction of cultural property, and legal aspects of sexual assault. The conclusions of the Bassiouni Commission were that serious crimes were being committed in B&H and Croatia.[255]

Unfortunately, Bassiouni does not acknowledge language professionals in the Commission Report or in any of his subsequent writings. Consequently, it is unclear where they came from and whether they had any other tasks but translation and interpreting. Elias-Bursać shared some personal communication with Bassiouni, but except for sharing that 11 interpreters were engaged in the work of the Commission in 32 field missions, it seems that Bassiouni himself did not know where these interpreters came from and how they ended up interpreting for the Commission. Bassiouni described these 11 people to Elias-Bursać as "UN interpreters and translators [who] applied UN standards."

Consistent with the fact that translation and interpretation in a legal context is a receiver-oriented exercise, Bassiouni does briefly refer to the relationship between these 11 interpreters and the investigators they were supporting, conveying to Elias-Bursać

---

254 UN, Security Council Resolution 780 Establishing a Commission of Experts to Examine and Analyze Information Submitted Pursuant to Resolution 771 (S/RES/780) (1992).

255 UN, Final report of Commission of Experts established pursuant to the UN Security Council Resolution 771 (S/1994/673) (1994).

that, under his chairmanship, discussions between 22 legal professionals and 11 interpreters involved "how the translators would address linguistic variants between the three ethnic groups."[256]

Since the Bassiouni Commission investigated ethnic conflict and since it had already acknowledged linguistic variants between the languages spoken by the three enemy ethnic groups, did the UN DGACM, UNPROFOR, or anyone take care of the other receiver, the victims and witnesses, by selecting Bassiouni Commission interpreters based on their ethnicity? Acknowledging "linguistic variants between the languages spoken by the three ethnic groups" would constitute a clear procedural and moral violation, if no provisions were taken by the Commission to refrain from engaging the members of an "attacking ethnicity" to interpret for a client with a "victim/witness ethnicity."

This is a very important point because interpreting is a very personal process, and even more so in the context of investigations. Mulayim and Lei explain that interpreters working in the investigative process are bound by the legal, pre-existing relationship between the parties which draws the boundaries within which an interpreter is able to move. It is essential for an interpreter to respect this pre-existing relationship between the clients and not engage in any activity that may interfere with this relationship.

Obviously, these 11 interpreters were not confined to offices but engaged in the field with investigators and clients and could be said to have been the most important part of the process. This is because they were *creating a pre-existing relationship* between investigators and subjects. Once subjects were identified, language professionals engaged them in a very sensitive *pas de trois*, both when it came to speaking to the Bassiouni Commission and then to "opening up" during the interviews. In all that, the communication between legal professionals and victims/witnesses is indirect: legal professionals are virtually powerless and cannot resort to their standard behavior because they do not speak the language of their client. But, the very ethnicity of interpreters may interfere in a relationship between the two.

---

[256] Elias-Bursać, Ellen (2015), Translating evidence and interpreting testimony at a war crimes tribunal. Palgrave Macmillan: London.

Mulayim and Lei consider that professional trust plays a significant role in influencing the views of society about a particular profession. They define professional trust as a commitment to those who benefit from the professional service so that they can rely on decisions and opinions provided by a professional and they will not be exploited or taken advantage of. Personal trust is the foundation of professional trust, but once that trust is broken, it is extremely difficult to re-establish. Professional trust, once achieved, results in respectful regard, which reflects how highly beneficiaries of a professional service and the broader public value and respect the services, opinions, and judgment afforded by the professional.[257]

It follows that, when investigating an ethnic conflict, professional trust and a successful relationship with victims/witnesses are essential, so one should care about the ethnicity of interpreters. This is because the subjects' personal trust in interpreters is a foundation of the relationship between the subjects and investigators. Conversely, interpreters are of paramount importance because they are creating the relationship between the subjects and investigators, but also developing it, maintaining it, and serve as the main catalyst during its culmination.

Here, it becomes apparent that the name of the language spoken is useless and that the attention is on an individual. In terms of dialectology, ethnic Serbs, Croats, and Muslims speak territorial, not ethnic, dialects. One can say whether a person is from Serbia, Croatia, or B&H, but one cannot say whether one is speaking with an ethnic Serb, ethnic Croat, or ethnic Bosniak. Also, one cannot establish the ethnicity of a B/C/S speaker by the way they speak, no matter how proficient they are in B/C/S, and that includes the members of the Bassiouni Commission. Should a B/C/S speaking individual have an ethnically unmarked Slavic name, it is also impossible to detect their ethnicity. It follows that if the clients were unhappy about the national background of their interpreter, they could have simply spread the word about his nationality among their community, thus preempting any attempt at communication through such interpreters. Selecting interpreters based on their nationality would have greatly helped in all such efforts.

---

[257] Mulayim, Sedat and Lai, Miranda (2016), Ethics for police translators and interpreters. CRC Press: Boca Raton.

Unfortunately, Elias-Bursać seems to have forgotten to ask Bassiouni about the nationality or ethnicity of these 11 "UN interpreters applying UN standards" interpreting for victims and witnesses of ethnic crimes and whether these 11 spoke the linguistic variant of the victims for whom they were interpreting.

As far as B&H is concerned, the Bassiouni Commission investigations were about Prijedor and concentration camps in the surrounding area (Serb perpetrators) and sexual assaults (Serb and Croat perpetrators): what was done to make sure that none of these 11 language professionals were put in a situation where their clients might perceive them as a member of attacking ethnicity because of their linguistic variant? Unfortunately, Elias-Bursać seems to have forgotten to ask Bassiouni about that. However, the Bassiouni Commission Report says that among the 146 interviewed victim-witnesses from B&H, 31 were raped women and two were suspected by the interviewer to have been victims themselves but were unwilling to speak of their own experience.[258] Here, it seems everybody forgot to ask why and no one followed up.

Recruitment of language professionals for the purposes of the Bassiouni Commission presented a pivotal moment for language professionals at the ICTY and set the tone for further recruitment. But so did immense changes brought on by the three management periods in the ICTY CLSS that followed.

Until about 2000, when CLSS management changed for the first time, the organization of the CLSS was rather logical despite the fact that the translation, interpreting, and transcription load just kept on growing because of the increased investigations and single and multi-accused trials. Field investigations involved language professionals who were mostly local to the area of investigations, and every in-house investigation team was assigned two CLSS language professionals and two Language Assistants (see below).

This allowed for prompt communication between all the parties and a strict separation of duties between different categories of language professionals: one group was working on court-related documents (CLSS translators, interpreters, and court reporters) and

---

[258] UN, Final report of Commission of Experts established pursuant to the UN Security Council Resolution 771 (S/1994/673) (1994).

the other group on investigation-related documents (Language Assistants). Both groups equally helped with interpreting for in-house witnesses and promptly responded to clients' needs. Field interpreters were hired and worked mostly in B&H and Croatia, where CLSS chiefs organized regular small-scale exams for field interpreters. Those CLSS language professionals who were not assigned to investigation teams worked in a pool and either "picked up" after the team language professionals or responded to the translation and interpreting needs of other ICTY clients.

The 1999 UN OIOS Audit Report was positive about the CLSS. The problems were revealed only in relation to allowing promotions without meeting the necessary seniority requirements and in recruiting interpreters and translators because of both the high standards required and the competition for qualified staff.[259]

However, all this changed once the CLSS management changed in/around 2000. Soon after the second Chief of the CLSS assumed that position, she organized a mission to Budapest to interview candidates for translator and interpreter positions at the ICTY, specifically from Serbia. The reason Budapest, Hungary, was chosen as a testing location is that the then-Milošević regime did not allow an ICTY presence in the territory of Serbia. The candidates from Serbia who were tested and interviewed in Budapest reached that location at their own cost and peril. Successful candidates were first employed at GS-level category positions in the ICTY OTP. All such candidates, excluding one known Hungarian hybrid, were ethnic Serbs and there were no fewer than 30 of them.

Soon after the successful candidates arrived in The Hague, the Chief of CLSS organized a second translation exam from English into B/C/S. Naturally, this examination was open to all new and old staff, but it seems the purpose of this exam was so that the Serb staff from Budapest who did not pass the P-level examination could transition from GS-level to P-level positions. Many candidates of all ethnicities from all regions of the former Yugoslavia, both old and new staff, actually passed the examination. However, only ethnic Serbs, the new recruits from Budapest, were offered P-level positions in the CLSS.

[259] UN, OIOS Report on the audit and investigation of the ICTY (A/54/120) (1999).

It also became obvious later that some of these ethnic Serbs from Budapest had prior family and/or personal connections to the CLSS management. Other Budapest hires of Serb ethnicity who were left at GS-level positions that first time around eventually found their way into the CLSS through three more exams organized in about 2005, 2006, and 2007 for English language translators.

Examinations organized by the CLSS were largely unmonitored and candidates had full access to the internet during the examination. Save that one time, the CLSS never organized an examination for B/C/S translators again in The Hague. The CLSS also never organized a similar mass examination for candidates from B&H and/or Croatia in B&H and/or Croatia or elsewhere into English or B/C/S.

Between 2000 and the present day, all the heads of sections at the ICTY CLSS have been ethnic Serbs, all their deputies were ethnic Serbs, all English and French revisers have been or are married to ethnic Serbs, and most B/C/S revisers were ethnic Serbs. One Bosnian Muslim reviser magically disappeared after pointing out the overwhelming number of Croatians in the CLSS during the first management period. One Croatian translator magically disappeared after pointing to the overwhelming number of Serbs in the CLSS during the second management period.

Since the ICTY was established in 1993 there have been a total of eight Bosnian Muslims working as P-level language professionals in the CLSS for anywhere between one to five years or longer than 10 years. The CLSS has had anywhere between 60 and 170 language staff since 1993.[260]

3.2.1. The CLSS

The 1999 Annan reforms conditioned the UN Secretariat to put more responsibility for staff selection in the hands of specific hiring

[260] There were four more Muslims who were employed at the P-level positions in the CLSS, but they have not been taken into consideration for the following reasons: two were Muslims from Croatia and from Serbia, respectively, one was from a mixed marriage Muslim/Serb, and one was a Dutch Muslim. There were three more Bosnians at P-level positions in the CLSS, but they have not been taken into consideration because they are Bosnian Serbs.

managers rather than the advisory bodies that had existed in the past, effectively turning it into a one-man recruitment show producing a core team of auxiliary players.[261]

Elias-Bursać, one of the core team players in the CLSS, reports to have gotten a job of a reviser at the ICTY after having received a call from the ICTY early one June morning in 1998 from a fellow translator who had recently taken a job in the CLSS, inviting her to come and try her hand at revising for six weeks that summer. If the revising suited her and she suited the English Translation Unit, they could discuss a longer stay.[262] The arrangement suited both and she stayed at the ICTY, on and off, until 2010. However, if the information in her LinkedIn account is correct, Elias-Bursać did not meet any educational or previous working experience requirements to even be remotely considered for this position.[263] Even if given the most generous of collegial allowances, her education and working experience made her a novice translator, at best. At any rate, at the ICTY, Elias-Bursać did not work as a translator whose work would be subjected to revision by more experienced colleagues in the field, but as an English language reviser in charge of the revision of translations from B/C/S into English: the final check and balance to all translational efforts.[264]

This is not the only *ex nihilo* recruitment to the CLSS management team. Phillip Hepburn, author of another paper that will be discussed here, is another one: whereas Elias-Bursać at least dabbled in language, Hepburn did not at all.[265]

The mass recruitment of candidates from Serbia in/around 2000 is also rather incongruent. Once staff from Serbia took over from Croatians with the change of management in/around 2000,

---

[261] Alexovičková, Iveta (2012), From hiring to firing: a comparative study on selected legal safeguards for the independence and impartiality of international civil servants serving in the United Nations Secretariat and in the European Commission. Wolf Legal Publishers: Nijmegen.
[262] Elias-Bursać, Ellen (2015), Translating evidence and interpreting testimony at a war crimes tribunal. Palgrave Macmillan: London.
[263] LinkedIn, Ellen Elias-Bursać: https://bit.ly/2RF8DBF.
[264] UN vacancies, ICTY, P-4 Translator/Reviser (English): https://bit.ly/2yjokYl.
[265] LinkedIn, Phillip Hepburn: https://bit.ly/3a5nJa4.

the existing staff was scandalized both because of the one-sidedness in the ethnicity of the new translators and interpreters and because the CLSS management gave jobs to people whose output had to be constantly double-checked because they had no working experience in conflict situations, post-conflict situations, or international criminal tribunals. Consequently, this had an effect on quality because new staff without any previous UN experience, in addition to having to be trained, had also to be taught UN-speak and the entire indoctrination-free background to the conflict.

Finally, since most verdicts clearly name the Serb perpetrator as the major attacker and instigator of attacks in the former Yugoslavia, this experience must have been extremely confusing and heartbreaking to these Serb staff who never stopped volunteering that they never knew about any events described in the evidence they were working on. Unfortunately, they voiced those feelings mostly when nobody asked for them, making it hard for staff directly affected by the war against B&H and Croatia to move on with their lives or, at the end, to believe their claims: *how* just *how* could you not have known?

As to the operational, substantive, and subject-matter reality at the ICTY with effect on provision of language services, the war in the former Yugoslavia was never fought in the territory of Serbia proper: the borders between the countries that once formed Yugoslavia were closed, people could not travel freely for work, and from 1990 onwards Serbia was notorious for arbitrarily allowing and then forbidding the presence of international organizations in its territory. Consequently, it is unclear where language professionals recruited from Serbia would have gained their previous working experience "in the context of the UN or an international organization" as requested in most ICTY vacancies.[266]

With that in mind, in addition to the professional assessment by Browne, the CLSS management has done an amazingly poor job in recruiting translators and interpreters who have had experience in translation and interpreting during conflict, namely those from B&H and Croatia where the war was actually fought, where all the peacekeeping and humanitarian agencies were

---

[266] UN vacancies, ICTY, P-2 Associate Translator (B/C/S): https://bit.ly/3elN3fi; UN vacancies, ICTY, P-3 Translator (B/C/S): https://bit.ly/2RHuJ6O.

actually deployed, and from where most victims and witnesses of the war against B&H and Croatia originate.

As to the substance, although hailed as seasoned translators and interpreters, most of the newly recruited and exclusively Serb staff that arrived with the change of management in/around 2000 had limited working experience (translation of literary texts or texts for publications). The reader will understand without much difficulty that translating literature is not comparable with translating the law or translation in a legal context because translating law requires painstaking precision to the point that translation delivered in a legal context must read like a translation and a legal translator cannot trick the reader into thinking that s/he is reading the original like one would when translating a literary piece, for example. So, the new translators had to be taught extreme discipline to leave the operational and factual information intact.

The new interpreters were no different either. Parties will normally furnish in-court interpreters with original and translated versions of documents they plan to use during the examination of witnesses. In one such instance, although furnished with an original and a translation, an in-court interpreter decided to substitute the existing translation with her own, translating the time-specific "hitherto" with time ambiguous "outgoing." The Prosecution rightfully complained. After all, all this in-court interpreter had to do was read from the existing translation. And for that, she needed discipline.[267]

The ICTY ARs and other publications mentioning ICTY language professionals only mention the CLSS professionals and overuse the expression "UN criteria and standards." I have already explained that the ones who were creating these criteria and standards were the ICTY language professionals, not the UN, because the UN had absolutely no experience in the realm of the international criminal tribunals before the ICTY. This phrase showing up again and again until the last annual, financial, and audit report analyzed for the purposes of this study, only creates a perception that the criteria for recruitment of language professionals were set, that standards for translation and interpreting were set, and that language professionals were afforded comprehensive

---

[267] ICTY, Cases, *Krstić*, T. 6910 (3 November 2000): https://bit.ly/3ci7Peo.

training in the subject-matter and translation and interpreting in the legal context once taking up their duties in The Hague or in the field.

If such criteria and standards were brought into existence at all at the ICTY, they would constitute the first set of criteria and standards for any type of translation and interpreting at an international criminal tribunal in the history of the world. Consequently, it is surprising that such criteria and standards were never published and/or presented during a conference and/or praised in any UN reports at the time or since and/or mentioned in any way by any other legal or investigating body or organization working with the assistance of language professionals or otherwise. Exhaustive, ten-year long research into the existence of such criteria and standards yielded no results.

The ICTY Manual on Established Practice dances around the issue of criteria and standards, as well, without ever actually mentioning these criteria and standards or taking credit for their establishment, development, or publication. In the part where it discusses translation and interpreting, the CLSS recommended certain measures to overcome challenges, but the way these have been worded cannot be said to constitute established practices or that they are appropriate for a manual on developed practices, as such. Indeed, they are but a series of recommendations for a next should-would-could language service at the next should-would-could international criminal tribunal.

Although it is a manual on established practices, the rest of the CLSS's contribution discusses obligations on the parties *vis-à-vis* translation and interpreting matters as if admitting the investigators, prosecutors, and defense took charge from the onset. Finally, it addressed matters that the CLSS *should* do. What they should do includes, according to the Manual, unfortunately, training on almost every aspect of their engagement with legal professionals and on translation and interpreting in the legal context 16 years into their existence.[268]

As to training, specialized schools for translators and interpreters leading to a degree did not exist in the former Yugoslavia

---

[268] ICTY, Press, Publications: Manual on Developed Practices (2009), UNICRI Publisher.

before 1992 when the wars started. The very few staff who did have a degree in translation or interpreting obtained them abroad. Given the fact that the former Yugoslavia was governed by the socialist system and that the countries that were created after the collapse of the former Yugoslavia became countries in transition, regular courses on, at least, the basics of continental or international criminal law should have been taught.[269]

Legal professionals very clearly and unambiguously distanced themselves from any training of ICTY language professionals in the I&T Code, stating that translators and interpreters shall maintain and continually improve their interpreting and translating skills, and

---

[269] Although the ICTY Recruitment and Training Office was established in 1993 with the establishment of the ICTY, it is completely unclear from the data how much staff training this office has actually provided or when they actually started providing training. At any rate, none of this stopped them from internally evolving: the "training" component of this Office had a Career Development Unit which transitioned into a Career Transition Unit. Again, it is hard to establish when these sections started with career development and career transitioning activities because they are scarcely mentioned in the ICTY ARs and, if at all, then in passing. The ICTY training was twofold: those targeting the region and those targeting ICTY staff, specifically legal professionals. As far as those trainings targeting the region are concerned, the 2012 ICTY AR exclaimed that a total of 14,000 people in the former Yugoslavia had been trained through seminars, workshops, and training (UN, Report of the ICTY (A/67/214) (2012), para. 91). As to the ICTY staff, both categories provided and received training both by in-house and by external resources. The first, and the only, time anything substantial has been said about any of these trainings was in the 2002 ICTY AR, where it has been stated that the in-house training courses which cover the history of the conflict, the warring factions, violations covered by the ICTY-S, individual criminal responsibility, and practice before the ICTY have been developed by the international legal advisers and given twice a year (UN, Report of the ICTY (A/57/379) (2002), para. 237). ICTY staff training numbers are reported as following: almost 30 staff (UN, Report of the ICTY (A/56/352) (2001), para. 274), over 400 (UN, Report of the ICTY (A/57/379) (2002), para. 316), 350 (UN, Report of the ICTY (A/58/297) (2003), para. 335), 568 (UN, Report of the ICTY (A/59/215) (2004), para. 383), more than 900 (UN, Report of the ICTY (A/60/267) (2005), para. 247), more than 900 (UN, Report of the ICTY (A/61/271) (2006), para. 110), 1,100 (UN, Report of the ICTY (A/62/172) (2007), para. 117) and 950 (UN, Report of the ICTY (A/63/210) (2008), para. 115). After 2008, information about the training abruptly stops. The ICTY ARs do not mention any training relating to languages, translation, interpreting, or transcribing.

increase their knowledge of court proceedings and technical vocabulary that might be encountered during the performance of their duties, also stating that it is incumbent on interpreters and translators to support and encourage the professional development of their colleagues, and that interpreters and translators should provide their colleagues, whenever possible, with any specialized knowledge they acquire which may be useful to the exercise of their duties.[270] If anything, they encouraged the ICTY Registry CLSS to foster collaborative effort and provide on-job training to language staff.

Indeed, as portrayed before, Bassiouni Commission legal professionals expected the language professionals to come prepared and so did the ICTY OTP.

The ICTY OTP legal professionals in charge of investigating sexual violence took the blame for the non-provision of training to ICTY language professionals off of themselves. According to the 2016 book "Prosecuting conflict-related sexual violence," the interpreters, investigators, and prosecutors who interviewed these victims stated to have been unprepared to do those jobs because nobody had previous experience with these types of cases or knew what to expect. None of the interpreters received any training before participating in interviews with sexual violence victims. They struggled when the investigators or lawyers used technical terminology for sexual acts. Interpreters were also not adequately prepared for dealing with traumatized victims. Some did not know that the witness would be talking about sexual violence, and the interpreter was sometimes the first person the victim had spoken to about the crimes.

The authors concluded that the interpreters should be briefed about these effects beforehand and learn mechanisms to handle the negative effects. The authors also concluded by saying that now, however, the situation is different and the pressing need to provide more training and support for interpreters and others involved in interviews of conflict-related sexual violence victims is clear, entirely feasible, and a crucial insight for the future. However, they fail to provide information on types of training provided or target audiences.[271]

---

[270] ICTY, Documents, Miscellaneous: The Code of Ethics for Interpreters and Translators Employed by the Tribunal (1999).

[271] Brammertz, Serge and Jarvis, Michelle (eds.) (2016), Prosecuting

The ICTY organized various types of in-house training courses for legal professionals in the field of advocacy and international humanitarian law in order to prepare them to conduct their duties, but it seems these training courses did not include language professionals.

The CLSS claims in its online presentation to have been staffed with "highly qualified and certified court interpreters and translators specializing in legal translation," but that is, for the reasons advanced before, more than stretching it. Institutional translators in the former Yugoslavia worked mostly in domestic companies that were doing business with foreign companies and could be classified as technical translators, at best.[272] Moreover, no ICTY vacancies to the position of translators and interpreters ever mentioned the requirement of court certification. This renders the claim about CLSS language professionals working at P-level positions as court certified moot and makes it clear they have been considered court certified only because they worked for the court; it is declarative pedantry amounting to deception, not a reality.

The CLSS staff report that CLSS management organized only one translation training session for B/C/S and English translators and three for English and French translators from its establishment in 1993 until today. This was further confirmed in Elias-Bursać's survey of CLSS language professionals, most of whom indicated that they had not received any further training while employed (56.5%).

But the way this information is presented may be misleading. As soon as the ICTY Completion Strategy was announced in about 2004, the ICTY started organizing all sorts of cross-training activities: language staff could be cross-trained in whatever ICTY section offered training. For example, a colleague who normally worked as a language professional in the UN Detention Unit (UNDU) requested and received cross-training in procurement, another one in administration, etc. So, it is not the case that 43.5% respondents to Elias-Bursać survey of CLSS language professionals received training in translation and interpreting: these respondents received *some* training within the overall ICTY cross-training drive aimed at making the soon-to-be-separated staff more competitive

conflict-related sexual violence. Oxford University Press: Oxford.
[272] ICTY, Translation and interpreting: https://bit.ly/2XDgtj2.

on the open market. There were some CLSS translators who cross-trained to become interpreters. That cross-training was open to CLSS staff only. Although many participated, thus being away from the office, only one successfully transitioned and was later used as a conference interpreter.

Field interpreters interviewed for the purposes of this study were adamant that they never received any training and that the only communication they ever had with the CLSS was when CLSS administrative staff would contact them for booking. A few field interpreters were confused when the CLSS was mentioned, stating that they did not know what CLSS was, as they were under the impression that investigators were in charge of field interpreters because they were the ones who called to book them and brought them their contracts to sign.

Elias-Bursać dedicated a significant portion of her study to discussing the results of her survey of 80 ICTY CLSS language professionals. Her survey clearly shows that CLSS language professionals did not have much experience in translation and interpreting or knowledge of the substantive subject-matter or the region prior to taking up their duties at the ICTY.

As to the actual training needs, respondents said they were there "to develop their skills" and had started dabbling "in testing and recruitment." Some self-complimented on the "progress made over two years of service at the ICTY as an in-house interpreter, and as freelance thereafter" saying "the initial lack of knowledge of the region and its recent history turned into an in-depth knowledge." Some shared that "what they preferred were the people: not only did I find quite a few friends from university, whom I had not seen for twenty years, but I also met new friends, many of whom will stay on for life."

As to the actual substance, some respondents literarily said they "did not have any knowledge of the roots and the dynamics of the conflict or the new legal concepts because they had no previous experiences in criminal law" and others "fought for the idea that international and Anglo Saxon legal terms which do not exist in ex-Yugoslav legal system have to be given new names in B/C/S instead of being reduced to the nearest existing terms."

The confession about "development of skills" and dabbling with testing and recruitment is particularly interesting. This trial-and-error approach to testing and recruitment was unfair for the actual candidates who were obviously "practiced on" by someone without prior experience in interpreting or testing and recruitment. The CLSS claimed to be conducting competitive examinations in The Hague and abroad in almost every ICTY AR under examination during the second CLSS management period between 2000 and 2007. Obviously, the reason why these exams yielded no satisfactory number of candidates was not because they were competitive but because they were made by the same people who claim to have been at the ICTY CLSS to develop their skills.[273]

The ICTY and CLSS administration were housed in a separate building which was an easy walk from the main building of the ICTY while the French translation unit was located at Scheveningen, which was a ten-minute car ride away. Respondents to Elias-Bursać's survey criticized being isolated from the rest of the organization: instead of immersing them in work, embedding them in teams with the parties, the CLSS management completely isolated them from the whole process. This isolation might have contributed to rather unhealthy working relations in the CLSS.

Elias-Bursać calls the following comments respondents made on the most challenging aspects of their work "administrative

[273] There was a lot of in-house criticism of CLSS management regarding the way they made these exams, because it could hardly be said that these were exams preparing language professionals for any form of legal environment. Most of these exams were excerpts from biographies of famous people or from Serbian surrealist literature of the 1980s and early 1990s. They had very little to do with language professionals working in a legal context. After contacting the ICTY Chief of Recruitment who told them only the people from the third world countries complain when they fail UN proctored exams, the failed staff started contacting internal UN criminal justice authorities *en masse*, complaining about the sheer inappropriate character of the translation exams and ethnic one-sidedness in preferred candidates to positions. The CLSS took all criticism on board and the new exams started incorporating excerpts from local laws. The CLSS put 614 people on their roster of freelancers based on these exams. The CLSS administrative staff report they regularly used about 10 and that those about 10 used to be in-house staff, rarely some of those 614 who passed competitive, rigorous, and stringent tests held around the world for the quality assurance.

matters." Respondents said they "could cope with war criminals, war victims, but they could not with stupid and insensitive management," "surviving in the culture of the CLSS," "politics and manipulation on a higher level," "favouritism (in the unit)," "lack of consistency," "dealing with people's vanities," "managerial incompetence all across the ICTY."

They are most certainly not the first or the last staff to say their managers are incompetent and hateful *éminences grises*. Unfortunately, things soon turned rather dark. Elias-Bursać introduces the following comments, calling them "criticism of the Tribunal's mission": "dissatisfaction with many ICTY judgments," "trying to persuade my peers that none of it mattered one jot, that the tribunal was deeply biased," "at times (I stress not all of time, but at certain times, particularly around 2005 onwards), I actually felt ashamed to work there, such was my discomfort with some of the judgments in later cases."[274]

The judgments from 2005 onwards included the acquittals of suspected war criminals in cases of alleged crimes against the Serbs in Croatia (*Gotovina et al.*), the Serbs in B&H (*Delić, Halilović, Orić*), and the Serbs in Kosovo (*Haradinaj et al.*). The Serb staff at the ICTY seems to have been in a permanent state of angry spasm over these acquittals. They also seemed confident enough in their position that they had no reservations committing their candid comments to a paper planned for publication.

Some would see the above comments as a matter of institutional allegiance: how can a translator voice an uninformed opinion about judgments? They could also be interpreted as instances of harassment: how could staff feel free to go around the office persuading colleagues that "none of it mattered one jot"? How could management have allowed that? Also, if "the tribunal was indeed deeply biased" and if one "actually felt ashamed to work there," why not quit and move on? It needs to be said that none of these people took a moral stand: there is no evidence that they quit over this.

So, it seems plausible to ask: was there an ulterior motive behind staying at the ICTY surrounded by all the documentary and

---

[274] Elias-Bursać, Ellen (2015), Translating evidence and interpreting testimony at a war crimes tribunal. Palgrave Macmillan: London.

other evidence, including information about insiders? The spirit behind these comments made by the CLSS staff reflects badly on every single language professional who has ever worked at the ICTY. It goes against the UN Charter, UN Rules and Regulations, and other international documents regulating the position and duties of language professionals. It denigrates the core reasons behind the establishment of the ICT, insists on reciprocity in punishment, and points at institutional disloyalty amounting to denialism.[275]

---

[275] I must admit that I was not in presence of such a glaring and shameless denialism even when I was interpreting for some of the most notorious war criminals of the late twentieth and early twenty-first century. I asked a colleague investigator who is presently working in an investigation unit setup in a system of internal UN justice to unofficially comment on the above statements: "One must consider those types of comments as personal opinion unless they are backed with facts and/or examples to show as evidence. In the UN System all around the world, I would guess, that a large percentage of its personnel have become disillusioned, frustrated, and even discouraged in relation to the UN's effectiveness, efficiency, and overall achievements over the last several decades. Yes, many of these comments may appear to be counterproductive to the UN in general and probably even more in specific missions and units. In my experience in the UN, I have seen some offices to be quite dysfunctional in terms of its interpersonal relationships and working environments which often leads to low productivity, stress-related incidences and high attrition. This goes a long way in damaging the organization's reputation and the morale of its employees. Some of it relates to abuse of authority by senior personnel and managers, low pay scale for national staff in comparison to the high pay scale of the internationals and as well the country context (war torn, poverty, disaster stricken, etc.). As an investigator conducting oversight investigations (some related to harassment and abuse of authority) it is important in my opinion to take into considerations the morale of the office's personnel, especially when I hear comments such as those you describe from the book. I think they should be a cause for worry especially among senior managers and it is their duty to make every effort to rectify the problems resulting in these negative comments. However, I can't see how those types of comments are grounds for dismissal unless an employee goes public in an attempt to damage the UN's reputation. There are rules about giving public opinions. But in order to prove some type of wrongdoing by that someone who makes such comments, it will be a difficult task in my opinion. Hearing comments with negative tones often occurs when our personnel feel that they have been shortchanged, either with career advancement, salary increases, or disciplinary issues. The UN

3.2.2. Seven ICTY units employing language professionals

Before I venture into analysis of the ancillary language units at the ICTY, I must explain two matters. The ICTY has been relying on donations and voluntary contributions from the very beginning of its existence. These donations and voluntary contributions included cash, in-kind, equipment, and staff as detailed and documented in the ICTY ARs. Whereas it is, perhaps, even normal that the ICTY "borrowed" Dutch guards for their Detention Unit, it would be unfair of the ICTY if they paid them according to the Dutch standards, because the UN does have an administrative category of Security guard. It is also strange that the organization which so heavily relies on language professionals could not make any standing and full arrangements for language professionals and had to depend on donations for most projects the next ancillary language professionals have been hired.

The second matter is Language Assistant. The UN DGACM does not recognize the category of Language Assistant as part of any of the existing three main categories of UN staff. The UN DGACM language professionals either translate or interpret or edit. However, there is a rise of hybrid positions in some non-UN DGACM-serviced UN entities that comprise a host of language-related duties whereby incumbents are expected to provide 3-in-1

---

has in place several systems for receiving complaints related to the topic of this discussion. Ethics, Ombudsman, and HR offices are now trained to deal with these issues. In addition, freedom of speech is one of the human rights that the UN fights to uphold, however, there may be contractual issues which prevent staff from speaking openly like this about their experiences, if they are specifically related to their work. Usually, I think ICTY lawyers should have a look at the book before it goes out. (I know people like "American Sniper" had to be cleared by the military before allowing the movie to go out because he had a special contract). Generally, the UN doesn't care about disenfranchised staff shooting their mouths off – it's usually from the lower ranks, and is gossip and banter, unsupported by facts. Remember the so-called female whistleblower who made the movie about Bosnia. This was very questionable. From my perspective, the comments you suggest are not surprising and personally I would not react to them all that much unless I was officially investigating an issue in an office affecting staff morale." (Email on file).

language services, i.e. translation, interpreting, and editing.[276]

Finally, some vacancies advertised by the non-UN DGACM-serviced UN System entities, besides the 3-in-1 language-related duties, increasingly request incumbents in language professionals' posts to perform other non-language-related duties, called (3-in-1)+ duties for the purposes of this study. These (3-in-1)+ vacancies to language posts abound throughout non-DGACM-serviced UN System entities, including the ICTY where they were provided by the ICTY Language Assistants.[277]

---

[276] For example, language professionals working in the Organization for the Prohibition of Chemical Weapons (OPCW) are given the title of "Linguist" and translate, interpret, and edit (UN vacancies, OPCW, P-3 Linguist (Chinese): https://bit.ly/2wL2Ao8). The following UNDP's English and Arabic "Translation/interpreting specialist" is supposed to translate, interpret, manage translation team, perform research, and take care of procurement and administration (UN vacancies, UNDP P-3 Interpreter/Translation Specialist: https://bit.ly/2yfesz6). ICRC "Translators/interpreters" are required to interpret and to translate. Both sets of professionals normally hold different academic degrees, but the ICRC does not have any other term for such positions (ICRC (grade not defied), Senior Arabic Translator/Reviser: https://bit.ly/2V8X9sf). A colleague shared that the Pacific Community in Noumea, New Caledonia, has four interpreter/translator posts. Basically, these are interpreters who translate when they are not on interpreting assignments (UN vacancies, Secretariat of the Pacific Community, Interpreter/Translator: https://bit.ly/2wFbmns).

[277] UN vacancies, IMF Editor (External relations officer) is a vacancy for an editor where the recruiter is looking for a production manager, editor, and software programmer with six to 12 years of experience: https://bit.ly/34AD6Gi; UN vacancies, AFRO/WHO, Interpreters (English, French, Portuguese) is a vacancy for unspecified number of "someones" to provide translation, editing and interpreting, but those "someones" would be preferred if they were members of AIIC which represents interpreters only: https://bit.ly/3bcrBHN; UN vacancies, UNOPS, IICA-2 Bilingual Communications Consultant/Translator (English and Somali) should have a "Bachelor's degree in Business Administration, or other relevant Social Science. MA in Business Administration, or other relevant Social Science fields is an advantage" and is supposed to produce "well-articulated French language editorial set of guidelines, revised web content on the event pages, media centre and related subsites, crisp public French language public information products, including content for advertorials, campaigns, media kits and visibility items, well written French subtitling on ECA multimedia content, well written French language media kits and coordination of francophone oriented Communication Section events, clearly articulated

Although completely illegal according to UN laws, Language Assistants were accepted and widely used throughout the ICTY. The ICTY Manual says "while the Tribunal's language services, CLSS, fall within the Registry, in practice the OTP has had to engage its own language assistants in an attempt to deal with the overall translation demands. Even so, translation work has to be done on the basis of strict priorities determined by the stage of the cases and the demands of the trial process."

The CLSS accepted them and offered and promoted their services through the Office of Document Management to defense teams, as well, saying unofficial OTP translations were produced by OTP Language Assistants in its Document and Video Unit, Military Analysis Team, or elsewhere for OTP use, and instructing defense teams that they might find unofficial translations useful for ascertainment of facts. Should it meet the defense's needs, the request for official translation from the CLSS could be cancelled.[278]

The ICTY Language Assistants are classified between GS-3 and GS-6 levels and are divided into several different groups without any precise delineation of their duties: they are data-entry clerks *cum* summarizers (G-3), research assistants *cum* evidence reviewers (G-4), "proper" Language Assistants *cum* translators, interpreters, and transcribers (G-5), and coordinators (G-6). Language Assistants are supervised by non-language professionals, mostly OTP team leaders who assign work personally or through translation coordinators or administrative assistants. They were assigned to some of the language units listed below. Language Assistants summarize and index documents, search and select evidence, transcribe audio and video material, translate and interpret mainly between B/C/S and English, but also other languages, such as Arabic, Dutch, French, Italian, and Spanish.[279]

Translations delivered by OTP Language Assistants were checked by what could be described as revisers for a while. This was a group of randomly picked staff who performed quality assurance

---

responses to francophone media inquiries on a variety of themes including flagship publications and ECA events and related products": https://bit.ly/2RE5kLa.

278 ICTY, Documents, Defense: Frequently asked questions on Translation Requests.

279 UN vacancies, ICTY, G-5 Language Assistant: https://bit.ly/2yehXpm.

and quality control of translated material. Except for Language Assistants in the OTP, there is no evidence other units mentioned below had any system of quality assurance and quality control for their product. The OTP never organized any language-related training for Language Assistants. The Registry did not, either.

The **Rules of the Road** could be seen as a first unit using Language Assistants fully independent from the official, ICTY-wide language service, the CLSS. This project was set up in 1996 and ran until 2005. Its purpose was to decide which perpetrators were going to be tried by the ICTY and which ones were going to be left to local jurisdictions.

All language-related work in this project was performed by the Rules of the Road's own Language Assistants in charge of making extended summaries of case files submitted for a review. The project relied heavily on donations to perform language-related work throughout. However, these donations were usually insufficient to clear the backlog of cases submitted for review. In 1999, the UK Foreign Minister Cook announced a donation to support the project and to fund the translation of documents seized by the OTP. The project continued thanks to funding from the donors. The 2001 ICTY AR established that since its commencement, the project received a total of 914 prosecution files from national prosecutors in B&H, including Republika Srpska, and reviewed close to 1,300 suspects. It has been reported that the project reviewed 190 files involving 1,055 suspects in 2001; 54 files involving 241 suspects in 2002; and 192 files involving 1,134 suspects by the end of 2002.

The Rules of the Road project was incorporated into the B&H OTP as part of external reforms in 2004. This closed a circle whereby the ICTY took full charge of all international criminal law- and international humanitarian law-related prosecutions in the territory of the former Yugoslavia, both by prosecuting those that it had already indicted, issuing new indictments, and reviewing national case files from the former Yugoslavia through the Rules of the Road project.[280]

---

[280] UN, Report of the ICTY (A/51/292) (1996), para. 80; UN, Report of the ICTY (A/52/375) (1997), para. 76; UN, Report of the ICTY (A/53/219) (1998), para. 129; UN, Report of the ICTY (A/54/187) (1999), paras. 136

The **UN Detention Unit** (UNDU) was established in 1994 and could be seen as a second unit using Language Assistants fully independent from the official, ICTY-wide language service, the CLSS.

The ICTY issued its first indictment on 7 November 1994, but, although the war was still raging in the territory of the former Yugoslavia and there were no detainees, the ICTY had already started making provisions for their accommodation. It was decided that the ICTY should not tolerate any discrimination on the basis of, *inter alia*, language and should provide each detainee with, *inter alia*, a copy of the rules of detention and any other regulations in his own language or interpreter in cases where the detainee did not speak or understand either of the working languages of the ICTY or those spoken by any of the staff of the UNDU. Since the 1994 Report establishes that the detainee is entitled to communicate freely and without restraint with his defense counsel, with the assistance of an interpreter where necessary, this also means that it was planned to provide the UNDU with interpreters.[281] However, they were provided with Language Assistants.[282]

The **ICTY Victims and Witnesses Unit** (VWU) was established in 1995 and could be seen as a third unit using Language Assistants fully independent from the official, ICTY-wide language service, the CLSS. It was planned that the VWU would employ its own interpreters to emphasize the impartial nature of its work and its independence from both prosecution and defense.[283]

---

and 181; UN, Report of the ICTY (A/55/273) (2000), paras. 188-189 and 260; UN, Report of the ICTY (A/56/352) (2001), para. 242; UN, Report of the ICTY (A/57/379) (2002), paras. 234-235 and 275; UN, Report of the ICTY (A/58/297) (2003), paras. 253 and 296; UN, Report of the ICTY (A/59/215) (2004), p. 3-5 and para. 329; UN, Report of the ICTY (A/60/267) (2005), paras. 10 and 214; UN, Report of the ICTY (A/61/271) (2006), para. 108.

[281] UN, Report of the ICTY (A/49/342) (1994), paras. 100, 107, and 109.

[282] UN vacancies, ICTY, G-5 UNDU Language Assistant (Albanian, B/C/S and English): https://bit.ly/2z2kgwc; UN vacancies, ICTY, G-5 UNDU Language Assistant (B/C/S and English): https://bit.ly/2V7I4Y1.

[283] UN, Report of the ICTY (A/50/365) (1995), para. 112; UN, Report of the ICTY (A/51/292) (1996), para. 196; UN, Report of the ICTY (A/52/375) (1997), para. 168; UN, Report of the ICTY (A/53/219) (1998), paras. 257, 264, and 267; UN, Report of the ICTY (A/54/187) (1999) para. 166, 192, and 200; UN, Report of the ICTY (A/59/215) (2004), para. 329; UN,

Witnesses were brought to testify from many countries, mostly from the former Yugoslavia. At first, some were brought to appear in hearings under ICTY RPE Rule 61 on procedure in case of failure to execute a warrant, then to appear in hearings *viva voce*, and then under ICTY RPE Rule 92*bis* where their statements would be admitted *in lieu* of their *viva voce* testimony. According to the ICTY ARs, between 1996 when witnesses first started appearing in hearings, and 2016, the ICTY hosted a total of 7,042 witnesses and people supporting them.[284]

As to the VWU language staff, although clearly named as "interpreters" by the 1995 ICTY AR, research into the VWU language professionals' jobs descriptions revealed that they did not have any language-related functional titles, and certainly not that of an interpreter. The VWU "interpreters" had the functional titles "Administrative Assistant" or "Witness Assistant" and they had duties to provide language assistance (B/C/S, English, Dutch) for the VWU and perform other *ad hoc* duties as required.[285] Naturally, these *ad hoc* duties amounted to a provision of (3+1)+ services, providing 24-hour live-in support, information, and assistance to their clients. The VWU has been financially and professionally supported by the EU and the Danish Rehabilitation and Research Center for Torture Victims since 1995.

Report of the ICTY (A/61/271) (2006), para. 108.

[284] Information extracted from: UN, Report of the ICTY (A/51/292) (1996), para. 118; UN, Report of the ICTY (A/52/375) (1997), p. 96; UN, Report of the ICTY (A/53/219) (1998), para. 154; UN, Report of the ICTY (A/54/187) (1999), para. 168; UN, Report of the ICTY (A/55/273) (2000), para. 224; UN, Report of the ICTY (A/56/352) (2001) para. 234; UN, Report of the ICTY (A/57/379) (2002) para. 268; UN, Report of the ICTY (A/58/297) (2003), p. 3; UN, Report of the ICTY (A/59/215) (2004) para. 351; UN, Report of the ICTY (A/60/267) (2005) para. 226; UN, Report of the ICTY (A/61/271) (2006), p. 4; UN, Report of the ICTY (A/62/172) (2007) para. 106; UN, Report of the ICTY (A/63/210) (2008) para. 92; UN, Report of the ICTY (A/64/205) (2009), para. 85; UN, Report of the ICTY (A/65/205) (2010) para. 91; UN, Report of the ICTY (A/66/210) (2011) para. 86; UN, Report of the ICTY (A/67/214) (2012) para. 98; UN, Report of the ICTY (A/68/255) (2013) para. 78; UN, Report of the ICTY (A/69/225) (2014) para. 62; UN, Report of the ICTY (A/70/226) (2015) para. 66; UN, Report of the ICTY (A/71/263) (2016) para. 64.

[285] UN vacancies, ICTY, G-5 VWU Administrative Assistant (Dutch, B/C/S and English): https://bit.ly/3bcHbD1; ICTY, G-5 VWU Witness Assistant (Dutch, B/C/S and English): https://bit.ly/2Vw245v.

The **ICTY court reporters** could be seen as a fourth unit fully independent from the official, ICTY-wide language service, the CLSS.

Generally, the court reporters belong to a category of officers of the court or, rather, they are an integral part of courts. However, court reporters were unknown in the UN System when the ICTY was established. The UN recognizes the category of Verbatim Reporters which are regularly used at standing UN courts (International Court of Justice, UN Dispute Tribunal, and Administrative Tribunal of the International Labor Organization) and the Secretariat. The difference between the ICTY and other court reporters and verbatim reporters in the UN System is that court reporters produce verbatim transcripts of court sessions, whereas "[c]ombining the skills of transcription, translation and editing, verbatim reporters ensure the substantive accuracy of all statements, while maintaining a uniformly high standard of style."[286] In other words, the end product of verbatim reporters' work is not a verbatim transcript, but an extended summary of facts, and they do not use any specialized equipment in the performance of their jobs. Naturally, this does not work for a court where every word uttered needs to be transcribed verbatim. It follows that the ICTY could not have used existing UN sources to find court reporters.

The practice has shown a certain curiosity to the engagement of court reporters at the ICTY which seems to have much to do with the type of contract they signed with the CLSS. In the beginning, court reporters were paid by page and then by court session. Obviously, if they were hired on a different type of contract or as in-house staff, the page and hour restriction would not figure in the equation. The ICTY ARs also state that the CLSS was responsible for hiring English and French court reporters. Here, it is unclear why the charge to hire and supervise court reporters was given to the CLSS as in most jurisdictions court reporters are hired and supervised directly by the courts. The ICTY ARs also state that the work in the courtroom requires the permanent services of court reporters for the ICTY's two working languages: English and French.[287] The CLSS understood "permanent services of court

---

[286] UN, Verbatim Reporters: https://bit.ly/3chon5R.

[287] UN, Report of the ICTY (A/50/365) (1995), para. 90; UN, Report of the

reporters" not as those stemming from the use of in-house sources, as the word "permanent" used in employment context normally suggests, but rather "permanently outsourced." So, the CLSS hired court reporters from outside companies from the very beginning.

As to them, the English language court reporters, in-house contractors of the outsourced company, work in teams of two: one sitting in the actual courtroom and the other one sitting in a nearby office, revising the work of his in-courtroom colleague (names, locations, misspellings, etc.). French language court reporters work(ed) off-site. Since they are located in Canada (-6 CET), they are able to respond to deadlines to submit camera-ready transcript two hours after the court ends the session.

The 1997 ICTY AR suggests the establishment of an **Outreach Program** which could be seen as a fifth unit using Language Assistants fully independent from the official, ICTY-wide language service, the CLSS.

The Outreach Program, with its related Internet Unit, would enable the ICTY to better inform the people of the former Yugoslavia of its work in the local languages and combat distortion of the ICTY's record. The Outreach Program falls under the Public Information Services whose activities include, *inter alia*, translation and distribution of information packets and systematic translation of all relevant public information materials into B/C/S. This program has been funded exclusively through voluntary contributions since its inception: the European Commission generously supported the program.

The Outreach Program published and widely distributed all available key and basic ICTY documents in B/C/S and Albanian (all public indictments, judgments, rules of procedure, press releases, leaflets, etc.) in print form and online at the B/C/S section of the ICTY's website. It also established and maintained live audio broadcasting of all public ICTY court sessions on the internet, which were later available in four languages (English, French, B/C/S, and Albanian), two of which came with a complete recording of the hearings (English and B/C/S). The program has also overseen the production of a series of documentaries in English and B/C/S that

---

ICTY (A/51/292) (1996), para. 134; UN, Report of the ICTY (A/52/375) (1997), para. 109.

provide audiences with an introduction to the work of the Tribunal and the crimes committed in the former Yugoslavia.[288]

The Outreach Program is the most important communicator of the Court's messages to the region. I have commented on their product heavily in the footnotes. Also, in all fairness, nothing could have been found in the Outreach Program's press releases or publications that was more than merely informing about the date, time, and subject of the ICTY's work. There was no deeper analysis as to what all this meant for the region. Most documents were written in legal language as if the communicators were communicating with their legal peers, not with common people.

As far as the Outreach Program language philosophy is concerned, there was no logic from the beginning: the OTP statement on the Judgment of Vojislav Šešelj dated 31 March 2016 was translated into Bosnian *ijekavian*, Information on the Partially Dissenting Opinion of Judge Lattanzi in Judgment in the case of Vojislav Šešelj from 31 March 2016 was translated into Serbian *ekavian*, and the OTP statement on the conviction of Radovan Karadžić from 24 March 2016 was translated into Bosnian *ijekavian*.[289] This seems to suggest the absence of any language or audience-related standards.

The 1999 ICTY AR hinted at the existence of yet another unit dedicated to some segments of language-related work at the ICTY: **Chamber Support Unit**. Language elements in the ICTY Chamber Support Unit could be seen as a sixth unit charged with language services fully independent from the official, ICTY-wide language service, the CLSS.

This unit started providing research and drafting assistance and editorial services in English and French to the judges. They

---

[288] UN, Report of the ICTY (A/52/375) (1997), para. 3; UN, Report of the ICTY (A/57/379) (2002), paras. 255 and 261; UN, Report of the ICTY (A/59/215) (2004), para. 329; UN, Report of the ICTY (A/62/172) (2007), para. 100.

[289] ICTY, Cases, *Šešelj*: B/C/S translation of the Statement of the OTP on the Judgement of Vojislav Šešelj (2016); ICTY, Cases, *Šešelj*: B/C/S translation of the Information on the Partially Dissenting Opinion of Judge Lattanzi in Judgement in the case of Vojislav Šešelj (2016); ICTY, Cases, *Karadžić*: B/C/S translation of the Statement of the OTP on the Conviction of Radovan Karadžić (2016).

continue with this engagement to date. The 2012 ICTY AR reports that the ICTY President implemented measures to expedite translations of final trial briefs and trial judgments to avoid delays on appeals, instructing both the ICTY and the ICTR Registrars to assign additional resources in order to halve the projected time needed for translation in four cases. Consequently, Trial Chambers expanded the practice of including translators in the judgment drafting process in order to expedite the translation of trial judgments, albeit 20 years into the ICTY's existence.[290] CLSS staff report that this was not a practice, but a one-off instance in which a French translator took part in the judgment drafting process.

As to the quality of their work, the Summary Judgment in *Šešelj* that was supposed to be edited by the Chamber Support Unit was riddled with typos and lacking basic proofreading.[291] This seems to suggest that this unit does not have ample time for editing and proofreading, or that services provided by the Chamber Support Unit in terms of proofreading and editing are non-existent and/or provided by linguistically incompetent staff. Not a single ICTY law or bylaw analyzed so far mentions this unit or its working methodology in any way. Finally, the above Summary Judgment that is still present on the ICTY site makes it uncertain which copy translators used to produce translation.

Finally, in addition to the Rules of the Road language professionals, VWU language professionals, UNDU language professionals, court reporters, Outreach Program language professionals, and Chamber Support Unit language professionals, the **OTP Language Unit** forms the seventh language-related unit that is completely separate from the CLSS and completely dependent on donations.

---

[290] UN, Report of the ICTY (A/67/214) (2012).

[291] The ICTY Judgment Summary in *Šešelj* was continuously checked every week from 31 March 2016 when it became publicly available. These are just some of many rather mistakes were still there the last time the text was checked in April 2020: making it futile impossible to make; criminal,,; which for the Prosecution consist of targeting all the possible modes; admitted through resulting from; is not binding over the Chamber only rests: UN, Cases, *Šešelj*, Judgment Summary (31 March 2016): https://bit.ly/3emZqrx.

The UN OIOS Internal Audit Division 2009 audit of the ICTY language services stated that the OTP Language Unit formed part of the Information, Evidence and Linguistic Section, which consisted of about 62 staff paid at GS-level where some 35-40 staff were deployed for translation purposes in 2009. The OTP explained this Language Unit was set up to meet an extremely tight deadline imposed by the Trial Chamber in the *Krajišnik* pre-trial proceedings, which left it with no alternative but to engage a team of translators. This coincided with the beginning of the second management period in the CLSS in/around 2000.

The OTP Language Unit was initially conceived as a temporary measure, but once the urgent work was completed, the OTP continued to maintain the Unit because of the advantages it offered. The OTP stated that without the resources of this Unit, if they had to wait for translations from the CLSS, the trials would come to a complete halt as the CLSS was busy with the defense phase of two multi-accused cases.

Indeed, at the time of this audit, the OTP quoted the Registry, which noted that in 2007 and 2008, the CLSS worked mostly for defense teams: 75% in 2007 and 80% in 2008. The OIOS Auditors noted that OTP's Language Unit lacked credible workload norms, performance indicators, and that the staffing requirements projected in the budget documents were not based on a sound justification. The 2006-2007 and 2008-2009 budget submission notes that the estimated number of pages requiring translation/transcription was expected to be 320,000 and staff requirements were projected based on a rate of 16 pages per person and 220 days per year. The auditors assessed that the yearly output of the OTP Language Unit ranged from 10,000 to 26,000 pages per year. Considering that these GTA staffing projections were based on 16 pages per day, the output of the language staff should typically yield some 140,800 pages per year. The OIOS Auditors concluded that either the staffing projections were incorrect, or the norm needed to be revised, reminding that the standard UN output for translators was 5.5 pages per day and that therefore the OTP Language Unit norm, nearly three times the standard UN norm, required reconsideration.

The auditors recommended that the OTP should review the existing workload norms, noted that maintaining the OTP Language Unit, with limited links to CLSS, represented a duplication of resources, and may not represent efficient allocation of resources. Considering that the CLSS and the OTP Language Unit essentially perform the same kind of work, there is a need for coordination between the two language service providers. Given that the CLSS is the official language services provider to the ICTY, the OIOS Auditors remarked that the OTP Language Unit needed to consult with the CLSS about administering, monitoring, and quality control within the OTP. Moreover, since translators at the ICTY range from GS-5 to P-4, the auditors said it was necessary to define and categorize the kinds of translation required and match these with the level of translator skill to ensure the most cost-effective use of translation resources. The auditors recommended that the ICTY Administration and the OTP should undertake a formal review to assess the justification to maintain separate language service resources within the OTP.

The OTP did not accept this recommendation, stating that it did not believe a formal review was warranted at this early stage: the amount of work that was being submitted together with the liaison/coordination between the OTP Language Unit and the CLSS made it abundantly clear that both language service resources were required, reiterating that the OTP depends on an instantly available and highly flexible service of Language Assistants where, by contrast, in many cases, the CLSS cannot accommodate the OTP's most immediate needs for assistance at short notice. Unlike CLSS translators, OTP Language Assistants are also involved in numerous other projects, such as processing intercepts, quality control of document coding, redaction of witness statements, reviewing video material, and other tasks. The OIOS Auditors replied they were unable to accept the assertion that it was too early for a formal review: the OTP's Language Unit had existed for a decade, though it was initially conceived of only as a temporary measure and the continuation of existing arrangements that are duplicative needed to be reviewed.[292] This never materialized.

During the 2002 plenary sessions, the ICTY Registrar set up a committee to examine translation requests on the basis of the urgency of the request and the capacity of the services in question.[293]

---

292 UN, OIOS Internal Audit Division, Audit of Language Services at ICTY (2009).

293 UN, Report of the ICTY (A/57/379) (2002).

The 2002-2003 UN Board of Auditors Report established that to allow defense counsel to select the documentation falling under the ICTY rules and regulations on disclosure of exculpatory and other material, the OTP opted for the scanning of documents and for web-based e-disclosure, which was launched late 2003. As a consequence, all documentation available at the OTP, regardless of its relevance, had to be translated. Since 2002, OTP Language Assistants have translated prosecution material at a preliminary stage to ascertain whether the material would be required for the Court proceedings. If the material was deemed to be required, the Tribunal requested that this already translated prosecution material be translated again before being used in Court. The second translation was provided by certified translators of the CLSS.[294]

Obviously, OTP Language Assistants were charged with language- and non-language duties. It seems that the requirement for language professionals to engage in non-strictly language professional affairs was inherited from the IMT: IMT language professionals were assigned to other departments between sessions, like investigation, translation, transcript correction, etc. Sometimes, interpreters would work for the prosecution as investigators. They were sent to countries in Europe to obtain affidavits from potential witnesses and their agreement to testify personally in court.[295] This has certainly not been the case at the ICTY, but selecting and analyzing documentary evidence has.

But primary duty to select and analyze documentary evidence lies with Military, Intelligence, and Research Analysts, classified between P-2 and P-4. Once documents reach them, Trial Teams would ask their team Language Assistants to select documents for evidence, which means that Language Assistants would start acting like investigators or Military, Intelligence, and Research Analysts. No job vacancies for the post of Language Assistant mention any educational requirements in legal or analytical fields, only language, if that at all.

It has been reasoned that Language Assistants were involved in these matters because most documents waiting to be

294 UN, UN BoA Financial report and audited financial statements for biennium 2002-2003 ended 31 December 2003 (A/59/5/Add.12) (2004).

295 Gaiba, Francesca (1998), The origins of simultaneous interpreting: the Nuremberg trial. University of Ottawa Press: Ottawa.

selected for evidence are in B/C/S and there is a lack of sufficient language capacity in the OTP to go through all of them. Language Assistants cannot review documents alone or in consultation because they are not professional Military, Intelligence, and Research Analysts. Likewise, Language Assistants cannot select relevant evidentiary materials because they are not lawyers.

The use of Language Assistants at the ICTY is a glaring example of how the UN poorly uses resources of the situation countries: after all the talk of multilingualism, all the ICTY needed to do to ensure good delivery of all these services provided by Language Assistants was to employ appropriate professionals with knowledge of B/C/S.[296]

3.3. Linguistic justice: the working institution towards language services providers

I am now in a position to examine whether linguistic justice has been served in the third line of communication with the judicial institution: the working institution towards the language service providers. My research shows that the CLSS, the ICTY language services provider, put ICTY language professionals in a rather bad position in terms of recruitment, professional criteria and standards, and training.

The international and ICTY laws and ICTY case law put ICTY language professionals in a pretty good situation providing them with protection from the legal conflict that normally goes on between the parties, independence to carry out their work, and a basic definition of a translational and interpretational product they can rely on both in the ICTY RPE and in the I&T Code. It was up to the language professionals' management, the CLSS, to deliver underlying policies on recruitment, training, and outputs.

Unfortunately, the ICTY CLSS has done very little, if anything at all.

[296] The following two vacancies from 2010 and 2015, respectfully, do require candidates to have a working knowledge of the B/C/S: UN vacancies, ICTY, Intelligence Analyst (Military): https://bit.ly/3enah4O, UN vacancies, ICTY, Intelligence Analyst (Criminal): https://bit.ly/3chltOs.

The 2009 ICTY Manual on Developed Practices admits that, although B/C/S effectively became a working language in many aspects of the ICTY work, many problems were caused by not having B/C/S as the Tribunal's working language.[297] By extension, the accused did not have transcripts of proceedings readily available in a language that s/he could understand and had to actually listen to the audio/visual tapes of the proceedings; the same goes for witnesses who came to testify more than once. Situation country courts, legal professionals, and other interested parties had to do the same. As to the situation country parties, the principles of transparency at any public or international organizations are extremely important. The ICTY had a reputation of being one-sided, biased, unfair, etc. in the situation countries. The lack of transcripts, materials, and publications in B/C/S could be said to have fueled those claims and fed the nationalist discourse currently thriving in the former Yugoslavia, contributing to a lack of transparency and perpetuating a popular image of the ICTY as a self-serving institution: the region did not see the proverbial black on white from the mouths of the proverbial babes.

As to the recruitment, the problems with language services started from the beginning, when Bassiouni confused the 11 language professionals who serviced the Bassiouni Commission for UN interpreters and translators who applied UN standards.[298] UN translators and interpreters from/into English and B/C/S were not readily available on the UN market. B/C/S did not figure into the official languages of the UN and the ICTY was the first international criminal tribunal since the IMT and the IMTFE. Accordingly, there could not have been any UN standards for translation and interpreting at international criminal tribunals when the ICTY was established. IMT scholars concerned with translation and interpretation do not explicitly mention any standards, stopping short from saying that these jobs were learned as staff went along, but if there were any standards, they were almost 50 years old. As for the UN, the ICSC standards for translation and editing were in existence, but these standards were geared toward the *translation* of, essentially, parliamentary and non-parliamentary documents

---

297 UN, Press, Publications: Manual on Developed Practices (2009), UNICRI Publisher.

298 Elias-Bursać, Ellen (2015), Translating evidence and interpreting testimony at a war crimes tribunal. Palgrave Macmillan: London.

and publications, and not at all toward *interpretation* in the context of international criminal tribunals that were engaged in investigations.

In 2015, the UN General Assembly adopted a resolution aiming at a more holistic approach to staffing and reemphasized mobility. The new mobility policy affects internationally recruited staff at P-level and FS-level positions and facilitates mobility, which is now defined as integral and a required part of a UN career.[299] This confirms that there is no impediment to moving trained UN DGACM language professionals elsewhere. In other words, after the obligatory six-month training in UN headquarters in New York City, a successful candidate of the LCE, for example, could have been moved to a position of an editor at the ICTY Chamber Support Unit, or French into English or English into French translators or interpreters could have been moved to a position at the ICTY CLSS, at least. There is no evidence in any ICTY, OIOS, UN BoA, or any other documents consulted for the purposes of this study that any of that has been done.

Searches were made into CLSS revisers and section heads, leading to the shocking discovery that for most of them working at the ICTY was the first working experience in their lives. Most of them worked as teaching assistants at the University of Belgrade. My contacts at the University of Sarajevo and the University of Zagreb confirmed there were teaching assistants there, as well, but that those people never found their way to the ICTY. Despite that, the ICTY CLSS staff climbed through the ranks pretty quickly and some of them became revisers or heads in less than five years. This was in clear violation of the previously discussed 1999 OIOS Report and its findings about the need for consistent application of placement and promotional policies for vacant positions and the need to stop allowing promotions without meeting the necessary seniority requirements.[300] However, since none of these CLSS managers and staff have written anything about their engagement at the ICTY, there is no point presenting their professional profiles here. The motivation for conducting that research was curiosity and the findings are presented just as they are: a curiosity.

---

[299] UN, Mobility framework (A/68/265) (2014).
[300] UN, OIOS Report on the audit and investigation of the ICTY (A/54/120) (1999).

The overall picture painted by the CLSS staff who responded to Elias-Bursać is of people who came to ICTY to learn, not of cutting-edge professionals putting their education to work while celebrating their previous working experience in delivery of a perfect service like one would rightfully expect from an institution with more than 50 years of institutional translation and interpreting.

Contrary to the ICTY reports, there was no competition for qualified staff. The International Association of Conference Interpreters (AIIC) and the International Association of Conference Translators (AITC) are recognized as partners by the UN and they have 917 and 214 members with French as the language of translation/interpreting into, respectively. French language professionals can, theoretically, work anywhere in the UN System, providing they pass the UN DGACM or other UN System entities' entrance exams, and they are widely available because French is a UN language. The ICTY CLSS would hire mostly young and inexperienced French language professionals, who they would then train to work in the context of an international criminal tribunal for about one year, just like all other staff. Once that year passed, the CLSS would lose these French language professionals to other UN System entities. CLSS management reports that they had about ten core French language professionals who had been with them since the beginning and that about 20 other staff changed every two years or so. After this two-year limit, staff would leave as soon as they could mostly because the ICTY is not a permanent organization. It is human nature to strive for certainty, so those motivations are more than understandable. But, it is highly illogical these other organizations would take CLSS's staff, as CLSS claimed: if you take staff who were trained to work in an international criminal tribunal and you are not working in that context, as is the case with almost all other UN System entities, you will have to retrain them anyway.

There were no other international criminal tribunals which could have "stolen" French staff from the CLSS until 2002 when the ICC was established, and 2006 and 2007 when the ECCC and STL were established, respectively. The ICC did, indeed, come as a pleasant surprise to the ICTY language professionals and almost everyone with ICC language combinations hoped to get a job at the ICC mostly because it is a permanent organization. However, it is my personal observation that the ICC has always been reluctant to take on ICTY staff. Fewer than ten former ICTY language, legal, and support staff colleagues work at the ICC and most them got those jobs after the change in ICC overall management in 2012. Most of them were hired at a lower grade or in different job profiles than that at which they worked at the ICTY.

There is more evidence that the recruitment into the CLSS was so botched that it is obvious that the main owners of the CLSS working methods, the ICTY revisers, have never understood legal professionals' process of arriving, accepting, and saving the legal facts and truth. For example, Hepburn, the former ICTY CLSS English Translation Unit Chief and reviser, acknowledges the search for terminological consistency is an endless task due to the duration and interconnectedness of proceedings. Because the same documents may be used again, the translators find existing translation of a term is inadequate once they finally discover the real meaning of a term which they have previously translated literally and revisers update the terminology database. If this results in discrepancies between new translations and translations of other documents that were done previously, it may become necessary to revise the old translations as they come up in the new trial.[301]

First of all, this is yet another proof of an absolute lack of any on-the-job training in the CLSS. Secondly, it clearly spells out that the CLSS revisers left their translators alone until they "finally discovered" an appropriate translation all on their own. Obviously, this is wrong because it hints at the non-existence of any collaborative effort, *a priori* knowledge of the trade, or understanding of the junior-senior system of patronage present in all organizations. And, finally, revising "old translations as they come up in the new trial" should send chills down the back of anyone working in the legal fora. Adjudicated facts of any trial are adjudicated facts: legal professionals are done with those facts in that trial and they have surrendered them to the realm of case law. If legal professionals want to change anything in adjudicated facts, then they declare a mistrial and issue an apology to everyone or the governmental system collapses. Here, it seems Hepburn suggests that CLSS

301 Hepburn, Phillip (2012), The Translation of Evidence at the ICTY: A Groundbreaking Institution. Translation and Interpreting Studies, 7(1):54-71.

translators or revisers went back and revised "old translations" to fit new cases.[302]

As to the criteria and standards, the problem here is that "criteria and standards" is not a mere buzzword or a platitude that one throws around, but an operational premise: it is a guideline for how something needs to be done in a specific context, supported by examples from practice and lessons learned. The organization simply must have it in the form of a document both for future in-house use and to assist future organizations.

Elias-Bursać mentions the Registry Policy Governing Translation Services (2006) which had been provided to her by the the ICTY Registry. Given that UN prides itself on transparency, this "policy" should be a public document available for scrutiny of language professionals. This "policy" should not be given under the table to any individual because having to request a document that should have been public to begin with implies secrecy. It is as if legal researchers had to write to the ICTY Registry asking if they could, please, be sent a copy of Statute and/or the Rules. There

---

[302] Exhaustive research of the official ICTY site and the ICTY Court Records revealed a series of documents where parties made motions at resubmission of wrong or corrected translations due to mistakes in filing (ICTY, Cases, *Šainović et al*, Order RE exhibits 6D202 (2008): https://bit.ly/3acmkOS; ICTY, Cases, *Šainović et al.*, Order RE exhibits 6D132 and 6D1496 (2008); ICTY, Cases, *Šainović et al.*, Second order on exhibits P2885, 1D279, 1D671, 4D3, 4D95, 4D106, and 5D272 (2008), and many others), where parties spotted a translation error (ICTY, Cases, *Šainović et al.*, Decision on Prosecution request for extension of time to submit corrected translation of exhibit P942 (2007); ICTY, Order RE exhibit P1999 (2007); ICTY, Cases, *Šainović et al.*, Order RE exhibits P2166 and P1506 (2008), and many others), or where parties requested submission of full instead of partial translation on the record (ICTY, Cases, *Hadžić*: Decision on matters relating to certain documents and transcripts (2014), and many others including the above), etc. Further research has shown that motions accepting revised translations were granted in cases where translation was replaced with the revised version because the previous versions were in draft format, where parties argued for different terminology, because the existing translation contained errors or omissions, where parties wanted the *viva voce* interpreting to be replaced by an official translation of the testifying witness' utterances, or most of the above. All these interventions by the parties are entirely normal. What is not normal is going back and revising translations once they were used to arrive at adjudicated facts.

cannot be secrecy surrounding basic documents in an institution established to find the truth.

The ICTY Manual can be looked at as a confessional of the CLSS's failures, but it cannot be said to constitute an acceptance or understanding of those failures on the part of the CLSS management. The CLSS management who contributed to the Manual forgot to say that it is their **legal obligation** under ICTY RPE 66(A)(i) and 66(A)(ii) to deliver specific documents in translation. They forgot to say that it is their **legal obligation** under ICTY-S Article 21(4)(b) to deliver those documents in time to enable proper defense. They forgot to say that it was their **legal obligation** under ICTY laws to inform all language policies on all those other documents which were not covered in the ICTY laws and other recruitment- and service delivery-related lacunae. Etc., etc., etc.

The CLSS management did not address the manner in which they overcame or coped with any of the established challenges they acknowledged in the ICTY Manual on Established Practice or elsewhere. The fact that they claim that "only certain documents need to be translated into the language of the accused" is a distortion of the OTPS's obligations under ICTY RPE Rule 66 which very clearly defines types of documents that have to be provided to the accused in their own language. The fact that the ICTY put its foot down on responsibility for translation remaining with the CLSS suggests the ICTY's acceptance of the CLSS's inability to self-regulate and confirms the finding of this study that language services at ICTY were highly over-segmented.

As to training, the legal client expected language professionals to come prepared to work in terms of their education, previous working experience, and training. There is very little evidence of CLSS-provided training, in turn.

The CLSS cannot be said to have contributed to the advancement of their profession. On the contrary. The 2009 OIOS Auditors established that ICTY language professionals were paid at between the GS-4 and P-4 level.[303] ICSC Standards were announced to eliminate situations in which some organizations placed certain

---

303 UN, OIOS Internal Audit Division, Audit of Language Services at ICTY (2009).

jobs in the P-level category while other organizations, sometimes within the same duty station, placed the same jobs within the GS-level category.[304] This means that the engagement of Language Assistants, documented as condoned by the CLSS, directly violates the core reasons for the establishment of the ICSC Standards: to eliminate differences in payment. However, this was done with the consent of the incumbent to the post of Language Assistant. At the ICTY, for example, Language Assistants were made to sign a document waiving their postgraduate degree.

The CLSS management not only allowed their colleagues to waive their diplomas, they surrendered them to the mercy of uninformed clients. The OTP's use of Language Assistants is an obvious example of how poorly the UN administration uses its internal resources and how poorly it enforces its own policies. The supercilious ICTY approach to OTP language professionals revolves around legal professionals commanding language professionals to conduct important legal duties for which they are absolutely unqualified. This approach is indicative of an institution that clearly ignores the local context and considers that speaking a local language qualifies a speaker to meddle in every aspect of the associated culture. The fact that a Language Assistant speaks B/C/S does not qualify him to perform the job of an analyst and reviewer of evidence to be used in a criminal context. This approach paints a picture of legal professionals who want to get through documents no matter what, including surrendering them to an unqualified group of people. This failure to plan properly constitutes a serious lack of due diligence.

None of this would be a problem if the ICTY gave Language Assistants with college degrees a title of Paralegal, for example, and paid them at P-level or gave all the others a title Bilingual Secretary. Instead, they gave their Language Assistants working titles that make no sense outside, or even in the UN System, and paid them as non-college diploma holders. This is a serious issue that has to do with the integrity and self-regulation of all included in this process.

---

304 Alexovičková, Iveta (2012), From hiring to firing: a comparative study on selected legal safeguards for the independence and impartiality of international civil servants serving in the United Nations Secretariat and in the European Commission. Wolf Legal Publishers: Nijmegen.

Although the 2009 OIOS Audit Report established that the CLSS has been able to ensure compliance through the provision of translation and interpreting services with the basic minimum guarantees in ICTY-S Article 21 on the rights of the accused, the OIOS Auditors also discovered that CLSS staff were not making the declaration under ICTY RPE Rule 76 which is to be solemnly made before performing any duties. In response, the CLSS stated that all ICTY staff must sign a solemn declaration before taking up their duties, i.e. when signing their employment contract. This declaration, the CLSS claimed, includes a reference to UN Staff Regulations and UN Rules which, in turn, require staff to act as foreseen in ICTY RPE Rule 76.

This reasoning is logically flawed, given the nature of language professionals' functions in the court, so as to ensure compliance with ICTY RPE, the OIOS Auditors recommended that translators and interpreters need to make a formal declaration and that the ICTY Administration should ensure that the CLSS obtains from its staff signed declarations affirming that they have read and understood the provisions contained in ICTY RPE Rule 76. The ICTY Administration accepted the recommendation and agreed that the signature of a specific statement provides an additional level of awareness of the obligations. This recommendation, made in 2009 or 16 years into the existence of ICTY, remained open pending confirmation that CLSS has commenced obtaining from its staff signed declarations signifying that they have read and understood the provisions contained in ICTY RPE Rule 76.[305]

Signing a declaration or affirmation is very important at any court, but, when it comes to the ICTY, as we have seen before, a declaration or affirmation signed by an interpreter attests to the reliability of the witness statement in the eyes of the Court (see Chapter 2.2.). The only evidence of interpreters making any declaration or affirmation is in the Interpreter Certification attached to ICTY Witness Statements. In the Interpreter Certification, the interpreter declares to be duly qualified and approved by the ICTY Registry to interpret from source to target language and vice versa, to have been informed by the witness s/he speaks one of those languages, to have orally translated all the

[305] UN, OIOS Internal Audit Division, Audit of Language Services at ICTY (2009).

statements appearing in the statement in the presence of the witness who appeared to have heard and understood his translation acknowledging that the facts and matters set out in statement provided, as translated by the interpreter, are true to the best of his knowledge and recollection and has accordingly signed the statement.

The problem in this Interpreter Certification lies in the wording "as translated by me." This interpreter *interpreted* the conversation, the investigator wrote it down as he heard it *in interpretation*, but the witness confirmed it by signature only after it was back-translated from English as written down by the investigator by the same interpreter who interpreted at the meeting, and, finally, by a different translator who translated it back into B/C/S in The Hague, after which the witness signed it as his own.

Procedurally, participation of at least two different language professionals and certification signed by only one of them is what the OIOS Auditors were talking about: whereas the original interpreter certified the interpretation of a witness statement as his own, the translator who translated it did not make a declaration under ICTY RPE Rule 76 to say it was his own translation nor a reviser who revised it to attest that it was double-checked before submitted for signature by the witness and offered as evidence. Skeptics interpreted this to mean that there were inherent untruths contained in witness statements. Academics questioned the reliability of double-translated statements. The judges thought the whole thing was so bullet-proof that they included interpreters "duly qualified and approved" by the ICTY Registry to interpret in the criteria of witness statement reliability (see Chapter 2.2.).

The Interpreter Certification gives too much leeway to the CLSS interpreter assigning authority. Draženović-Carrieri, who was quoted earlier, stated, *inter alia*, that interpreters were handpicked to work with victims and witnesses based on their ethnicity.[306]

I examined interpreting for victims and witnesses during the witness statement taking process under Draženović-Carrieri's management. I searched the ICTY court records for witness

306 Draženović-Carrieri, Maja (2002), B/C/S-A practical approach. Lexicography and language policy in south-slavic languages after 1989. Verlag Otto Sagner: Munich.

statements between 1 January 1994 and 31 December 1999; the results yielded 54 different witness statements. The research showed that Draženović-Carrieri might have got carried away with such absolute statements: examination of her statement that interpreters were handpicked as to their ethnicity cannot be proven or disproven because the witness statement form does not contain a field where the interpreter could explicitly enter his or her ethnicity; only witnesses declared their ethnicity. Therefore, these interpreters were assigned to interpret for witnesses on the discretion of the assigning authority.

As far as interpreters assisting during the witness statement taking process are concerned, Interpreter Certification obliges them to state the languages from/into which they are qualified to interpret by the ICTY and the language the witness informed them s/he can speak and understand. Most interpreters put the language a witness can speak and understand as a language for which they were qualified to interpret from/into by the ICTY. As a result, several interpreters declared that they were qualified for both Bosnian and Serbo-Croatian (ERN 00300299 and ERN 00300314) and for both Bosnian and Croatian (ERN 00336795 and ERN 00391643). There are also several witness statements on which witnesses entered their language as Bosnian, but interpreters certified that they interpreted their statement into and from Croatian (ERN 00311490, ERN 00325377, ERN 00325427, ERN 00337976, ERN 00337927, ERN 00337894). This is in direct violation of Draženović-Carrieri's promises and the witnesses' right to the use of their own language under ICTY RPE Rule 3(C).

This examination only establishes that interpreters were assigned to interpret for witnesses at the discretion of the assigning authority, i.e. CLSS management. It does not establish that the interpreting was victim and witness-centric as claimed. It does establish that interpreters did not enter their own language on the witness statement form at all: interpreters would routinely agree that they interpreted from/into whatever language the witness entered he spoke and understood therefore only creating the perception and appearance of language services being victim and witness-centric. It does establish a rather sloppy, if non-existent, job of CLSS authorities on assigning interpreters as to their ethnicity.

Finally, this Interpreter Certification might be a legal fiction. This is because there were three different categories of language professionals who were potentially working on witness statements: CLSS language professionals representing the official ICTY language services working under the auspices of the Registry, Language Assistants representing the parties' semi-official language service working under the auspices of the OTP or the defense, and field interpreters who have been declaratively qualified and approved by the Registrar to conduct these duties. In other words, not all categories of interpreters who took witness statements have actually been "duly qualified and approved" by the ICTY Registry to interpret. The Registry merely declared to have duly qualified and approved them, but they could not have duly qualified and approved OTP Language Assistants, for example, because OTP Language Assistants did not fall organizationally under the Registry.

There were no security-related checks on Language Assistants, either. Language Assistants are not impartial or independent, by definition, because they are an integral part of the OTP or the defense and have to mediate as part of their job description. This affects their neutrality because their loyalty is to the OTP or the defense, not to the client. This approach to language professionals puts them in between their clients, which is the last place where they should be as language professionals. Finally, Language Assistants were not subject to any codes of ethics or codes of conduct, and were left legally unregulated in performance of their tasks. This is a serious failure in the laws because Language Assistants are the first link to documents in B/C/S.

Language professionals are privy to much confidential information and should be bound by specific standards of conduct with the emphasis on safeguarding such confidentiality. Sometimes they are explicitly told that documents on which they are working are confidential, but they are rarely informed for which side: the UN or the submitter. Most ICTY language professionals come from the former Yugoslavia and they work on documents and information considered sensitive, classified, or secret in their countries of origin. The ICTY was established to adjudicate on ethnic crimes and the selection of interpreters in terms of their ethnicity, citizenship, or nationality should be *de rigueur* at international criminal tribunals adjudicating on ethnic crimes.

The research conducted so far has established that the ICTY laws did not safeguard against language professionals of the attacking ethnicity freely engaging with victims and witnesses of the attacked ethnicity at all levels of the investigative and judicial process. It now establishes that the ICTY laws allowed for language professionals of the attacking ethnicity a free access to documents and information considered sensitive, classified, or secret in their countries of origin.

The UN bases its overall approach to classifying information entrusted to or originating from the UN on the understanding that the work of the UN should be open and transparent, except insofar as the nature of information concerned is deemed confidential. The Secretary-General's bulletin on Information Sensitivity, Classification and Handling classifies sensitive documents. It also authorizes the originator or the UN recipient to decide whether the information is sensitive, to clearly mark documents, and authorize the heads of departments or offices to make sure certain standards are fulfilled when handling sensitive information without prejudice to the authority of heads of departments or offices to put in place stricter controls over the handling of classified information so long as such controls are consistent with the present bulletin.[307]

In other words, there was no institutional impediment to international criminal tribunals making their own internal rules and regulations governing marking and handling of classified and sensitive information in that the heads of departments and offices could decide that their staff should sign certain confidentiality undertakings. This has been confirmed by the ICTY Human Resources Unit who said they "require staff to sign the oath of office and that confidentiality documents would have been internally done and kept by the unit. This information would not be in your file but kept by the unit" (email on file).[308]

ICTY OTP, ICTY UNDU, and VWU management contacted for purposes of this study could not confirm that their language staff also signed a separate confidentiality undertaking about their communications with detainees, victims, and witnesses after signing an Oath of Office at the signing of contract, just like all other ICTY staff.

---

[307] UN, Information sensitivity, classification and handling (ST/SGB/2007/6) (2007).

[308] UN, Staff Rules and Staff Regulations (ST/SGB/2014/1) (2015).

It is on the basis of my research that I strongly recommend the relationship between legal and language professionals and that between language professionals engaged in legal transactions or legal professionals and their non-legal clients from the investigations phase via proofing to testifying must be firmly regulated and it must be binding on both parties in the form of actual written standards of translation, interpreting, and transcription at international criminal tribunals.

It is on the basis of my research that I strongly recommend the UN, in general, and international criminal tribunals in particular, must start recruiting professionally educated translators and interpreters. It must be made clear that staff recruited to language positions at international criminal tribunals should never perform any other jobs: the use of Language Assistants must disappear from international criminal tribunals.

CHAPTER 4

MAY WE CONSULT THE COURT RECORD, PLEASE

ICTY ARs provide a rather incongruous picture of ICTY language services during the second management period between approximately 2000 and 2007. Whereas the OTP complains of having the largest collection of evidentiary documents of about 1.5 million pages and a backlog of about 185,000 pages and the ICTY Bureau (the ICTY President, the Vice-President, and the Presiding Judges of the Trial Chambers) is busy discussing various translation emergencies with impact on expeditious trials and ICTY budget, the CLSS management is busy travelling the world, looking for French translators willing to work in The Hague, and conducting competitive examinations to update their list of freelancers. They found 641.

Then, in about 2008, during the third management period, a CLSS translation support staff member told me it was bewildering the "CLSS would bring [in an external translator], give [that external translator] €20,000 a month, [that the external translator] barely translates 5 pages by the end of the month and then the CLSS brings [that same external translator] again in a couple of months."

In January 2020, I gave a series of lectures on selected portions of this study and ICTY to first- and second-year students of law and humanities in B&H. They described the ICTY as a place where Šešelj huffed and puffed and cussed and cursed while they laughed.

In Chapter 4, I am examining whether linguistic justice has been served along the fourth line of communication with the judicial institution: the working institution towards the situation country. I am showing in practice first overall outputs in translation and interpretation, and overall ethnicity- and nationality-based language service delivery. Then I am analyzing the permanent court record: translation of evidence, exhibits, and court documents; court

Table 4. CLSS translation outputs as reported in ICTY ARs

Year	2004	2005	2008	2009	2010	2011	2012	2013	2015	2016	2017
No. of pages	75,000	75,000	75,000	70,000	60,000	66,000	67,500	59,000	45,000	18,200	10,200

interpreting; and court transcripts. I am doing this to establish whether the ICTY Registry CLSS delivered language services.

4.1. Linguistic justice: overall production in translation and interpretation

The ICTY CLSS output in translation and interpretation has been documented as subpar in many internal ICTY sources.

As to their workload, it seems the CLSS had to translate only court documents. In that, according to the ICTY ARs, priority was given to translation into English and French to ensure bilingual parity of documents in accordance with the UN policies on multilingualism. Evidence and exhibits parties planned to use in court were translated both by the CLSS and OTP Language Assistants where, according to the OIOS Audit report quoted earlier, the CLSS worked mostly for the defense. Operational documents of the parties were translated by OTP/Defense Language Assistants.

Translational output can be planned and is measurable. Practice direction on the length of briefs and motions (2001, 2002, 2005) provides guidelines for predictability of incoming court documents for translation.[309] CLSS management should have been governed by it in all subsequent staff allocation.

The UN translation exams have around 500 words which must be translated in 2 hours.[310] This means that UN conveys their expectations regarding outputs from the very beginning and discourages slow producers.

The UN daily output standards for translators are set at 1,650 words per day (5.5 pages at 300 words per page) subject to revision, 1,815 words per day (6 pages) for self-revised translations, and 3,960 words (13 pages) per day for revisers, as discussed before. The CLSS management reported the following outputs in translation to drafters of ICTY ARs.[311]

---

309 ICTY, Documents, Practice directions: Practice direction on the length of briefs and motions (2001, 2002, 2005).
310 UN, LCEs: sample examinations: https://bit.ly/2VxDT6H.
311 UN, Report of the ICTY (A/59/215) (2004), para. 368; UN, Report of the

This production seems subpar, bearing in mind the number of internal and external staff at the disposal of the CLSS.

Elias-Bursać, former CLSS reviser, says little about the official UN translation outputs in her study and claims that the output for the average English Translation Unit translator working on evidence was five to seven pages of finished translation per day, or roughly a thousand pages per year, whereas a reviser might revise between 4,000 and 5,000 pages per year. However, these numbers are presented in a non-uniformed way, are too approximate, and must be calculated properly.

A UN month has 21 days, a year has 12 months, the UN allows 30 days of annual leave, 10 days of uncertified sick leave annually, and 10 days of official holidays annually; the latter must be taken. These criteria allow for the following combinations and calculations of annual output in translation:

N*(DAILY OUTPUT*((12*21)-50))

where N staff took all 30 days of annual leave, obligatory 10 days of official holidays, and all 10 days of uncertified sick leave to calculate an absolute annual minimum output in translation.

N*(DAILY OUTPUT*((12*21)-40))

where N staff took all 30 days of annual leave and obligatory 10 days of official holidays or all 10 days of uncertified sick leave to calculate a lower median output in translation.

N*(DAILY OUTPUT*((12*21)-20))

where N staff took obligatory 10 days of official holidays and all 10 days of uncertified sick leave to calculate an upper median output in translation.

ICTY (A/60/267) (2005), para. 238; UN, Report of the ICTY (A/63/210) (2008), para. 100; UN, Report of the ICTY (A/64/205) (2009), para. 84; UN, Report of the ICTY (A/65/205) (2010), para. 90; UN, Report of the ICTY (A/66/210) (2011), para. 85; UN, Report of the ICTY (A/67/214) (2012), para. 97; UN, Report of the ICTY (A/68/255) (2013), para. 71; UN, Report of the ICTY (A/70/226) (2015), para. 72; UN, Report of the ICTY (A/71/263) (2016), para. 69; UN, Report of the ICTY (A/72/266) (2017), para. 67.

N*(DAILY OUTPUT*((12*21)-10))

where N staff took obligatory 10 days of official holidays allowed to calculate an absolute maximum output in translation.

Using the above formula and UN daily outputs for translators, self-revised translators, and revisers, I calculated the following annual outputs for the three categories of language staff.

Table 5. Minimum, upper median, lower median, and maximum output in translation for UN System language professionals

N=service providers	ABS MIN	LOWER MED	UPPER MED	ABS MAX
Translators	1,111	1,166	1,276	1,331
Self-revised translators	1,212	1,272	1,392	1,452
Revisers	2,626	2,756	3,016	3,146

According to this formula, one translator should be able to produce between 1,111 and 1,331 pages annually, self-revised translator between 1,212 and 1,452 annually, and reviser between 2,626 and 3,146 pages annually.

Elias-Bursać claims the CLSS had a total of 60-80 (1997-2004) and 150-170 (2005-2013) in-house staff.[312] They will be taken into consideration for the following calculations. So will 614 external staff mentioned in the ICTY ARs. This is because there must have been a reason why the time out of the office, travel expenses, hotel expenses, and DSA reimbursements were approved by the ICTY Procurement on the orders of the ICTY Registrar in charge of Human Resources and CLSS for the CLSS management to travel around the world searching for and, finally, finding the 614th external staff member.

Table 6 presents a calculation of the annual minimum, upper median, lower median, and maximum output in translation of N number of translators as reported by Elias-Bursać.

312 Elias-Bursać, Ellen (2015), Translating evidence and interpreting testimony at a war crimes tribunal. Palgrave Macmillan: London.

Table 6. Minimum, upper median, lower median, and maximum output in translation for CLSS

N	ABS MIN	LOWER MED	UPPER MED	ABS MAX
60	66,660	69,960	76,560	79,860
80	88,880	93,280	102,080	106,480
150	166,650	174,900	191,400	199,650
170	188,870	198,220	216,920	226,170
614	851,004			

The 2009 UN OIOS Internal Audit Division, mentioned before, established that the CLSS had 65 translators on its rolls (excluding revisers) whose yearly output was expected at some 78,650 pages. However, the output for in-house CLSS translators has ranged from 58,115 to 64,565, indicating a shortfall of between 18-26%.

Table 7 presents expected and found annual output by the OIOS cross-referenced with my calculation of the annual minimum, upper median, lower median, and maximum output in translation.

Table 7. Minimum, upper median, lower median, and maximum output in translation for CLSS vs. expected and found output in translation by the UN OIOS

N=65	Expected by OIOS	Found by OIOS (incl. external staff)	ABS MIN	LOWER MED	UPPER MED	ABS MAX
2004	78,650	71,950 (7,385)	72,215	75,790	82,940	86,515
2005		76,193 (17,376)				
2006		71,730 (13,615)				
2007		74,254 (14,175)				

The findings of the OIOS Auditors show that N=65 did not meet the OIOS's expectations of minimum output in translation at all. Using my formula and comparing it with the findings of the OIOS Auditors shows that N=65 did not reach even the bare minimum of my calculations in 2004 and 2006, they got close to the lower median in 2007, and barely went above the lower median in 2005.

Obviously, the authors of the 2004 ICTY AR who reported the annual CLSS translation output at 75,000 must have misread the memo the CLSS sent them as their contribution to the ICTY ARs. And then they must have misread the numbers the CLSS sent them as their contribution to the 2005 ICTY AR again. Clearly, due to this miscommunication, one cannot be sure about the outputs reported to the ICTY AR drafters for other years as copied from ICTY ARs into Table 4, either.

The 2009 OIOS Report Auditors proposed measures for improvement. The CLSS responded, proposing reduced norms, but the OIOS Auditors concluded that even with the reduced norms suggested by the CLSS for the English and French translation units, the average productivity would still be below UN norms.

OIOS Auditors tracked the production of 16 translators in the English Translation Unit and established that only two translators achieved the required productivity norm during three years of tracking. The OIOS Auditors concluded that the output levels for translators in the English Translation Unit were sub-optimal and that they needed to become more efficient.

OIOS Auditors tracked the production of 10 translators in the French Translation Unit and established that productivity levels were below UN standards because only four translators achieved an annual output of more than 1,000 pages; the French revisers also did not meet their targets. The OIOS Auditors concluded that the output levels for translators in the French Translation Unit were sub-optimal and that they needed to improve their efficiency.

The output for the B/C/S Translation Unit in three years of tracking for 11 selected translators and revisers showed that the average output per staff member was far higher: two translators had exceptionally high outputs of 13.3 and 8.6 pages per day and the B/C/S revisers met their targets. The CLSS responded that this is because those people were assigned easy documents to translate.

All in all, the OIOS 2009 Report established that between January 2004 and June 2008, the ICTY spent $70.8 million on salaries and allowances for CLSS staff and $19 million on outsourced services including external interpreting, translation, and court reporting.[313]

---

[313] UN, OIOS Internal Audit Division, Audit of Language Services at ICTY

As to the output in interpretation, the number of interpreter days is calculated on the basis of one interpreter being equal to one day. For example, if there are trials five days a week for which seven interpreters are hired to man three interpreting booths for one hearing lasting from 09:00 to 14:00, that one week of engagement of seven staff equals 35 interpreter days (7x5). If the court met in both sessions throughout a week (09:00 to 14:00 and 14:00 to 19:00) and if seven interpreters were assigned to each session, the CLSS would have registered 70 interpreters' days. At that rate, 8,500 conference interpreter days would mean interpreters worked 121.42 days in a given year.

The CLSS management reported the following outputs in interpreting to drafters of the ICTY ARs.[314]

Table 8. CLSS output in interpretation as reported in the ICTY ARs

Year	2008	2009	2010	2011	2012	2013	2015	2016	2017
No. of days	8,500	7,000	6,000	4,400	3,600	3,600	1,350	710	173

It is worth remembering that the UN working year has 251 working days, which means that the CLSS interpreters did not work for even half a year.

This finding was also substantiated in the 2009 UN OIOS audit of language services at the ICTY. The OIOS Audit Report repeated the standard UN workload norms for interpreting were seven sessions of three hours or 21 hours per week, with a two-hour break between sessions, and preparing for assignments the remaining hours. The 2009 OIOS Report established that CLSS interpreters provided interpreting for four court sessions per week

(2009).

314 UN, Report of the ICTY (A/59/215) (2004), para. 368; UN, Report of the ICTY (A/60/267) (2005), para. 238; UN, Report of the ICTY (A/63/210) (2008), para. 100; UN, Report of the ICTY (A/64/205) (2009), para. 84; UN, Report of the ICTY (A/65/205) (2010), para. 90; UN, Report of the ICTY (A/66/210) (2011), para. 85; UN, Report of the ICTY (A/67/214) (2012), para. 97; UN, Report of the ICTY (A/68/255) (2013), para. 71; UN, Report of the ICTY (A/70/226) (2015), para. 72; UN, Report of the ICTY (A/71/263) (2016), para. 69; UN, Report of the ICTY (A/72/266) (2017), para. 67.

and were undertaking interpreting work on average between 16 to 19 hours, which nearly matches the norms, based on the sample taken for testing.

However, OIOS Auditors also reviewed entry and exit times for CLSS interpreters for the month of September 2008 and determined that interpreters usually left the office once they completed their shift and did not come back for the rest of the day. Most interpreters attended the office for an average of 20 to 22 hours per week, compared to the standard 37½-hour work week in the ICTY. Moreover, they worked four days a week: they did not come to the office on the fifth day and did not apply for leave for this day.

For the month of September 2008, the OIOS Auditors calculated that interpreters were absent from the office for around 143 days a year, even though they were paid a salary of approximately $60,000 for these days. The auditors concluded that, on an annual basis, the same trend of absence would imply an expenditure of around $720,000 on interpreters' salaries for days when they were not in the office.[315]

Several ICTY ARs claim that the CLSS language professionals assisted in field interpreting of interviews by investigation teams and witness-proofing sessions by legal professionals prior to testimony and interviews with suspects.

The ICTY had liaison and field offices in Zagreb, Sarajevo, Banja Luka, Priština, and Belgrade. All these offices were manned by Language Assistants and only one of them, the Sarajevo office, had a CLSS language professional as well. It is unclear why the CLSS language professionals would go to interview clients in the first place because, as is clear from the ARs examined, they were barely coping with the work they already had on their plate. The clients could have been interviewed either by the existing staff in the field offices (Belgrade, Zagreb, Sarajevo, and Banja Luka) or by field interpreters. This makes even more sense because both staff categories are paid at the local level and their engagement would have saved the organization significant costs, in addition to

[315] UN, OIOS Internal Audit Division, Audit of Language Services at ICTY (2009).

all these other savings identified by the OIOS Auditors.[316]

However, many CLSS language professionals, translators and interpreters alike, did go out on missions. Given their existing workload, this use of CLSS language professionals was unreasonable and, given the costs of CLSS language professionals, it represented additional expenditure. Finally, given their isolation from the rest of the organization, and, quite frankly, their ethnicity, nationality, and language variant, it is unclear how effective CLSS language professionals would be both *vis-à-vis* a *pas de trois* with suspects, victims, witnesses, insiders, investigation, and the prosecution facts-wise, since some of them already voiced dissatisfaction about being away from the prosecutorial and investigatory action. On the other hand, it is only natural that CLSS language professionals would be motivated to go on missions because this provided them with an opportunity to make money on top of their regular earnings.

As a rule, CLSS language professionals *would not* assist during the witness proofing, which is normally done prior to the victim's or witness's testimony in The Hague. Witness proofing included working weekends and staying after 17:30, so CLSS language professionals probably had no financial or other interest in assisting with witness proofing. For comparison: witnesses were interviewed by an OTP investigator, lawyer and/or analyst who were also P-level staff and who were also not paid overtime if they stayed after 17:30 or if they came in during the weekends. So, it seems plausible to ask why CLSS language professionals couldn't have done the same?

If any CLSS staff participated in witness proofing, those would be the CLSS's Language Assistants who were normally charged with administrative duties and, when needed, as consecutive interpreters in a legal context. It is easy to understand why they would be motivated to come in on the weekends because they were paid at GS-level and entitled to overtime. It would *not at all* be an exaggeration to say that 95% of all witness proofing was conducted by OTP Language Assistants and that CLSS support staff were used only when the existing OTP Language Assistant staff were used to full capacity.

316 UN, Travel Allowance: https://bit.ly/2wCOQvo.

4.2. Linguistic justice: overall ethnicity- and nationality-based provision of language services

We learned in Chapter 1 that the ICTY management, the CLSS management, and the judges were aware the language spoken in the former Yugoslavia was vested with ethnic and national affiliations and used as a tool in the conflict. The language experts confirmed it. The problem is that the ICTY Registry did not hire appropriate language service managers to act on any of it in practice: they "invented" the B/C/S and hoped for the best.

I am moving to the analysis of the linguistic justice served to defendants during initial appearances before the court, to the region during reading of verdicts, and to the B/C/S speaking victims and witnesses who came to testify at the ICTY.

Appendix 3 contains full data on the ethnicity of defendants and language of interpreters during the initial appearance of defendants. This data has been extracted from the available videos on the ICTY YouTube channel, which are limited to the initial appearances of the accused. The ethnicity of the accused is recorded as appearing on the Case Information Sheet, and the language of the interpreters was recorded as heard.

The first examination will establish whether linguistic justice was served to defendants during their initial appearances by the ICTY Registry CLSS in combination English and B/C/S.

This examination shows that there were 81 recorded initial appearances of individuals and groups to enter a plea between 1996 and 2001, namely: 43 Bosnian Serbs, 18 Serbian Serbs, 9 Bosnian Croats, 5 Croatian Serbs, 4 Bosnian Muslims, and 2 Croatian Croats. Interpretation was provided by 81 teams of interpreters: 36 one-interpreter teams and 45 two-interpreter teams.

In 43 individual and group initial appearances of Bosnian Serbs, they were provided with interpreting by:

- 1 one-interpreter team speaking Bosnian
- 7 one-interpreter teams speaking Croatian
- 11 one-interpreter teams speaking Serbian
- 9 two-interpreter teams speaking Croatian and Serbian
- 7 two-interpreter teams speaking Croatian

- 6 two-interpreter teams speaking Bosnian and Serbian
- 1 two-interpreter team speaking Serbian
- 1 two-interpreter team speaking Bosnian and Croatian.

In 18 individual and group initial appearances of Serbian Serbs, they were provided with interpreting by:

- 5 one-interpreter teams speaking Serbian
- 5 one-interpreter teams speaking Croatian
- 6 two-interpreter teams speaking Croatian and Serbian
- 1 two-interpreter team speaking Bosnian and Croatian
- 1 two-interpreter team speaking Serbian.

In 9 individual and group initial appearances of Bosnian Croats, they were provided with interpreting by:

- 1 one-interpreter team speaking Croatian
- 1 one-interpreter team speaking Bosnian
- 5 two-interpreter teams speaking Croatian and Serbian
- 1 two-interpreter team speaking Bosnian and Serbian
- 1 two-interpreter team speaking Croatian.

In 5 individual and group initial appearances of Croatian Serbs, they were provided with interpreting by:

- 3 one-interpreter teams speaking Croatian
- 2 one-interpreter teams speaking Serbian.

In 4 individual and group initial appearances of Bosnian Muslims, they were provided with interpreting by:

- 2 one-interpreter teams speaking Bosnian
- 1 one-interpreter team speaking Croatian
- 1 two-interpreter team speaking Bosnian and Serbian.

In 2 individual and group initial appearances of Croatian Croats, they were provided with interpreting by:

- 1 two-interpreter team speaking Bosnian and Croatian
- 1 two-interpreter team speaking Croatian and Serbian.

Was linguistic justice served in 81 recorded initial appearances of individuals and groups who entered a plea between 1996 and 2001, namely: 43 Bosnian Serbs, 18 Serbian Serbs, 9 Bosnian Croats, 5 Croatian Serbs, 4 Bosnian Muslims, and 2 Croatian Croats?

Those defendants who originated from B&H were served linguistic justice only in those instances where they were provided with interpreting to/from Bosnian. However, out of 56 one- or two-interpreter teams, interpretation into Bosnian language figures in 4/56 instances alone and 9/56 instances together with Croatian or Serbian languages; interpretation into Bosnian language is completely missing in 43/56 instances.

Those defendants who originated from Serbia were served linguistic justice only in those instances where they were provided with interpreting to/from Serbian. However, out of 18 one- or two-interpreter teams, interpretation into Serbian language figures in 6/18 instances alone and 6/18 instances together with Bosnian or Croatian languages; interpretation into Serbian language is completely missing in 6/18 instances.

Those defendants who originated from Croatia were served linguistic justice only in those instances where they were provided with interpreting to/from Croatian. Out of 2 one- or two-interpreter teams, interpretation into Croatian language figures in 2/2 instances together with Bosnian or Serbian languages, but never alone.

Was linguistic justice served in 81 recorded initial appearances of individuals and groups who entered a plea between 1996 and 2001, namely: 56 initial appearances of *ijekavian* speaking defendants from B&H; 18 initial appearances of *ekavian* speaking defendants from Serbia; and 7 initial appearances of *ijekavian* speaking defendants from Croatia?

In 56 individual and group initial appearances of *ijekavian* speaking defendants from B&H, they were provided with interpreting by:

- 23 one- or two-interpreter teams providing interpreting into *ijekavian* only
- 21 one- or two-interpreter teams providing interpreting into *ijekavian* and *ekavian*
- 12 one- or two-interpreter teams providing interpreting into *ekavian* only.

In 18 individual and group initial appearances of *ekavian* speaking defendants from Serbia, they were provided with interpreting by:

- 6 one- or two-interpreter teams providing interpreting into *ijekavian* only
- 6 one- or two-interpreter teams providing interpreting into *ijekavian* and *ekavian*
- 6 one- or two-interpreter teams providing interpreting into *ekavian* only.

In 7 individual and group initial appearances of *ijekavian* speaking defendants from Croatia, they were provided with interpreting by:

- 4 one- or two-interpreter teams providing interpreting into *ijekavian* only
- 3 one- or two-interpreter teams providing interpreting into *ekavian* only.

Dialectally, out of 56 one- or two-interpreter teams working on the initial appearances of defendants from B&H, *ijekavian* figures in 23/56 instances alone, in 21/56 instances *ekavian* and *ijekavian* were used together, and in 12/56 instances *ekavian* was used alone. In all those 33/56 instances where *ekavian* appears alone or together with Croatian *ijekavian*, the ICTY Registry CLSS has made a strong national, ethnic, and political identity statement against B&H and the peoples of B&H.

In 56 individual and group initial appearances of *ijekavian* speaking defendants from B&H, Bosnian *ijekavian* features in the initial appearances of 8/43 Bosnian Serbs, 2/9 Bosnian Croats, 3/4 Bosnian Muslims. In all of those 43/56 instances Bosnian *ijekavian* does not appear, the ICTY Registry CLSS has made a strong national, ethnic, and political identity statement against B&H and the peoples of B&H. In all these instances, 56/56, interpretation into Bosnian language was performed by one and the same woman.

In all of those 6/18 instances where Serbian *ekavian* does not appear, the ICTY Registry CLSS has made a strong national, ethnic, and political identity statement against Serbia and the peoples of Serbia.

In all of those 3/7 instances where Croatian *ijekavian* does not appear, the ICTY Registry CLSS has made a strong national, ethnic, and political identity statement against Croatia and the peoples of Croatia.

The second examination will establish whether linguistic justice was served by the ICTY Registry CLSS in communication with the region during the reading of the verdicts in combination English and B/C/S.

Appendix 4 contains full data on the language of interpreters and the location of crimes and ethnicity of victims during the reading of trial, appeals, sentencing, and revised judgments. This data has been extracted from the available videos on the ICTY YouTube channel, which are limited to the reading of the 49 trial judgments (TJ), 41 appeals judgments (AJ), 6 sentencing judgments (SJ), 1 sentencing appeal (SA), and 1 revised judgment (RJ) delivered to a total of 98 groups and individuals between 1997 and 2016. The ethnicity of the accused, the location of crimes and the ethnicity of victims is recorded as appearing on the Case Information Sheet, and the language of the interpreters was recorded as heard. The audiences in B&H, Croatia, and Kosovo were provided interpretation by 98 teams of interpreters: 5 one-interpreter teams and 93 two-interpreter teams.

As a location of crimes, B&H figures in 74 instances. The B&H audiences were provided interpretation by:

- 1 one-interpreter team speaking Bosnian
- 4 one-interpreter teams speaking Croatian
- 6 two-interpreter teams speaking Croatian
- 9 two-interpreter teams speaking Bosnian and Serbian
- 12 two-interpreter teams speaking Bosnian and Croatian
- 42 two-interpreter teams speaking Croatian and Serbian.

As a location of crimes, Croatia figures in 12 instances. The Croatian audiences were provided interpretation by:

- 10 two-interpreter teams speaking Croatian and Serbian
- 1 two-interpreter team speaking Bosnian and Croatian
- 1 two-interpreter team speaking Bosnian and Serbian.

As a location of crimes, all regions figure in 8 instances. These audiences were provided interpretation by:

- 1 three-interpreter team speaking Bosnian, Croatian, and Serbian
- 1 two-interpreter team speaking Bosnian and Croatian
- 3 two-interpreter teams speaking Bosnian and Serbian
- 3 two-interpreter teams speaking Croatian and Serbian.

As a location of crimes, Kosovo figures in 4 instances. The Kosovar audiences were provided interpretation by:

- 1 two-interpreter team speaking Croatian
- 1 two-interpreter team speaking Bosnian and Serbian
- 2 two-interpreter teams speaking Croatian and Serbian.

Was linguistic justice served to the audiences in B&H, Croatia, and Kosovo by the 98 teams of interpreters?

B&H audiences were served linguistic justice only in those instances where they were provided with interpreting to/from Bosnian. However, out of 74 one- or two-interpreter teams, interpretation into Bosnian language figures in 1/74 instances alone and 21/74 instances together with Croatian or Serbian languages; interpretation into Bosnian language is completely missing in 52/74 instances.

Audiences from Croatia were served linguistic justice only in those instances where they were provided with interpreting to/from Croatian. However, out of 12 two-interpreter teams, interpretation into Croatian language figures in 0/12 instances alone and 11/12 instances together with Bosnian or Serbian languages; interpretation into Croatian language is completely missing in 1/12 instances.

Audiences from all regions were served linguistic justice only in those instances where they were provided with interpreting to/from Bosnian and Croatian and Serbian. However, out of 8 two- or three-interpreter teams, interpretation into Bosnian and Croatian and Serbian together figures in 1/8 instances alone and is completely missing in 7/8 instances.

Kosovar audiences were served linguistic justice only in those instances where they were provided with interpreting to/from Serbian. However, out of 4 two-interpreter teams, interpretation into Serbian language figures in 0/4 instances alone and 3/74 instances together with Bosnian or Croatian languages; interpretation into Serbian language is completely missing in 1/4 instances.

Was linguistic justice served to 74 *ijekavian* audiences in B&H, 12 *ijekavian* audiences in Croatia, 8 *ijekavian and ekavian* audiences in all regions, and 4 *ekavian* audiences in Kosovo by 98 teams of interpreters in dialectal terms during the reading of the above verdicts?

In 74 individual and group appearances of *ijekavian* speaking audiences in B&H for the reading of the verdicts, they were provided with interpreting into following dialects:

- 23 one- or two-interpreter teams providing interpreting into *ijekavian* only
- 51 one- or two-interpreter teams providing interpreting into *ijekavian* and *ekavian*.

In 12 individual and group appearances of *ijekavian* speaking audiences in Croatia for the reading of the verdicts, they were provided with interpreting into following dialects:

- 1 one- or two-interpreter teams providing interpreting into *ijekavian* only
- 11 one- or two-interpreter teams providing interpreting into *ijekavian* and *ekavian*.

In 8 individual and group appearances of *ijekavian* and *ekavian* audiences in all regions for the reading of the verdicts, they were provided with interpreting into following dialects:

- 1 one- or two-interpreter teams providing interpreting into *ijekavian* only
- 7 one- or two-interpreter teams providing interpreting into *ijekavian* and *ekavian*.

In 4 individual and group appearances of *ekavian* speaking audiences in Kosovo for the reading of the verdicts, they were provided with interpreting into following dialects:

- 1 two-interpreter team providing interpreting into *ijekavian* only

- 3 one- or two-interpreter teams providing interpreting into *ijekavian* and *ekavian*.

Dialectally, out of 74 one- or two-interpreter teams reading the verdicts to the audiences in *ijekavian* speaking B&H, *ijekavian* figures in 22/74 instances alone and in 52/74 instances *ekavian* and *ijekavian* were used together. In all those 52/74 instances where *ekavian* appears together with Croatian *ijekavian,* the ICTY Registry CLSS has made a strong national, ethnic, and political identity statement against B&H and the peoples of B&H.

Dialectally, out of 12 two-interpreter teams reading the verdicts to the audiences in *ijekavian* speaking Croatia, in all of those 11/12 instances where Serbian *ekavian* appears, the ICTY Registry CLSS has made a strong national, ethnic, and political identity statement against Croatia and the peoples of Croatia.

Dialectally, out of 4 two-interpreter teams reading the verdicts to the audiences in *ekavian* speaking Kosovo, in all of those 1/4 instances where Serbian *ekavian* does not appear, the ICTY Registry CLSS has made a strong national, ethnic, and political identity statement against Kosovo and the peoples of Kosovo.

The third examination will establish whether linguistic justice was served by the ICTY Registry CLSS to the B/C/S speaking victims and witnesses who came to testify.

Appendix 6 contains full data on the situation country, the ethnicity of testifying witnesses, language of interpreters, and language of the transcript in 590 cases of B/C/S speaking victims and witnesses came to testify as recorded in the ICTY Registry B/C/S transcripts. The situation country was taken from the Case Information Sheet of the case in which the individual testified, the ethnicity of testifying witnesses was recorded as self-declared in the transcripts, and language of interpreters of language of the transcript were recorded as appearing in the transcript.[317] Protected

317 In examining languages of interpreters in the transcripts, the major concern revolved around the fact that the analysis was made without relying on the audio recording where I could even recognize some of the interpreters' voices. So, the main problem I faced during this examination was: what if this person interpreting was actually a Bosnian language interpreter preferring a Croatian variant? This is because, owing to the

witnesses were not considered.

Pursuant to the UN policies on multilingualism, the ICTY did not make transcripts into B/C/S; B/C/S is neither an official UN language nor an ICTY official or working language. It was only in 2008 that the ICTY started an 18-month long project of transcribing court sessions into B/C/S off the available recordings. (More about that in the next sections.) Some OSCE reports claim more than 18,500 pages of transcripts were produced in response to specific requests from courts and prosecutors in the region.[318] But, if we take a closer look at the transcripts, this statement becomes somewhat incongruent.

In order to make clear this incongruence, I examined the language of the transcript. This is the language used to annotate court transcripts, such as: court session (*sudska sednica* in Serbian *ekavian* vs. *sudska sjednica* in Bosnian and Croatian *ijekavian*); day of session (*ponedeljak, sreda* in Serbian *ekavian* vs. *ponedjeljak, srijeda* in Bosnian and Croatian *ijekavian*); time of break (*vreme pauze* in Serbian *ekavian* vs. *vrijeme pauze* in Bosnian and Croatian *ijekavian*); witness (*svedok* in Serbian *ekavian* vs. *svjedok* in Bosnian and Croatian *ijekavian*), etc. It would have been incongruous to send Serbian *ekavian* to the

---

wars, the politics of the standard Bosnian language started preferring the Croatian variant, meaning instead of *opšti* people are encouraged to say *opći*, and so on. However, whereas a Croatian speaker must say *opći* and a Serbian speaker must say *opšti*, both *opći* and *opšti* are correct in the Bosnian language and a Bosnian speaker can choose which overlapping *ijekavian* vocabulary to use. Thankfully, the Bosnian language is a language separate from both Serbian and Croatian, so Croatian speaking interpreters were identified by specific vocabulary a Bosnian speaker would not use, such as: *tjedan* vs. *sedmica, tajnik* vs. *sekretar, točka* vs. *tačka, stanka* vs. *pauza, unatoč* vs. *uprkos, osobno* vs. *lično, prevoditelj* vs. *prevodilac, preformulirati* vs. *preformulisati*, etc. So, for instance, if I found the word "točka," I concluded the speaker speaks Croatian language. In determination of the Bosnian language, it was usually necessary to find more than one clue. So, if I found "tačka," I had to search for other words pointing to either *ekavian* or *ijekavian*. None of this was an issue with Serbian speaking interpreters because the main feature of Serbian language is *ekavian* pronunciation to which Serbian speaking interpreters stuck throughout. The same overarching criterion was used determining the language of the transcript.

[318] OSCE, War Crimes Justice Project (undated): https://bit.ly/2VfRuj2.

Republic of B&H or the Republic of Croatia judicial authorities who requested them.

As a situation country, B&H appears in 457 instances, Croatia in 87 instances, all countries in the region appear in 46 instances, and Kosovo appears in 5 instances in the ICTY Registry-made transcripts. Out of 457 instances where B&H appears as a situation country and where B&H judicial authorities requested transcripts, the language of the transcript is Serbian *ekavian* in 239 transcripts and Bosnian *ijekavian* in 218 transcripts.

Out of 87 instances where Croatia appears as a situation country and where Croatian judicial authorities requested transcripts, the language of the transcript is Serbian *ekavian* in 13 transcripts and Bosnian *ijekavian* in 74 transcripts.

Out of 46 instances where all countries in the region appear as a situation country and judicial authorities from all these countries probably requested transcripts, the language of the transcript is Serbian *ekavian* in 20 transcripts and Croatian *ijekavian* in 26 transcripts.

Out of 5 instances where Kosovo appears as a situation country and where Serbian judicial authorities requested transcripts, the language of the transcript is Serbian *ekavian* in all 5 transcripts.

Appendix 6 shows that the ICTY Registry B/C/S transcript team transcribed testimonies of witnesses who had been called to testify once and more than once, and that some testified during several days. I cannot comment on this choice by the former Yugoslavia authorities except to say that, as it concerns my data, it is provided for each and every day of testimony.

As to B&H, the ICTY Registry B/C/S transcript team transcribed testimonies of witnesses where interpretation to Bosnian Serbs was provided by:

- 149 two-interpreter teams speaking Croatian and Serbian
- 70 two-interpreter teams speaking Bosnian and Croatian
- 49 one-interpreter teams speaking Croatian
- 42 two-interpreter teams speaking Bosnian and Serbian
- 38 two-interpreter teams speaking Serbian
- 17 one-interpreter teams speaking Bosnian.

As to B&H, the ICTY Registry B/C/S transcript team transcribed testimonies of witnesses where interpretation to Bosnian Muslims was provided by:

- 30 two-interpreter teams speaking Croatian and Serbian
- 17 one-interpreter teams speaking Croatian
- 13 two-interpreter teams speaking Bosnian and Croatian
- 12 one-interpreter teams speaking Serbian
- 7 two-interpreter teams speaking Bosnian and Serbian
- 2 one-interpreter teams speaking Bosnian.

As to B&H, the ICTY Registry B/C/S transcript team transcribed testimonies of witnesses where interpretation to Bosnian Croats was provided by:

- 6 two-interpreter teams speaking Croatian and Serbian
- 2 one-interpreter teams speaking Croatian
- 2 one-interpreter teams speaking Serbian
- 1 two-interpreter team speaking Bosnian and Serbian.

As to Croatia, the ICTY Registry B/C/S transcript team transcribed testimonies of witnesses where interpretation to Croatian Croats was provided by:

- 7 two-interpreter teams speaking Croatian and Serbian
- 5 one-interpreter teams speaking Serbian
- 4 one-interpreter teams speaking Bosnian and Croatian
- 4 one-interpreter teams speaking Croatian
- 3 one-interpreter teams speaking Bosnian
- 3 two-interpreter teams speaking Bosnian and Serbian.

As to Croatia, the ICTY Registry B/C/S transcript team transcribed testimonies of witnesses where interpretation to Croatian Serbs was provided by:

- 18 two-interpreter teams speaking Croatian and Serbian
- 14 two-interpreter teams speaking Bosnian and Croatian
- 9 two-interpreter teams speaking Bosnian and Serbian
- 8 one-interpreter teams speaking Croatian
- 7 one-interpreter teams speaking Bosnian
- 4 two-interpreter teams speaking Serbian.

As to Croatia, the ICTY Registry B/C/S transcript team transcribed testimonies of witnesses where interpretation to one Croatian Muslim was provided by:

- 1 two-interpreter team speaking Croatian and Serbian.

As to cases and transcripts concerning all the countries in the region, the ICTY Registry B/C/S transcript team transcribed testimonies of witnesses where interpretation to Bosnian Muslims was provided by:

- 5 two-interpreter teams speaking Croatian and Serbian
- 4 two-interpreter teams speaking Bosnian and Croatian
- 1 one-interpreter team speaking Croatian
- 1 one-interpreter team speaking Serbian.

As to cases and transcripts concerning all the countries in the region, the ICTY Registry B/C/S transcript team transcribed testimonies of witnesses where interpretation to Bosnian Serbs was provided by:

- 4 two-interpreter teams speaking Bosnian and Croatian
- 2 two-interpreter teams speaking Croatian and Serbian
- 2 two-interpreter teams speaking Bosnian and Serbian
- 2 one-interpreter teams speaking Serbian
- 1 one-interpreter team speaking Bosnian
- 1 one-interpreter team speaking Croatian.

As to cases and transcripts concerning all the countries in the region, the ICTY Registry B/C/S transcript team transcribed testimonies of witnesses where interpretation to Serbian Serbs was provided by:

- 13 two-interpreter teams speaking Croatian and Serbian
- 5 two-interpreter teams speaking Bosnian and Croatian
- 3 one-interpreter teams speaking Croatian
- 2 two-interpreter teams speaking Bosnian and Serbian.

As to Kosovo, the ICTY Registry B/C/S transcript team transcribed testimonies of witnesses where interpretation to one Serbian Serb (who testified over 5 days) was provided by:

- 5 two-interpreter teams speaking Croatian and Serbian.

It can be said that linguistic justice to these witnesses from B&H, for example, was served only in cases where they have been interpreted into Bosnian in court (152/457). In all other 305 instances where witnesses from B&H were provided interpretation, the ICTY Registry CLSS has made a strong national, ethnic, and political identity statement to these witnesses *á la* Big Brother watching over their testimonies for the good or the bad. The same goes for witnesses from other countries.

This Big Brother is best exemplified in the case of Mr Dražen Erdemović, a Bosnian Croat who committed crimes in Srebrenica as a soldier of the Army of Bosnian Serbs: he decided to come forward about his crimes while in Serbia, got in touch with the ICTY authorities, got the entire system of international criminal justice on their feet and, quite honestly, cracked the Srebrenica case with the information he provided to the ICTY investigators. When he finally got to the ICTY courtroom to testify, put on his headphones to look at the welcoming judges, the language he heard through interpretation was Serbian, the language of the authority against which he was testifying.

The same goes for Bosnian Muslim witnesses who testified against their former torturers or rapists and whose language variant was the reason they were victims in the first place, or Bosnian Serb witnesses who testified about bad apples in their own ranks. They should all be lauded for continuing with their testimony once their heard the language of the Big Brother for better or for worse even though the morally vacuous ICTY Registry CLSS interpreter selection must have mortified them.

It is on the basis of my research that I strongly recommend the recruitment of language professionals at international criminal tribunals adjudicating on ethnic crimes must be entirely governed by citizenship and ethnicity concerns.

4.3. Linguistic justice: translation of evidence, exhibits, and court documents

Now, I will perform a twofold examination of the CLSS's output: submission of court documents in time as per ICTY-S and ICTY RPE on expeditious and fair trials and bilingual parity of court documents as per UN Policies on multilingualism. I will do this in the example of trial documents which make a small part of the overall court record and which are referred to in the Practice direction on the length of briefs and motions from 2001, 2002, and 2005.[319] These documents are mentioned and available on the internet pages of each and every trial conducted at the ICTY.

As to the "in time" portion of my examination, strict deadlines for legal translators are a legal requirement, not a recommendation of how much time should be taken on a document. ICTY-S Article 20 sets the fair and expeditious trials as the fundamental object and purpose of the ICTY. As far as translation is concerned, delivery of translation in time would imply the accused has been served with documents in adequate time for the preparation of his defense as set in ICTY-S, Article 21 (4)(b).

As to the bilingual parity of court documents, we have seen throughout the study the effects UN-wide multilingualism policies have had on recruitment. Now we are going to see the full extent of how misplaced those policies were in an international criminal tribunal targeting a situation country that has very little to do with a UN official language translated/interpreted into/from, here French.

The purpose of the next two examinations is to see whether the trial documents were served in time and in full in both the ICTY working languages, English and French.

The first examination is in the practical example of the English-speaking *Stanišić and Župljanin*. It is hard to say when investigation in this case started, but the Case Information Sheet is pretty explicit about the following: the initial indictment in *Stanišić* was issued on 25 February 2005, the operational indictment was filed on 10 September 2009, the initial indictment in *Župljanin* was issued on 14 March 1999, the operational indictment was filed on 10 September 2009. The trial of these two began on 14 September 2009. This means that the prosecution in this case had an advantage of several years over the defense. This is considered normal: once an international criminal investigation begins it is not the case that the prosecutor has a suspect right from the outset. However, such a prosecutor may already begin issuing requests for translation and, if good and prudent, can have all support

[319] ICTY, Documents, Practice directions: Practice direction on the length of briefs and motions (2001, 2002, 2005).

documents translated by the beginning of the trial either by his own Language Assistants or by the CLSS. On the other hand, the defense's job has only just begun.

Table 9 below shows the type and number of documents pending translation into B/C/S or French in *Stanišić and Župljanin* even after the completion of this English-speaking trial. It was drawn up by counting and comparing available versions of documents.

The next summary table consists of: 7 indictments, 2 Appeals Chamber judgments, 4 trial judgments, 112 Trial Chamber decisions, 47 Trial Chamber orders, 29 Appeals Chamber decisions, 25 Appeals Chamber orders, 1 President's decision, 16 President's orders, 12 Registry decisions, 5 pre-trial briefs, 7 final briefs, 5 appeal briefs, 7 videos, transcripts, 11 press releases, and 1 miscellaneous document to a total of 291 documents produced in English. Since videos, press releases, and transcripts have not been considered, the total of number of documents pending translation under examination came to 273 documents produced in English.[320]

Table 9. Documents pending translation after the completion of the English-speaking trial (Stanišić and Župljanin)

Type of document	English	French	B/C/S
Indictments	7	2	8
Appeals Chamber judgment	2	1	1
Trial judgment	4	4	4
Trial Chamber decisions	112	9	50
Trial Chamber orders	47	1	13
Appeals Chamber decisions	29	0	2
Appeals Chamber orders	25	0	2
President's decisions	1	0	0
President's orders	16	0	4
Registry decisions	12	2	4
Pre-trial briefs	5	0	0
Final briefs	7	0	0
Appeal briefs	5	0	0
Miscellaneous	1	0	0
Total	273	18	88
Missing	0	255	185
Percentage requiring translation	0	93.40%	67.66%

[320] ICTY, Cases, *Stanišić and Župljanin*.

Of 273 documents in English, 255 have not been translated into French and 185 have not been translated into B/C/S. Trial briefs have not been translated into French or B/C/S at all.

Given the percentage of missing documents in French, it cannot be said that the CLSS ensured bilingual parity of court documents in the English-speaking *Stanišić and Župljanin* as required by UN policies on multilingualism.

Given the percentage of missing documents in B/C/S, it is clear the CLSS infringed on the rights of the accused stemming from ICTY-S, Article 21 (4)(b).

The second examination is in the practical example of the French-speaking *Šešelj*.

Again, it is hard to say when investigation in this case started, but the Case Information Sheet is pretty explicit about the following: the initial indictment in *Šešelj* was issued on 14 February 2003, the operational indictment was filed on 7 December 2007, and the trial began on 7 November 2007. Given that Šešelj was a self-representing defendant and that he surrendered on 23 February 2003, about seven days after the indictment was issued, this means that both the prosecution and the defense had equal time to prepare for trial.

Table 10 below shows the type and number of documents pending translation into B/C/S or French in *Šešelj* even after the completion of this French-speaking trial.

Table 10 has also been made by counting and comparing available versions of documents. However, it has been noticed that although this was a French-speaking trial, documents submitted in English outnumbered those in the French language. The next summary table consists of: 7 indictments, 0 Appeals Chamber judgments, 5 trial judgments, 231 Trial Chamber decisions, 149 Trial Chamber orders, 16 Appeals Chamber decisions, 2 Appeals Chamber orders, 17 President's decision, 39 President's orders, 19 Registry decisions, 0 pre-trial briefs, 2 final briefs, 0 appeal briefs, 0 prosecution documents, 1 submissions and requests, 9 videos, transcripts, 24 press releases, and 1 miscellaneous document to a total of 522 documents produced in English. Since videos, press releases, and transcripts have not been considered, total of number of documents pending translation under examination came to 489 documents produced in English.[321]

Table 10. Documents pending translation after the completion of the French-speaking trial (Šešelj)

Type of document	English	French	B/C/S
Indictments	7	4	6
Appeals Chamber judgment	0	0	0
Trial judgment	5	5	5
Trial Chamber decisions	231	248	123
Trial Chamber orders	149	111	70
Appeals Chamber decisions	16	12	7
Appeals Chamber orders	2	0	2
President's decisions	17	29	6
President's orders	39	22	19
Registry decisions	19	18	1
Pre-trial briefs	0	0	0
Final briefs	2	1	0
Appeal briefs	0	0	0
Prosecution documents	0	0	24
Submissions and requests	1	0	4
Miscellaneous	1	0	0
Total	489	450	267
Missing	0	39	222
Percentage requiring translation	0	7.97%	45.39%

Of 489 documents in English, 39 are missing in French and 185 have not been translated into B/C/S.[322]

---

321 ICTY, Cases, *Šešelj*.
322 Note in Table 8 that the ICTY Registry, Outreach Program misnamed, misfiled, and broke down in several parts otherwise single files on the individual pages of cases concerned. This user-unfriendly approach made the making of the Appendix 1 extremely difficult and cannot be said to make researchers' work easy at all. This resulted in discrepancies in the actual number of documents (final briefs have been, indeed, translated into the language of the accused and into French, but the Outreach Office misfiled them under *Nalozi pretresnog vijeća* (Orders of the Trial Chambers) in the B/C/S site). The Outreach Office seems to have forgotten to file some, as well, hence the uneven number of even the most used documents that had to be translated.

Given the percentage of missing documents in French, it cannot be said that the CLSS ensured bilingual parity of court documents in the French-speaking *Šešelj* as required by UN policies on multilingualism.

Given the percentage of missing documents in B/C/S, it is clear the CLSS infringed on the rights of the accused stemming from ICTY-S, Article 21(4)(b).

Finally, these two examples also show the linguistic equality of arms between prosecution and defense was but in letter only, at least for the two trials presented here.

This examination may only be called complete once future researchers conduct similar comparisons for every single case heard before the ICTY.

For now, may these two examples showing the CLSS did not succeed in translating the full court record in these two cases into French or B/C/S thereby infringing on the rights of the accused to translation in time serve as the last practical examples of the sheer senselessness of the UN policies on multilingualism at international criminal tribunals.

4.4. Linguistic justice: court interpreting

This study argues throughout for ethnicity- and nationality-based recruitment of language professionals working at international criminal tribunals that are adjudicating on ethnic crimes. By extension, the study advances arguments that interpreters from B&H should interpret for clients from B&H, and so on. The linguistic and legal background to this argumentation is provided in the earlier chapters of this study.

Here, the study will turn to victims and witnesses commenting on interpretation, then to a practical example of a non-Bosnian interpreter interpreting a Bosnian language-speaking witness into English, before finishing with a practical example of how much goes missing in interpretation even when provided during a highly visible trial and what is done about it.

Overall, the receivers of in-court and interpretation services during proofing, victims and witnesses, were aware of linguistic variants and commented on it. In June 2016, the ICTY VWU published a report entitled "Echoes of Testimonies: A Pilot Study into the long-term impact of bearing witness before the ICTY." This project, which was conducted in cooperation with the Castleberry Peace Institute of the University of North Texas, was designed to examine the impact that testifying before the Tribunal has had on 300 fact witnesses from B&H, Croatia, Kosovo, and Serbia, including those who experienced severe emotional or physical trauma during the war. Based on the findings of this study, the VWU and the authors recommended that international judicial institutions should further develop and standardize support mechanisms to safeguard witnesses' wellbeing. They also called on courts to implement follow-up programs for those who testified and to develop strong relationships with the communities where witnesses live. In relation to translation and interpreting and its impact on witnesses, the report reasons these issues were examined because they have consequences for all stakeholders in the courtroom and implications for how the law is ultimately interpreted.

Witnesses recalled that interpreting did not accurately reflect their meaning and that there were language differences between them and the interpreter. Witnesses also expressed concern about the pace of interpreting, the distracting nature of the interpreting process, and auditory issues associated with hearing what was interpreted. Witnesses suggested that better information needed to be provided about what to expect or that the interpreting process had been problematic. Some witnesses also complained about interpreting difficulties and the accuracy of the interpreting between native speakers and the interpreters. This could be taken to mean that these 300 fact witnesses did say that a selection of in-court interpreters has mostly been wrong as to their language variant, knowledge of the merits of the case, and their ethnicity or nationality.[323]

---

323 University of Texas and ICTY Victims and Witnesses Unit (2016), Echoes of Testimonies: A Pilot Study into the long-term impact of bearing witness before the ICTY: https://bit.ly/3acryu9.

Before moving to the analysis, I must make several comments on the overall attitude of interpreters which, so far, resemble the one often found with novice interpreters or those who do not fully understand their service to the society.

Quoting I&T Code, Article 10, Accuracy, para. 1 Truth and Completeness, former ICTY interpreter Hajdu argues that it is okay to interpret an obvious slip of tongue "bio sam kindapovan" with "I was kindapped." However, although not reprimanded here for elitism or laughing behind her client's backs, such interpreters and such interpreting seems to contradict the overall impression that a witness should leave on the Trial Chambers: should such a witness be unable to tell the obvious difference between "kindapped" and "kidnapped," could he be trusted to know the difference between being in remand, being detained, being imprisoned, and being in a concentration camp, and, ultimately, could his experience be accepted as genuine and trustworthy by the Trial Chamber that evaluates it.[324]

Whereas it is completely acceptable to pay attention to accuracy, being excessive about it can have legal effects. Being kidnapped, detained, raped, subjected to watching the killing or the rape of one's own children is as traumatic as it gets. Do interpreters really have to make a show about it? Careful readers will have noticed that whenever the ICTY originals were quoted, either in the shape of a transcript or a document, they are full of typos and lack editing. The ICTY language staff have worked with many legal professionals who even 20 years into working on the former Yugoslavia have not been able to properly spell or pronounce toponyms or personal names they encountered in their daily work day in and day out, bless them. Interpreters spelling or pronouncing those same toponyms the same way legal professionals do would send very unflattering messages about themselves, the legal professionals, and the court. So why pick on a victim?

The next example of an overall attitude of misunderstanding one's service to society is even more disturbing. Elias-Bursać reports on two serious interpreting incidents that she noticed at the ICTY, calling it "an impressive record" for 10,000 trial days.[325] One

---

324 Hajdu, Nata (undated), The kindapper and the kidnapped: Interpreting at the ICTY: https://bit.ly/2REGUBn.

325 Elias-Bursać, Ellen (2015), Translating evidence and interpreting

of these instances occurred when a court interpreter into English, during the court session, on hearing what the client had to say completed her interpreting and then exclaimed into the microphone in a language the client could understand "*Jao, što sere!*" (Is he bullshitting or what!) Naturally, the client heard her and complained right there in the courtroom.

The Trial Chamber called this "an interpreting incident" and confirmed that the CLSS carried out an "inquiry and [provided an] explanation" that an offensive comment had, indeed been made by one of the interpreters "in reaction to a statement made by the witness in a video clip presented as evidence" and that it was inadvertently broadcast. The Trial Chamber concluded that "it does not appear to the Chamber [that the comment made by an interpreter] arise[s] from any ethnic prejudice or hostility to the Defence, [but that] the comment was entirely inappropriate. Such comments are not acceptable in this Chamber or at the Tribunal." As for the results of the CLSS inquiry, "[t]he Chamber is satisfied that appropriate action was taken in respect of the interpreter in question in order to prevent future incidents of this nature." The whole thing suggests a certain degree of misplaced generosity, because the Chamber concluded the case by establishing "Furthermore, this interpreter offered to be removed from this case. This interpreter will no longer be assigned to work on the *Krajišnik* trial."[326]

Speaking from hindsight, Elias-Bursać clarifies that the "procedure at the ICTY [...] was to move the interpreter to another case." The actual procedure has been described in the I&T Code, Preamble. The B/C/S transcript of this session is not available on the ICTY internet page of *Krajišnik* trial. It should be added that B/C/S transcripts for 22 and 24 March 2006 in the *Krajišnik* trial, the day before and the day after this incident, are available. This confirms the ICTY Registry CLSS caused the UN reputational damage and embarrassment.

This is just another proof that the ICTY CLSS checks and balances were lacking as this case could have been disciplined differently, more so because the interpreter in question was a

---

testimony at a war crimes tribunal. Palgrave Macmillan: London.
[326] ICTY, Cases, *Krajišnik*, T. 21867-21868 (23 March 2006): https://bit.ly/2V8Gois.

member of CLSS management who, due to the virtue of her position, should have known better and should have been disciplined more severely.

This is more so because the client was a high-ranking wartime Serb official who testified in open court, thus literally putting the rest of his life in peril seeing as he still lived in the Serb-dominant part of B&H. The behavior of this interpreter reflected badly on all parties to the proceedings. As to victims and witnesses, those insiders who might have thought about coming to testify may have seen, and have definitely heard about this, and probably changed their minds, discouraged from being disrespected. The lack of disciplinary action in this case might have signaled to them that such behavior is institutionally acceptable. The ICTY Registry CLSS sent very unflattering messages to the region about respect for the bravery of the parties' testifying clients and might have precluded other insiders from stepping forward.

I am now in position to examine in-court interpreting for a Bosnian language speaker by a non-Bosnian language speaker. The witness from the next example is a fact witness Witness B-1054, a Bosnian Muslim, testifying in *Milošević* about the events in Višegrad; the interpreter is not a speaker of the Bosnian language. The mistakes in interpreting are marked in **bold**; the "Author's translation" refers to a translation of the original.

Table 11. Interpreting during testimony of a fact witness

Original	As interpreted	Author's translation
1. Pa kad smo tuj došli, ćilimi što su bili prostrti: oni su nečim bili posuti, kao nekom naftom, gorivom, tako da je...	1. When we reached **this Omeragic house**, the carpets had been – some oil or fuel had been poured on the carpets.	1. When we got there, those carpets that were spread, they have been doused with something like oil, like fuel.
2. Tuj smo i našli toga naroda osim nas što su nas prećerali iz kuće u kuću i tuj su nas popalili.	**2. [...]** And **that is when** they set fire to us.	2. This is where we joined other people apart from us they collected from our homes along the way. This is where they set fire on us.
3. Među nama je bila beba od dva dana starosti.	3. Amongst us was a two-day-old baby.	3. There was a two days old baby among us.
4. Uglavnom da su djeca vrištala, žene, starci pomagali.	4. The children were screaming. The women, the old men, **were trying to help.**	4. Children were screaming, women, elderly were wailing.
5. Ja sam do prozora odma prešla tako da sam izbacila sina od trinaest i po godina kroz prozor i da sam i ja za njim **do dva-tri minuta iskočila kroz prozor**.	**5. I was right next to the window**, and I threw out my **13-year-old son** out the window, and then I followed him **a couple of minutes** later.	5. I got to the window at once and I threw my 13.5 years old son out the window. I followed him jumping through the window in about two-three minutes.
6. **U to** me **ranio**: lijeva ruka lijeva noga.	6. **Then** I was wounded in my left arm and left leg.	6. I got wounded during: left arm, left leg.
7. Tako da sam u potok otišla **i u kanalizaciju**.	7, 8, 9. I went into the **stream and the sewage canal** where I stayed for three nights and three days.	7. I ended up in the creek, in the sewage water.
8. U toj sam kanalizaciji ostala tri dana i tri noći.		8. I stayed in the sewage water for three days and three nights.
9. Tuj sam se ucrvala.		9. My injuries got infected by maggots.

Although interpreting into English, it is obvious from delivery this interpreter has not been educated in an English- speaking country (*tu su nas popalili* has been wrongly translated as "that is *when* they set fire to us" whereas it should be "that is *where* they set fire on us"). Other mistakes included additions, omissions, and misinterpretations.

There was one contextual addition: "this Omeragic house" was not mentioned in the original at all, but it was obvious from the previous examination of this witness that this is the location of the crime.

But there were some serious omissions, as well. The first one, *tuj sam se ucrvala* meaning "this is where maggots started coming out my injuries" is completely missing at the end of the discourse. This omission encroaches on the overall picture of horror and the aftermath of related desperation. Obviously, omitting this information, this interpreter did not succeed in painting the same picture to the Chambers as painted by the B/C/S speaker.

The second one, [in the house where they set fire on us] "this is where we joined other people apart from us they collected from our homes along the way" directly encroaches on facts of the case trying to prove extermination: the Lukić cousins went on a killing spree collecting Muslims from nearby villages from their homes, first separating ladies to dance naked for them and to rape them, and then merging them all together with people from the houses surrounding this particular house. Since the prosecution provides summary testimonies to in-court interpreters, this interpreter just read out all this information uttered by the examining prosecutor; it is unclear how s/he could not have picked up on it contextually from this witness's testimony.

As to the substance, it could be understood from Witness B-1054's previous testimony that it was Milan Lukić who was standing at the door while these people were devoured by fire and it could be taken that Witness B-1054 was referring to him in Line 6 as an actual person who wounded her. This is an example of sheer untranslatability of even the most vital information.

But there was a mistake due to the lack of knowledge about the topology of Višegrad. The city always had problems due to the rain and outdated sewage system: the rain would create small creeks and sewage would spill over into those creeks. The victim was sitting for three days and three nights in such conditions, not in a proper sewage canal with a dry spot here and there.

Other mistakes included numbers: this interpreter did not convey the proper age of a son the witness threw out the burning home or the time it took the witness to escape from the room.

Finally, there were two mistakes due to misunderstanding of the Bosnian language. The first one was *U to me ranio* which was interpreted as "then I was wounded." However, the literal meaning of *u to* is "in that." If we see the previous sentence, it is obvious that she was jumping through the window. Contextually, this "in that" could mean that she was wounded mid air, en route, or, as I have suggested, *during*.

The second mistake is rather serious because it encroaches directly on facts. *Uglavnom da su djeca vrištala, žene, starci* ***pomagali*** was interpreted as "The children were screaming. The women, the old men, **were trying to help.**" Trying to help what? These people were doused with fuel and set on fire, there was no evidence of a fire extinguisher being among them. They were completely helpless. Ergo, this *pomagali* could not have been "helping," but a short version of *zapomagati* or "to wail" and the whole segment should have been "The women, the old men, **were wailing**," "The women, the old men **wailed**," or "The women, the old men **called for help**" as the Bosnian term *pomagati* suggests.

These mistakes in interpreting are not at all innocent because of the loss of operational and factual data. Perpetrators in this case were accused of extermination. Instead, saying that "people were trying to help" suggests that these people had an option to defend themselves. In reality, they were wailing, just like this witness has said, meaning they were lamenting the fact that the Serb perpetrator doused them with petrol, was about to light the match, and burn them and their children alive.[327]

[327] The fact that these people were helpless was corroborated by a survivor who testified that "the room was extremely crowded." The Trial Chamber accepted that this witness's "view was unobstructed because the people in the Omeragić House were sitting down" and that this witness's testimony "provided a logical explanation as to how she was able to see Milan Lukić in

Obviously, once academics and practitioners start analyzing ICTY court transcripts it will become clear what has been established here and everywhere: that Wayles was right about the Croatian and Serbian speakers not necessarily understanding all the ins and outs of the Bosnian language and that Bosnian speakers should have interpreted for people from B&H all along.

As to collegial allowances to this interpreter, there should be none. It is human nature to accept, get upset for pointing out, and oversee these mistakes because this interpreter was in shock as the event was beyond horrific. However, this interpreter is not the reader of these humble lines. This interpreter had time to prepare mentally, emotionally, and factually given s/he worked 3 to 4 hours a day 4 days a week as established by the 2009 OIOS Audit Report. The fact that interpreters did not know the basic facts of the case or the topological features of the venue means they had not used the half day off four days a week and the one full day off to prepare for their assignment.

I am now turning to a practical example of a Serbian interpreter interpreting for a highly visible Serbian client. The purpose of the next examination is to show mistakes happen even during highly publicized and visible trials.

Parties know evidence which they are presenting in the court and should one make a serious mistake interpreting, it does go noticed. Let us look at the example of the following misinterpretation during the initial appearance of Mr. Milošević at the ICTY on 3 July 2001.

Table 12 contains the B/C/S and English transcript I made from the ICTY recording of Milošević's initial appearance. The mistakes in interpreting are marked in **bold**; the "Author's back-translation" refers to a translation of the interpreting. The interpreter started one second behind the speaker and finished three seconds after him.[328]

---

the doorway with the device." ICTY, Cases, *Lukić*, Judgment on Appeals (2012).

[328] ICTY, Cases, *Milošević*, Initial Appearance (3 July 2001).

Table 12. Interpreting during the initial appearance of a defendant

Original	Interpreting	Author's back-translation
JUDGE MAY:	SUDIJA MAY:	JUDGE MAY:
1. Mr. Milosevic, I see that you're not represented by counsel today.	1. Gospodine Miloševiću, vidim da nemate pravnog zastupnika **danas ovde.**	1. Mr. Milošević, I see you do not have a legal representative here, today.
2. We understand that this is of your own choice.	**2. Koliko smo obavešteni**, to je Vaš vlastiti izbor.	2. As far as we have been informed, that is of your own choice.
3. You do have the right, of course, to defend yourself.	3. Vi, naravno, imate pravo **da se sami branite**, ali, takođe imate pravo i na pravnog zastupnika.	3. You, naturally, have the right to self-representation, but, you also have the right to a legal representative.
4. You also have a right to counsel, and you should consider carefully whether it's **in your own best interests** not to be represented.	**4. Mislim da treba dobro da razmislite** da li je u **Vašem interesu, Vašem najboljem interesu** da nemate pravnog zastupnika.	4. I think you should think well whether it is in your own interest, your own best interest to not have a legal representative.
5. These proceedings will be long and complex and you may wish to reconsider the position.	5. Ovaj postupak će biti veoma dug i složen i **možda ćete razmotriti situaciju i promeniti mišljenje**.	5. This procedure shall be very long and complex and perhaps you will reconsider the situation and change your opinion.
6. In these circumstances, if you wish to have time to consider whether you want to have counsel or not, **we would be prepared to give it to you**.	**6. Ukoliko želite dodatno vreme** kako biste razmislili da li Vam je potreban pravni zastupnik ili ne, **mi smo spremni da Vam omogućimo neko dodatno vreme**.	6. Should you wish additional time to consider whether you require legal representative or not, we are ready to provide you some additional time.
7. Now, do you want **some time** to **consider** now whether you wish to be represented?	7. Dakle, da li želite **neko dodatno vreme** da **razmislite** sada da li želite da Vas neko zastupa **pravno**?	7. So, do you want some additional time now to think over whether you want a person to legally represent you?

Given that interpreters into B/C/S also have the benefit of a live transcript of proceedings in English appearing before them to help them with their interpreting, and that they work four hours a day with one full working day off to prepare, interpreting from this example is subpar.

This is because the whole style of interpreting is awkward (You may wish to reconsider the position → *možda ćete razmotriti situaciju i promeniti mišljenje* (perhaps you will reconsider the situation and change your opinion), if you wish to have time→ *Ukoliko želite dodatno vreme* (Should you wish additional time), we would be prepared to give it to you → *mi smo spremni da Vam omogućimo neko dodatno vreme* (we are ready to provide you some additional time), today → *danas, ovde* (here, today)).

There were misinterpretations – right to defend yourself → *pravo da se sami branite* (right to self-representation) and We understand → *Koliko smo obavešteni* (As far as we have been informed) – including one self-correction – in your own best interests → *Vašem interesu, Vašem najboljem interesu* (your own interest, your own best interest) There was also one omission (Line 6, "in these circumstances"), and several additions.

Register is a variety of language that a language user considers appropriate to a specific situation. Register depends on field of discourse, tenor of discourse, and mode of discourse. Within register, the field of discourse refers to what is going on that is relevant to the language user's choice of linguistic terms. This is an initial appearance of the defendant before the court. This is the venue where the Presiding Judge informs the defendant of his/her rights and where the defendant may enter a plea.

Unfortunately, major mistakes in the field of discourse completely distorted the Presiding Judge's take on Milošević's legal rights. Although the Presiding Judge very clearly informed Milošević that he had a right to "a defense," the interpreter informed him that he had a right to "self-representation." Naturally, defendants also have a right to self-representation (ICTY-S, Article 21(d)), but the judges only have a duty to inform the defendant of his rights under ICTY RPE 62(A)(ii), one of which is the right to a defense, during the initial appearance. It is worth asking whether this erroneous interpreting is to blame for the fact that Milošević chose to represent himself, which caused many issues later on for all the parties.

Within register, the mode of discourse abstractly refers to the role that language plays (speech, essay, lecture, etc.) and to its medium of transmission (spoken or written). Here, after having informed him of his rights, the Presiding Judge informs Milošević that, with those rights in mind, considering he does not have legal representation, he can take some time to reconsider his right to defense:

> **Now** (conclusive), do you want some time to consider now whether you wish to be represented?
>
> Dakle, da li želite neko dodatno vreme da razmislite sada da li želite da Vas neko zastupa pravno?
>
> So, do you want **some additional time now** (temporal) to consider whether you want a person to legally represent you?

This interpreter misinterpreted the second "now," which was clearly a conclusive and was not meant as "take some time now (here in the courtroom) to rethink your position," but "now that I have explained your rights to you, do you want some time to rethink your position."

This interpreter not only distorted original messages, but she also omitted two important segments of the original speech and misinterpreted "some time" meant in general for "some additional time" as here in the courtroom now and, despite having the opportunity to correct herself, she stuck with it to the end where the subpar interpreting gave Milošević the impression of time pressure.

Within register, the tone of a discourse abstractly refers to the relationship between the people who are taking part in the discourse.[329] Here, the tone of the Presiding Judge was informative, he is informing his client about the proceedings and his related rights. His position is that of a legal, not a moral authority. This interpreter did not distinguish between these two messages and, instead, she mistook it for condescension: "consider carefully" is a standard legal expression which has its legal equivalent in B/C/S (*pažljivo razmotriti*), but this interpreter said, "you should think well" (*dobro razmislite*) which is a dreaded B/C/S expression that parents use with their children when they are being naughty.

---

329 Baker, M. (2011), In other words: a coursebook on translation (second edition), Routledge: London and New York.

The misinterpretation of "we understand" into *koliko smo obavešteni* or "as far as we have been informed" is also rather serious, because it gives an impression of a "Big Brother" watching over the trial. Serbian nationalist discourse, as explained earlier, heavily reposes on the absence of critical analysis, on semi-truths, and on unidentified but menacing external factors, so this misinterpretation could be an evidence of such an indoctrination by this interpreter.

In that, it is also worth mentioning that Serbian liberals hailed the arrest of Milošević whom they blamed for everything wrong with the country, and continue to do so, more specifically because Serbia suffered under UN sanctions (1992-1995) and, in their view, NATO bombings (1999). Interestingly, public opinion rarely blamed Milošević for the atrocities that Serbian and Serb troops committed in Croatia, B&H, and Kosovo, and are very careful to avoid the issue altogether to this day or constantly pitch the idea that everyone was equally guilty. Serbian liberals were very happy to see Milošević in The Hague, so this condescending and patronizing choice of words could also be interpreted as an accidental reflection of public opinion on the part of interpreter ("Gotcha!") and is an example of a biased preconception about the client and a collective paranoia.

The second problem with the tone of discourse is in the designation of the Presiding Judge as a speaker in interpreting. The Presiding Judge speaks on behalf of a Trial Chamber, not in his personal capacity. This interpretation completely disregarded that: the insertion *mislim* (I think) makes it seem like the Presiding Judge is offering his own personal opinion regarding the choices Mr. Milošević has *vis-à-vis* his legal representation. However, the Presiding Judge clearly said, "you should consider/reconsider/take time" without involving himself in the client's choices and making it clear the client should consider/reconsider/take time, not somebody else on his behalf. The way this was interpreted makes it seem like a Presiding Judge is saying: "I see you are here without defense. Sure, you can defend yourself alone. But if I were you, I would take some time to think it over. So, take that time here and now and think it over, okay?" whereas the Presiding Judge said: "According to your rights under ICTY RPE, you have a right to a defense. I don't see your defense counsel. This will be a long ride: take time and think that choice over." This subpar interpretation gave the impression of the Presiding Judge's personal agenda toward this client. It is worth saying that the relationship between these two was never respectful, from this very beginning up until the Presiding Judge's demise in 2004.

How could this go unnoticed? How could the defendant be misinformed of his rights in the presence of a judge, prosecution, defense, media, region, etc., and how could he be bullied into time pressure at the international criminal tribunal during such a high-profile case (or any case, for that matter)?

In addition to all that has been established previously in this study regarding ICTY and CLSS recruitment, quality and quantity control, etc., nobody challenged the interpretation. Who could challenge interpreting? Since his rights were being encroached and violated and he was the one being time pressured in interpreting, Milošević or his defense counsel could have challenged the interpreting. However, Milošević did not do that because he relied on interpreting and the interpreting, as shown above, was completely wrong.

How many mistakes are there like this in tens of thousands of court hours? Who knows? Maybe these examples will serve as an invitation to all those willing to do more research on the quality of court interpreting at the ICTY.

Gaiba shares that the IMT was aware of the shortcomings of simultaneous interpreting even before the trials had begun, but that it was impossible for the speakers to check the accuracy of interpreting. In such highly critical proceedings, defendants and speakers in general would need to be sure that translations of their testimony were accurate. Interpreters were working two days and resting up the third. Later in the trial, this arrangement was changed so that day off meant off court, but not at rest: interpreters spent the third day checking the transcripts of their translation against the verbatim recording. Since it was discovered that the interpreting system needed someone to supervise its smooth functioning, the IMT invented the role of an Interpretation Monitor, who was not chosen among interpreters because they completely devoted their attention to translating. The Interpretation Monitor was an army officer chosen from the Translation Division. The Interpretation Monitor was present at all times in court to supervise interpreters and facilitate their tasks by reminding the IMT to speak at the proper pace by manning the "yellow light" letting the speakers know they need to slow down and the "red light" which would require interruption of proceedings. The Interpretation Monitor sat between the English desk and the Marshal of the Court (the military court version of the Registrar) and was assigned a team of interpreters to supervise.[330]

It arises from Gaiba's discussions of the qualities of the Interpretation Monitor that this person could be partly described as a "linguistic project manager" in today's terms. The ICTY had no red or yellow lights or systems of checks and balances to ensure the accuracy of interpreting, as it was incumbent on parties to determine this on their own.

An Interpretation Monitor should have been in place from the very beginning of the ICTY due to the reasons advanced so far in this study and all the examples discussed here, both to monitor exchange by manning the lights, to assign interpreters to check their interpreting on the fifth day and the second half of their working day, or to assign them to interpret for witnesses during preparation for court testimony in the proofing which would eliminate the need for otherwise unqualified and legally unregulated Language Assistants to interpret for clients.

Previous discussions of the CLSS interpreters working hours and work load show that they could have checked the accuracy of interpreting. Since they were not used for those purposes, their absence for half a day every day and no-show on Fridays was an incredible waste of in-house resources. This waste resulted in incredible doubling and tripling of jobs as evidenced throughout this study.

Most importantly, since none of them worked at the international war crimes tribunal before getting a job with the ICTY, by interpreting for witnesses before their testimony, court interpreters would establish contact with them, learn their speech pattern, and, consequently, learn how to avoid or deal with linguistic traps. Those who were not Bosnian language speakers could have learned some new words, since most witnesses were from B&H. Overall, court interpreters would start improving their

330 Gaiba, Francesca (1998), The origins of simultaneous interpreting: the Nuremberg trial. University of Ottawa Press: Ottawa.

overall performance, listening to themselves, learning from their mistakes, and they would not be in position to interpret for someone they have never met before.

It is on the basis of my research that I strongly recommend international criminal tribunals reinstate the IMT's institution of appointing an Interpretation Monitor as a quality check on language professionals' output.

4.5. Linguistic justice: court transcripts

It was clear from the very beginning of the engagement of court reporters at the ICTY that they were primarily to cater to the Court by creating English and French court transcripts. This lack of transcripts in B/C/S primarily created problems for non-English and non-French-speaking defenses, self-representing defendants, and other defendants as some instances described already show.

Could the ICTY transcripts have been made in B/C/S from the very beginning? Here, this study will first turn to the equipment used to transcribe the court proceedings because it is crucial for the use of languages. There were two options for making transcripts in B/C/S: classical stenography notetaking, followed by transcribing and computer stenography on the stenotype machine, and a computer program for simultaneously recording and transcribing speech. This stenotype machine is regularly used by court reporters in Common Law countries, including at the ICTY. Unfortunately, none of those stenotype machines were adapted for use in B/C/S languages, despite all the best efforts of the local practitioners in the former Yugoslavia. Could the court reporters using the stenotype machine and related computer software have been used to make B/C/S transcripts? The answer is: no, such machines and such practitioners do not exist for any of the B/C/S languages.

Now, could the manual stenographers be used to record proceedings in B/C/S? The manual stenographers were working as court reporters throughout the First and the Second Yugoslavia; the Yugoslavian Association of Stenographers and Dactylographers was functional between 1945 and 1990, bringing together all professional associations from all the republics, but the collapse of Yugoslavia led to the demise of this Association. Could the manual stenographers have been used to record proceedings in B/C/S from the very beginning of the ICTY? Yes, they could. Could manual stenographers be used to record proceedings in B/C/S right now? Yes, they could.

However, none of them were used to transcribe ICTY court proceedings in B/C/S then and they are still not used now. There were no attempts made to recruit B/C/S court reporters or create ICTY court transcripts in B/C/S until 2010.

In 2008, a team of experts, led by the OSCE's Office for Democratic Institutions and Human Rights in conjunction with the ICTY and the UN Interregional Crime and Justice Research Institute, carried out a needs assessment among the judiciaries in the former Yugoslavia in order to transfer the wealth of knowledge from the ICTY and build the capacity of local judiciaries before the ICTY completes its mandate. In 2009, these findings were published in a report entitled "Final Report: Supporting the Transition Process: Lessons Learned and Best Practices in Knowledge Transfer." One of the key findings in relation to the needs of local judiciaries in order to efficiently process the war crimes on the local level was a lack of ICTY court transcripts available in local languages. The three organizations jointly started an 18-month long "War Crimes Justice Project" in order to address those needs.

In July 2010, the ICTY Registry recruited a team who began creating verbatim transcripts of ICTY court proceedings in B/C/S from B/C/S audio recordings of ICTY court proceedings. The ICTY engaged a team of 20 transcribers, who transcribed a total of over 60,000 pages in B/C/S in those 18 months. The transcription project mainly addressed the most pressing needs of the local judiciaries in terms of assisting their ongoing trials and investigations within the available funding, time, and resource restraints. Unfortunately, on the project's completion in December 2011, the transcription project was discontinued due to a lack of additional funding. Currently, it is not clear whether the project would be continued.[331]

These ICTY Registry transcripts were made only in B/C/S, not in Albanian or Macedonian, the languages of some defendants and some audiences in the situation country. The B/C/S transcripts of some, though not all, court sessions were made in trials:

---

331 OSCE, Supporting the Transition Process: Lessons Learned and Best Practices in Knowledge Transfer: Final Report (2009): https://bit.ly/3cj6Dab.

Blagojević and Jokić, Brđanin, Erdemović, Halilović, Karadžić, Krajišnik, Krstić, Lukić, Nikolić, Popović, Stanišić and Župljanin, Tolimir, and *Vasiljević* (B&H as a situation country), *Martić* (Croatia as a situation country), *Đorđević and Šainović* (Kosovo as a situation country), and *Perišić* and *Milošević* (the influence of the Serbian political and military leadership over Serb rebels and Serb(ian) insurgents in B&H, Croatia and Kosovo).

Appendix 5 contains the time of court sessions, ERN ranges, and actual ERN pages of the ICTY court sessions transcribed by the ICTY Registry B/C/S transcript team. Matters such as typos and others are duly recorded in the footnotes in Appendix 5 only if they affected data.

Table 13. Total number of trial days vs. the days available in B/C/S transcripts

Trial	Total trial days	Days transcribed by the ICTY Registry B/C/S transcript team	Trial	Total days	Days transcribed by the ICTY Registry B/C/S transcript team
Blagojević and Jokić	145	12	Popović	425	222
Brđanin	284	7	Stanišić and Župljanin	354	116
Erdemović	n/a	2	Tolimir	242	3
Halilović	77	4	Vasiljević	54	1
Karadžić	499	11	Martić	148	156
Krajišnik	314	164	Đorđević	199	5
Krstić	98	3	Šainović et al	285	3
Lukić	85	10	Perišić	198	4
Nikolić	n/a	1	Milošević	n/a	42

The data on total trial days in the above cases from Table 13 was taken as recorded in the Case Information Sheet; I counted the days transcribed as they appear in the B/C/S transcripts. The value n/a means that there were no trials in this case because the defendant pleaded guilty or that he died before the trial was over. The discrepancy in the total days of trial and the days in the B/C/S transcripts in Martić might be because there is an error in Martić Case Information Sheet: 156 days in the B/C/S transcripts correspond to 156 days in the English language transcript; this case seems to be the only trial that has been transcribed in full.

Table 13 also shows the ICTY Registry B/C/S transcript team produced a total of 766 days of transcripts.

A total of 29 transcribed days are recorded as below 15 pages. I established those court sessions are heavily redacted, meaning that the transcript contains no operational or other data that could be of interest to the judiciary of the former Yugoslavia or anyone, such as in *Krajišnik* on 22 and 23 June 2005 or *Martić* on 20 March 2006 or 9 June 2006 (see Appendix 5). Why waste funds, staff, and effort to make them at all? However, although containing below 15 pages, all these days are recorded as containing above 100 pages of transcripts. I will address this below.

Finally, I was surprised at the report which proudly said that the ICTY Registry B/C/S transcript team had reached a goal of producing 60,000 pages of transcript. It reminded me I also read ICTY ARs which threw around the number of pages of court transcript produced that year as if the actual number of transcript pages meant anything instead of saying the English and French transcripts had been done on time and delivered.[332]

These production indicators in pages of transcript are not helpful at all. Transcribers' production is measured in minutes of recorded material, not in the number of pages produced. In other words: how many minutes of recorded material they transcribed, not how many pages they can produce. This is because the number of words appearing on a page is unpredictable: one single page may have a series of "Uh-huhs" or it may have full text from top to bottom, in addition to transcribing tags identifying speakers and the proceedings. Given all the constraints with the actual recording, the transcription industry accepted minimum is four hours of transcription time for one hour of clear audio, or a 4:1 ratio. In

[332] UN, Report of the ICTY (A/64/205) (2009), para. 84: 70,000 pgs; UN, Report of the ICTY (A/65/205) (2010), para. 90: 100,000 pgs; UN, Report of the ICTY (A/66/210) (2011), para. 85: 88,000 pgs; UN, Report of the ICTY (A/67/214) (2012), para. 97: 58,000 pgs; UN, Report of the ICTY (A/68/255) (2013), para. 71: 71,000 pgs; UN, Report of the ICTY (A/70/226) (2015), para. 72: 28,000 pgs; UN, Report of the ICTY (A/71/263) (2016), para. 69: 14,000 pgs.

other words, 15 minutes of audio per one hour of work or 120 minutes of transcribed audio material in an 8-hour working day.[333]

As to the pages of transcripts subject to the work of the ICTY Registry B/C/S transcript team, Excel spreadsheet counted all the ERN ranges and came up to a total of 62,610 pages. This means the ICTY Registry B/C/S transcript team managers rounded the number down to 60,000 when reporting to the donors.

Next, after I recorded the number of pages in each court session as given by the PDF Viewer to which they were posted, added 1 to account for the actual number of pages, the Excel spreadsheet counted them all and came up with 59,903 actual pages. This means the ICTY Registry B/C/S transcript team managers did not report properly to the donors that they produced 60,000 pages of transcript because they were short 97 pages of achieving that goal.

As to the number of pages that had been actually transcribed, there were several constraints calculating them. English and French transcript templates have 25 lines per page; the ICTY Registry B/C/S transcript team template had 30. Although I counted all the lines in the latter, I did not have a proper reference with which to compare: to the B/C/S or the English and French transcript?

This is because unlike the English and French transcript teams, the ICTY Registry B/C/S transcript team never went all the way down to the 30th line on the page to produce a properly full page of transcript. For example, although there were sufficient lines available on the preceding page, the new page contains only a few lines which could have easily fitted on the preceding page, such as: T. 28109 (3 lines on the new page although 6 lines available on the preceding page); T. 28206 (1-3); T. 28977 (1-6); T. 29245 (5-9); T. 30643 (5-9); T. 30721 (3-6); T. 31017 (2-4); T. 34956 (2-7); T. 5442 (6-9); T. 1411 (2-5); T. 6513 (3-6); T. 995 (4-10); T. 1544 (6-11); T. 4778 (1-4), etc. in *Popović* and *Krajišnik*.

---

333 Brittain, Chloe (undated). Transcription time per audio hour: how long should transcribing actually make? Opal Transcription Services: https://bit.ly/3emrMCj.

I did the following research to show how much is already lost due to not going all the way down to the 30th line. The shortest transcript was 3 pages long (6 March 2006, *Martić*) and the longest was 151 pages long (23 June 2005, *Krajišnik*) which could be taken to mean that the average transcript was about 74 pages long. One such transcript of 74 pages was spotted in *Krajišnik* on 25 April 2006. As stated before, one page of ICTY Registry B/C/S transcript has 30 lines, but in this particular transcript of 74 pages, the transcribers ended page on following lines: 25, 19, 19, 15, 18, 11, 17, 14, 19, 20, 20, 20, 22, 20, 20, 17, 18, 22, 15, 15, 15, 17, 22, 17, 13, 17, 13, 18, 20, 15, 17, 20, 18, 18, 17, 25, 22, 22, 18, 17, 21, 14, 23, 22, 22, 22, 21, 22, 26, 24, 22, 23, 21, 21, 20, 19, 21, 24, 22, 22, 21, 14, 24, 16, 24, 21, 23, 15, 13, 16, 18, 18, 21, and 17. A 30-line 74-page transcript should have 2,220 lines, but this one has just 1,420 lines, which means a 74-page transcript, taken as an average lenght transcript, has a shortfall of about 35%.

In addition, the ICTY Registry B/C/S transcript team consolidated the pagination of their transcripts with those in English and French. However, there are two problems with that: these transcripts were made for the use of the local judiciary in the former Yugoslavia who had no need of citing or quoting English and French pages in the B/C/S speaking court; there was no need for this consolidation due to the lack of an English- and French-speaking audience.

Also, these ICTY Registry B/C/S transcripts already contain a certain number of blank pages inserted to consolidate the B/C/S transcripts with the pagination of the English and French transcripts. Why is this done twice?

I recorded and duly counted the full blank pages and full ERN ranges inserted into the ICTY Registry B/C/S transcripts to consolidate between the English and the French transcripts: 15 in *Brđanin*; 480 and 6 in *Krajišnik*; 1 in *Krstić*; 1 in *Lukić*; 6 and 50 in *Popović*; 4 in *Tolimir*; 15 in *Martić*; 1 in *Đorđević*; 1 in *Perišić*; and 329 and 40 in *Milošević*. The total number of full blank pages and full ERN ranges inserted into the ICTY Registry B/C/S transcripts to consolidate between the English and the French transcripts came to a total of 949 blank pages of consolidation. This brings the grand total of actually transcribed pages of the ICTY Registry B/C/S transcripts from 59,903 down to 58,954.

Finally, a total number of the ICTY Registry B/C/S transcripts contain a certain number of blank pages of redacted material. I decided to define the redacted material as a whole page or range of pages of redacted material as clearly named as such in the actual transcripts. Although it is customary to transcribe redacted material, as well, the ICTY Registry B/C/S transcript team claims they did not transcribe redacted material because they did not have the recordings.

I recorded and duly counted full blank pages and full ERN ranges of redacted material in the ICTY Registry B/C/S transcripts: 9 and 29 in *Blagojević and Jokić*; 10 and 140 in *Brđanin*; 3 in *Halilović*; 33 in *Karadžić*; 14 and 432 in *Krajišnik*; 1 in *Krstić*; 19 and 149 in *Lukić*; 89 and 245 in *Popović*; 23 and 84 in *Stanišić and Župljanin*; 139 and 1,464 in *Martić*; 3 and 5 in *Đorđević*; 1 in *Perišić*; 30 and 116 in *Milošević*. The total number of full blank pages and full ERN ranges of redacted material in the ICTY Registry B/C/S transcripts came to a total of 3,038 blank pages of redacted material. Given that there were several lines of redacted material in almost every court session transcribed, and given that at least half of preceding page and a half of the page following the clear annotation on redacting have also been redacted, this number of 3,038 could very well be triple. But, I counted only clearly marked full redacted pages which brings the grand total of actually transcribed pages of ICTY Registry B/C/S transcripts from 58,954 down to 55,916.

Internal ICTY and OSCE reports, including the donor reports citing the number of pages transcribed by the ICTY Registry B/C/S transcript team as “more than 60,000”, should now correct their information to “a little bit above 55,000.”

Appendix 5 also shows recorded and calculated times of court sessions, the ERN ranges and pages, and contents for all trial sessions transcribed as part of the B/C/S transcription project.

The general ICTY court transcript format, adopted by the ICTY Registry B/C/S transcription project, recorded the starting and ending times of court sessions and every single page was assigned an ERN number. There is a plenty of reasons to assume these have been merely copied from the existing transcripts in the English language.

After I recorded the times of court sessions, the Excel duly performed times calculations for me whereupon I established that the ICTY Registry B/C/S transcription team transcribed a total of 2,657 hours and 41 minutes of audio material during the 18-month life of this project.

Considering the number of staff in the ICTY Registry B/C/S transcription team, the time at their disposal, and the audio quality of court sessions, this number seems subpar.

A UN month has 21 days, the UN allows 45 days of annual leave, 15 days of uncertified sick leave, and 15 days of official holidays in 18 months; the latter must be taken. Although the minimum transcription industry standard is 15 minutes of transcribed material an hour, I decided to calculate the daily output based on a 7-hour working day which brought me to a minimum of 105 minutes of transcribed material a day. These criteria allow for the following combinations and calculations:

20*(105*((18*21)-75))=636,300 minutes or 10,605 hours

where 20 staff took all 45 days of annual leave and obligatory 15 days of official holidays allowed in 18 months and all 15 days of uncertified sick leave to transcribe an absolute minimum output.

20*(105*((18*21)-60))=667,800 minutes or 11,130 hours

where 20 staff took all 45 days of annual leave and obligatory 15 days of official holidays or all 15 days of uncertified sick leave allowed in 18 months to transcribe an upper median output.

20*(105*((18*21)-30))=730,800 minutes or 12,180 hours

where 20 staff took obligatory 15 days of official holidays and all 15 days of uncertified sick leave allowed in 18 months to transcribe a lower median output.

20*(105*((18*21)-15))=762,300 minutes or 12,705 hours.

where staff took obligatory 15 days of official holidays allowed in 18 months to transcribe an absolute maximum output.

Table 14. The ICTY Registry B/C/S transcription team output: produced vs. minimum, median, and maximum output (in hours)

	PRODUCED	ABS MIN	LOWER MED	UPPER MED	ABS MAX
Hours	2,657	10,605	11,130	12,180	12,705

Obviously, the ICTY Registry B/C/S transcription team did not reach the bare minimum of transcription output according to the transcription industry standards even with my overly liberal calculations of a 7-hour workday and the bare industry minimum of 15 minutes per hour indicating a shortfall of around 75%.

In 2018, the "Om3ga Solutions" developed an application called "Daktilograf" (typist or dactylographer). This application converts speech originally delivered in B/C/S to text with an accuracy of more than 95% in the real-time operation. The company already has a wide clientele using this application ranging from various industries to institutions of public administration in the former Yugoslavia. As the human work on the BCS transcripts would amount to revising, this application promises results in a rather short period of time, as well.[334] Could this application be used to complete pending work on B/C/S transcripts? The answer is: yes, it could.

---

334 Om3ga solutions, Daktilograf: https://bit.ly/2wEZMbW.

CONCLUSIONS

ALL RISE

This book has attempted to provide some normative guidelines and recommendations to adjudicating linguistic justice at international criminal tribunals in the example of the ICTY, the first of many nonmilitary international criminal tribunals. Exhaustive conclusions and recommendations have already been given at the end of each chapter. Here, I will only highlight the most glaring direct and indirect consequences of ICTY Registry CLSS management failures at communication along the four lines I defined before. My research confirmed Weiss's statement that the UN is a feudal kingdom and that the UN System organizations are a dysfunctional family.

Subscribing under Bassiouni's motto that "to criticize is to improve," this book never set out to be a complimentary one. Collegial allowances and benefits of the doubt were given wherever deserved throughout the study. The very fact that no ICTY trials were declared mistrials due to poor language services makes the CLSS a successful language service provider. However, there is much more to the provision of language services at an international criminal tribunal adjudicating on ethnically motivated war crimes. And those other things were exactly what my book is about.

The UN's work should be scrutinized at every corner and the data they present to donors and the public should be always rechecked because the UN is the organization that has the final say on everything international. Criticizing administration of the organization with more than 50 years in the field of administration will, inevitably, fall on deaf ears. However, it is worth saying that any administration that thinks in stereotypes and speaks in platitudes while delivering service is exhausting, dangerous, and anti-progress and there is very little sense in anyone financially supporting it. The donors and the public are overdue in saying "Time's up!" to an administration that does not respect its own rules, that ignores the recommendations and conclusions of its own internal audit and investigation authorities, and whose sheer incompetence and lack of punishment of the incompetent constantly leads to limited or no service delivery. May the next all-encompassing, comprehensive, strict, and top-down UN reform revolve around purging the incompetents.

However, it is hoped that pointing to the direct and indirect consequences of shortcomings and failures of the administration of the first in the long – and seemingly neverending – row of international criminal tribunals will result in some changes in the way linguistic justice is adjudicated at the level of the laws and of the practice in these international criminal tribunals.

The provision of language services at the institution that was ICTY was a precedent in that the ICTY was the first independent international criminal tribunal. That is where all similarities between the ICTY and precedents stop. There were war crimes tribunals before the ICTY and they all had language services. The UN under whose auspices the ICTY was created existed in various forms since the 1920s and had, and it still has, rather extensive and experienced language services. Legal and language professionals existed and worked together since Hammurabi. There were so many precedents and lessons learned for the ICTY Registry CLSS management that the provision of language services at the ICTY was supposed to be a short, sweet, and highly efficient celebration of these actors' abilities to work together and of institutional lessons learned. Instead, it is genuinely baffling that it was such a failure at almost every turn.

As to the first line of communication with the judicial organization, the situation country towards the working institution, it is clear from discussions and examinations in Chapter 1 that the ICTY management, the CLSS management, and the judges were aware the language spoken in the former Yugoslavia was vested with ethnic and national affiliations and used as a tool in the conflict. The language experts confirmed it. The problem is that the ICTY Registry did not hire appropriate language service managers to act on any of it in practice.

The "invention" of the neutrally-perceived B/C/S did not have any place in Court as the judges used the phrase "[your] language" when speaking to their clients about their language and did not mention the Serbian, Croatian, Serbo-Croatian, Bosnian, etc. language, save to refer to documents. This "invention" did not have any place in the practice of translation and interpreting because the interpreters routinely agreed they spoke and wrote the language of the victims and witnesses.

The "invention" of B/C/S accounted for a name but did not account for any of the differences in languages remarked on by Browne, did not account for staff-related due diligence at war crimes tribunals adjudicating on ethnic crimes, and did not account for the history of language and identity-related conflicts in the former Yugoslavia. The ICTY CLSS botched the provision of language services from the very beginning and did very little, if anything, to fix it during the next 25-plus years.

This study must remark it is unfortunate the ICTY legal professionals never indicted anyone for speech atrocity crimes or that the OTP did not question further the appropriation of all of B&H that is non-Serb or non-Croat by the Serb(ian) and Croat(ian) nationalists wherever it cropped up during trials. This oversight and mere allowing of facts to speak for themselves made Bosnian Muslims remain invisible and gave the impression ethnic crimes against them were committed in a vacuum, rather than in a continuum.

Direct consequences of these failures and oversights are felt throughout the region since the sophistry advanced by the in-court nationalists remained unchallenged and nationalist arguments only resumed and continue to persist to this day. In the best traditions of Munchausen's trilemma, the countries of the former Yugoslavia still defend their wartime choices, centering them around arguments that either the reason to commit the crimes was predicated on a series of sub-reasons leading to an infinite regression, or, that those reasons were tracked back to arbitrary axiomatic statements, or, that the reasons were circular, i.e. crimes were committed because they were committed.

Indirect consequences are felt the most in B&H: the 1992-1995 war is given two short paragraphs in the history books in B&H and remains a topic for manipulation in the history books taught in the Republic of Serbia and the Republic of Croatia. Obviously, the entire region is devoid of all attempts at critical analysis or critical thinking.

The oversight in prosecution and arguing of facts by legal professionals whose job is to anticipate situations and events and to argue for a living is unacceptable. Given that the IMT and IMTFE trials left the ICTY with a legacy that celebrating war criminals was unacceptable, given that there was a precedent in prosecution of speech atrocity crimes, the ICTY could be said to have set back the realm of international criminal justice in that regard. The post-2019 efforts to issue gag orders against the released war criminals, specifically banning them from speaking in public, made by the ICTY are commendable, but they are a little bit too little and came a little bit too late.

As to the second line of communication with the judicial organization, the working institution towards the parties to the proceedings, it is clear from Chapter 2 that the ICTY CLSS management did very little, if anything at all, to inform the language laws at the ICTY despite the existing legal facets enabling them to do so.

Normative procedural due process language-related rights, obligations, and requirements in the ICTY laws, language-related case law, and procedural linguistic equality of arms between the ICTY prosecution and defense were grossly misinformed as detailed throughout the study.

A direct consequence of the CLSS's failure to inform the language laws was that communication between the prosecution and defense was effected which led to the scarce to non-existent procedural linguistic equality of arms between the two.

Failing to inform on the length of documents which could be reasonably handled by the parties to the proceedings, the ICTY Registry CLSS added on to the length of already lengthy trials, infringing not only on the rights of defendants and their defense attorneys, but also making a significant impact on the length of trials making it impossible for the victims to get expeditious justice and realize their rights in domestic jurisdictions.

Indirect consequences of this failure are felt throughout the region.

All these normative procedural language inequalities were sold to the region by defendants and their defense teams as a proof that defendants are *agnus dei* of the local authorities who surrendered them and/or the international community that tried them at the ICTY so nationalist arguments got validation from the public, resumed uninterrupted, and continue to persist to this day.

For victims, the end of protracted trials meant that, on hearing the ICTY judgments, if still alive, they could declare that justice had been served. And that was about that: the fact that the ICTY may have recognized them as a testifying victim had no bearing on their status in their home country whatsoever. If a woman was raped in 1992 and with a child, by the end of the trial the child might have already been a young adult.

As to the third line of communication with the judicial organization, the working institution towards language services providers, it is clear from Chapter 3 that the ICTY CLSS management did very little, if anything at all, to set recruitment, professional criteria and standards, and training for any ICTY language professionals. It remains entirely unclear why no one was sent from the UN DGACM to advise on criteria and standards and proper delivery of multilingual language services as part of UN mobility policies.

Direct consequences of these failures are numerous and dangerous.

The ICTY CLSS management did not set any clear criteria and standards for translation and interpreting at international criminal tribunals adjudicating on ethnic crimes. It must be said that this would not be a guide on whether to spell "/sic/" or "*sic*." It is a document or a series of documents promoting one's own profession; arrangements behind mingling between language professionals and clients of different ethnicities; security-related arrangements behind language professionals' access to documents of the other side; practical arrangements behind not putting language professionals in the arena of conflict with the other parties to the proceedings, etc.

The ICTY CLSS management allowed for segmentation of language services where almost every unit at the ICTY had its own language services provider with limited, if any, links to the ICTY. This category of language professionals, Language Assistants, were not paid as proper language professionals, in violation of ICSC laws, and their clients made them provide the so-called (3+1)+ comprising a host of language and non-language related services. It seems like the whole ICTY got behind ignoring the existence of Language Assistants as they were not covered in any laws, including security-related ones.

The ICTY laws did not safeguard against language professionals of the attacking ethnicity freely engaging with victims and witnesses of the attacked ethnicity at all levels of the investigative and judicial process. The ICTY laws allowed for language professionals of the attacking ethnicity a free access to documents and information considered sensitive, classified, or secret in their countries of origin.

Indirect consequences of these failures are equally dangerous because the ICTY Registry CLSS management's failures and shortcomings strike against the core status of UN language professionals.

The UN language staff worked assiduously since the creation of UN to garner and keep professional respect and equal pay to other professionals in the Organization. The ICTY Registry CLSS management allowed, promoted, and even depended on Language Assistants who provided the (3+1)+ language and non-language services at different pay scales to their CLSS colleagues. This has shown the ICTY that language staff is expendable, that their output can be achieved by anyone, and that their status is fluid.

The ICTY Registry CLSS management set back UN language professionals to the beginnings of the Organization. This approach to language professionals needs to be condemned by the ICSC, the AITC, the AIIC, and recipients of language professionals' product throughout the Organization until Language Assistants are no longer found in the UN System as a whole.

As to the fourth line of communication with the judicial organization, the working institution towards the situation country, it was clear from Chapter 4 that the CLSS did very little to fulfill its legal obligations under ICTY RPE 66(A)(i) and 66(A)(ii) to deliver specific documents in translation or their legal obligation under ICTY-S Article 21(4)(b) to deliver those documents in time to enable proper defense.

The ICTY Registry CLSS has made a strong national, ethnic, and political identity statement against B&H, Croatia, and Kosovo and its peoples as they failed to provide proper language or language variant interpreting services to defendants during initial appearance, to the region during the reading of verdicts, or to the testifying B/C/S victims and witnesses from the region.

As a matter of fact, by failing to properly punish the misconduct in their own ranks, the ICTY Registry CLSS sent very unflattering messages to the region about respect for the bravery of the parties' testifying clients and might have precluded other insiders from stepping forward, thereby causing the UN reputational damage and embarrassment.

The ICTY Registry B/C/S transcript project from 2008 literally provided too little and came too late in all its politically incorrect glory thus contributing to the distortion of the ICTY's historical record and the wealth of knowledge.

Take away the shelling, the concentration camps, and the Serbs moving from one end of the country to another waiting hand and foot on megalomaniac war criminals, the countries of the former Yugoslavia are exactly where they were in the 1990s. The war criminals who served their sentences are regular guests on local TV political, historical, and reality shows, they themselves normalized in the eyes of the viewers and their crimes and victims ignored like a fart in an overcrowded ex-Yugoslav elevator. Sadly, even 150 years after, fra Knežević could send the same message "to our brothers residing and living in B&H for many centuries, still wishing [they] were Serbs or Croats." The self-hate reigns supreme in B&H where everyone would rather be anything else than a B&H citizen.

The former Yugoslavian audiences had a job to read and watch the ICTY trials, but very little was provided to them by the ICTY Registry CLSS in their language and in watch- and read-friendly ways, so they could not have used the ICTY's legal truths established by the parties to the proceedings and their clients and adjudicated by the judges to start eliminating the causes that led to the situation in the first place, to start gaining critical perspectives on the issues discussed, and to start neutralizing all causes perpetuating the situation in the present.

My examinations based on the lines of communication defining the service delivery have established that the ICTY was an institution that barely succeeded in communicating with any of its French- or B/C/S-speaking audiences through its language services, CLSS, despite its mission to give victims voice and many legal facets that enabled the CLSS to provide service delivery.

The ICTY Registry CLSS was set for failure from the start because its management was a failure. And CLSS management was a failure because *not* planning for staff recruitment, languages and linguistic variants concerns, criteria and standards, and staff training *is* planning to fail. The ethnicity-based recruitment was practiced by the ICTY Registry CLSS at the international criminal tribunal adjudicating on ethnic crimes but it had a major sinister flaw. Whereas it could be true that good professionals know other good professionals, once they start recommending other good professionals from a particular country and with a particular ethnicity that amounts to brazen and rampant ethnic discrimination, right under the nose of a variety of legal professionals who had all got together to adjudicate on ethnically motivated crimes for which language was one of the indices.

Indeed, war atrocities on the one side, but it seems that the real problems for the situation countries start once the UN administration gets involved. For all these reasons, all those who find themselves in the future dealing with the UN Administration or the Administration of the contemporary international criminal tribunals, as they are, in any way, must be warned: *timeo, timeo Danaos et dona ferentes*.

APPENDICES

Appendix 1. The pre-trial, final, and appeal briefs: the word/page count and status of translation into B/C/S and French

Trial	Pre-trial, final and appeals brief	Date	Length in pages and/or words	B/C/S	FRE
Đorđević	Public Redacted Final Trial Brief and Corrigendum (Part 1)	20/12/2011	201 p.	-	-
Đorđević	Public Redacted Final Trial Brief and Corrigendum (Part 2)	20/12/2011	164 p.	-	-
Đorđević	Appeal Brief - Redacted Version	15/08/2011	44,330 w.	-	-
Galić[335]	Prosecution pre-trial brief	23/10/2001	53,083 w.	-	-
Gotovina et al[336]	Pre-trial brief of General Ante Gotovina	5/04/2007	53 p. 14,807 w.	-	-
Gotovina et al	Mladen Markac's pre-trial brief	5/04/2007	37 p. 11,568 w.	-	-
Gotovina et al	Pre-trial brief of Ivan Cermak	5/04/2007	27 p. 6,754 w.	-	-
Gotovina et al	Prosecution pre-trial brief	23/03/2007	64 p. 14,739 w.	-	-

[335] ICTY, Cases, *Galić*: https://bit.ly/34C1esd.
[336] ICTY, Cases, *Gotovina et al.*: https://bit.ly/2XCSyAc.

Trial	Pre-trial, final and appeals brief	Date	Length in pages and/or words	B/C/S	FRE
Gotovina et al	Ante Gotovina's supplemental brief pursuant to the oral order of the Appeals Chamber of 14 May 2012	17/05/2012	9 p. 2,722 w.	-	-
Gotovina et al	Ivan Čermak's Public Redacted Final Brief	13/09/2010	357 p. 87,094 w.	-	-
Gotovina et al	Prosecution's public redacted Final Trial Brief	2/08/2010	408 p. 88,783 w	-	-
Gotovina et al	Gotovina Defence Final Trial Brief	27/07/2010	315 p. 86,164 w	-	-
Gotovina et al	Mladen Markac's public redacted Appeal Brief	5/10/2011	119 p. 38,574 w.	-	-
Gotovina et al	Appellant's Brief of Ante Gotovina (Public Redacted)	2/08/2011	143 p. 39,044 w	-	-
Hadžić	Defence pre-trial brief	31/07/2012	13 p. 3,768 w	-	-
Hadžić	Prosecution's redacted pre-trial brief	3/07/2012	156 p.	-	-
Lukić	Prosecution's Pre-Trial Brief Pursuant to Rule 65 ter (E) (I)	14/03/2008	44 p. 14,099 w.	-	-
Lukić	Milan Lukić's final trial brief and submissions	13/05/2009	151 p. 50,607 w.	-	-
Lukić	Prosecution Final Trial Brief	12/05/2009	213 p. 59,551 w.	-	-
Lukić	Sredoje Lukić's Defence Final Brief	12/05/2009	198 p. 59,988 w.	-	-
Lukić	Redacted Appeal Brief - Milan Lukic	17/03/2010	113 p. 29,891 w.	-	-
Lukić	Appeal Brief on behalf of Sredoje Lukic	2/11/2009	115 p. 29,941 w.	-	-

Trial	Pre-trial, final and appeals brief	Date	Length in pages and/or words	B/C/S	FRE
Lukić	Prosecution Appeal Brief	2/11/2009	10 p. 1,721 w.	-	-
Milošević, D.[337]	Dragomir Milosevic - Defence Appeal Brief	14/08/2008	94 p. 26,657 w.	-	-
Perišić[338]	Public redacted version of the Appeal brief of Momčilo Perišić	10/04/2012	135 p. 37,810 w.	-	-
Popović et al	Pre-Trial Brief - Milan Gvero	12/07/2006	25 p.	-	-
Popović et al	Pre-Trial Brief - Vinko Pandurević	12/07/2006	11 p. 2,496 w.	-	-
Popović et al	Pre-Trial Brief - Drago Nikolić	12/07/2006	16 p. 5,119 w.	-	-
Popović et al	Pre-Trial Brief - Vujadin Popović	12/07/2006	22 p.	-	-
Popović et al	Public redacted version of the Final Trial Brief - Drago Nikolić	30/07/2010	357 p.	-	-
Popović et al	Final Brief - Milan Gvero	30/07/2010	285 p.	-	-
Popović et al	Defendant, Ljubisa Beara's notice of filing a public redacted version of the Beara Final Trial Brief	28/07/2010	295 p.	-	-
Popović et al	Public redacted version of Vujadin Popovic's Final Brief	28/07/2010	291 p. 93,000 w.	-	-
Popović et al	Pandurevic notice of filing a public redacted version of the Pandurevic final trial brief	26/07/2010	264 p.	-	-
Popović et al	Prosecution's notice of filing a public redacted version of the prosecution Final Trial Brief	14/07/2010	850 p.	-	-

337 ICTY, Cases, *Dragomir Milošević*: https://bit.ly/3elDNI5.
338 ICTY, Cases, *Perišić*: https://bit.ly/3ckOLvD.

Trial	Pre-trial, final and appeals brief	Date	Length in pages and/or words	B/C/S	FRE
Popović et al	Ljubomir Borovcanin - Public and Corrected Final Trial Brief	23/04/2010	310 p.	-	-
Popović et al	Public redacted version of Appeal Brief on behalf of Milan Gvero against the trial judgment of 10/06/e 2010	19/02/2013	94 p.	-	-
Popović et al	Prosecution Appeal Brief (Grounds Against Milan Gvero)	18/02/2013	27 p. 6,650 w.	-	-
Popović et al	Appellant's brief on behalf of Drago Nikolić	3/08/2011	116 p. 30,281 w.	-	-
Popović et al	Public redacted version of brief in reply on behalf of Drago Nikolić	18/07/2011	53 p. 7,831 w	-	-
Popović et al	Appellant Ljubiša Beara's notice of reclassification and re-filing of the public redacted version of Appeal Brief	16/06/2011	128 p. 39,229 w.	-	-
Prlić et al[339]	Redacted Final Trial Brief	1/04/2011	614 p.	-	-
Prlić et al	Berislav Pušić's Final Brief (Public Redacted Version)	31/03/2011	150 p. 39,133 w.	-	-
Prlić et al	Bruno Stojić's redacted final trial brief	31/03/2011	212 p.	-	-
Prlić et al	Slobodan Praljak's Redacted Final Trial Brief	31/03/2011	187 p.	-	-
Prlić et al	Petković defence final brief	31/03/2011	260 p.	-	-
Prlić et al	Jadranko Prlić's Final Brief	29/03/2011	197 p.	-	-
Prlić et al	Valentin Ćorić's Final Trial Brief	28/03/2011	211 p.	-	-
Stanišić & Župljanin	Pre-trial brief of the defence of Mico Stanisic	29/06/2009	17 p.	-	-
Stanišić & Župljanin	Defence pre-trial brief on behalf of Mr. Stojan Župljanin pursuant to rule 65ter (f)	29/06/2009	23 p. 10,340 w.	-	-
Stanišić & Župljanin	Prosecutor's Pre-trial brief	1/12/2006	57 p.	-	-
Stanišić & Župljanin	Prosecution Final Trial Brief - part 3	12/07/2012	65 p.	-	-

339 ICTY, Cases, *Prlić et al.*: https://bit.ly/2wFoMQm.

Trial	Pre-trial, final and appeals brief	Date	Length in pages and/or words	B/C/S	FRE
Stanišić & Župljanin	Prosecution Final Trial Brief - part 1	12/07/2012	170 p.	-	-
Stanišić & Župljanin	Prosecution Final Trial Brief - part 2	12/07/2012	172 p.	-	-
Stanišić & Župljanin	Prosecution Final Trial Brief - part 5	12/07/2012	34 p.	-	-
Stanišić & Župljanin	Prosecution Final Trial Brief - part 4	12/07/2012	34 p.	-	-
Stanišić & Župljanin	Defence Final Trial Brief (Redacted) - Stojan Župljanin	12/07/2012	168 p. 58,893 w.	-	-
Stanišić & Župljanin	Stojan Župljanin's Appeal Brief	20/04/2016	150 p. 36,725 w.	-	-
Stanišić & Župljanin	Appellant's Brief on Behalf of Mićo Stanišić	19/08/2013	157 p. 39,423 w.	-	-
Stanišić & Župljanin	Prosecution Appeal Brief	19/08/2013	36 p. 10,058 w.	-	-
Strugar[340]	Prosecutor's pre-trial brief pursuant to rule 65ter (E) (i)	27/08/2003	50 p.	-	-
Šainović et al	Prosecution Public Redacted Final Trial Brief and Corrigendum	28/07/2008	388 p. 98,819 w.	-	-
Šainović et al	Prosecution's pre-trial brief	10/05/2006	137 p. 54,481 w.	-	-
Šainović et al	Vladimir Lazarevic's Final Trial Brief	29/07/2008	232 p. 69,402 w.	-	-
Šainović et al	Nikola Šainović- Public redacted version of "Defence Brief in reply"	21/07/2010	38 p. 11,964 w.	-	-
Šainović et al	General Ojdanić's Amended Appeal Brief	11/12/2009	308 p. 47,927 w.	-	-
Šainović et al	Prosecution's consolidated reply brief	17/11/2009	39 p. 9,151 w.	-	-

[340] ICTY, Cases, *Strugar*: https://bit.ly/2xy7zIZ.

Trial	Pre-trial, final and appeals brief	Date	Length in pages and/or words	B/C/S	FRE
Šainović et al	Sreten Lukic - Defense Appelant's Brief Refiled	7/10/2009	199 p. 59,998 w.	-	-
Šainović et al	General Pavković's submission of his amended Appeal Brief	30/09/2009	172 p. 42,552 w.	-	-
Šainović et al	Ojdanic's Appeal Brief	23/09/2009	143 p. 44,916 w.	-	-
Šainović et al	Pavkovic's Appeal Brief	23/09/2009	166 p. 41,667 w.	-	-
Šainović et al	Sainovic Defence Appeal Brief	23/09/2009	144 p. 44,857 w.	-	-
Šainović et al	Prosecution Appeal Brief	21/08/2009	89 p. 22,097 w.	-	-
Tolimir	Zdravko Tolimir's submission with a pre-trial brief pursuant to rule 65 ter (f) and notification of the defence of alibi in respect of some charges	30/09/2009	192 p. 55,879 w.	-	-
Tolimir	Prosecution filing of public version of Pre-trial Brief	29/09/2009	132 p. 55,708 w.	+	-
Tolimir	Prosecution Public Redacted Final Trial Brief	28//11/2012	323 p.	+	-
Tolimir	Defence Final Trial Brief	1/10/2012	149 p.	+	-
Tolimir	Public Redacted Version of the Consolidated Appeal Brief	28/02/2014	131 p. 44,997 w.	-	-

Appendix 2. Decisions on requests for time and/or word extension to submit the pre-trial, final, and appeal briefs

Trial	Language-related request	Date	+/-
Blagojević & Jokić[341]	Decision on Accused Blagojevic's Request for Extension of Time to File Defence Pre-trial Brief	8/01/2003	-
Blagojević & Jokić	Decision on Accused Dragan Jokic's Request for Extension of Time to File Defence Pre-trial Brief	8/09/2003	-
Blagojević & Jokić	Decision on Vidoje Blagojevic's Motion for Extension of Time in Which to File his Notice of Appeal and on Dragan Jokic's Motion for Extension of Time in Which to File his Appeal Brief	14/04/2005	+
Blagojević & Jokić	Decision on Blagojevic's and Jokic's Motions for Extension of Time to File Their Appeal Brief	21/07/2005	+
Blagojević & Jokić	Decision on Prosecution's Motion to Extend Word Limit of Consolidated Response Brief	6/12/2005	-
Blaškić[342]	Decision on Appellant's Motion to Extend Deadline for Filing Appellant's Brief and Request for Authorization to Exceed the Page Limit for Appellant's Brief	7/11/2001	+
Blaškić	Decision on Prosecution's Request for an Extension of Time and for Authorisation to Exceed the Page Limit for its Response to the Appellant's Brief	29/01/2002	+
Blaškić	Decision on Appellant's Application for Extension of Page Limits for Supplementary Brief on Appeal	24/11/2003	+
Boškoski & Tarčulovski[343]	Decision on joint defence motion for extension of word-limit for final trial brief	23/04/2008	+/-
Boškoski & Tarčulovski	Decision on johan Tarčulovski's motion for extension of time to file appeal brief	16/10/2008	-
Boškoski & Tarčulovski	Decision on Johan Tarčulovski's second motion for extention of time to file appeal brief	22/10/2008	+

341 ICTY, Cases, *Blagojević & Jokić*: https://bit.ly/2xvikfd.
342 ICTY, Cases, *Blaškić*: https://bit.ly/34HeFqL.
343 ICTY, Cases, *Boškoski & Tarčulovski*: https://bit.ly/2Katjxa.

Trial	**Language-related request**	**Date**	**+/-**
Boškoski & Tarčulovski	Decision on Tarčulovski's urgent motion for extension of time to file his reply brief	16/04/2009	-
Brđanin	Decision on Prosecution's Request for Variation of Page Limit on Final Brief	30/03/2004	+
Brđanin	Further Decision on Variation of Page Limit on Final Brief	31/03/2004	+
Brđanin	Decision on Appellant's Motion for Extension of Time to File a Consolidated Brief and for Enlargement of Page Limit	22/06/2005	+
Brđanin	Decision on Motion for Extension of Time for the Filing of Prosecution Response Brief	20/07/2005	+
Delić	Decision on the Prosecution motion to exceed word limits imposed by the Practice Direction On The Length Of Briefs And Motions	20/09/2006	+
Delić	Decision on the prosecution motion to exceed word limits imposed by the Practice Direction On The Length Of Briefs And Motions	26/09/1996	+
Delić	Decision on urgent defence motion to exceed word limit for final trial brief	8/05/2008	+
Galić	Decision on "Urgent Prosecution Motion for an Order Requiring the Appellant to Re-file his Appeal Brief and Request for Leave to Exceed Word-limit for Motion"	2/09/t 2004	+/-
Galić	Decision on Defence's Request for Leave to Exceed Page Limit in Defence's Appellant's Brief	19/05/2004	-
Hadžić	Decision on prosecution motion for extension of word limit for pre-trial brief	26/06/2012	+
Hadžihasanović & Kubura[344]	Decision on Prosecution's Application Seeking Authorization to Exceed the Page Limits of the Pre-trial Brief	2/10/2003	+
Kordić & Čerkez	Decision on Second Motions to extend Time for filing Appellant's Briefs	2/07/2001	-
Kordić & Čerkez	Decision Authorising Reply Brief to Exceed the Limit Imposed by the Practice Direction on the Length of Briefs and Motions	26/09/2001	+
Kordić & Čerkez	Decision authorising Respondent's Brief to exceed the Limit impose by the Practice Direction on the Length of Briefs and Motions and granting an Extension of Time to file Brief	30/08/2001	+
Kordić & Čerkez	Decision authorising Appellant's Briefs to exceed the Limit imposed by the Practice Direction on the Length of Briefs and Motions	29/08/2001	+

344 ICTY, Cases, *Hadžihasanović & Kubura*: https://bit.ly/2xn79Fz.

Trial	Language-related request	Date	+/-
Kordić & Čerkez	Decision on Motions to extend Time for filing Appellant's Briefs	11/05/2001	+
Kovačević[345]	Decision on Prosection's Motion for Variation of length of Pre-trial Brief	14/11/2001	-
Krajišnik	Decision on request by Momcilo Krajisnik for extension of time to comply with appeal brief word limit	7/01/2008	+
Krajišnik	Order to comply with appeal brief word limit	3/12/2007	+
Krajišnik	Order on amicus curiaes motions regarding word limits and ordering of his appeal brief	31/07/2007	+
Krajišnik	Decision on Prosecution's Motion for Extension of Limit of Length of Pre-Trial Brief	27/07/2001	+
Kunarac et al[346]	Decision on Prosecution Request for Extension of time, Notice of filing Respondent briefs over 100 pages and, if necessary Motion to Exceed page limit of Prosecution's response briefs	3/09/t 2001	+
Kvočka et al	Decision on Appellant Request for Variant of length of Appellant's Brief	22/03/2002	+
Limaj et al	Decision on Defence's Applications for Extension of Time to File Pre-trial Briefs and Order for Filing of Expert Reports and Notice under Rule 94 bis	7/05/2004	+
Limaj et al	Decision on "Motion on Behalf of Haradin Bala to Join 'Defence Application for Further Extension of Time to File Response to Prosecution Brief on Appeal' Filed on 25 April 2006"	27/04/2006	-
Limaj et al	Decision On Defence Application For Further Extension Of Time To File Response To Prosecution Brief On Appeal	26/04/2006	-
Lukić Milan & Lukić Sredoje	Decision on Milan Lukic's motion seeking extension of time to file appeal brief and motion for stay of proceedings	30/10/2009	+/-
Lukić Milan & Lukić Sredoje	Decision on Milan Lukic's motion for leave to file an amended notice of Appeal and for an extension of time for filing his Appeal brief'	5/06/2007	+/-
Martić[347]	Decision on Motion for Extension of Time for Filing the Respondent's brief	31/10/2007	+/-

345 ICTY, Cases, *Kovačević*: https://bit.ly/2yiLrSU.
346 ICTY, Cases, *Kunarac et al.*: https://bit.ly/2V7DeKi.
347 ICTY, Cases, *Martić*: https://bit.ly/2Vwd2bq.

Trial	Language-related request	Date	+/-
Martić	Decision on Prosecution's Motion for Leave to File Pre-trial Brief of Sixty Pages	5/05/2004	-
Milošević, D.	Decision on defence motion for extension of time to file appellate brief and to increase the word limit	11/08/2008	-
Milošević, S.	Decision on Prosecution's Motion for Extension of limit of length of Pre-Trial brief	17/04/2002	+
Mucić et al	Order relating to Appeal Brief filed on behalf of Zejnil Delalic	26/05/2000	+
Naletilić & Martinović[348]	Decision on Motion for an Extension to submit the Pre-trial Brief	21/11/2000	+
Naletilić & Martinović	Decision on the Prosecution Request to Vary Lenght of Final Trial Brief	26/09/2002	+/-
Naletilić & Martinović	Decision on Martinovic Motion for Extension of Time for Filing the Respondent's Brief and on Naletilic Motion for Enlargement of Time for Filing Rule 115 Motion, Appeals Brief, and Response to Prosecutor's Appeal Brief	18/08/2003	+/-
Nikolić, M.[349]	Decision on Appelant's Request to Withdraw Previous Motions to Revise Appelant's Brief and to Amend Notice of Appeal	19/07/2005	+
Orić[350]	Order on Defence Motion for Variation of the Word Limit for Final Trial Brief	9/03/2006	+
Perišić	Decision on counsel's request to exceed word limit for pre-trial brief	28/03/2007	+
Perišić	Decision on Momcilo Perisićs motion for leave to exceed the word limit for the appeal brief	30/01/2012	+
Prlić et al	Decision on Defence Motions to extend time and/or exceed word limits for Appeal Briefs and Prosecution motion for extension of time to file respondent's Briefs	22/08/2014	+/-
Prlić et al	Decision on requests for extension of word limit for respondent's briefs and reply briefs and for time limit for reply briefs	9/04/2015	-
Prlić et al	Decision on Motions for extension of time to file Appeal Briefs and for authorization to exceed word limit	22/08/2013	+/-

348 ICTY, Cases, *Naletilić & Martinović*: https://bit.ly/2yXyqyt.
349 ICTY, Cases, *Nikolić*: https://bit.ly/3chElNl.
350 ICTY, Cases, *Orić*: https://bit.ly/3aejWro.

Trial	**Language-related request**	**Date**	**+/-**
Prlić et al	Order Granting the Defence Counsel for the Accused Valentin Coric Leave to Exceed the Number of Words in the Pre-Trial Brief	22/02/2006	+
Šainović et al	Decision on defence requests for extension of time and word limits to file reply briefs	20/01/2010	+/-
Simić et al	Decision on Motion of Blagoje Simic for Extension of Time to File Appellate Brief and Request for Expedited Decision	19/01/2004	+
Stakić[351]	Decision on Prosecution Motion for Extension of Time to File Reply Brief and for Extension of Pages	12/01/2004	+
Stakić	Decision on Second Motion for Extension of Time to File Appellant's Brief	19/12/2003	+
Stakić	Order on Prosecution's Motion for Reconsideration of prior Motion for Variation of length of Pre-trial Brief	15/01/2002	+
Stakić	Decision on Prosecution's Urgent Motion Regarding Defects in Milomir Stakic's Brief on Appeal	23/02/2004	+
Stanišić & Župljanin	Decision denying prosecution motion for extension of word limit for final trial brief	11/05/2012	-
Stanišić & Župljanin	Decision denying Prosecution motion for extension of word limit for final trial brief	1/05/2012	-
Stanišić & Župljanin	Decision denying Stanišić defence motion for extension of word limit for final Trial Brief	27/04/2012	-
Stanišić & Župljanin	Decision on denying Župljanin defence motion for extension of word limit for Final Brief	25/04/2012	-
Stanišić & Župljanin	Decision granting in part prosecution's motion for extension of time to file the final trial brief and order on final trial briefs and closing arguments	25/04/2012	+/-
Stanišić & Župljanin	Decision on Mico Stanisic's motion seeking reconsideration of decision on variation of time and word limits to file appellant's brief	21/06/2013	-
Stanišić & Župljanin	Decision on Mico Stanisic's and Stojan Zupljanin's motions seeking variation of time and word limits to file appeal briefs	4/06/2013	+/-

[351] ICTY, Cases, *Stakić*: https://bit.ly/3ciqMNG.

Trial	Language-related request	Date	+/-
Stanišić & Župljanin	Decision on Mico Stanisic's motion seeking reconsideration of decision on variation of time and word limits to file appellant's brief	21/06/2013	-
Stanišić & Župljanin	Decision on Mico Stanisic's and Stojan Zupljanin's motions seeking variation of time and word limits to file appeal briefs	4/06/2013	+/-
Strugar	Decision on "Defence request for variation of time limit to file response to prosecution's appeal brief"	13/06/2005	-
Tolimir	Decision on the prosecution request for extension of time to file public redacted version of the prosecution Final Brief	10/10/2012	+/-
Tolimir	Decision on Tolimir's motion for extension of time for filing amendments to the brief in reply	20/02/2014	+
Tolimir	Decision on Tolimir's request for extension of time for filing an appellant's brief	17/06/2013	+
Tolimir	Decision on motion for setting a time limit for filing an appellant's brief and for an extension of word limit	17/05/2013	+
Tolimir	Decision on Tolimir's request for a time limit to amend his notice of appeal and his Appeal brief	9/07/2013	+/-
Tolimir	Decision on motion for setting a time limit for filing an appellant's brief and for an extension of word limit	17/05/2013	+/-
Tolimir	Decision on prosecution's motion for variation of the word limit for its final trial brief	12/01/2012	+/-
Tolimir	Order regarding response to request of the prosecution relating to the length of the pre-trial brief	2/03/2009	+

Appendix 3. Ethnicity of defendants vs. language of interpreters during the initial appearance of defendants

Accused	Ethnicity of the accused	Date of initial appearance	Duration of proceedings	Interpreters language
Tihomir Blaškić	Bosnian Croat	3/04/1996	00:58:22	Croatian (*ijekavian*)
Slavko Dokmanović	Croatian Serb	4/07/1997	00:24:08	Serbian (*ekavian*)
Milan Kovačević	Bosnian Serb	30/07/1997	00:36:38	Croatian (*ijekavian*) Serbian (*ekavian*)
Dario Kordić	Bosnian Croat	8/10/1997	01:09:23	Croatian (*ijekavian*) Serbian (*ekavian*)
Zoran Kupreškić	Bosnian Croat	8/10/1997	01:09:23	Croatian (*ijekavian*) Serbian (*ekavian*)
Anto Furundžija[352]	Bosnian Croat	19/12/1997	00:22:56	Croatian (*ijekavian*) Serbian (*ekavian*)
Goran Jelisić[353]	Bosnian Serb	26/01/1998	01:34:39	Croatian (*ijekavian*) Croatian (*ijekavian*)
Miroslav Tadić (see *Simić et al*)	Bosnian Serb	17/02/1998	00:59:22	Croatian (*ijekavian*) Croatian (*ijekavian*)
Milan Simić (see *Simić et al*)	Bosnian Serb	17/02/1998	00:45:15	Croatian (*ijekavian*) Croatian (*ijekavian*)
Simo Zarić (see *Simić et al*)	Bosnian Serb	26/02/1998	00:35:42	Croatian (*ijekavian*) Croatian (*ijekavian*)
Dragoljub Kunarac	Bosnian Serb	9/03/1998	00:16:52	Serbian (*ekavian*)
Stevan Todorović[354]	Bosnian Serb	30/09/1998	00:52:34	Croatian (*ijekavian*) Croatian (*ijekavian*)

352 ICTY, Cases, *Furundžija*: https://bit.ly/2Vti6gx.
353 ICTY, Cases, *Jelisić*: https://bit.ly/2xzee5R.
354 ICTY, Cases, *Todorović*: https://bit.ly/3ckVhCw.

Accused	Ethnicity of the accused	Date of initial appearance	Duration of proceedings	Interpreters language
Dragan Kolundžija (see *Sikirica et al*)	Bosnian Serb	14/06/1999	00:15:58	Croatian (*ijekavian*) Croatian (*ijekavian*)
Radoslav Brđanin	Bosnian Serb	12/07/1999	00:42:22	Serbian (*ekavian*) Croatian (*ijekavian*)
Vinko Martinović	Bosnian Croat	12/08/1999	00:42:22	Bosnian (*ijekavian*) Serbian (*ekavian*)
Damir Došen (see *Sikirica et al*)	Bosnian Croat	8/11/1999	00:14:46	Bosnian (*ijekavian*)
Stanislav Galić	Bosnian Serb	29/12/1999	00:30:31	Serbian (*ekavian*) Croatian (*ijekavian*)
Mitar Vasiljević	Bosnian Serb	28/01/2000	00:10:39	Serbian (*ekavian*)
Dragoljub Prcać (see *Kvočka et al*)	Bosnian Serb	10/03/2000	00:41:41	Croatian (*ijekavian*) Serbian (*ekavian*)
Mladen Naletelić	Bosnian Croat	24/03/2000	01:16:37	Croatian (*ijekavian*) Serbian (*ekavian*)
Momčilo Krajišnik	Bosnian Serb	7/04/2000	00:27:24	Bosnian (*ijekavian*) Serbian (*ekavian*)
Dragan Nikolić	Bosnian Serb	24/04/2000	00:07:31	Serbian (*ekavian*)
Duško Sikirica[355]	Bosnian Serb	7/07/2000	00:24:45	Serbian (*ekavian*)
Biljana Plavšić[356]	Bosnian Serb	11/01/2001	00:18:45	Serbian (*ekavian*)
Blagoje Simić	Bosnian Serb	15/03/2001	00:16:50	Serbian (*ekavian*) Serbian (*ekavian*)
Milomir Stakić	Bosnian Serb	28/03/2001	00:38:02	Croatian (*ijekavian*) Croatian (*ijekavian*)
Dragan Obrenović[357]	Bosnian Serb	18/04/2001	00:10:06	Croatian (*ijekavian*)

[355] ICTY, Cases, *Sikirica et al.*: https://bit.ly/2K84Cl6.
[356] ICTY, Cases, *Plavšić*: https://bit.ly/2yiieaG.

Accused	Ethnicity of the accused	Date of initial appearance	Duration of proceedings	Interpreters language
Slobodan Milošević	Serbian Serb	3/07/2001	00:09:25	Serbian (*ekavian*)
Enver Hadžihasanović Mehmed Alagić Amir Kubura	Bosnian Muslim Bosnian Muslim Bosnian Muslim	9/08/2001	00:21:26	Bosnian (*ijekavian*) Serbian (*ekavian*)
Vidoje Blagojević	Bosnian Serb	16/08/2001	00:10:08	Bosnian (*ijekavian*)
Dragan Jokić	Bosnian Serb	21/08/2001	00:09:48	Serbian (*ekavian*)
Sefer Halilović	Bosnian Muslim	27/09/2001	00:11:06	Bosnian (*ijekavian*)
Pavle Strugar	Serbian Serb	25/10/2001	01:08:37	Croatian (*ijekavian*) Serbian (*ekavian*)
Slobodan Milošević	Serbian Serb	29/10/2001	02:45:22	Croatian (*ijekavian*) Serbian (*ekavian*)
Miodrag Jokić[358]	Serbian Serb	14/11/2001	00:45:40	Croatian (*ijekavian*) Serbian (*ekavian*)
Nenad Banović Predrag Banović[359]	Bosnian Serb Bosnian Serb	16/11/2001	00:20:50	Croatian (*ijekavian*)
Slobodan Milošević	Serbian Serb	11/12/2001	02:00:25	Croatian (*ijekavian*) Bosnian (*ijekavian*)
Momir Nikolić[360]	Bosnian Serb	3/04/2002	01:16:07	Croatian (*ijekavian*) Serbian (*ekavian*)
Dragoljub Ojdanić (see *Šainović et al*)	Serbian Serb	26/04/2002	00:10:10	Croatian (*ijekavian*)
Nikola Šainović	Serbian Serb	3/05/2002	00:10:58	Croatian (*ijekavian*)
Mile Mrkšić[361]	Serbian Serb	16/05/2002	00:18:21	Croatian (*ijekavian*)

357 ICTY, Cases, *Obrenović*: https://bit.ly/3bfQt1e.
358 ICTY, Cases, *Jokić*: https://bit.ly/3erVyFU.
359 ICTY, Cases, *Nenad Banović and Predrag Banović*: https://bit.ly/2VvW1Or.
360 ICTY, Cases, *Nikolić, M.*: https://bit.ly/2VcaKPH.

Accused	Ethnicity of the accused	Date of initial appearance	Duration of proceedings	Interpreters language
Milan Martić	Croatian Serb	21/05/2002	00:35:57	Croatian (*ijekavian*)
Darko Mrđa[362]	Bosnian Serb	17/06/2002	00:26:17[363]	Serbian (*ekavian*)
Ranko Češić[364]	Bosnian Serb	20/06/2002	00:17:42	Bosnian (*ijekavian*) Serbian (*ekavian*)
Miroslav Deronjić[365]	Bosnian Serb	10/07/2002	00:43:58	Serbian (*ekavian*) Serbian (*ekavian*)
Vojislav Šešelj	Bosnian Serb	26/02/2003	02:24:54	Bosnian (*ijekavian*) Croatian (*ijekavian*)
Vojislav Šešelj	Bosnian Serb	25/03/2003	01:00:50	Serbian (*ekavian*) Croatian (*ijekavian*)
Naser Orić	Bosnian Muslim	15/04/2003	00:12:42	Croatian (*ijekavian*)
Miroslav Radić (see *Kvočka et al*)	Serbian Serb	21/05/2003	00:41:59	Serbian (*ekavian*) Croatian (*ijekavian*)
Franko Simatović	Serbian Serb	2/06/2003	00:11:25	Serbian (*ekavian*)
Jovica Stanišić[366]	Serbian Serb	13/06/2003	00:11:57	Serbian (*ekavian*)
Veselin Šljivančanin (see Mrkšić et al)	Serbian Serb	3/07/2003	00:13:23	Croatian (*ijekavian*)
Milan Babić[367]	Croatian Serb	26/11/2003	00:23:06[368]	Croatian (*ijekavian*)
Ivan Čermak	Croatian Croat	12/03/2004	00:56:51	Croatian (*ijekavian*)

[361] ICTY, Cases, *Mrkšić et al.*: https://bit.ly/3baYqF5.
[362] ICTY, Cases, *Mrđa*: https://bit.ly/3bbuyIB.
[363] Note the ICTY Registry, Outreach Program misfiled the "IA" video under "TJ" in both language versions.
[364] ICTY, Cases, *Češić*: https://bit.ly/2REgnUC.
[365] ICTY, Case, *Deronjić*: https://bit.ly/34FhWXv.
[366] ICTY, Cases, *Stanišić and Simatović*: https://bit.ly/3acGxUK.
[367] ICTY, Cases, *Babić*: https://bit.ly/2xu5nlK.
[368] Note the ICTY Registry, Outreach Program misfiled the "IA" video under "TJ" in B/C/S.

Accused	Ethnicity of the accused	Date of initial appearance	Duration of proceedings	Interpreters language
Mladen Markač (see Gotovina et al)	Croatian Croat			Bosnian (*ijekavian*)
Jadranko Prlić Bruno Stojić Slobodan Praljak Milivoj Petković Valentin Čorić Berislav Pušić	Bosnian Croat Bosnian Croat Bosnian Croat Bosnian Croat Bosnian Croat Bosnian Croat	6/04/2004	01:21:40	Croatian (*ijekavian*) Serbian (*ekavian*)
Ljubiša Beara (see *Popović et al*)	Bosnian Serb	12/10/2004	00:06:16	Serbian (*ekavian*)
Miroslav Bralo[369]	Bosnian Croat	15/11/2004	00:31:55	Croatian (*ijekavian*) Croatian (*ijekavian*)
Dragomir Milošević	Bosnian Serb	7/12/2004	00:31:08	Croatian (*ijekavian*) Croatian (*ijekavian*)
Milan Milutinović (see *Šainović et al*)	Serbian Serb	27/01/2005	00:07:05	Serbian (*ekavian*)
Vladimir Lazarević (see *Šainović et al*)	Serbian Serb	7/02/2005	00:51:24	Croatian (*ijekavian*) Serbian (*ekavian*)
Radivoje Miletić Milan Gvero (see *Popović et al*)	Bosnian Serb Bosnian Serb	2/03/2005	01:40:23	Serbian (*ekavian*) Serbian (*ekavian*)
Rasim Delić	Bosnian Muslim	3/03/2005	00:17:13	Bosnian (*ijekavian*)
Momčilo Perišić	Serbian Serb	9/03/2005	00:10:07	Croatian (*ijekavian*)
Drago Nikolić (see *Popović et al*)	Bosnian Serb	23/03/2005	00:07:08	Croatian (*ijekavian*)
Vinko Pandurević (see *Popović et al*)	Bosnian Serb	31/03/2005	00:28:21	Croatian (*ijekavian*) Serbian (*ekavian*)

[369] ICTY, Cases, *Bralo*: https://bit.ly/3exZx3I.

Accused	Ethnicity of the accused	Date of initial appearance	Duration of proceedings	Interpreters language
Sreten Lukić (see *Šainović et al*)	Serbian Serb	6/04/2005	00:11:30	Croatian (*ijekavian*) Serbian (*ekavian*)
Ljubomir Borovčanin (see *Popović et al*)	Bosnian Serb	7/04/2005	00:56:52	Croatian (*ijekavian*) Serbian (*ekavian*)
Vujadin Popović	Bosnian Serb	18/04/2005	00:12:59	Croatian (*ijekavian*)
Nebojša Pavković (see *Šainović et al*)	Serbian Serb	28/04/2005	00:22:12	Serbian (*ekavian*) Serbian (*ekavian*)
Ante Gotovina	Croatian Croat	12/12/2005	01:33:35	Croatian (*ijekavian*) Serbian (*ekavian*)
Sredoje Lukić	Bosnian Serb	13/02/2006	00:06:55	Croatian (*ijekavian*)
Milan Lukić	Bosnian Serb	31/03/2006	00:21:55	Serbian (*ekavian*)
Vlastimir Đorđević	Serbian Serb	19/06/2007	00:17:02	Serbian (*ekavian*)
Zdravko Tolimir	Bosnian Serb	3/07/2007	00:41:52	Serbian (*ekavian*) Croatian (*ijekavian*)
Radovan Karadžić	Bosnian Serb	31/07/2008	01:06:26	Bosnian (*ijekavian*) Serbian (*ekavian*)
Radovan Karadžić	Bosnian Serb	29/08/2008	00:24:09	Bosnian (*ijekavian*) Serbian (*ekavian*)
Mićo Stanišić Stojan Župljanin	Bosnian Serb Bosnian Serb	20/11/2008	00:10:30	Croatian (*ijekavian*)
Ratko Mladić	Bosnian Serb	3/06/2011	01:02:50	Bosnian (*ijekavian*) Serbian (*ekavian*)
Ratko Mladić	Bosnian Serb	4/07/2011	00:48:49	Serbian (*ekavian*) Bosnian (*ijekavian*)
Goran Hadžić	Croatian Serb	25/07/2011	00:11:21	Serbian (*ekavian*)
Goran Hadžić	Croatian Serb	24/08/2011	00:08:29	Croatian (*ijekavian*)

Appendix 4. Language of interpreters vs. location of crimes and ethnicity of victims during the reading of trial, appeals, sentencing, and revised judgments

Date	Type	Duration	Accused	Ethnicity of the accused	Location of crimes	Ethnicity of victims	Interpreters language
14/07/1997	TJ	00:13:05	Tadić	B&H Serb	B&H	B&H Muslims	Croatian (*ijekavian*)* Serbian (*ekavian*)
7/10/1997	AJ	00:22:50	Erdemović	B&H Serb	B&H	B&H Muslims	Croatian (*ijekavian*) Serbian (*ekavian*)
7/05/1999	TJ	00:32:31	Aleksovski	B&H Croat	B&H	B&H Muslims	Croatian (*ijekavian*) Croatian (*ijekavian*)
15/07/1999	AJ	00:26:46	Tadić	B&H Serb	B&H	B&H Muslims	Croatian (*ijekavian*)* Croatian (*ijekavian*)*
14/12/1999	TJ	00:26:35	Jelisić	B&H Serb	B&H	B&H Muslims	Croatian (*ijekavian*) Serbian (*ekavian*)
14/12/1999	TJ	00:57:51	Delalić Mucić Delić Landžo	B&H Muslim B&H Croat B&H Muslim B&H Muslim	B&H	B&H Serbs	Serbian (*ekavian*) Croatian (*ijekavian*)
14/01/2000	TJ	00:37:46	Kupreškić, Z. Kupreškić, M. Kupreškić, V. Josipović Papić Šantić	B&H Croat B&H Croat B&H Croat B&H Croat B&H Croat B&H Croat	B&H	B&H Muslims	Croatian (*ijekavian*)* Croatian (*ijekavian*)
3/03/2000	TJ	01:06:15	Blaškić	B&H Croat	B&H	B&H Muslims	Croatian (*ijekavian*) Croatian (*ijekavian*)
24/03/2000	TJ	00:28:41	Aleksovski	B&H Croat	B&H	B&H Muslims	Serbian (*ekavian*) Croatian (*ijekavian*)
21/07/2000	AJ	00:13:32	Furundžija	B&H Croat	B&H	B&H Muslims	Croatian (*ijekavian*)

Date	Type	Duration	Accused	Ethnicity of the accused	Location of crimes	Ethnicity of victims	Interpreters language
20/02/2001	AJ	00:40:58	Delalić Mucić Delić Landžo	B&H Muslim B&H Croat B&H Muslim B&H Muslim	B&H	B&H Serbs	Serbian (*ekavian*) Bosnian (*ijekavian*)
22/02/2001	TJ	00:32:23	Kunarac Kovač Vuković	B&H Serb B&H Serb B&H Serb	B&H	B&H Muslims	Bosnian (*ijekavian*) Croatian (*ijekavian*)*
26/02/2001	TJ	00:35:31	Kordić Čerkez	B&H Croat B&H Croat	B&H	B&H Muslims	Croatian (*ijekavian*) Serbian (*ekavian*)
5/07/2001	AJ	00:23:40	Jelisić	B&H Serb	B&H	B&H Muslims	Croatian (*ijekavian*)
31/07/2001	SJ	00:16:02	Todorović	B&H Serb	B&H	B&H Muslims	Serbian (*ekavian*) Croatian (*ijekavian*)
2/08/2001	TJ	01:26:34	Krstić	B&H Serb	B&H	B&H Muslims	Croatian (*ijekavian*)* Serbian (*ekavian*)
23/10/2001	AJ	00:57:57	Kupreškić, Z. Kupreškić, M. Kupreškić, V. Josipović Šantić	B&H Croat B&H Croat B&H Croat B&H Croat B&H Croat	B&H	B&H Muslims	Bosnian (*ijekavian*) Croatian (*ijekavian*)*
2/11/2001	TJ	00:59:34	Kvočka Kos Radić Žigić Prcać	B&H Serb B&H Serb B&H Serb B&H Serb B&H Serb	B&H	B&H Muslims	Croatian (*ijekavian*)* Serbian (*ekavian*)
13/11/2001	SJ	00:25:28	Sikirica Došen Kulundžija	B&H Serb B&H Serb B&H Serb	B&H	B&H Muslims	Croatian (*ijekavian*)*
15/03/2002	TJ	00:28:04	Krnojelac	B&H Serb	B&H	B&H Muslims	Croatian (*ijekavian*) Serbian (*ekavian*)

Date	Type	Duration	Accused	Ethnicity of the accused	Location of crimes	Ethnicity of victims	Interpreters language
22/06/2002	AJ	00:43:54	Kunarac Kovač Vuković	B&H Serb B&H Serb B&H Serb	B&H	B&H Muslims	Croatian (*ijekavian*) Serbian (*ekavian*)
17/10/2002	TJ	00:23:06	Simić	B&H Serb	B&H	B&H Muslims	Croatian (*ijekavian*)* Serbian (*ekavian*)
28/11/2002	TJ	00:26:13	Vasiljević	B&H Serb	B&H	B&H Muslims	Serbian (*ekavian*) Croatian (*ijekavian*)*
27/02/2003	TJ	00:32:56	Plavšić	B&H Serb	B&H	B&H non-Serbs	Serbian (*ekavian*) Bosnian (*ijekavian*)
31/03/2003	TJ	01:29:21	Naletelić Martinović	B&H Croat B&H Croat	B&H	B&H Muslims	Croatian (*ijekavian*) Bosnian (*ijekavian*)
31/07/2003	TJ	00:58:56	Stakić	B&H Serb	B&H	B&H Muslims	Bosnian (*ijekavian*) Serbian (*ekavian*)
17/09/2003	AJ	01:12:22	Krnojelac	B&H Serb	B&H	B&H Muslims	Croatian (*ijekavian*)* Serbian (*ekavian*)
17/10/2003	TJ	00:25:28	Simić Tadić Zarić	B&H Serb B&H Serb B&H Serb	B&H	B&H Muslims	Croatian (*ijekavian*) Serbian (*ekavian*)
28/10/2003	SJ	00:26:47	Banović	B&H Serb	B&H	B&H Muslims	Croatian (*ijekavian*) Serbian (*ekavian*)
2/12/2003	TJ	00:32:05	Nikolić	B&H Serb	B&H	B&H Muslims	Croatian (*ijekavian*) Serbian (*ekavian*)
5/12/2003	TJ	00:44:36	Galić	B&H Serb	B&H	B&H Muslims	Serbian (*ekavian*) Croatian (*ijekavian*)
10/12/2003	TJ	00:28:15	Obrenović	B&H Serb	B&H	B&H Muslims	Serbian (*ekavian*) Croatian (*ijekavian*)
18/12/2003	TJ	00:46:18	Nikolić	B&H Serb	B&H	B&H Muslims	Croatian (*ijekavian*) Serbian (*ekavian*)

Date	Type	Duration	Accused	Ethnicity of the accused	Location of crimes	Ethnicity of victims	Interpreters language
2/02/2004	AJ	00:45:49	Vasiljević	B&H Serb	B&H	B&H Muslims	Bosnian (*ijekavian*) Croatian (*ijekavian*)*
18/03/2004	TJ	00:17:29	Jokić	SR Serb	CRO	Croats	Bosnian (*ijekavian*)* Croatian (*ijekavian*)
30/03/2004	SJ	00:36:32	Deronjić	B&H Serb	B&H	B&H Muslims	Serbian (*ekavian*) Croatian (*ijekavian*)
31/03/2004	TJ	00:22:07	Mrđa	B&H Serb	B&H	B&H Muslims	Serbian (*ekavian*) Croatian (*ijekavian*)
19/04/2004	AJ	01:17:57	Krstić	B&H Serb	B&H	B&H Muslims	Serbian (*ekavian*) Croatian (*ijekavian*)
29/06/2004	SJ	00:20:38	Babić	CRO Serb	CRO	Croats	Croatian (*ijekavian*) Serbian (*ekavian*)
29/07/2004	AJ	01:43:14	Blaškić	B&H Croat	B&H	B&H Muslims	Croatian (*ijekavian*) Croatian (*ijekavian*)
1/09/2004	TJ	01:37:13	Brđanin	B&H Serb	B&H	B&H Muslims	Bosnian (*ijekavian*) Croatian (*ijekavian*)
17/12/2004	AJ	01:12:22	Kordić Čerkez	B&H Croat B&H Croat	B&H	B&H Muslims	Croatian (*ijekavian*) Bosnian (*ijekavian*)
17/01/2005	TJ	00:55:47	Jokić Blagojević	B&H Serb B&H Serb	B&H	B&H Muslims	Bosnian (*ijekavian*) Croatian (*ijekavian*)
31/01/2005	TJ	00:47:14	Strugar	SR Serb	CRO	Croats	Serbian (*ekavian*) Croatian (*ijekavian*)
4/02/2005	AJ	00:29:04	Nikolić	B&H Serb	B&H	B&H Muslims	Croatian (*ijekavian*) Serbian (*ekavian*)
28/02/2005	AJ	01:28:22	Kvočka Radić Žigić Prcać	B&H Serb B&H Serb B&H Serb B&H Serb	B&H	B&H Muslims	Croatian (*ijekavian*)* Serbian (*ekavian*)*

Date	Type	Duration	Accused	Ethnicity of the accused	Location of crimes	Ethnicity of victims	Interpreters language
18/07/2005	SA	00:30:56	Babić	CRO Serb	CRO	Croats	Bosnian (*ijekavian*)* Serbian (*ekavian*)
20/07/2005	AJ	00:23:28	Deronjić	B&H Serb	B&H	B&H Muslims	Bosnian (*ijekavian*) Serbian (*ekavian*)
16/11/2005	TJ	00:46:50	Halilović	B&H Muslim	B&H	B&H Serbs	Croatian (*ijekavian*) Bosnian (*ijekavian*)
7/12/2005	TJ	00:14:15	Bralo	B&H Croat	B&H	B&H Muslims	Bosnian (*ijekavian*)
8/03/2006	AJ	00:32:45	Nikolić	B&H Serb	B&H	B&H Muslims	Serbian (*ekavian*) Bosnian (*ijekavian*)
22/03/2006	AJ	00:55:08	Stakić	B&H Serb	B&H	B&H Muslims	Croatian (*ijekavian*)* Serbian (*ekavian*)
3/05/2006	AJ	00:52:13	Naletelić Martinović	B&H Croat B&H Croat	B&H	B&H Muslims	Croatian (*ijekavian*) Bosnian (*ijekavian*)
8/05/2006	TJ	00:21:56	Rajić[370]	B&H Croat	B&H	B&H Muslims	Croatian (*ijekavian*)* Bosnian (*ijekavian*)
30/06/2006	TJ	01:17:56	Orić	B&H Muslim	B&H	B&H Muslims	Serbian (*ekavian*) Bosnian (*ijekavian*)
27/09/2006	TJ	00:35:13	Krajišnik	B&H Serbs	B&H	B&H Muslims	Bosnian (*ijekavian*) Serbian (*ekavian*)
28/11/2006	AJ	00:58:01	Simić	B&H Serbs	B&H	B&H Muslims	Serbian (*ekavian*) Croatian (*ijekavian*)*
30/11/2006	AJ	01:12:52	Galić	B&H Serb	B&H	B&H Muslims	Croatian (*ijekavian*) Serbian (*ekavian*)
2/04/2007	AJ	00:50:52	Bralo	B&H Croat	B&H	B&H Muslims	Croatian (*ijekavian*) Serbian (*ekavian*)
3/04/2007	AJ	00:35:53	Brđanin	B&H Serb	B&H	B&H Muslims	Croatian (*ijekavian*) Serbian (*ekavian*)

[370] ICTY, Cases, *Rajić*: https://bit.ly/2XyM1Xv.

Date	Type	Duration	Accused	Ethnicity of the accused	Location of crimes	Ethnicity of victims	Interpreters language
3/04/2007	SJ	00:23:06	Češić	B&H Serb	B&H	B&H Muslims	Bosnian (*ijekavian*) Croatian (*ijekavian*)
4/04/2007	TJ	00:21:46	Zelenović[371]	B&H Serb	B&H	B&H Muslims	Serbian (*ekavian*) Croatian (*ijekavian*)*
9/05/2007	AJ	00:52:02	Jokić Blagojević	B&H Serb B&H Serb	B&H	B&H Muslims	Serbian (*ijekavian*) Croatian (*ijekavian*)
12/06/2007	TJ	01:17:02	Martić	CRO Serb	CRO	Croats	Serbian (*ekavian*) Croatian (*ijekavian*)
27/09/2007	TJ	01:00:52	Mrkšić Radić Šljivančanin	SR Serb SR Serb SR Serb	CRO	Croats	Croatian (*ijekavian*) Serbian (*ekavian*)
16/10/2007	AJ	00:26:42	Halilović	B&H Muslim	B&H	B&H Serbs	Croatian (*ijekavian*) Croatian (*ijekavian*)
31/10/2007	AJ	00:15:36	Zelenović	B&H Serb	B&H	B&H Muslims	Croatian (*ijekavian*)*
12/12/2007	TJ	00:25:00	Milošević	B&H Serb	B&H	B&H Muslims	Croatian (*ijekavian*) Serbian (*ekavian*)
22/04/2008	AJ	00:47:21	Hadžihasanović Kubura	B&H Muslim B&H Muslim	B&H	B&H Serbs	Croatian (*ijekavian*) Serbian (*ekavian*)
3/07/2008	AJ	00:35:08	Orić	B&H Muslim	B&H	B&H Serbs	Croatian (*ijekavian*)* Serbian (*ekavian*)
17/07/2008	AJ	00:47:51	Strugar	SR Serb	CRO	Croats	Serbian (*ekavian*) Croatian (*ijekavian*)
15/09/2008	TJ	00:57:58	Delić	B&H Muslim	B&H	B&H Serbs	Croatian (*ijekavian*) Serbian (*ekavian*)
8/10/2008	AJ	00:28:46	Martić	CRO Serb	CRO	Croats	Croatian (*ijekavian*) Serbian (*ekavian*)

[371] ICTY, Cases, *Zelenović*: https://bit.ly/3acIdho.

Date	Type	Duration	Accused	Ethnicity of the accused	Location of crimes	Ethnicity of victims	Interpreters language
26/02/2009	TJ	01:28:27	Milutinović Šainović Ojdanić Pavković Lazarević Lukić, Sreten	SR Serb SR Serb SR Serb SR Serb SR Serb SR Serb	Kosovo	Albanians	Serbian (*ekavian*) Croatian (*ijekavian*)
17/03/2009	AJ	00:42:42	Krajišnik	B&H Serb	B&H	B&H Muslims	Croatian (*ijekavian*)* Serbian (*ekavian*)
5/05/2009	AJ	01:10:17	Mrkšić Šljivančanin	SR Serbs SR Serb	CRO	Croats	Serbian (*ekavian*) Croatian (*ijekavian*) Croatian (*ijekavian*)
20/07/2009	TJ	00:42:33	Lukić, M. Lukić, S.	B&H Serb B&H Serb	B&H	B&H Muslims	Croatian (*ijekavian*) Serbian (*ekavian*)
12/11/2009	AJ	00:46:38	Milošević	B&H Serb	B&H	B&H Muslims	Bosnian (*ijekavian*) Serbian (*ekavian*)
10/06/2010	TJ	01:26:12	Popović Beara Nikolić, M. Borovčanin Miletić Gvero Pandurević	B&H Serb B&H Serb B&H Serb B&H Serb B&H Serb B&H Serb B&H Serb	B&H	B&H Muslims	Bosnian (*ijekavian*) Serbian (*ekavian*)*
8/12/2010	RJ	00:27:52	Šljivančanin	SR Serb	CRO	Croats	Croatian (*ijekavian*) Serbian (*ekavian*)
23/02/2011	TJ	00:50:57	Đorđević	SR Serb	Kosovo	Albanians	Serbian (*ekavian*) Bosnian (*ijekavian*)*
6/12/2011	TJ	00:32:40	Perišić	SR Serb	B&H	B&H Muslims	Serbian (*ekavian*) Croatian (*ijekavian*)*

Date	Type	Duration	Accused	Ethnicity of the accused	Location of crimes	Ethnicity of victims	Interpreters language
15/04/2012	TJ	00:50:02	Gotovina Čermak Markač	CRO Croat CRO Croat CRO Croat	CRO	CRO Serbs	Croatian (*ijekavian*) Serbian (*ekavian*)
16/11/2012	AJ	00:37:59	Gotovina Markač	CRO Croat CRO Croat	CRO	CRO Serbs	Croatian (*ijekavian*) Serbian (*ekavian*)
4/12/2012	AJ	00:36:44	Lukić, M. Lukić, S.	B&H Serb B&H Serb	B&H	B&H Muslims	Croatian (*ijekavian*) Serbian (*ekavian*)
12/12/2012	TJ	01:03:59	Tolimir	B&H Serb	B&H	B&H Muslims	Croatian (*ijekavian*)* Serbian (*ekavian*)*
28/02/2013	AJ	00:54:18	Perišić	SR Serb	B&H	B&H Muslims	Serbian (*ekavian*) Croatian (*ijekavian*)
27/03/2013	TJ	01:05:58	Stanišić Župljanin	B&H Serb B&H Serb	B&H	B&H Muslims	Serbian (*ekavian*) Bosnian (*ijekavian*)
30/05/2013	TJ	00:45:01	Stanišić Simatović	SR Serb SR Serb	B&H and CRO	Non-Serbs	Serbian (*ekavian*) Croatian (*ijekavian*)
23/01/2014	AJ	01:26:37	Šainović Pavković Lazarević Lukić, Sreten	SR Serb SR Serb SR Serb SR Serb	Kosovo	Albanians	Serbian (*ekavian*) Croatian (*ijekavian*)
27/01/2014	AJ	00:38:18	Đorđević	SR Serb	Kosovo	Albanians	Serbian (*ekavian*) Serbian (*ekavian*)
30/01/2015	AJ	02:04:20	Popović Beara Nikolić, Drago Miletić Pandurević	B&H Serb B&H Serb B&H Serb B&H Serb B&H Serb	B&H	B&H Muslims	Serbian (*ekavian*) Croatian (*ijekavian*)
8/04/2015	AJ	01:12:37	Tolimir	B&H Serb	B&H	B&H Muslims	Bosnian (*ijekavian*) Croatian (*ijekavian*)*

Date	Type	Duration	Accused	Ethnicity of the accused	Location of crimes	Ethnicity of victims	Interpreters language
15/12/2015	AJ	00:31:27	Stanišić Simatović	SR Serb SR Serb	B&H and CRO	Non-Serbs	Bosnian (*ijekavian*) Serbian (*ekavian*)
24/03/2016	TJ	01:42:47	Karadžić	B&H Serb	B&H	Non-Serbs	Croatian (*ijekavian*)* Bosnian (*ijekavian*)
24/03/2016	TJ	01:42:49	Prlić Stojić Praljak Petković Ćorić Pušić	B&H Croat B&H Croat B&H Croat B&H Croat B&H Croat B&H Croat	B&H	B&H Muslims	Croatian (*ijekavian*) Serbian (*ekavian*) Croatian (*ijekavian*)
31/03/2016	TJ	01:26:08	Šešelj	B&H Serb	Serbia, CRO, B&H	Non-Serbs	Serbian (*ekavian*) Bosnian (*ijekavian*) Croatian (*ijekavian*)
30/06/2016	AJ	00:54:08	Stanišić Župljanin	B&H Serb B&H Serb	B&H	B&H Muslims	Croatian (*ijekavian*) Bosnian (*ijekavian*)

Appendix 5. The ICTY Registry B/C/S transcript team times, ERN ranges, and ERN pages

Trial	Date	Time	Total time	ERN range	ERN pages	Total pages
Blagojević and Jokić	21/07/2003	0909-1022 1051-1208 1242-1343	01:13:00 01:17:00 01:01:00	1335-1411	77	77
Blagojević and Jokić	13/11/2003	0901-1016 1046-1207 1243-1345	01:15:00 01:21:00 01:02:00	4460-4544	85	85
Blagojević and Jokić	14/11/2003	0901-1016 1046-1159 1231-1401	01:15:00 01:13:00 01:30:00	4545-4638	94	94
Blagojević and Jokić	21/11/2003	0903-1015 1047-1158 1231-1350	01:12:00 01:11:00 01:19:00	5016-5119	104	104
Blagojević and Jokić	1/12/2003	0904-1015 1048-1200 1232-1353	01:11:00 01:12:00 01:21:00	5357- 5442	86	86
Blagojević and Jokić	19/01/2004	0900-1005 1037-1159 1232-1351	01:05:00 01:22:00 01:19:00	6116- 6207	92	85
Blagojević and Jokić	20/01/2004	0907-1020 1051-1210 1242-1350	01:13:00 01:19:00 01:08:00	6208- 6300	93	93
Blagojević and Jokić	21/01/2004	0902-1017 1051-1201 1231-1355	01:15:00 01:10:00 01:24:00	6301- 6392	92	92

Trial	Date	Time	Total time	ERN range	ERN pages	Total pages
Blagojević and Jokić	22/01/2004	0901-1016 1047-1205 1237-1342 1503-1640	01:15:00 01:18:00 01:05:00 01:37:00	6393- 6513	121	101
Blagojević and Jokić	8/06/2004	1416-1532 1602-1710 1741-1902	01:16:00 01:08:00 01:21:00	10486-10541 6189-6223[372]	56/35	91
Blagojević and Jokić	9/06/2004	0901-1036 1101-1202 1233-1350	01:35:00 01:01:00 01:17:00	10577-10669	93	93
Blagojević and Jokić	19/07/2004	0902-1014 1048-1159 1233-1249	01:12:00 01:11:00 01:16:00	12042-12104	63	63
Blagojević and Jokić			**46:20:00**	**1,090**		**1,064**[373]
Brđanin	25/04/2002	1417-1423 1447-1547 1623-1758	00:06:00 01:00:00 01:35:00	4954-5012	59	59
Brđanin	26/04/2002	1423-1530 1557-1745	01:07:00 01:48:00	5056-5120[374]	65	65
Brđanin	15/05/2002	0901-1028 1105-1225 1301-1348	01:29:00 01:20:00 00:47:00	5623-5709	87	87
Brđanin	8/12/2003	0907-1342	03:35:00	23290-23373	84	7

372 Pagination is off: if the transcript on 9 June begins with T. 10577, the previous one should have ended on T. 10576.

373 This number includes: 9 full blank pages and 29 redacted ERN range pages (6122-6129; 6476; 6477; 6478; 6479; 6481-6501; 10578; 10579; 10580) to a total of a minimum of 38 untranscribed pages.

374 Pagination is off: the session from 25 April ends at T. 5012 and session from 26 April begins at T. 5056.

Trial	Date	Time	Total time	ERN range	ERN pages	Total pages
Brđanin	9/12/2003	0900-1211 1241-1334	01:16:00 00:53:00	23374-23464	91	31
Brđanin	20/02/2004	0905-1037 1123-1245 1307-1347	01:32:00 01:22:00 00:40:00	24839-24933	95	95
Brđanin	23/02/2004	0905-1027 1100-1232 1302-1348	01:22:00 01:32:00 00:46:00	24934-25033	100	100
Brđanin			**22:10:00**	**581**		**444**[375]
Erdemović	19/11/1996	1000-1140 1200-1230 1430-1545 1600-1643	01:40:00 01:30:00 01:15:00 00:43:00	114-219	106	94
Erdemović	20/11/1996	1010-1055 1110-1330 1515-1630	00:45:00 02:20:00 01:15:00	220-341	122	106
Erdemović			**09:28:00**	**228**		**200**[376]
Halilović	23/05/2005	1434-1602 1632-1745 1811-1908	01:28:00 01:13:00 00:57:00	1--80	80	80

375 This number includes: 15 blank pages inserted to consolidate pagination with English and French transcripts (5087, 5119, 5709, 23438, 23451, 24851, 24864, 24877, 24890, 24903, 24916, 24933, 24939, 24945, 24951), and 10 full blank pages and 140 redacted ERN range pages (23295-23373, 23375-23435, 24962, 24963, 24964, 25014, 25015, 25016, 25030, 25031) to a total of a minimum of 165 untranscribed pages.

376 This number includes: 2 full blank pages and 28 redacted ERN range pages (161-173, 272-288) to a total of a minimum of 30 untranscribed pages.

Trial	Date	Time	Total time	ERN range	ERN pages	Total pages
Halilović	24/05/2005	0907-1027 1103-1216 1246-1356	01:20:00 01:13:00 01:10:00	1--77	77	77
Halilović	26/05/2005	0909-1021 1057-1218 1253-1349	01:12:00 01:21:00 00:56:00	1--76	76	76
Halilović	27/05/2005	0901-1028 1106-1210 1245-1349	01:27:00 01:04:00 01:04:00	1—82	82	82
Halilović			**14:25:00**	**315**		**315**[377]
Karadžić	8/10/2010	1418-1537 1603-1720 1746-1906	01:09:00 01:17:00 01:20:00	7506-7606	101	101
Karadžić	9/06/2011	0903-1031 1102-1230 1302-1431	01:28:00 01:04:00 01:04:00	14489-14604	116	116
Karadžić	14/06/2011	0901-1022 1047-1201 1233-1345	01:21:00 01:14:00 01:12:00	14605-14700	96	96
Karadžić	15/06/2011	0903-1029 1101-1230 1302-1434	01:26:00 01:29:00 01:32:00	14701-14812	112	112
Karadžić	17/06/2011	0902-1031 1100-1236 1311-1430	01:29:00 01:36:00 01:19:00	14813-14924	112	103

377 This number includes: 3 full blank pages (75, 76, 77) to a total of a minimum of 3 untranscribed pages.

Trial	Date	Time	Total time	ERN range	ERN pages	Total pages
Karadžić	20/06/2011	0902-1028 1100-1231 1302-1431	01:26:00 01:31:00 01:29:00	14925-15032	108	108
Karadžić	22/08/2011	1415-1753 1811-1855	02:38:00 00:44:00	17578-17672	95	43
Karadžić	23/08/2011	1416-1535 1606-1736 1801-1908	01:19:00 01:30:00 01:07:00	17673-17773	101	101
Karadžić	24/08/2011	1427-1541 1609-1729 1757-1912	01:14:00 01:20:00 01:15:00	17774-17865	92	92
Karadžić	29/08/2011	0900-1021 1042-1144 1217-1345	01:21:00 01:02:00 01:28:00	17953-18046	94	63
Karadžić	6/09/2011	0902-0948 1007-1036 1103-1223 1329-1419 1433-1459	01:46:00 00:29:00 01:20:00 00:50:00 00:26:00	18405-18500	96	94
Karadžić			**44:15:00**	**1,123**		**1,029**[378]
Krajišnik	7/04/2000	1002-1030	00:28:00	1-15	15	15
Krajišnik	12/03/2003	1502-1615	01:13:00	88-120	33	33
Krajišnik	3/02/2004	1518-1644 1719-1902	01:26:00 01:43:00	296-373	78	78
Krajišnik	3/02/2004	1420-1437	00:17:00	287-295	9	9

[378] Unfortunately, when I was checking this data just before submitting this book to the publisher, I discovered Karadžić transcripts have been taken offline. I am certain this number includes: 33 blank pages of redacted material to a total of a minimum of 33 untranscribed pages, but I cannot say exactly which ones like I did for all the others.

Trial	Date	Time	Total time	ERN range	ERN pages	Total pages
Krajišnik	5/02/2004	1419-1547 1610-1730 1759-1901	01:28:00 01:20:00 01:02:00	481-583	103	103
Krajišnik	10/02/2004	0914-1033 1059-1150	01:19:00 00:51:00	681-731	51	51
Krajišnik	11/02/2004	0904-1032 1109-1119 1141-1240 1258-1353	01:28:00 00:10:00 00:59:00 00:55:00	732-821	90	90
Krajišnik	12/02/2004	0915-0951 1013-1037 1103-1119 1122-1231 1256-1347	00:36:00 00:24:00 00:16:00 01:09:00 00:51:00	822-902	81	81
Krajišnik	13/02/2004	0905-1032 1101-1223 1246-1351	01:27:00 01:22:00 01:05:00	903-995	93	93
Krajišnik	16/02/2004	0904-1028 1056-1219 1244-1351	01:24:00 01:23:00 01:07:00	996-1090	95	95
Krajišnik	18/02/2004	1420-1545 1612-1728 1752-1902	01:25:00 01:16:00 01:10:00	1091-1181	91	91
Krajišnik	19/02/2004	1419-1545 1609-1747 1820-1903	01:26:00 01:41:00 00:43:00	1182-1266	85	85
Krajišnik	20/02/2004	1419-1544 1607-1737 1801-1901	01:25:00 01:30:00 01:00:00	1267-1348	82	82

Trial	Date	Time	Total time	ERN range	ERN pages	Total pages
Krajišnik	23/02/2004	1421-1547 1609-1729 1753-1904	01:26:00 01:20:00 01:11:00	1349-1451	103	103
Krajišnik	24/02/2004	0905-1030 1054-1222 1247-1346	01:25:00 01:28:00 00:59:00	1452-1544	93	93
Krajišnik	25/02/2004	0905-1030 1054-1215 1243-1354	01:25:00 01:21:00 01:09:00	1545-1641	97	97
Krajišnik	26/02/2004	0903-0915 1002-1146 1219-1349	00:12:00 01:44:00 01:30:00	1642-1725	84	84
Krajišnik	27/02/2004	0909-1026 1049-1221 1243-1348 1603-1713	01:17:00 01:32:00 01:05:00 01:10:00	1726-1841	116	116
Krajišnik	13/04/2004	0907-0945 1001-1042 1109-1234 1257-1347	00:38:00 00:41:00 01:25:00 00:50:00	1842-1938	97	97
Krajišnik	14/04/2004	0906-1030 1059-1225 1248-1342	01:24:00 01:26:00 01:54:00	1939-2034	96	96
Krajišnik	16/04/2004	0903-1030 1057-1231 1253-1350	01:27:00 01:34:00 01:57:00	2132-2225	94	94
Krajišnik	20/04/2004	0906-1028 1054-1201	01:22:00 01:07:00	2300-2363	64	64

Trial	Date	Time	Total time	ERN range	ERN pages	Total pages
Krajišnik	21/04/2004	0904-1031 1057-1220 1252-1346	01:27:00 01:23:00 00:53:00	2364-2447	84	84
Krajišnik	23/04/2004	0906-1100 1112-1216 1314-1356	01:04:00 01:04:00 00:42:00	2588-2671	84	84
Krajišnik	25/05/2004	0907-1030 1100-1215 1239-1349	01:23:00 01:15:00 01:10:00	2778-2880	103	103
Krajišnik	26/05/2004	0907-0956 1002-1032 1102-1232 1300-1345	00:49:00 00:30:00 01:30:00 00:45:00	2881-2976	96	96
Krajišnik	27/05/2004	0907-1020 1051-1220 1253-1359	01:13:00 01:29:00 01:06:00	2977-3070	94	94
Krajišnik	28/05/2004	0914-1030 1108-1226 1256-1348	01:16:00 01:18:00 00:52:00	3071-3163	93	93
Krajišnik	1/06/2004	0907-1030 1058-1230 1250-1345	01:23:00 01:32:00 00:55:00	3164-3264	101	101
Krajišnik	23/06/2004	1420-1545 1618-1730 1755-1903	01:25:00 01:12:00 01:08:00	4183-4271	89	89
Krajišnik	24/06/2004	0906-1030 1058-1225 1253-1347	01:24:00 01:27:00 00:54:00	4272-4363	92	92

Trial	Date	Time	Total time	ERN range	ERN pages	Total pages
Krajišnik	25/06/2004	0908-1016 1047-1211 1244-1339	01:08:00 01:24:00 00:55:00	4364-4447	84	84
Krajišnik	16/07/2004	1427-1546 1616-1705 1755-1812	01:19:00 00:49:00 00:17:00	4448-4522	75	75
Krajišnik	28/07/2004	0904-1037 1105-1230 1255-1400	01:33:00 01:25:00 01:05:00	4718-4801	84	84
Krajišnik	29/07/2004	1424-1549 1623-1746 1810-1906[379]	01:25:00 01:23:00 00:56:00	4802-4893	92	92
Krajišnik	30/08/2004	1425-1536 1601-1903	01:11:00 03:01:00	5001-5095	95	89
Krajišnik	31/08/2004	0909-1034 1106-1229 1253-1346	01:25:00 01:23:00 00:53:00	5096-5192	97	97
Krajišnik	1/09/2004	1425-1535 1611-1711 1732-1847	01:10:00 01:00:00 01:15:00	5193-5286	94	94
Krajišnik	2/09/2004	0902-1032 1057-1231 1252-1349	01:30:00 01:34:00 00:56:00	5287-5383	97	97
Krajišnik	27/09/2004	0907-1020 1053-1158 1223-1405	01:13:00 01:05:00 01:42:00	6061-6168	108	108

[379] T. 4893 reads “7.06h”, but it is clear from the context it should read “19:06,” instead.

Trial	Date	Time	Total time	ERN range	ERN pages	Total pages
Krajišnik	28/09/2004	0906-1007 1037-1159 1223-1350	01:01:00 01:22:00 01:27:00	6169-4778[380]	107	107
Krajišnik	29/09/2004	0906-1037 1103-1228 1254-1359	01:31:00 01:25:00 01:05:00	6276-6390	115	115
Krajišnik	5/10/2004	1102-1217 1257-1327 1342-1358	01:15:00 00:30:00 00:16:00	6654-6708	55	55
Krajišnik	20/10/2004	1423-1425 1449-1607 1633-1745 1808-1902	00:02:00 01:18:00 01:12:00 00:54:00	7180-7265	86	86
Krajišnik	26/10/2004	1426-1529 1559-1727 1756-1856[381]	01:03:00 01:28:00 01:00:00	7356-7445	90	90
Krajišnik	2/11/2004	0910-1038 1116-1230 1258-1359	01:28:00 01:14:00 01:01:00	7820-7918	99	99
Krajišnik	3/11/2004	0906-1031 1059-1231 1256-1400	01:25:00 01:32:00 01:04:00	7919-8033	115	115

[380] Pagination is off: the session on 28 September is said to have ended on T. 4778 when it would be logical it ended on T. 6275 if the session on 29 September started on T. 6276.

[381] T.7444 reads the session ended at 16:56 hrs which is illogical given that the last break ended at 17:56 hrs; T. 7444 of the English transcripts confirmed it ended at 18:56 hrs.

Trial	Date	Time	Total time	ERN range	ERN pages	Total pages
Krajišnik	8/11/2004	1415-1602 1634-1744 1811-1830	01:47:00 01:10:00 00:09:00	8034-8126	93	93
Krajišnik	9/11/2004	1421-1545 1621-1749 1816-1903	01:24:00 01:28:00 00:47:00	8127-8226	100	100
Krajišnik	10/11/2004	1420-1543 1624-1729 1755-1902	01:23:00 01:05:00 01:07:00	8227-8336	110	110
Krajišnik	22/11/2004	0907-1024 1059-1148 1206-1253 1314-1338 1341-1358	01:17:00 00:49:00 00:48:00 00:24:00 00:17:00	8440-8543	104	104
Krajišnik	24/11/2004	0909-1040 1110-1228 1255-1343	01:31:00 01:18:00 00:48:00	8637-8725	89	89
Krajišnik	25/11/2004	0908-1032 1106-1229 1254-1345	01:24:00 01:23:00 00:51:00	8726-8815	90	90
Krajišnik	29/11/2004	0909-1032 1105-1223 1252-1349	01:23:00 01:18:00 00:57:00	8910-8995	86	86
Krajišnik	30/11/2004	0909-1032 1103-1238 1302-1349	01:23:00 01:35:00 00:47:00	8996-9089	94	94
Krajišnik	6/12/2004	1423-1548 1621-1724	01:25:00 01:03:00	9197-9257	61	61

Trial	Date	Time	Total time	ERN range	ERN pages	Total pages
Krajišnik	7/12/2004	1421-1543 1616-1734 1758-1903	01:22:00 01:18:00 01:05:00	9258-9342	85	85
Krajišnik	9/12/2004	1429-1554 1624-1724 1804-1902	01:25:00 01:00:00 00:58:00	9343-9422	80	80
Krajišnik	10/12/2004	1420-1548 1621-1717 1725-1746	01:28:00 00:56:00 00:21:00	9423-9490	68	68
Krajišnik	15/12/2004	1453-1622 1702-1729	00:29:00 00:27:00	9491-9542	52	52
Krajišnik	1/03/2005	0906-1030 1100-1225 1255-1345	01:24:00 01:25:00 00:50:00	9606-9715	110	110
Krajišnik	2/03/2005	0910-1030 1110-1235 1300-1343	01:20:00 01:25:00 00:43:00	9716-9818	103	103
Krajišnik	3/03/2005	1002-1110 1135-1230 1255-1345	01:08:00 00:55:00 00:50:00	9819-9900	82	82
Krajišnik	4/03/2005	0917-1030 1105-1230 1258-1350	01:12:00 01:25:00 00:52:00	9901-9995	95	95
Krajišnik	7/03/2005	0908-1025 1055-1230 1255-1347	01:17:00 01:35:00 00:52:00	9996-10095	100	100
Krajišnik	8/03/2005	0908-1035 1110-1219 1247-1346	01:17:00 01:09:00 00:59:00	10096-10191	96	96

Trial	Date	Time	Total time	ERN range	ERN pages	Total pages
Krajišnik	14/03/2005	0904-1030 1057-1220 1244-1348	01:26:00 01:23:00 01:04:00	10431-10533	103	103
Krajišnik	15/03/2005	0904-1034 1102-1239 1305-1400	01:30:00 01:37:00 00:55:00	10534-10638	105	105
Krajišnik	17/03/2005	1034-1158 1230-1357	01:24:00 01:27:00	10639-10711	73	73
Krajišnik	22/03/2005	1430-1550 1621-1707	01:20:00 00:46:00	10897-10954	58	58
Krajišnik	23/03/2005	1421-1507	00:46:00	10955-10974	20	20
Krajišnik	29/03/2005	0903-1030 1057-1228 1252-1350	01:27:00 01:31:00 00:58:00	10975-11080	106	106
Krajišnik	1/04/2005	0907-1402	04:55:00	11272-11376	105	33
Krajišnik	4/04/2005	0912-1030 1101-1235 1302-1345	01:18:00 01:34:00 00:43:00	11377-11460	84	84
Krajišnik	5/04/2005	0916-1030 1058-1243 1307-1357	01:14:00 01:45:00 00:50:00	11461-11539	79	79
Krajišnik	6/04/2005	1421-1550 1619-1726 1749-1905	01:29:00 01:07:00 01:16:00	11540-11621	82	82
Krajišnik	7/04/2005	1419-1552 1622-1741 1803-1910	01:33:00 01:19:00 01:07:00	11622-11704	83	83

Trial	Date	Time	Total time	ERN range	ERN pages	Total pages
Krajišnik	8/04/2005	1418-1549 1617-1752 1812-1908	01:31:00 01:35:00 00:56:00	11705-11794	90	90
Krajišnik	11/04/2005	0945-1003 1008-1040 1112-1240 1306-1347	00:18:00 00:32:00 01:28:00 00:41:00	11795-11877	83	83
Krajišnik	12/04/2005	0933-1028 1100-1204 1232-1353	00:55:00 01:04:00 01:21:00	11878-11964	87	87
Krajišnik	13/04/2005	0907-1032 1101-1227 1254-1354	01:25:00 01:26:00 01:00:00	11965-12056	92	92
Krajišnik	15/04/2005	0904-1035 1104-1212	01:31:00 01:08:00	12154-12219	66	66
Krajišnik	21/04/2005	1422-1826	04:04:00	12463-12548	86	35
Krajišnik	25/04/2005	0907-1004 1018-1046 1121-1147 1236-1258	00:57:00 00:28:00 00:26:00 00:22:00	12549-12602	54	54
Krajišnik	26/04/2005	0912-1035 1107-1227 1248-1321	01:23:00 01:20:00 01:33:00	12603-12682	80	80
Krajišnik	17/05/2005	1423-1543 1619-1715	01:20:00 00:56:00	13028-13089	62	62
Krajišnik	18/05/2005	1422-1532 1609-1646	01:10:00 00:37:00	13090-13142	53	53
Krajišnik	23/05/2005	0907-1029 1106-1134	01:22:00 00:28:00	13267-13323	57	57

Trial	Date	Time	Total time	ERN range	ERN pages	Total pages
Krajišnik	24/05/2005	0937-1035 1108-1244	00:58:00 01:36:00	13324-13392	69	69
Krajišnik	25/05/2005	0912-0920 0927-1033 1250-1301	00:08:00 01:06:00 00:11:00	13393-13414	22	22
Krajišnik	26/05/2005	1014-1108 1214-1244	00:54:00 00:30:00	13415-13450	36	36
Krajišnik	1/06/2005	1425-1551 1619-1732 1759-1913	01:26:00 01:13:00 01:14:00	13741-13853	113	113
Krajišnik	2/06/2005	1426-1555 1634-1751 1614-1906	01:29:00 01:17:00 02:50:00	13854-13940	87	87
Krajišnik	3/06/2005	1315-1443 1518-1658 1721-1818	01:28:00 01:40:00 00:57:00	13941-14046	106	106
Krajišnik	6/06/2005	0911-1027 1103-1216 1245-1354	01:16:00 01:13:00 01:09:00	14047-14136	90	90
Krajišnik	9/06/2005	0905-1025 1058-1226 1252-1355	01:20:00 01:28:00 01:03:00	14137-14242	106	106
Krajišnik	10/06/2005	0952-1059 1131-1250 1316-1418	01:07:00 01:19:00 01:02:00	14243-14332	90	90
Krajišnik	15/06/2005	0925-1032 1056-1232 1253-1357	01:07:00 01:36:00 01:04:00	14524-14614	91	91

Trial	Date	Time	Total time	ERN range	ERN pages	Total pages
Krajišnik	16/06/2005	0907-1042 1113-1235 1301-1346	01:35:00 01:12:00 00:45:00	14615-14700	86	86
Krajišnik	17/06/2005	0907-1035 1105-1201 1225-1354	01:25:00 00:56:00 01:29:00	14701-14800	100	100
Krajišnik	22/06/2005	0906-1343	04:37:00	14964-15068	105	3
Krajišnik	23/06/2005	0909-1744	08:35:00	15069-15219	151	10
Krajišnik	28/06/2005	0909-1031 1100-1240 1306-1350	01:22:00 01:40:00 00:44:00	15315-15406	92	92
Krajišnik	29/06/2005	1423-1547 1617-1746 1812-1908	01:24:00 01:29:00 00:56:00	15407-15504	98	98
Krajišnik	30/06/2005	0908-1012 1045-1227 1249-1355	01:04:00 01:42:00 01:06:00	15504-15617[382]	114	114
Krajišnik	8/07/2005	0909-1211 1218-1240 1307-1346 1511-1634	03:02:00 00:22:00 00:39:00 01:23:00	16039-16164	126	77
Krajišnik	12/07/2005	1423-1549 1623-1741 1802-1904	01:26:00 01:18:00 01:02:00	16262-16363	102	102
Krajišnik	13/07/2005	1437-1609 1644-1758 1827-1938	01:22:00 01:14:00 01:11:00	16364-16473	110	110

[382] This is not a typo: the session on 29 June ends and session on 30 June begins with T. 15504 as recorded.

Trial	Date	Time	Total time	ERN range	ERN pages	Total pages
Krajišnik	14/07/2005	0903-1031 1059-1154 1242-1259 1304-1402	01:28:00 00:55:00 00:17:00 00:58:00	16474-16577	104	104
Krajišnik	19/07/2005	0914-1034 1109-1241 1304-1349	01:20:00 01:32:00 00:45:00	16667-16756	90	90
Krajišnik	20/07/2005	0911-1031 1112-1306 1333-1401	01:20:00 01:54:00 00:28:00	16757-16860	104	104
Krajišnik	16/08/2005	1044-1146 1221-1336	01:02:00 01:15:00	17057-17111	55	55
Krajišnik	19/08/2005	1409-1511	01:02:00	17112-17138	27	27
Krajišnik	28/09/2005	0939-1020 1107-1211 1226-1333	00:41:00 01:04:00 01:07:00	17139-17217	79	79
Krajišnik	6/10/2005	0937-1109 1148-1334	01:32:00 01:46:00	17218-17310	93	93
Krajišnik	10/10/2005	0908-1034 1113-1214 1244-1348	01:26:00 01:01:00 01:04:00	17311-17398	88	88
Krajišnik	11/10/2005	0909-1035 1111-1231 1301-1348	01:26:00 01:20:00 00:47:00	17399-17490	92	92
Krajišnik	27/10/2005	0909-1024 1103-1218 1255-1347	01:15:00 01:15:00 00:52:00	17804-17890	87	87

Trial	Date	Time	Total time	ERN range	ERN pages	Total pages
Krajišnik	31/10/2005	1422-1547 1618-1802 1833-1857	01:25:00 01:44:00 00:24:00	17891-17975	85	85
Krajišnik	2/11/2005	1419-1533 1620-1813	01:14:00 01:53:00	18058-18139	82	82
Krajišnik	7/11/2005	0905-1033 1104-1231 1252-1354	01:28:00 01:27:00 01:02:00	18140-18239	100	100
Krajišnik	9/11/2005	1420-1547 1615-1750 1817-1906	01:27:00 01:35:00 00:49:00	18322-18414	93	93
Krajišnik	10/11/2005	1422-1543 1616-1741 1818-1851	01:21:00 01:25:00 00:33:00	18415-18503	89	89
Krajišnik	15/11/2005	1423-1507 1559-1623	00:54:00 00:24:00	18504-18535	32	32
Krajišnik	16/11/2005	1422-1547 1615-1733 1801-1914	01:25:00 01:18:00 01:13:00	18536-18623	88	88
Krajišnik	17/11/2005	1420-1554 1629-1536 1802-1903	01:34:00 01:07:00 01:01:00	18624-18710	87	87
Krajišnik	18/11/2005	0905-1039 1111-1235 1308-1422	01:34:00 01:24:00 01:14:00	18711-18806	96	96
Krajišnik	21/11/2005	0921-1036 1106-1240 1305-1356	01:15:00 01:34:00 00:51:00	18807-18892	86	86

Trial	Date	Time	Total time	ERN range	ERN pages	Total pages
Krajišnik	5/12/2005	0907-1031 1102-1230 1255-1345	01:24:00 01:28:00 00:50:00	19152-19240	89	89
Krajišnik	6/12/2005	1439-1541 1612-1746 1816-1901	01:02:00 01:34:00 00:45:00	19241-19318	78	78
Krajišnik	8/12/2005	1425-1608	01:43:00	19319-19360	42	42
Krajišnik	12/12/2005	1508-1701 1739-1903	01:53:00 01:24:00	19361-19436	76	76
Krajišnik	13/12/2005	1423-1520 1558-1648 1723-1908	00:57:00 00:50:00 01:45:00	19437-19514	78	78
Krajišnik	17/01/2006	1417-1546 1620-1753 1821-1901	01:29:00 01:33:00 00:40:00	19870-19955	86	86
Krajišnik	27/01/2006	0905-1035 1105-1229 1305-1355	01:30:00 01:24:00 00:50:00	20560-20643	84	84
Krajišnik	31/01/2006	0909-1037 1111-1256	01:28:00 01:45:00	20729-20806	78	78
Krajišnik	8/03/2006	0908-0934 1025-1154 1228-1348	01:25:00 01:19:00 01:20:00	20899-20971	73	73
Krajišnik	9/03/2006	1433-1611 1643-1815 1840-1910	01:38:00 01:32:00 00:30:00	20972-21063	92	92
Krajišnik	10/03/2006	0907-1037 1112-1254 1320-1418	01:30:00 01:42:00 00:58:00	21064-21173	110	110

Trial	Date	Time	Total time	ERN range	ERN pages	Total pages
Krajišnik	13/03/2006	1422-1552 1622-1730 1759-1901	01:30:00 01:08:00 01:02:00	21174-21264	91	91
Krajišnik	14/03/2006	1424-1557 1626-1724 1751-1911	01:33:00 00:58:00 01:20:00	21265-21360	96	96
Krajišnik	17/03/2006	1422-1537 1631-1726 1801-1823	01:15:00 00:55:00 00:22:00	21537-21595	59	59
Krajišnik	20/03/2006	0914-1053 1123-1323	01:39:00 02:00:00	21596-21671	76	76
Krajišnik	21/03/2006	0906-1041 1122-1227 1301-1352	01:35:00 01:05:00 00:51:00	21672-21746	75	75
Krajišnik	22/03/2006	0907-1023 1054-1229 1258-1349	01:16:00 01:35:00 01:51:00	21747-21835	89	89
Krajišnik	24/03/2006	0905-1029 1110-1212 1241-1346	01:24:00 01:02:00 01:05:00	21913-21991	79	79
Krajišnik	27/03/2006	1430-1606 1636-1730 1756-1906	01:36:00 00:54:00 01:10:00	21992-22081	90	80
Krajišnik	30/03/2006	1422-1554 1628-1741 1807-1911	01:32:00 01:13:00 01:04:00	22160-22235	76	76
Krajišnik	5/04/2006	0910-1040 1111-1132 1209-1346	01:30:00 00:21:00 01:37:00	22481-22566	86	86

Trial	Date	Time	Total time	ERN range	ERN pages	Total pages
Krajišnik	6/04/2006	0912-1037 1112-1228 1302-1350	01:25:00 01:26:00 00:48:00	22567-22654	88	88
Krajišnik	7/04/2006	0928-1022 1031-1108 1140-1338 1413-1425	00:56:00 00:37:00 01:58:00 00:12:00	22655-22747	93	93
Krajišnik	25/04/2006	0910-0955 1046-1115 1204-1307 1324-1346	00:45:00 00:29:00 01:03:00 01:22:00	22942-23015	74	74
Krajišnik	26/04/2006	0909-1033 1107-1226 1256-1347	01:24:00 01:19:00 00:51:00	23016-23103	88	88
Krajišnik	27/04/2006	1424-1550 1620-1735 1804-1859	01:26:00 01:15:00 00:55:00	23104-23195	92	92
Krajišnik	2/05/2006	0909-1029 1104-1225 1253-1348	01:20:00 01:21:00 00:55:00	23286-23367	82	82
Krajišnik	8/05/2006	1527-1552 1627-1728 1800-1903	00:25:00 01:01:00 01:03:00	23630-23709	80	80
Krajišnik	27/06/2006	0941-1102 1131-1305 1336-1352 1425-1531	01:21:00 01:34:00 00:16:00 01:06:00	26326-26409	84	83
Krajišnik	6/07/2006	1110-1136 1205-1324 1345-1421	00:26:00 01:19:00 00:36:00	26821-26875	55	55

Trial	Date	Time	Total time	ERN range	ERN pages	Total pages
Krajišnik	7/07/2006	0901-1036 1104-1236 1259-1407	01:35:00 01:32:00 01:08:00	26876-26976	101	101
Krajišnik	12/07/2006	1423-1557 1635-1812 1833-1912	01:34:00 01:37:00 00:39:00	27054-27130	77	77
Krajišnik	13/07/2006	1426-1555 1630-1755 1820-1905	01:29:00 01:25:00 00:45:00	27131-27208	78	78
Krajišnik	30/08/2006	0905-1037 1107-1236 1301-1349	01:32:00 01:29:00 00:48:00	27364-27450	87	87
Krajišnik	31/08/2006	1437-1534 1602-1712 1744-1859	00:57:00 01:10:00 01:15:00	27451-27534	84	84
Krajišnik	27/09/2006	1306-1343	00:37:00	27535-27549	15	15
Krajišnik			**565:51:00**	**13,917**		**13,485**[383]

383 This number includes: 480 full blank pages and 6 full ERN ranges inserted to consolidate pagination with English and French transcripts (100, 113, 301, 307, 486, 492, 498, 504, 510, 706, 1019, 1043, 1067, 1352, 1356, 1360, 1364, 1368, 1372, 1376, 1380, 1384, 1388, 1392, 1396, 1400, 1404, 1408, 1412, 1416, 1420, 1424, 1428, 1432, 1436, 1440, 1444, 1460, 1469, 1478, 1487, 1496, 1505, 1514, 1523, 1532, 1541, 1553, 1562, 1571, 1580, 1589, 1598, 1607, 1616, 1625, 1634, 1640, 1649, 1657, 1665, 1673, 1681, 1689, 1697, 1705, 1713, 1735, 1745, 1755, 1765, 1775, 1785, 1795, 1805, 1815, 1825, 1835, 1857, 1873, 1889, 1905, 1921, 1952, 1966, 1980, 1994, 2008, 2022, 2154, 2177, 2200, 2308, 2317, 2326, 2335, 2344, 2353, 2389, 2415, 2792, 2807, 2822, 2837, 2852, 2867, 2894, 2908, 2922, 2936, 2950, 2964, 3022, 3085, 3100, 3115, 3130, 3145, 3177, 3191, 3205, 3219, 3233, 3247, 4197, 4212, 4227, 4242, 4257, 4294, 4317, 4340, 4734, 4751, 4768, 4785, 4811, 4821, 4831, 4841, 4851, 4861, 4871, 4881, 5009, 5018, 5027, 5045, 5054, 5063, 5072, 5081, 5090, 5094, 5108, 5121, 5134, 5147, 5160, 5173, 5186, 5215, 5238, 5261, 5284, 5311, 5336, 5361, 6110-6112, 6161-6163, 4689, 4707, 4725, 4743, 4761, 6286, 6297, 6308, 6319, 6330, 6341, 6352, 6363, 6374, 6664, 6675,

Trial	Date	Time	Total time	ERN range	ERN pages	Total pages
Krstić	14/04/2000	0933-1008 1021-1123 1134-1220 1256-1405 1421-1433	00:35:00 01:02:00 00:46:00 01:09:00 00:12:00	2940-3053	114	114

6686, 7185, 7191, 7197, 7203, 7368, 7381, 7394, 7407, 7420, 7433, 7924, 7930, 7936, 7942, 7948, 7954, 8136, 8146, 8156, 8166, 8176, 8186, 8196, 8206, 8216, 8238, 8250, 8262, 8274, 8286, 8298, 8310, 8322, 8334, 8713, 8719, 8915, 8921, 9202, 9208, 9214, 9220, 9263, 9269, 9348, 9353, 9360, 9443, 9464, 9485, 9835, 9852, 9869, 9916, 9932, 9948, 9964, 9980, 10144, 10456, 10482, 10508, 10546, 10559, 10572, 10585, 10598, 10611, 10624, 10659, 10680, 10701, 10904, 10911, 10925, 10939, 10953, 10960, 10966, 10986, 10998, 11010, 11022, 11034, 11046, 11058, 11070, 11287, 11390, 11404, 11418, 11432, 11446, 11471, 11482, 14493, 11504, 11515, 11526, 11565, 11591, 11635, 11649, 11663, 11677, 11691, 11719, 11734, 11749, 11764, 11779, 11806, 11818, 11830, 11842, 11854, 11866, 11888, 11899, 11910, 11921, 11932, 11943, 11954, 11985, 12006, 12027, 12164, 12175, 12186, 12197, 12208, 12474, 12510, 12566, 12584, 12638, 13037, 13047, 13057, 13067, 13077, 13098, 13107, 13116, 13125, 13134, 13277, 13288, 13299, 13310, 13335, 13347, 13359, 13371, 13383, 13425, 13436, 13447, 13761, 13782, 13803, 13824, 13845, 13852, 13874, 13895, 13994, 14064, 14082, 14100, 14118, 14536, 14549, 14562, 14575, 14588, 14601, 14613, 14628, 14642, 14656, 14670, 14684, 14711, 14722, 14733, 14744, 14755, 14766, 14777, 14788, 15325, 15336, 15347, 15358, 15369, 15380, 15391, 15423, 15439, 15455, 15471, 15487, 15544, 15585, 16113, 16138, 16287, 16313, 16339, 16385, 16407, 16429, 16451, 16490, 16507, 16524, 16541, 16558, 16681, 16696, 16711, 16726, 16741, 16777, 16798, 16819, 16840, 17074, 17092, 17117, 17123, 17129, 17135, 17323, 17336, 17349, 17362, 17375, 17388, 17408, 17418, 17428, 17438, 17448, 17458, 17468, 17478, 17818, 17833, 17848, 17863, 17878, 17918, 17946, 18071, 18085, 18099, 18113, 18127, 18150, 18161, 18172, 18183, 18194, 18205, 18216, 18227, 18333, 18345, 18357, 18369, 18381, 18393, 18405, 18422, 18430, 18438, 18446, 18454, 18462, 18470, 18478, 18486, 18494, 18640, 18657, 18674, 18691, 18734, 18758, 18782), 15 blank pages inserted to consolidate pagination with English and French transcripts (5087, 5119, 5709, 23438, 23451, 24851, 24864, 24877, 24890, 24903, 24916, 24933, 24939, 24945, 24951), and 14 full blank pages and 432 redacted ERN range pages (5032-5038, 5080, 5082, 5083, 11292-11307, 11318-11375, 12468, 12479-12505, 12513-12538, 14965-15067, 15070-15153, 15156-15214, 16040-16089, 26327-26328) (23295-23373, 23375-23435, 24962, 24963, 24964, 25014, 25015, 25016, 25030, 25031) to a total of a minimum of 932 untranscribed pages.

Trial	Date	Time	Total time	ERN range	ERN pages	Total pages
Krstić	22/05/2000	0938-1100 1120-1240 1300-1403	01:22:00 01:20:00 01:03:00	3065-3184	120	109
Krstić	21/11/2003	1003-1149 1319-1426 1449-1535 1606-1658	01:46:00 01:07:00 00:46:00 00:52:00	95-208	114	109
Krstić			**12:00:00**	**348**		**332**[384]
Lukić	27/08/2008	0854-1013 1034-1210 1242-1347	01:19:00 01:36:00 01:05:00	602-690	89	87
Lukić	28/08/2008	0857-1209 1243-1342	03:12:00 00:59:00	691-769	79	68
Lukić	29/08/2008	0823-0950 1015-1140 1217-1313	01:27:00 01:25:00 00:56:00	770-868	99	95
Lukić	17/09/2008	0851-1012 1037-1210 1242-1341	01:21:00 01:33:00 00:59:00	1732-1825	94	87
Lukić	18/09/2008	0854-1401	05:07:00	1826-1912	87	10
Lukić	19/09/2008	0850-1211 1246-1347	03:21:00 01:01:00	1913-2012	100	67
Lukić	23/09/2008	1419-1545 1608-1844	01:26:00 02:38:00	2116-2205	90	86
Lukić	24/09/2008	0850-1021 1043-1201	01:31:00 01:18:00	2206-2286	81	81

384 This number includes: 1 blank page inserted to consolidate English and French transcript pagination (148) and 1 blank redacted page (3013) to a total of a minimum of 2 untranscribed pages.

Trial	Date	Time	Total time	ERN range	ERN pages	Total pages
Lukić	25/09/2008	0851-1021 1049-1212 1248-1350 1419-1426	01:30:00 01:23:00 01:02:00 01:07:00	2287-2382	96	96
Lukić	2/10/2008	1415-1546 1612-1736 1812-1915	01:29:00 01:24:00 01:03:00	2469-2569	101	101
Lukić			**41:12:00**	**916**		**778**[385]
Nikolić	10/10/1995	1004-1117 1130-1300 1430-1615 1630-1730	01:13:00 01:30:00 00:45:00 01:00:00	234-376	143	143
Nikolić			**04:28:00**	**143**		**143**
Popović	10/11/2005	1436-1612	01:36:00	1-46	46	46
Popović	4/04/2006	1418-1550 1614-1708	01:32:00 00:54:00	77-139	63	62
Popović	19/05/2006	1103-1236	01:33:00	140-174	35	33
Popović	6/07/2006	1440-1610 1638-1731	01:30:00 00:53:00	175-236	62	57
Popović	13/07/2006	1420-1542 1615-1743 1816-1855	01:22:00 01:28:00 00:39:00	238-327	90	89
Popović	14/07/2006	0905-1020	01:15:00	328-358	31	31

[385] This number includes: 1 blank pages inserted to consolidate English and French transcript pagination (2205), and 19 full blank pages and 149 redacted ERN range pages (643, 651-653, 707-711, 714-715, 741-743, 763-767, 785-789, 1817-1824, 1832-1833, 1835-1911, 1914-1947, 1973, 2011, 2189-2193, 2269, 2381, 2470, 2543, 2564) to a total of a minimum of 169 untranscribed pages.

Trial	Date	Time	Total time	ERN range	ERN pages	Total pages
Popović	21/08/2006	0902-0927 0933-1019 1043-1145 1212-1342	00:25:00 00:46:00 01:02:00 01:30:00	359-452	94	93
Popović	22/08/2006	0902-0957 1021-1137 1206-1323	00:55:00 01:16:00 01:17:00	453-545	93	93
Popović	23/08/2006	0903-1008 1035-1124 1150-1254	01:05:00 00:59:00 01:04:00	546-622	77	77
Popović	24/08/2006	0903-1024 1058-1229 1253-1345	01:21:00 01:31:00 00:52:00	623-726	104	99
Popović	25/08/2006	0900-1005 1034-1338	01:05:00 01:04:00	727-830	104	85
Popović	28/08/2006	0903-1023 1049-1212 1240-1336	01:20:00 01:23:00 00:56:00	831-920	90	90
Popović	29/08/2006	1432-1540 1603-1708 1732-1829	01:08:00 01:05:00 00:57:00	921-992	72	72
Popović	30/08/2006	1422-1544 1607-1729 1756-1901	01:22:00 01:22:00 01:05:00	993-1082	90	90
Popović	31/08/2006	1420-1545 1619[386]-1741 1815-1857	01:25:00 01:22:00 00:42:00	1083-1167	85	84

[386] T. 1115 stating the start of court break has a typo: it says 14:19 hrs where it should be 16:19.

Trial	Date	Time	Total time	ERN range	ERN pages	Total pages
Popović	6/09/2006	0907-1047 1121-1303	01:40:00 01:42:00	1168-1246	79	76
Popović	7/09/2006	0902-1031 1101-1227 1304-1345	01:29:00 01:26:00 00:41:00	1247-1327	81	80
Popović	8/09/2006	0903-1024 1054-1233 1302-1347	01:21:00 01:39:00 00:45:00	1328-1416	89	68
Popović	11/09/2006	0906-1030 1059-1225 1258-1346	01:24:00 01:26:00 00:48:00	1417-1502	86	85
Popović	12/09/2006	1420-1542 1616-1742 1813-1901	01:22:00 01:26:00 00:48:00	1503-1580	78	78
Popović	14/09/2006	1419-1540 1616-1646 1702-1745 1812-1902	01:21:00 00:30:00 00:43:00 00:50:00	1581-1667	87	74
Popović	15/09/2006	0933-1030 1059-1230 1259-1350	00:57:00 01:31:00 00:51:00	1668-1760	93	83
Popović	18/09/2006	0903-1032 1105-1233 1306-1350	01:30:00 01:28:00 00:44:00	1761-1853	93	93
Popović	19/09/2006	0904-1028 1106-1223 1255-1346	01:24:00 01:17:00 00:51:00	1854-1932	79	79
Popović	21/09/2006	0914-1030 1103-1224 1256-1344	01:16:00 01:21:00 00:48:00	1933-1978	46	46

Trial	Date	Time	Total time	ERN range	ERN pages	Total pages
Popović	22/09/2006	0906-1032 1059-1229 1300-1344	01:26:00 01:30:00 00:44:00	2006-2083	78	78
Popović	25/09/2006	0904-1029 1101-1232 1300-1347	01:25:00 01:31:00 00:47:00	2084-2164	81	81
Popović	27/09/2006	1425-1545 1615-1659 1733-1858	01:20:00 00:44:00 01:26:00	2234-2311	78	78
Popović	28/09/2006	1419-1506 1540-1711 1741-1852	00:47:00 00:31:00 01:11:00	2312-2387	76	76
Popović	29/09/2006	0910-1037	01:27:00	2388-2424	37	37
Popović	16/10/2006	0906-1027 1100-1224 1302-1345	01:21:00 01:24:00 00:43:00	2425-2520	96	96
Popović	17/10/2006	0906-1027 1059-1226 1257-1348	01:21:00 01:27:00 00:51:00	2521-2624	104	104
Popović	18/10/2006	0903-1028 1101-1109 1111-1226 1256-1347	01:25:00 00:08:00 01:15:00 00:51:00	2625-2727	103	102
Popović	19/10/2006	0903-0933 0939-1031 1103-1229 1305-1346	00:30:00 00:52:00 01:26:00 00:41:00	2728-2844	117	117
Popović	26/10/2006	1431-1546 1616-1724 1757-1903	01:15:00 01:08:00 01:06:00	3031-3111	81	81

Trial	Date	Time	Total time	ERN range	ERN pages	Total pages
Popović	27/10/2006	1427-1552 1618-1847	01:25:00 01:29:00	3112-3196	85	84
Popović	30/10/2006	0902-1029 1059-1230 1304-1348	01:27:00 01:31:00 00:44:00	3197-3293	97	82
Popović	31/10/2006	0913-1025 1104-1229 1302-1347	01:12:00 01:25:00 00:45:00	3294-3374	81	79
Popović	1/11/2006	0905-1040 1113-1229 1303-1346	01:35:00 01:16:00 00:43:00	3375-3469	95	81
Popović	2/11/2006	0905-1029 1106-1228 1306-1345	01:24:00 01:22:00 00:39:00	3470-3551	82	82
Popović	3/11/2006	0908-1030 1105-1128	01:22:00 00:23:00	3552-3591	40	39
Popović	30/11/2006	0904-1031 1105-1227 1254-1331	01:27:00 01:22:00 00:37:00	4819-4909	91	91
Popović	4/12/2006	1012-1142 1210-1344	01:30:00 01:34:00	4910-4998	89	89
Popović	7/12/2006	0903-1027 1100-1231 1259-1353	01:24:00 01:31:00 00:54:00	5172-5281	110	110
Popović	18/01/2007	1416-1558	01:42:00	6026-6063	38	38
Popović	30/01/2007	1417-1547 1614-1702 1728-1859	01:30:00 00:48:00 01:31:00	6518-6622	105	86

Trial	Date	Time	Total time	ERN range	ERN pages	Total pages
Popović	31/01/2007	1415-1554 1621-1747 1817-1900	01:39:00 01:26:00 00:43:00	6623-6719	97	97
Popović	6/02/2007	0904-0957 1028-1200 1228-1346	00:53:00 01:32:00 01:18:00	6906-6984	79	79
Popović	7/02/2007	0905-1030 1100-1227 1256-1343	01:25:00 01:27:00 00:47:00	6985-7069	85	81
Popović	8/02/2007	0906-1001 1028-1127 1140-1212 1244-1340	00:55:00 00:59:00 00:32:00 00:56:00	7070-7157	88	85
Popović	9/02/2007	0904-1028 1058-1231 1300-1347	01:24:00 00:33:00 00:47:00	7158-7246	89	89
Popović	19/02/2007	0905-1031 1101-1236 1304-1345	01:26:00 01:35:00 00:41:00	7247-7336	90	90
Popović	21/02/2007	0913-1031 1058-1229 1258-1346	01:18:00 01:31:00 01:48:00	7444-7546	103	103
Popović	14/03/2007	1423-1544 1614-1745 1812-1900	01:21:00 01:31:00 00:48:00	8789-8898	110	110
Popović	15/03/2007	1422-1547 1616-1738 1808-1859	01:25:00 01:22:00 00:51:00	8899-9009	111	111

Trial	Date	Time	Total time	ERN range	ERN pages	Total pages
Popović	30/03/2007	0905-1030 1058-1234 1301-1346	01:25:00 01:36:00 00:45:00	9720-9785	66	66
Popović	2/04/2007	0903-1034 1104-1230 1300-1346	01:31:00 01:26:00 00:46:00	9786-9858	73	73
Popović	16/04/2007	0905-1030 1100-1222 1253-1347	01:25:00 01:22:00 00:54:00	10032-10112	81	81
Popović	17/04/2007	0906-1031 1100-1232 1300-1346	01:25:00 01:32:00 00:46:00	10113-10188	76	76
Popović	18/04/2007	0906-1031 1059-1215 1245-1305	01:25:00 01:16:00 00:20:00	10189-10257	69	69
Popović	19/04/2007	0906-1020 1031-1046 1117-1211	01:14:00 01:15:00 01:04:00	10258-10311	54	54
Popović	24/04/2007	1418-1531 1600-1729 1756-1902	01:13:00 01:29:00 01:06:00	10399-10476	78	78
Popović	25/04/2007	1425-1542 1612-1733 1800-1903	01:17:00 01:21:00 01:03:00	10477-10557	81	81
Popović	1/05/2007	0904-0947 1001-1031 1055-1232 1310-1345	01:43:00 00:30:00 01:37:00 00:35:00	10723-10800	78	78

Trial	Date	Time	Total time	ERN range	ERN pages	Total pages
Popović	2/05/2007	0905-1027 1057-1228 1257-1344	01:22:00 01:31:00 00:47:00	10801-10879	79	79
Popović	4/05/2007	0907-1029 1100-1232 1301-1346	01:22:00 01:32:00 00:45:00	10919-10997	79	79
Popović	7/05/2007	0905-1019 1021-1029 1059-1235 1307-1320	01:14:00 00:08:00 01:36:00 00:13:00	10998-11069	72	72
Popović	10/05/2007	1422-1546 1615-1742 1813-1902	01:24:00 01:27:00 00:49:00	11253-11347	95	95
Popović	14/05/2007	0940-1033 1059-1218 1250-1339	00:53:00 01:19:00 00:49:00	11427-11496	70	70
Popović	16/05/2007	0905-1030 1059-1230 1258-1348	01:25:00 01:31:00 00:50:00	11579-11664	86	86
Popović	17/05/2007	0903-1027 1057-1213 1243-1347	01:24:00 01:16:00 01:04:00	11665-11740	76	76
Popović	18/05/2007	0904-1027 1100-1230 1300-1347	01:23:00 01:30:00 00:47:00	11741-11820	80	80
Popović	21/05/2007	0910-1030 1100-1225 1255-1347	01:20:00 01:25:00 00:52:00	11821-11891	71	71

Trial	Date	Time	Total time	ERN range	ERN pages	Total pages
Popović	23/05/2007	1420-1544 1612-1747 1813-1903	01:24:00 01:35:00 00:50:00	11967-12049	83	83
Popović	24/05/2007	1420-1537 1620-1739 1806-1904	01:17:00 01:19:00 00:58:00	12050-12130	81	81
Popović	29/05/2007	0928-1031 1055-1230 1259-1345	01:03:00 01:35:00 00:46:00	12131-12206	76	76
Popović	30/05/2007	0906-1024 1056-1229 1258-1345	01:18:00 01:33:00 01:47:00	12207-12284	78	78
Popović	31/05/2007	0904-1033 1102-1232 1259-1347	01:29:00 01:30:00 00:48:00	12285-12364	80	80
Popović	12/06/2007	0906-1034 1107-1220 1252-1347	01:28:00 01:13:00 00:55:00	12452-12531	80	80
Popović	14/06/2007	0906-1033 1105-1230 1300-1348	01:27:00 01:25:00 00:48:00	12594-12668	75	75
Popović	15/06/2007	0911-1021 1051-1227 1256-1347	01:10:00 01:36:00 00:51:00	12669-12741	73	73
Popović	19/06/2007	1424-1532 1608-1733 1805-1901	01:08:00 01:25:00 00:56:00	12829-12910	82	75
Popović	20/06/2007	1421-1501 1527-1647 1709-1800	00:40:00 01:20:00 00:51:00	12911-12973	63	59

Trial	Date	Time	Total time	ERN range	ERN pages	Total pages
Popović	21/06/2007	1425-1540 1611-1722 1753-1857	01:15:00 01:11:00 01:04:00	12974-13062	89	85
Popović	22/06/2007	0906-1033 1058-1222 1251-1351	01:27:00 01:24:00 01:00:00	13063-13159	97	83
Popović	26/06/2007	0905-1029 1057-1225 1306-1345	01:24:00 01:28:00 00:39:00	13270-13368	99	99
Popović	28/06/2007	0908-1024 1054-1230 1258-1347	01:16:00 01:36:00 01:49:00	13451-13531	81	81
Popović	9/07/2007	0907-1026 1058-1233 1300-1347	01:19:00 01:35:00 00:47:00	13532-13611	80	80
Popović	18/07/2007	1422-1545 1616-1707 1724-1733	01:23:00 00:51:00 00:09:00	13893-13954	62	62
Popović	19/07/2007	1533-1633	01:00:00	13955-13979	25	25
Popović	21/08/2007	0906-1027 1058-1221 1251-1333	01:21:00 01:23:00 01:42:00	13980-14066	87	86
Popović	23/08/2007	0908-1029 1100-1228 1302-1345	01:21:00 01:28:00 00:43:00	14159-14250	92	92
Popović	24/08/2007	0907-1030 1100-1233 1306-1345	01:23:00 01:33:00 00:39:00	14251-14344	94	94

Trial	Date	Time	Total time	ERN range	ERN pages	Total pages
Popović	27/08/2007	0904-1028 1100-1231 1300-1305[387]	01:24:00 01:31:00 00:05:00	14345-14421	77	77
Popović	30/08/2007	1421-1550 1618-1739 1803-1843	01:29:00 01:21:00 00:40:00	14492-14575	84	84
Popović	13/09/2007	1420-1540 1612-1747 1814-1902	01:20:00 01:35:00 00:48:00	15312-15396	85	85
Popović	14/09/2007	0906-1034 1100-1142	01:28:00 00:42:00	15397-15451	55	55
Popović	17/09/2007	0908-1024 1054-1232 1259-1348	01:16:00 01:38:00 00:49:00	15452-15527	76	76
Popović	19/09/2007	0906-1015 1033-1107	01:09:00 00:34:00	15610-15647	38	38
Popović	15/10/2007	0904-1028 1051-1224 1249-1332	01:24:00 01:33:00 00:43:00	16260-16359	100	100
Popović	5/11/2007	1000-1139 1212-1415	01:39:00 01:03:00	17457-17520	64	64
Popović	6/11/2007	1422-1542 1610-1710 1745-1855	01:20:00 01:00:00 01:10:00	17521-17595	75	75
Popović	7/11/2007	1422-1545 1615-1741 1807-1852	01:23:00 01:26:00 00:45:00	17596-17671	76	76

[387] T. 14381 stating there was audio missing 10:57:00 to 11:06:00.

Trial	Date	Time	Total time	ERN range	ERN pages	Total pages
Popović	8/11/2007	1428-1545 1614-1744 1812-1900	01:17:00 01:30:00 00:48:00	17672-17752	81	81
Popović	20/11/2007	0907-1031 1100-1235 1305-1345	01:24:00 01:35:00 00:40:00	17922-18008	87	87
Popović	22/11/2007	1421-1545 1620-1635	01:24:00 00:15:00	18094-18135	42	42
Popović	29/11/2007	1419-1545 1615-1746 1814-1900	01:26:00 01:31:00 00:46:00	18444-18520	77	77
Popović	30/11/2007	0904-1028 1100-1231 1258-1333	01:24:00 01:31:00 00:35:00	18521-18593	73	73
Popović	3/12/2007	0904-1029 1059-1231 1300-1350	01:25:00 01:32:00 00:50:00	18594-18665	72	72
Popović	6/12/2007	1409-1543 1613-1701	00:34:00 00:48:00	18844-18892	49	49
Popović	10/12/2007	0914-1036 1105-1232 1300-1345	01:22:00 01:27:00 00:45:00	18893-18988	96	96
Popović	11/12/2007	0907-1018 1049-1229 1258-1347	01:11:00 01:40:00 00:49:00	18989-19074	86	84
Popović	12/12/2007	0907-1030 1100-1232 1302-1345	01:23:00 01:32:00 00:43:00	19075-19165	91	90

Trial	Date	Time	Total time	ERN range	ERN pages	Total pages
Popović	13/12/2007	0908-1037 1059-1230 1303-1345	01:29:00 01:31:00 00:42:00	19166-19261	96	66
Popović	14/12/2007	0907-1030 1102-1205 1215-1240	01:23:00 01:03:00 00:25:00	19262-19328	67	67
Popović	10/01/2008	0907-1025 1058-1215 1248-1345	01:18:00 01:17:00 01:57:00	19329-19411	83	83
Popović	11/01/2008	0907-1030 1102-1207 1235-1348 1425-1549	01:23:00 01:05:00 01:13:00 01:24:00	19412-19544	133	133
Popović	15/01/2008	0911-1031 1106-1229 1301-1348	01:20:00 01:23:00 00:47:00	19666-19757	92	92
Popović	16/01/2008	0906-1030 1102-1218 1249-1345	01:24:00 01:16:00 00:56:00	19758-19858	101	101
Popović	17/01/2008	0908-1016 1050-1219 1250-1340	01:08:00 01:29:00 00:50:00	19859-19951	93	93
Popović	22/01/2008	0907-1031 1103-1232 1304-1345	01:24:00 01:29:00 00:41:00	20121-20211	91	91
Popović	24/01/2008	1424-1545 1617-1745 1814-1902	01:21:00 01:28:00 00:48:00	20316-20419	104	104

Trial	Date	Time	Total time	ERN range	ERN pages	Total pages
Popović	28/01/2008	0920-1030 1055-1147 1150-1214 1240-1343	01:10:00 00:52:00 00:34:00 01:03:00	20505-20582	78	78
Popović	29/01/2008	0906-1030 1105-1231 1313-1358	01:24:00 01:26:00 00:45:00	20583-20663	81	81
Popović	14/02/2008	0907-1032 1104-1221 1250-1339	01:25:00 01:17:00 00:49:00	21224-21304	81	81
Popović	3/03/2008	1423-1504	00:41:00	21459-21474	16	16
Popović	3/06/2008	0904-1026 1055-1228 1255-1343	01:22:00 01:33:00 00:48:00	21629-21707	79	79
Popović	5/06/2008	0904-1029 1058-1233 1258-1348	01:25:00 01:35:00 00:50:00	21792-21868	77	77
Popović	9/06/2008	0905-1030 1058-1228 1258-1346	01:25:00 01:30:00 00:48:00	21949-22028	80	80
Popović	10/06/2008	1421-1531 1604-1620 1633-1728 1758-1901	01:10:00 00:16:00 00:55:00 01:03:00	22029-22102	74	74
Popović	11/06/2008	1420-1540 1613-1726 1758-1823	01:20:00 01:13:00 00:26:00	22103-22175	73	73
Popović	17/06/2008	0905-1031 1101-1236 1303-1357	01:26:00 01:35:00 00:54:00	22261-22348	88	88

Trial	Date	Time	Total time	ERN range	ERN pages	Total pages
Popović	18/06/2008	0907-1018 1049-1230 1301-1346	01:11:00 01:41:00 00:45:00	22349-22429	81	81
Popović	24/06/2008	1420-1545 1615-1746 1815-1902	01:25:00 01:31:00 00:47:00	22672-22754	83	83
Popović	25/06/2008	1418-1545 1616-1748 1815-1900	01:27:00 01:32:00 00:45:00	22755-22835	81	81
Popović	26/06/2008	1422-1543 1615-1744 1814-1902	01:21:00 01:29:00 00:48:00	22836-22913	78	78
Popović	30/06/2008	0904-1010 1038-1215 1246-1345	01:06:00 01:37:00 00:59:00	23005-23087	83	83
Popović	1/07/2008	0905-1027 1059-1230 1300-1345	01:22:00 01:31:00 00:45:00	23088- 23159	72	72
Popović	3/07/2008	0905-1026 1057-1200 1232-1245	01:21:00 01:03:00 00:12:00	23230-23279	50	50
Popović	7/07/2008	0909-1033 1101-1233 1301-1331	01:24:00 01:32:00 00:30:00	23358-23431	74	74
Popović	10/07/2008	0906-1028 1102-1231 1258-1344	01:22:00 01:29:00 00:46:00	23510-23589	80	80
Popović	11/07/2008	0902-0944 1017-1149 1223-1352	00:42:00 01:32:00 01:29:00	23590-23675	86	86

Trial	Date	Time	Total time	ERN range	ERN pages	Total pages
Popović	22/07/2008	0903-1025 1058-1217 1246-1342	01:22:00 01:19:00 00:56:00	23752-23839	88	88
Popović	23/07/2008	0904-1023 1056-1110 1121-1228 1256-1345	01:19:00 00:14:00 01:07:00 00:49:00	23840-23936	97	97
Popović	25/07/2008	0906-1025 1100-1229 1259-1353	01:19:00 01:29:00 00:54:00	24055-24139	85	85
Popović	28/07/2008	0906-1041 1114-1249 1357-1517	01:35:00 01:35:00 01:20:00	24140-24248	109	109
Popović	29/07/2008	0907-1029 1100-1200 1237-1345	01:22:00 01:00:00 01:08:00	24249-24341	93	93
Popović	25/08/2008	1420-1546 1620-1748 1823-1900	01:26:00 01:28:00 00:37:00	24540-24618	79	79
Popović	29/08/2008	0905-1030 1100-1232 1301-1347	01:25:00 01:32:00 00:46:00	24862-24959	98	96
Popović	1/09/2008	0905-1029 1103-1229 1302-1341	01:24:00 01:26:00 00:39:00	24960-25036	77	77
Popović	10/09/2008	0904-1039 1110-1228 1300-1337	01:35:00 01:18:00 00:37:00	25498-25583	86	86

Trial	Date	Time	Total time	ERN range	ERN pages	Total pages
Popović	17/09/2008	1420-1539 1603-1718 1746-1840	01:19:00 01:15:00 00:54:00	25822-25909	88	88
Popović	24/09/2008	1004-1110 1131-1236	01:06:00 01:05:00	26141-26194	54	54
Popović	1/10/2008	1417-1547 1614-1723 1743-1845	01:30:00 01:09:00 01:02:00	26464-26545	82	82
Popović	6/10/2008	0904-1019 1043-1201 1223-1322	01:15:00 01:18:00 00:59:00	26635-26704	70	70
Popović	7/10/2008	0905-1023 1058-1224 1252-1344	01:18:00 01:26:00 00:52:00	26705-26779	75	75
Popović	8/10/2008	0904-1029 1058-1234 1302-1346	01:25:00 01:36:00 00:42:00	26780-26864	85	85
Popović	9/10/2008	0900-1028 1105-1132 1140-1226 1249-1343	01:28:00 00:27:00 00:46:00 00:54:00	26865-26941	77	77
Popović	10/10/2008	0905-1030 1059-1220 1248-1351	01:25:00 01:21:00 01:03:00	26942-27021	80	80
Popović	20/10/2008	0904-1022 1052-1231 1259-1345	01:18:00 01:39:00 00:46:00	27022-27105	84	84
Popović	23/10/2008	0907-1030 1053-1206 1239-1340	01:23:00 01:13:00 01:01:00	27267-27356	90	90

Trial	Date	Time	Total time	ERN range	ERN pages	Total pages
Popović	28/10/2008	1421-1502 1521-1615 1635-1745 1808-1348[388]	00:41:00 00:54:00 01:10:00 00:40:00	27428-27511	84	84
Popović	30/10/2008	1420-1544 1617-1710 1741-1850	01:24:00 00:53:00 01:09:00	27587-27654	68	68
Popović	31/10/2008	0904-1031 1058-1235 1303-1353	01:27:00 01:37:00 00:50:00	27655-27741	87	87
Popović	7/11/2008	0905-1029 1104-1230 1335-1500	01:24:00 01:26:00 01:25:00	27921-28013	93	93
Popović	12/11/2008	1422-1545 1613-1751 1816-1854	01:23:00 01:38:00 00:38:00	28014-28109	96	96
Popović	13/11/2008	1417-1552 1631-1716 1741-1855	01:35:00 00:45:00 01:14:00	28110-28206	97	97
Popović	14/11/2008	0903-1029 1057-1232 1259-1347	01:26:00 01:35:00 00:48:00	28207-28281	75	75
Popović	17/11/2008	0904-1026 1102-1235 1302-1346	01:22:00 01:32:00 00:44:00	28282-28359	78	78

388 T. 27511 stating the time the court adjourned is an obvious typo: it should be 18:48 hrs, not 13:48 hrs.

Trial	Date	Time	Total time	ERN range	ERN pages	Total pages
Popović	18/11/2008	0904-1030 1059-1230 1302-1347	01:26:00 01:31:00 00:45:00	28360-28442	83	83
Popović	19/11/2008	0904-1029 1058-1231 1258-1344	01:25:00 01:33:00 00:46:00	28443-28519	77	77
Popović	20/11/2008	0905-1020 1042-1202 1225-1316	01:15:00 01:20:00 00:51:00	28520-28587	68	68
Popović	21/11/2008	0905-1020 1044-1205 1228-1316	01:15:00 01:21:00 01:48:00	28588-28662	75	75
Popović	24/11/2008	0904-1029 1059-1231 1259-1345	01:25:00 01:32:00 00:46:00	28663-28745	83	83
Popović	26/11/2008	1420-1545 1615-1747 1815-1858	01:45:00 01:32:00 00:43:00	28823-28902	80	80
Popović	27/11/2008	0904-1031 1058-1216 1246-1346	01:27:00 01:18:00 01:00:00	28903-28977	75	75
Popović	28/11/2008	0904-1031 1100-1228 1259-1323	01:27:00 01:28:00 00:24:00	28978-29040	63	63
Popović	1/12/2008	0903-1018 1043-1159 1234-1343	01:15:00 01:16:00 01:09:00	29041-29111	71	71
Popović	3/12/2008	0904-1034 1108-1233 1301-1346	01:30:00 01:15:00 00:45:00	29183-29245	63	63

Trial	Date	Time	Total time	ERN range	ERN pages	Total pages
Popović	4/12/2008	0908-1031 1100-1231 1259-1345	00:23:00 01:31:00 00:46:00	29246-29305	60	60
Popović	5/12/2008	0904-1033 1102-1231 1259-1350	01:29:00 01:29:00 00:51:00	29306-29382	77	77
Popović	9/12/2008	0932-1041 1106-1151 1219-1315	01:09:00 00:45:00 00:56:00	29383-29444	62	62
Popović	11/12/2008	1420-1545 1608-1742 1805-1748	01:25:00 01:34:00 00:43:00	29520-29592	73	73
Popović	15/12/2008	0905-1031 1059-1235 1307-1347	01:26:00 01:36:00 00:40:00	29677-29763	87	87
Popović	12/01/2009	0922-1027 1059-1232 1303-1345	01:05:00 01:33:00 00:42:00	29948-30015	68	68
Popović	13/01/2009	0906-1029 1156-1344	01:23:00 01:48:00	30016-30073	58	58
Popović	14/01/2009	0904-1028 1059-1229 1258-1345	01:24:00 01:30:00 00:47:00	30074-30135	62	62
Popović	15/01/2009	0907-1031 1101-1233 1300-1344	01:24:00 01:32:00 00:44:00	30136-30199	64	64
Popović	16/01/2009	0909-1030 1102-1225 1301-1326	01:21:00 01:23:00 00:25:00	30200-30270	71	71

Trial	Date	Time	Total time	ERN range	ERN pages	Total pages
Popović	19/01/2009	0905-1027 1058-1227 1259-1348	01:22:00 01:29:00 00:49:00	30271-30348	78	78
Popović	20/01/2009	1423-1545 1614-1754 1829-1859	01:22:00 01:40:00 00:30:00	30349-30425	77	77
Popović	21/01/2009	1421-1538 1611-1740 1810-1900	01:17:00 01:29:00 00:50:00	30426-30505	80	80
Popović	22/01/2009	1419-1545 1614-1742 1805-1902	01:26:00 01:28:00 00:57:00	30506-30594	89	89
Popović	26/01/2009	0905-0958 1035-1121 1239-1254	00:53:00 00:46:00 00:15:00	30595-30643	49	49
Popović	27/01/2009	0907-1030 1101-1219 1250-1357	01:23:00 01:18:00 01:07:00	30644-30721	78	78
Popović	28/01/2009	0907-1021 1050-1209 1243-1347	01:14:00 01:19:00 01:04:00	30722-30796	75	75
Popović	29/01/2009	0905-1020 1049-1209 1238-1343	01:15:00 01:20:00 01:05:00	30797-30869	73	73
Popović	30/01/2009	0906-1022 1053-1215 1245-1345	01:16:00 01:22:00 01:00:00	30870-30944	75	75
Popović	2/02/2009	0907-1025 1054-1212 1240-1345	01:18:00 01:18:00 01:05:00	30945-31017	73	73

Trial	Date	Time	Total time	ERN range	ERN pages	Total pages
Popović	3/02/2009	1421-1533 1559-1700 1725-1815	01:12:00 01:01:00 00:50:00	31018-31081	64	64
Popović	9/02/2009	0905-1020 1049-1209 1238-1343	01:15:00 01:20:00 01:05:00	31082-31155	74	74
Popović	10/02/2009	0904-1021 1049-1209 1238-1345	01:17:00 01:20:00 01:07:00	31156-31231	76	76
Popović	11/02/2009	0905-1022 1052-1212 1240-1345	01:17:00 01:20:00 01:05:00	31232-31308	77	77
Popović	12/02/2009	0907-1018 1047-1206 1238-1345	01:11:00 01:19:00 01:07:00	31309-31387	79	72
Popović	13/02/2009	0903-1022 1048-1210 1238-1345	01:19:00 01:22:00 01:07:00	31388-31479	92	92
Popović	16/02/2009	0904-1020 1049-1211 1242-1345	01:16:00 01:22:00 01:03:00	31480-31570	91	90
Popović	17/02/2009	1420-1537 1607-1716 1749-1901	01:17:00 01:09:00 01:12:00	31571-31661	91	86
Popović	18/02/2009	1426-1534 1606-1722 1752-1858	01:08:00 01:16:00 01:06:00	31662-31744	83	82
Popović	19/02/2009	1420-1535 1605-1720 1750-1900	01:15:00 01:15:00 01:10:00	31745-31835	91	91

Trial	Date	Time	Total time	ERN range	ERN pages	Total pages
Popović	20/02/2009	0905-1018 1050-1208 1239-1342	01:13:00 01:18:00 01:03:00	31836-31939	104	104
Popović	23/02/2009	0904-1020 1049-1200 1230-1345	01:16:00 01:11:00 01:15:00	31940-32031	92	88
Popović	25/02/2009	0905-1018 1048-1212 1240-1346	01:15:00 01:24:00 01:06:00	32032-32111	80	80
Popović	26/02/2009	0905-1001 1029-1148 1220-1343	00:56:00 01:19:00 01:23:00	32112-32197	86	81
Popović	27/02/2009	0905-1019 1050-1209 1242-1337	01:14:00 01:19:00 00:55:00	32198-32283	86	86
Popović	2/03/2009	0904-1020 1048-1200 1230-1346	01:16:00 01:12:00 01:16:00	32284-32378	95	91
Popović	3/03/2009	1418-1534 1605-1725 1753-1856	01:16:00 01:19:00 01:03:00	32379-32470	92	90
Popović	11/03/2009	1035-1101	00:26:00	32609-32619	11	11
Popović	21/04/2009	0907-1021 1051-1232 1302-1348	01:14:00 01:41:00 00:46:00	32894-32969	76	76
Popović	22/04/2009	1420-1548 1618-1746 1817-1902	01:28:00 01:28:00 00:45:00	32970-33053	84	84

Trial	Date	Time	Total time	ERN range	ERN pages	Total pages
Popović	6/07/2009	0906-1017	01:11:00	33927-33952	26	26
Popović	15/07/2009	1424-1603 1625-1751 1804-1855	00:39:00 01:26:00 00:51:00	33953-34041	89	89
Popović	10/06/2010	1006-1133	01:27:00	34917-34956	40	40
Popović			**758:16:00**	**17,564**		**17,326**[389]
Stanišić and Župljanin	9/06/2009	1429-1508	00:29:00	21-35	15	15
Stanišić and Župljanin	4/09/2009	1422-1537 1619-1744	01:15:00 01:25:00	83-150	68	68
Stanišić and Župljanin	15/09/2009	1420-1545 1610-1732 1756-1829 1857-1903	01:25:00 01:22:00 00:33:00 00:06:00	247-337	91	91
Stanišić and Župljanin	16/09/2009	1417-1545 1606-1720 1742-1900	01:28:00 01:14:00 01:18:00	338-437	100	100

[389] This number includes: 6 blank pages and 50 ERN ranges inserted to consolidate English and French transcript pagination (24, 1395-1416, 1978-2005, 7157, 22175, 32378), and 89 full blank pages and 245 redacted ERN range pages (91-92, 152-154, 207-212, 214-215, 264-265, 449-450, 633-637, 644, 718-719, 731, 779-782, 786-792, 815-825, 1131-1132, 1209-1212, 1288-1289, 1457, 1464-1465, 1516, 1588-1601, 1669-1679, 1887, 2423, 2527, 2631-2632, 3150-3151, 3215-3216, 3239-3242, 3250-3255, 3268-3273, 3275-3276, 3304, 3316-3317, 3361-3362, 3390-3391, 3424-3425, 3428-3429, 3432-3440, 3453-3456, 3490, 3500, 3519, 3522, 3544, 3568-3569, 3574, 3578, 6525, 6550, 6561, 6577-6579, 6596-6601, 6606-6615, 6618-6621, 7029, 7036, 7062-7066, 7093, 7125-7128, 7146, 12841-12848, 12856, 12861, 12967-12971, 12981-12984, 13018-13019, 13023, 13095-13096, 13101, 13110-13120, 13135-13136, 13155-13157, 13984-13985, 14000, 19003-19005, 19117-19118, 31365-31372, 31557-31558, 31616-31618, 31635-31637, 31642-31643, 31667-31668, 31898, 31944-31948, 32175-32180, 32325-32329, 32402, 32404-32406, 32438) to a total of a minimum of 390 untranscribed pages.

Trial	Date	Time	Total time	ERN range	ERN pages	Total pages
Stanišić and Župljanin	17/09/2009	0905-1026 1047-1156 1256-1349	01:21:00 01:09:00 00:53:00	438-515	78	78
Stanišić and Župljanin	6/10/2009	1418-1543 1606-1725 1750-1855	01:25:00 01:19:00 01:05:00	880-967	88	88
Stanišić and Župljanin	7/10/2009	1427-1547 1609-1730 1757-1904	01:20:00 01:21:00 01:07:00	968-1052	85	85
Stanišić and Župljanin	8/10/2009	0901-1018 1059-1234 1303-1346	01:17:00 01:35:00 00:43:00	1053-1136	84	84
Stanišić and Župljanin	12/10/2009	0919-1028 1053-1219 1243-1344	01:09:00 01:26:00 01:01:00	1219-1299	81	81
Stanišić and Župljanin	13/10/2009	0903-1023 1047-1202 1227-1347	01:20:00 01:15:00 01:20:00	1300-1388	89	89
Stanišić and Župljanin	15/10/2009	0903-1024 1100-1204 1228-1340	01:21:00 01:04:00 01:12:00	1475-1553	79	79
Stanišić and Župljanin	19/10/2009	0940-1024 1048-1207 1233-1348 1454-1617	00:44:00 01:19:00 01:15:00 00:23:00	1554-1659	106	106
Stanišić and Župljanin	20/10/2009	0906-1023 1059-1207 1234-1341 1448-1625	01:17:00 01:08:00 01:07:00 01:37:00	1660-1774	115	115

Trial	Date	Time	Total time	ERN range	ERN pages	Total pages
Stanišić and Župljanin	21/10/2009	0908-1027 1059-1204 1229-1346 1450-1616	01:19:00 01:05:00 01:17:00 00:26:00	1775-1896	122	122
Stanišić and Župljanin	26/10/2009	0905-1024 1105-1214 1237-1345	01:19:00 01:09:00 01:08:00	1963-2045	83	83
Stanišić and Župljanin	27/10/2009	1419-1540 1605-1720 1742-1904	01:21:00 01:15:00 00:22:00	2046-2136	91	91
Stanišić and Župljanin	28/10/2009	0907-1025 1047-1208 1230-1347	01:18:00 01:21:00 01:17:00	2137-2232	96	96
Stanišić and Župljanin	30/10/2009	0902-1017 1043-1159 1224-1345	01:15:00 01:16:00 01:21:00	2322-2409	88	88
Stanišić and Župljanin	3/11/2009	1418-1539 1603-1720 1743-1901	01:21:00 01:17:00 01:18:00	2497-2585	89	89
Stanišić and Župljanin	11/11/2009	0906-1022 1050-1205 1227-1345	01:16:00 01:15:00 01:18:00	2864-2945	82	82
Stanišić and Župljanin	12/11/2009	0904-1024 1056-1204 1229-1344	01:20:00 01:08:00 01:15:00	2946-3028	83	83
Stanišić and Župljanin	13/11/2009	0903-1023 1058-1208 1232-1348	01:20:00 01:10:00 01:16:00	3029-3116	88	88

Trial	Date	Time	Total time	ERN range	ERN pages	Total pages
Stanišić and Župljanin	16/11/2009	0906-1028 1051-1213 1244-1346	01:22:00 01:22:00 01:02:00	3117-3204	88	88
Stanišić and Župljanin	2/12/2009	0904-1026 1053-1159 1225-1344	01:22:00 01:06:00 01:19:00	4019-4108	90	90
Stanišić and Župljanin	8/12/2009	0914-1026 1125-1231 1253-1349	01:12:00 01:06:00 00:56:00	4362-4446	85	85
Stanišić and Župljanin	9/12/2009	0908-1023 1049-1214 1242-1343	02:15:00 01:25:00 01:01:00	4447-4526	80	80
Stanišić and Župljanin	1/02/2010	0903-1030 1051-1208 1229-1351 1439-1553 1530-1637	01:27:00 01:17:00 01:22:00 01:14:00 01:07:00	5845-5975	131	131
Stanišić and Župljanin	2/02/2010	1424-1510 1518-1542 1613-1724 1750-1908	00:46:00 00:24:00 01:11:00 01:18:00	5976-6050	75	75
Stanišić and Župljanin	3/02/2010	1425-1541 1604-1639 1656-1722 1744-1901	01:16:00 00:35:00 01:26:00 01:17:00	6051-6131	81	81
Stanišić and Župljanin	5/02/2010	0905-1033 1059-1159 1223-1258	01:28:00 01:00:00 00:35:00	6211-6280	70	70

Trial	Date	Time	Total time	ERN range	ERN pages	Total pages
Stanišić and Župljanin	15/02/2010	1426-1547 1629-1727 1751-1902	01:21:00 00:58:00 01:11:00	6281-6360	80	80
Stanišić and Župljanin	17/02/2010	1416-1540 1603-1656	01:34:00 00:53:00	6445-6497	53	53
Stanišić and Župljanin	18/02/2010	1418-1541 1603-1721 1747-1836	01:23:00 01:18:00 00:49:00	6498-6578	81	81
Stanišić and Župljanin	19/02/2010	1017-1108	00:51:00	6579-6598	20	20
Stanišić and Župljanin	23/02/2010	0904-1029 1055-1215 1237-1343	01:25:00 01:20:00 01:06:00	6667-6751	85	85
Stanišić and Župljanin	24/02/2010	0907-1025 1110-1207 1230-1349 1422-1553	01:18:00 00:57:00 01:19:00 01:31:00	6752-6855	104	104
Stanišić and Župljanin	25/02/2010	1416-1540 1604-1720 1742-1855	01:24:00 01:16:00 01:13:00	6856-6943	88	88
Stanišić and Župljanin	8/03/2010	0906-1020 1045-1128	01:14:00 00:43:00	7247-7342	96	46
Stanišić and Župljanin	11/03/2010	1024-1205 1227-1321	01:31:00 00:54:00	7471-7528	58	58
Stanišić and Župljanin	12/03/2010	0925-1024 1108-1141	00:59:00 00:33:00	7529-7562	34	34

Trial	Date	Time	Total time	ERN range	ERN pages	Total pages
Stanišić and Župljanin	15/03/2010	1426-1543 1619-1727 1753-1905	01:15:00 01:08:00 01:12:00	7563-7645	83	83
Stanišić and Župljanin	18/03/2010	0905-1026 1050-1205 1232-1345	01:21:00 01:15:00 01:13:00	7727-7818	92	92
Stanišić and Župljanin	19/03/2010	1427-1543 1607-1720 1753-1909	01:16:00 01:13:00 01:16:00	7819-7899	81	81
Stanišić and Župljanin	30/03/2010	0911-1036 1059-1210 1231-1348	01:25:00 01:11:00 01:17:00	8278-8361	84	84
Stanišić and Župljanin	31/03/2010	0908-0927 0951-1038 1059-1209 1234-1347	00:19:00 00:47:00 01:10:00 01:13:00	8362-8439	78	78
Stanišić and Župljanin	16/04/2010	0905-1025 1056-1206 1232-1337	01:20:00 01:10:00 01:05:00	8790-8863	74	74
Stanišić and Župljanin	26/04/2010	1421-1557 1603-1720 1745-1832	01:36:00 01:17:00 00:37:00	9200-9278	79	79
Stanišić and Župljanin	27/04/2010	0904-1027 1055-1159 1224-1332	01:23:00 01:04:00 01:08:00	9279-9361	83	83
Stanišić and Župljanin	28/04/2010	0905-0955	00:50:00	9362-9380	19	19
Stanišić and Župljanin	4/05/2010	0905-1026 1050-1210 1238-1346	01:21:00 01:20:00 01:08:00	9473-9564	92	92

Trial	Date	Time	Total time	ERN range	ERN pages	Total pages
Stanišić and Župljanin	5/05/2010	0907-1023 1053-1205 1231-1348	01:16:00 01:12:00 01:17:00	9565-9644	80	80
Stanišić and Župljanin	6/05/2010	0904-1028 1055-1204 1228-1347	01:24:00 01:09:00 01:19:00	9645-9733	89	89
Stanišić and Župljanin	7/05/2010	0906-1025 1051-1206 1230-1350	01:19:00 01:15:00 01:20:00	9734-9821	88	88
Stanišić and Župljanin	10/05/2010	0906-1024 1049-1204 1228-1335	01:18:00 01:15:00 01:07:00	9822-9903	82	82
Stanišić and Župljanin	11/05/2010	0907-1021 1052-1205 1231-1347	01:14:00 01:12:00 01:16:00	9904-9987	84	84
Stanišić and Župljanin	12/05/2010	0907-1020 1105-1207 1238-1354	01:13:00 01:02:00 01:16:00	9988-10066	79	74
Stanišić and Župljanin	18/05/2010	1017-1146 1219-1348	01:29:00 01:29:00	10394-10470	77	77
Stanišić and Župljanin	19/05/2010	1424-1543 1609-1724 1751-1855	01:19:00 01:15:00 01:04:00	10471-10552	82	82
Stanišić and Župljanin	20/05/2010	0905-1030 1057-1211 1235-1346	01:25:00 01:14:00 01:11:00	10553-10638	86	86
Stanišić and Župljanin	21/05/2010	0905-1022 1056-1213	01:17:00 01:17:00	10639-10705	67	67

Trial	Date	Time	Total time	ERN range	ERN pages	Total pages
Stanišić and Župljanin	25/05/2010	0909-1026 1054-1202 1229-1347	01:17:00 01:08:00 01:18:00	10706-10789	84	82
Stanišić and Župljanin	26/05/2010	0908-1025 1055-1206 1234-1349	01:17:00 01:11:00 01:15:00	10790-10872	83	83
Stanišić and Župljanin	27/05/2010	0906-1024 1101-1208 1242-1347	01:18:00 01:07:00 01:05:00	10873-10955	83	77
Stanišić and Župljanin	28/05/2010	0908-1025 1058-1209 1234-1343	01:17:00 01:11:00 01:09:00	10956-11033	78	71
Stanišić and Župljanin	31/05/2010	0905-1025 1050-1208 1232-1351	01:20:00 01:18:00 01:19:00	11034-11112	79	79
Stanišić and Župljanin	1/06/2010	0909-1022 1100-1208 1231-1345	01:13:00 01:08:00 01:14:00	11113-11194	82	82
Stanišić and Župljanin	2/06/2010	0907-1030 1054-1203 1232-1347	01:23:00 01:09:00 01:15:00	11195-11285	91	91
Stanišić and Župljanin	8/06/2010	1425-1540 1608-1721 1745-1859	01:15:00 01:13:00 01:14:00	11356-11437	82	82
Stanišić and Župljanin	10/06/2010	0904-1024 1049-1204 1229-1344	01:20:00 01:15:00 01:15:00	11514-11596	83	83
Stanišić and Župljanin	11/06/2010	0910-1025 1050-1205 1230-1342	01:15:00 01:15:00 01:12:00	11597-11676	80	80

Trial	Date	Time	Total time	ERN range	ERN pages	Total pages
Stanišić and Župljanin	14/06/2010	0906-1025 1049-1202	01:19:00 01:13:00	11677-11735	59	59
Stanišić and Župljanin	17/06/2010	0906-1028 1054-1207 1230-1303	01:22:00 01:13:00 00:33:00	11880-11950	71	71
Stanišić and Župljanin	21/06/2010	0903-0908 1103-1212 1237-1347	00:05:00 01:09:00 01:10:00	11951-12007	57	57
Stanišić and Župljanin	22/06/2010	0929-1026 1054-1206 1229-1341	00:57:00 01:12:00 01:12:00	12008-12086	79	79
Stanišić and Župljanin	16/07/2010	0906-1000 1030-1118 1126-1147	00:54:00 00:48:00 01:21:00	12897-12939	43	43
Stanišić and Župljanin	22/07/2010	0908-0922	00:14:00	13165-13171	7	7
Stanišić and Župljanin	16/08/2010	1425-1542 1607-1723 1752-1901	01:17:00 01:16:00 01:09:00	13172-13260	89	89
Stanišić and Župljanin	17/08/2010	1421-1538 1631-1721 1747-1912	01:17:00 00:50:00 01:25:00	13261-13346	86	86
Stanišić and Župljanin	19/08/2010	1430-1542 1607-1700	01:12:00 00:53:00	13430-13478	49	49
Stanišić and Župljanin	20/08/2010	0916-1027 1054-1102	01:09:00 00:08:00	13479-13510	32	32
Stanišić and Župljanin	24/08/2010	0915-1036 1059-1134	01:11:00 00:35:00	13599-13646	48	48

Trial	Date	Time	Total time	ERN range	ERN pages	Total pages
Stanišić and Župljanin	25/08/2010	0913-1025 1110-1207 1237-1351	01:12:00 00:57:00 01:14:00	13647-13717	71	71
Stanišić and Župljanin	1/09/2010	1436-1540 1622-1729 1800-1900	01:04:00 01:07:00 01:00:00	14017-14081	65	65
Stanišić and Župljanin	2/09/2010	1439-1547 1618-1727 1802-1907	01:08:00 01:09:00 01:05:00	14082-14153	72	72
Stanišić and Župljanin	3/09/2010	0900-1026 1100-1207 1231-1344	01:26:00 01:07:00 01:13:00	14154-14229	76	76
Stanišić and Župljanin	6/09/2010	0904-1027 1057-1208 1231-1346	01:23:00 01:11:00 01:15:00	14230-14309	80	80
Stanišić and Župljanin	27/09/2010	0908-1025 1051-1203 1234-1347	01:17:00 01:12:00 01:13:00	14842-14925	84	79
Stanišić and Župljanin	28/09/2010	1422-1534 1604-1730 1759-1846	01:12:00 01:24:00 00:47:00	14926-15006	81	68
Stanišić and Župljanin	29/09/2010	0905-1007 1031-1204	01:02:00 01:33:00	15007-15063	57	57
Stanišić and Župljanin	30/09/2010	1420-1540 1607-1721 1748-1901	01:20:00 01:14:00 01:13:00	15064-15147	84	84
Stanišić and Župljanin	1/10/2010	0907-1022 1050-1209 1246-1346	01:15:00 01:19:00 01:00:00	15148-15224	77	77

Trial	Date	Time	Total time	ERN range	ERN pages	Total pages
Stanišić and Župljanin	4/10/2010	0906-1025 1050-1207 1233-1349	01:16:00 01:17:00 01:16:00	15225-15310	86	86
Stanišić and Župljanin	6/10/2010	0909-1030 1057-1206 1237-1347	01:21:00 01:09:00 01:10:00	15401-15494	94	94
Stanišić and Župljanin	7/10/2010	0903-1023 1052-1208 1231-1346 1435-1607	01:20:00 01:16:00 01:15:00 00:32:00	15495-15614	120	120
Stanišić and Župljanin	8/10/2010	0904-1025 1049-1206 1312-1409	00:21:00 01:17:00 00:57:00	15615-15695	81	81
Stanišić and Župljanin	12/04/2011	0903-1026 1057-1205 1228-1350	01:23:00 01:08:00 01:22:00	19407-19486	80	80
Stanišić and Župljanin	13/04/2011	0907-1030 1057-1206 1232-1348	01:23:00 01:09:00 01:16:00	19487-19567	81	81
Stanišić and Župljanin	14/04/2011	0902-1007 1029-1150 1211-1324	01:05:00 01:21:00 01:13:00	19568-19646	79	79
Stanišić and Župljanin	15/04/2011	0904-1024 1048-1205 1228-1340	01:20:00 00:17:00 01:12:00	19647-19724	78	78
Stanišić and Župljanin	18/04/2011	0904-1030 1055-1209 1231-1347	01:26:00 01:14:00 01:16:00	19725-19801	77	76

Trial	Date	Time	Total time	ERN range	ERN pages	Total pages
Stanišić and Župljanin	19/04/2011	0907-1028 1102-1206 1228-1348	01:21:00 01:04:00 01:20:00	19802-19874	73	73
Stanišić and Župljanin	20/04/2011	0903-1025 1052-1212 1236-1346	01:22:00 01:20:00 01:10:00	19875-19951	77	77
Stanišić and Župljanin	21/04/2011	0905-1025 1050-1157	01:20:00 01:07:00	19952-20005	54	54
Stanišić and Župljanin	17/05/2011	0925-1023 1055-1208 1238-1345	00:58:00 01:13:00 01:07:00	20742-20811	70	61
Stanišić and Župljanin	18/05/2011	0904-1025 1049-1207 1230-1348	01:21:00 01:18:00 01:18:00	20812-20894	83	83
Stanišić and Župljanin	19/05/2011	0907-1028 1101-1202 1232-1350 1438-1552	01:21:00 01:01:00 01:18:00 01:14:00	20895-20997	103	103
Stanišić and Župljanin	20/05/2011	0906-1026 1050-1214 1237-1345	01:20:00 01:24:00 01:08:00	20998-21084	87	87
Stanišić and Župljanin	23/05/2011	0914-1029 1056-1203 1228-1417	01:15:00 01:07:00 00:49:00	21085-21178	94	94
Stanišić and Župljanin	24/05/2011	0903-1021 1046-1159 1225-1345	01:18:00 01:13:00 01:20:00	21179-21252	74	74
Stanišić and Župljanin	25/05/2011	0903-1025 1053-1208 1232-1338	01:22:00 01:15:00 01:06:00	21253-21331	79	63

Trial	Date	Time	Total time	ERN range	ERN pages	Total pages
Stanišić and Župljanin	27/05/2011	0903-1025 1051-1203 1229-1345	01:22:00 01:12:00 01:16:00	21405-21481	77	77
Stanišić and Župljanin	30/05/2011	0909-1025 1052-1205 1234-1347	01:16:00 01:12:00 01:13:00	21482-21555	74	74
Stanišić and Župljanin	31/05/2011	0903-1022 1054-1205 1226-1344	01:19:00 01:11:00 01:18:00	21556-21633	78	78
Stanišić and Župljanin	1/06/2011	0902-1025 1049-1205 1231-1343	01:23:00 01:16:00 01:12:00	21634-21714	81	81
Stanišić and Župljanin	2/06/2011	0904-1024 1055-1205 1230-1331	01:20:00 01:10:00 01:01:00	21715-21794	80	80
Stanišić and Župljanin	3/06/2011	0900-1026 1047-1113	01:26:00 00:26:00	21795-21831	37	37
Stanišić and Župljanin			**188:37:00**	**9,068**		**8,954**[390]
Tolimir	17/05/2010	1421-1544 1622-1747 1819-1901	01:23:00 01:25:00 00:42:00	1861-1943	83	83

[390] This number includes: 23 full blank pages and 184 redacted ERN range pages (9989, 10058, 10060-10065, 10725-10727, 10761, 10774, 10866, 10899-10902, 10931-10933, 10949-10950, 11020-11027, 11051, 11081, 14845-14849, 14856, 14901-14902, 14942-14944, 14964-14975, 19727-19728, 20749-20755, 20766-20769, 21296-21303, 21310-21319) to a total of a minimum of 207 untranscribed pages.

Trial	Date	Time	Total time	ERN range	ERN pages	Total pages
Tolimir	17/05/2011	0903-1031 1105-1209 1244-1346	01:28:00 01:04:00 01:02:00	14173-14250	78	78
Tolimir	18/05/2011	0901-1029 1103-1230 1302-1353	01:28:00 01:27:00 01:52:00	14251-14334	84	84
Tolimir			**11:51:00**	**245**		**245**
Vasiljević	18/09/2001	0930-1100 1133-1300 1430-1536	01:30:00 01:27:00 01:06:00	628-731	104	104
Vasiljević			**04:03:00**	**104**		**104**[391]
Martić	21/05/2002	0900-1456[392]	05:46:00	1-17	16	16
Martić	23/09/2002	1102-1228	01:26:00	17-53	37	37
Martić	23/09/2002	1251-1333	00:41:00	54-70	17	17
Martić	28/01/2003	1500-1533	00:33:00	71-86	16	16
Martić	29/05/2003	1500-1517	00:17:00	87-94	8	8
Martić	29/09/2003	1503-1523	00:22:00	95-103	9	9
Martić	22/01/2004	1432-1517	00:45:00	104-123	20	20
Martić	20/05/2004	1507-1618	01:11:00	124-153	30	30
Martić	21/09/2004	1550-1626	00:36:00	154-169	16	16
Martić	18/01/2005	1504-1524	00:20:00	170-179	10	10
Martić	19/05/2005	1419-1442	00:23:00	180-190	11	11
Martić	15/09/2005	1418-1500	00:42:00	191-210	20	20

[391] This number includes: 4 blank pages inserted to consolidate English and French transcript pagination (653, 679, 705, 730) to a total of a minimum of 4 untranscribed pages.

[392] The B/C/S contains an error: the English version says the trial commenced at 14:19 and the French version says 14:20, not 09:00 as stated in the B/C/S transcript.

Trial	Date	Time	Total time	ERN range	ERN pages	Total pages
Martić	12/12/2005	1804-1936	01:32:00	211-256	46	46
Martić	13/12/2005	1415-1531 1551-1719	01:16:00 01:28:00	257-319	63	63
Martić	16/01/2006	1433-1558 1622-1748 1817-1858	01:25:00 01:22:00 00:41:00	320-408	89	89
Martić	17/01/2006	1420-1544 1620-1626 1649-1806 1836-1909	01:24:00 00:06:00 01:17:00 00:33:00	409 - 494	86	86
Martić	18/01/2006	1421-1531 1602-1710 1740-1902	01:10:00 01:08:00 01:22:00	495-586	92	92
Martić	19/01/2006	1421-1536 1606-1650	01:15:00 00:44:00	587-634	48	48
Martić	26/01/2006	1431-1545 1616-1730 1801-1904	01:14:00 01:14:00 01:03:00	635-727	93	93
Martić	27/01/2006	0900-1014 1048-1200 1233-1547	01:14:00 01:12:00 03:14:00	728-851	124	124
Martić	30/01/2006	0902-1018 1047-1202 1231-1352	01:16:00 01:15:00 01:21:00	852-931 19:03:00	80	80
Martić	31/01/2006	0906-1016 1051-1159	01:10:00 01:08:00	932-1005	**74**	**74**

Trial	Date	Time	Total time	ERN range	ERN pages	Total pages
Martić	03/02/2006	0917-1051 1049-1203 1231-1346 1433-1550	01:34:00 01:14:00 01:15:00 01:17:00	1006-1115	110	110
Martić	06/02/2006	0907-1014 1050-1205 1230-1730	01:07:00 01:15:00 05:00:00	1116-1187	72	72
Martić	07/02/2006	0904-1016 1048-1200 1232-1354	01:12:00 01:12:00 01:22:00	1188-1267	80	80
Martić	09/02/2006	0906-1015 1045-1203	01:09:00 01:18:00	1268-1320	49	49
Martić	15/02/2006	1418-1535 1602-1715 1746-1900	01:17:00 01:13:00 01:14:00	1321-1411	91	91
Martić	16/02/2006	1428-1533 1601-1717 1747-1900	01:05:00 01:16:00 01:03:00	1412-1495	84	84
Martić	17/02/2006	0901-1016 1047-1158 1232-1343	01:15:00 01:11:00 01:11:00	1496-1577	82	82
Martić	20/02/2006	0903-1020 1046-1202 1236-1346	01:17:00 01:16:00 01:10:00	1578-1658	81	81
Martić	21/02/2006	0903-1017 1052-1201 1231-1349	01:14:00 01:09:00 01:18:00	1659-1749	91	91
Martić	2/03/2006	1418-1533 1600-1716 1746-1906	01:15:00 01:16:00 01:20:00	1750-1849	100	100

Trial	Date	Time	Total time	ERN range	ERN pages	Total pages
Martić	3/03/2006	1416-1531 1601-1716 1745-1901	01:15:00 01:15:00 01:16:00	1850-1934	85	85
Martić	6/03/2006	0923-0937	00:14:00	1935-1937	3	3
Martić	8/03/2006	1417-1531 1602-1715 1746-1902	01:14:00 01:13:00 01:16:00	1938-2028	91	74
Martić	9/03/2006	0901-1159 1231-1353	01:58:00 01:22:00	2029 - 2128	100	86
Martić	10/03/2006	1444-1514 1604-1906	00:30:00 03:02:00	2129-2218	90	71
Martić	13/03/2006	0902-0936 1100-1109	00:34:00 00:09:00	2219- 2236	18	18
Martić	14/03/2006	0900-1312	04:12:00	2237-2256	19	3
Martić	15/03/2006	0902-0941	00:39:00	2257-2271	15	11
Martić	20/03/2006	1416-1915	04:59:00	2272 - 2374	103	3
Martić	21/03/2006	1425-1523	00:58:00	2375-2401	27	27
Martić	22/03/2006	1417-1531 1601-1703	01:14:00 01:02:00	2402-2461	60	60
Martić	23/03/2006	0903-1014 1040-1345	01:11:00 03:05:00	2462-2557	96	51
Martić	24/03/2006	1415-1530 1604-1715 1746-1842	01:15:00 01:11:00 00:56:00	2558-2637	80	74
Martić	27/03/2006	0906-1016 1046-1202 1233-1349	01:10:00 01:16:00 01:16:00	2638-2720	83	76

Trial	Date	Time	Total time	ERN range	ERN pages	Total pages
Martić	28/03/2006	0902-1102 1122-1221 1240-1347	02:00:00 00:59:00 01:07:00	2721-2806	86	65
Martić	29/03/2006	0901-1018 1047-1143 1232-1436	01:17:00 00:56:00 02:04:00	2807-2887	81	70
Martić	30/03/2006	0901-1017 1046-1202 1231-1345	01:16:00 01:16:00 01:14:00	2888-2977	90	90
Martić	31/03/2006	0904-1024 1051-1344	01:20:00 02:53:00	2978-3058	81	65
Martić	3/04/2006	0905-1202 1234-1346	02:57:00 01:12:00	3059-3130	72	42
Martić	4/04/2006	0900-1203 1235-1342	03:03:00 01:07:00	3131-3214	84	48
Martić	5/04/2006	1416-1531 1602-1717 1751-1831	01:15:00 01:15:00 00:40:00	3215-3292	78	78
Martić	6/04/2006	1419-1530 1604-1701 1731-1856	01:11:00 00:57:00 01:25:00	3293-3369	77	77
Martić	7/04/2006	1001-1131 1202-1339	01:30:00 01:27:00	3370-3444	75	75
Martić	10/04/2006	0902-1018 1046-1404	01:16:00 04:40:00	3445-3515	71	68
Martić	11/04/2006	0902-1019 1047-1204 1233-1349	01:17:00 01:17:00 01:16:00	3516-3594	79	79

Trial	Date	Time	Total time	ERN range	ERN pages	Total pages
Martić	12/04/2006	0901-1016 1048-1203 1233-1345	01:15:00 01:15:00 01:12:00	3594-3672	78	78
Martić	13/04/2006	0901-1018 1053-1222	01:17:00 01:29:00	3673-3735	63	55
Martić	25/04/2006	0901-1014 1046-1201 1232-1348	01:13:00 01:15:00 01:16:00	3736-3824	89	89
Martić	26/04/2006	0905-1016 1048-1204 1233-1247	01:11:00 01:16:00 00:14:00	3825-3888	64	64
Martić	2/05/2006	1426-1500 1602-1713 1745-1903	00:34:00 01:11:00 01:18:00	3889-3965	77	77
Martić	3/05/2006	1414-1522	01:08:00	3966-3994	29	29
Martić	4/05/2006	1416-1528 1602-1719 1749-1902	01:12:00 01:17:00 01:13:00	3995-4072	78	78
Martić	5/05/2006	1413-1532 1603-1716 1746-1903	01:19:00 01:13:00 01:17:00	4073-4139	67	67
Martić	8/05/2006	0903-1053	01:50:00	4140 - 4148	9	6
Martić	9/05/2006	0907-1016 1050-1206 1233-1306	01:09:00 01:16:00 00:29:00	4149-4209	61	58
Martić	11/05/2006	1013-1026	00:13:00	4210-4215	6	6
Martić	22/05/2006	0902-1347	04:45:00	4216-4300	85	3
Martić	23/05/2006	0900-1348	04:46:00	4301-4385	85	14

Trial	Date	Time	Total time	ERN range	ERN pages	Total pages
Martić	24/05/2006	0900-1203 1231-1346	03:03:00 01:15:00	4386-4462	77	49
Martić	25/05/2006	0901-1404	05:03:00	4463-4549	87	13
Martić	26/05/2006	0901-1015 1040-1207 1232-1244	01:14:00 01:27:00 00:12:00	4550-4626	77	77
Martić	29/05/2006	1417-1532 1610-1718 1746-1903	01:15:00 01:08:00 01:17:00	4627-4709	83	83
Martić	30/05/2006	1427-1531 1602-1719 1753-1904	01:04:00 01:17:00 01:11:00	4710-4794	85	85
Martić	31/05/2006	1417-1531 1602-1717 1744-1904	01:14:00 01:15:00 01:20:00	4795-4890	96	96
Martić	1/06/2006	1417-1546 1605-1736 1757-1921	01:29:00 01:31:00 01:24:00	4891-4988	98	98
Martić	2/06/2006	1423-1530 1539-1726	01:07:00 01:47:00	4989-5056	68	68
Martić	6/06/2006	0902-1017 1046-1202 1229-1354	01:15:00 01:16:00 01:25:00	5057-5144	88	88
Martić	7/06/2006	0906-1015 1046-1202 1231-1344	01:09:00 01:16:00 01:13:00	5145-5236	92	92
Martić	8/06/2006	0902-1347	04:45:00	5237-5326	90	63
Martić	9/06/2006	0905-1150	02:45:00	5327-5384	58	8

Trial	Date	Time	Total time	ERN range	ERN pages	Total pages
Martić	12/06/2006	1416-1530 1600-1719 1751-1902	01:14:00 01:19:00 01:11:00	5385-5477	93	93
Martić	13/06/2006	1422-1530 1601-1719 1747-1920	01:08:00 01:18:00 01:33:00	5478-5568	91	91
Martić	14/06/2006	1423-1458 1523-1531 1600-1904	01:35:00 01:09:00 03:04:00	5569-5643	75	75
Martić	15/06/2006	1424-1529 1558-1714 1745-1916	01:05:00 01:16:00 01:31:00	5644-5724	81	81
Martić	16/06/2006	1440-1543 1600-1615	01:03:00 00:15:00	5725-5758	34	22
Martić	19/06/2006	0910-1013 1043-1147	01:03:00 01:03:00	5759-5807	49	49
Martić	20/06/2006	0900-1025	01:25:00	5808-5839	32	32
Martić	26/06/2006	1415-1530 1605-1716 1746-1903	01:15:00 01:11:00 01:17:00	5840-5926	87	87
Martić	27/06/2006	1430-1524	00:54:00	5927-5956	30	30
Martić	3/07/2006	0900-1008	01:08:00	5958-5982	25	26
Martić	7/07/2006	0900-1016 1046-1112	01:16:00 00:26:00	5983-6023	41	41
Martić	11/07/2006	0901-1016 1046-1201 1230-1407	01:15:00 01:15:00 01:37:00	6024-6106	83	84

Trial	Date	Time	Total time	ERN range	ERN pages	Total pages
Martić	12/07/2006	0900-1015 1047-1200 1232-1346	01:15:00 01:13:00 01:14:00	6107-6189	83	83
Martić	13/07/2006	0923-1020 1047-1205 1231-1346	00:57:00 01:18:00 01:15:00	6189-6273	85	85
Martić	14/07/2006	0903-1015 1050-1204 1232-1255	01:12:00 01:14:00 00:33:00	6274-6341	68	68
Martić	14/08/2006	1418-1530 1601-1716 1746-1904	01:12:00 01:15:00 01:18:00	6342-6431	90	90
Martić	15/08/2006	0902-1015 1049-1203 1232-1355	01:13:00 01:14:00 01:23:00	6432-6523	92	92
Martić	16/08/2006	0902-1009 1047-1157 1232-1345	01:07:00 01:10:00 01:13:00	6524-6618	95	95
Martić	18/08/2006	0902-1016 1048-1203 1230-1348	01:14:00 01:15:00 01:18:00	6704-6786	83	77
Martić	17/08/2006	0915-1015 1046-1200 1230-1348	01:00:00 01:14:00 01:18:00	6619-6703	85	85
Martić	21/08/2006	1415-1530 1558-1711 1744-1858	01:15:00 01:13:00 01:14:00	6787-6871	85	74
Martić	22/08/2006	0906-1017 1054-1200 1232-1348	01:11:00 01:06:00 01:16:00	6872-6950	79	79

Trial	Date	Time	Total time	ERN range	ERN pages	Total pages
Martić	23/08/2006	0859-1014 1046-1156 1228-1304	01:15:00 01:10:00 00:36:00	6951-7037	87	87
Martić	24/08/2006	0903-1015 1047-1352	01:12:00 03:05:00	7038-7126	89	71
Martić	25/08/2006	1417-1532 1603-1720 1748-1903	01:15:00 01:17:00 01:15:00	7127-7214	88	83
Martić	28/08/2006	1428-1532 1604-1717 1746-1900	01:04:00 01:13:00 01:14:00	7215-7304	90	79
Martić	29/08/2006	0900-1117 1046-1348	02:17:00 03:02:00	7305-7393	89	32
Martić	30/08/2006	1030-1346	03:16:00	7394-7440	47	3
Martić	31/08/2006	0900-1356	04:56:00	7441-7528	88	3
Martić	1/09/2006	0900-1348	04:48:00	7529-7622	94	3
Martić	4/09/2006	1415-1900	04:45:00	7623-7711	89	3
Martić	5/09/2006	0900-1352	04:52:00	7712-7798	87	8
Martić	6/09/2006	0913-1015 1044-1200 1233-1347	01:12:00 01:16:00 01:14:00	7799-7873	75	75
Martić	7/09/2006	0901-1010 1045-1200 1230-1345	01:09:00 01:15:00 01:15:00	7873-7962	90	90
Martić	8/09/2006	1420-1510 1610-1715 1745-1905	00:50:00 01:05:00 01:20:00	7963-8030	68	68

Trial	Date	Time	Total time	ERN range	ERN pages	Total pages
Martić	11/09/2006	1414-1530 1558-1715 1744-1945	01:16:00 01:17:00 02:01:00	8031-8120	90	90
Martić	12/09/2006	0900-1013 1045-1200 1230-1348	01:13:00 01:15:00 01:18:00	8121-8212	92	92
Martić	13/09/2006	0900-1014 1044-1200 1229-1342	01:14:00 01:16:00 01:13:00	8213-8309	97	97
Martić	14/09/2006	0900-0920 0934-1015 1046-1200 1230-1346	00:20:00 00:41:00 01:14:00 01:16:00	8310-8399	90	90
Martić	15/09/2006	1417-1531 1600-1716 1752-1902	01:14:00 01:16:00 01:10:00	8400-8483	84	84
Martić	18/09/2006	1418-1530 1600-1718 1745-1900	01:12:00 01:18:00 01:15:00	8484-8575	92	92
Martić	19/09/2006	0900-1015 1055-1200 1230-1350	01:15:00 01:05:00 01:20:00	8576-8662	87	87
Martić	20/09/2006	0901-1015 1045-1200 1230-1346	01:15:00 01:15:00 01:16:00	8663-8753	91	91
Martić	21/09/2006	0900-1000 1100-1200 1230-1350	01:00:00 01:00:00 01:20:00	8754-8843	90	90

Trial	Date	Time	Total time	ERN range	ERN pages	Total pages
Martić	22/09/2006	1418-1531 1601-1714 1745-1907	01:13:00 01:13:00 01:22:00	8844-8936	93	93
Martić	9/10/2006	1418-1530 1601-1715 1745-1905	01:12:00 01:14:00 01:20:00	8937-9032	96	96
Martić	10/10/2006	0905-1015 1045-1200 1230-1730	01:10:00 01:15:00 05:00:00	9033-9128	96	96
Martić	11/10/2006	1422-1533 1600-1649 1654-1715 1744-1901	01:11:00 00:49:00 00:19:00 01:16:00	9129-9224	96	96
Martić	12/10/2006	0908-1017 1047-1203 1231-1346	01:09:00 01:16:00 01:15:00	9225-9317	93	93
Martić	13/10/2006	0901-1014 1046-1159 1230-1351	01:13:00 01:13:00 01:21:00	9318-9410	93	87
Martić	16/10/2006	1416-1529 1600-1719 1748-1900	01:13:00 01:19:00 01:12:00	9411-9512	102	69
Martić	17/10/2006	1415-1535 1605-1718 1746-1906	01:20:00 01:13:00 01:20:00	9513-9614	102	91
Martić	18/10/2006	1420-1530 1559-1716 1745-1901	01:10:00 01:17:00 01:16:00	9615-9709	95	89

Trial	Date	Time	Total time	ERN range	ERN pages	Total pages
Martić	19/10/2006	1416-1532 1559-1716 1745-1859	01:16:00 01:17:00 01:14:00	9710-9798	89	89
Martić	20/10/2006	1413-1513 1601-1715 1745-1859	01:00:00 01:14:00 01:14:00	9799-9900	102	102
Martić	23/10/2006	0901-1017 1045-1201 1229-1344	01:16:00 01:16:00 01:15:00	9901-9995	95	95
Martić	25/10/2006	0919-1015 1108-1202 1231-1349	00:56:00 00:54:00 01:18:00	9996-10079	84	84
Martić	26/10/2006	0901-1017 1047-1158 1231-1345	01:16:00 01:11:00 01:14:00	10080-10171	92	92
Martić	27/10/2006	0901-1015 1044-1159 1230-1347	01:14:00 01:15:00 01:17:00	10172-10269	98	98
Martić	30/10/2006	1414-1528 1600-1713 1746-1906	01:14:00 01:13:00 01:20:00	10270-10361	92	92
Martić	31/10/2006	1425-1526 1600-1713 1745-1859	01:01:00 01:13:00 01:14:00	10362-10454	93	93
Martić	1/11/2006	1415-1513 1559-1715 1746-1901	00:58:00 01:16:00 01:15:00	10455-10545	91	70
Martić	2/11/2006	1416-1846	04:30:00	10564-10637	74	9

Trial	Date	Time	Total time	ERN range	ERN pages	Total pages
Martić	3/11/2006	1421-1529 1600-1715 1744-1918	01:08:00 01:15:00 01:32:00	10638-10741	104	104
Martić	09/11/2006	0903-1014 1045-1201 1233-1348	01:11:00 01:16:00 01:15:00	10742-10837	96	96
Martić	10/11/2006	1423-1532 1602-1714 1743-1904	01:09:00 01:12:00 01:21:00	10838-10931	94	94
Martić	13/11/2006	1416-1531 1601-1715 1745-1852	01:15:00 01:14:00 01:07:00	10932-11031	100	100
Martić	14/11/2006	1420-1430 1449-1530 1601-1715 1746-1907	00:10:00 00:41:00 01:14:00 01:21:00	11032-11115	84	84
Martić	15/11/2006	1419-1506	00:47:00	11116-11137	22	22
Martić	16/11/2006	1420-1459	01:39:00	11138-11155	18	18
Martić	29/11/2006	1601-1620	00:19:00	11156-11164	9	9
Martić	10/01/2007	0904-1000 1029-1159 1230-1345	00:56:00 01:30:00 01.15:00	11165-11249	85	84
Martić	11/01/2007	0905-1016 1047-1202 1229-1353	01:11:00 01:15:00 01:24:00	11250-11342	93	93
Martić	12/01/2007	0907-1015 1045-1206 1231-1412	01:08:00 01:21:00 01:41:00	11343-11447	105	105
Martić	12/06/2007	0859-1017	01:18:00	11448-11476	29	29

Trial	Date	Time	Total time	ERN range	ERN pages	Total pages
Martić			**519:16:00**	**11,458**		**10,117**[393]
Đorđević	6/05/2009	0905-1030 1106-1229 1306-1347	01:25:00 01:23:00 00:41:00	3977-4052	76	76
Đorđević	15/05/2009	0902-1030 1107-1230 1302-1356	01:28:00 01:23:00 00:54:00	4521-4598	78	74
Đorđević	18/05/2009	1417-1541 1611-1743 1810-1855	01:24:00 01:32:00 00:45:00	4599-4674	76	76

---

393 This number includes: 15 blank pages inserted to consolidate English and French transcript pagination (8, 33, 51, 61, 78, 99, 109, 115, 134, 135, 175, 195, 200, 205, 2128), and 139 full blank pages and 1,464 redacted ERN range pages (333, 334, 1313-1317, 1939-1943, 1951-1955, 1959, 1965-1967, 1976, 1993, 2000, 2001, 2014-2021, 2038, 2039, 2048-2062, 2078, 2118, 2119, 2125, 2126, 2137-2143, 2151, 2163, 2176-2187, 2203, 2204, 2215-2217, 2238-2255, 2258, 2266-2270, 2273-2373, 2463-2467, 2515-2556, 2559-2565, 2639-2646, 2735, 2736, 2758-2761, 2787-2805, 2808-2819, 3014-3016, 3022-3028, 3038-3046, 3060-3067, 3080-3088, 3096, 3114-3129, 3132-3150, 3154-3160, 3172-3178, 3183, 3192-3195, 3210-3213, 3490-3493, 3623, 3716, 3720-3728, 3882-3883, 3983, 3988-3989, 4074, 4141-4144, 4146, 4150, 4204-4207, 4212-4213, 4217-4299, 4302-4363, 4374-4384, 4387-4410, 4419-4420, 4430-4432, 4437, 4447-4449, 4459, 4471-4533, 4536-4548, 5238, 5240-5244, 5248-5249, 5256-5257, 5264-5270, 5279-5283, 5285-5289, 5292, 5305-5307, 5309, 5318-5323, 5328-5377, 5382-5383, 5387-5389, 5412, 5415, 5425, 5482-5483, 5726-5729, 5737-5746, 5751, 6302, 6361-6363, 6711-6712, 6735-6738, 6745-6747, 6788-6791, 6859-6867, 6876-6877, 6999, 7081-7084, 7092-7104, 7111-7114, 7141, 7169-7170, 7202-7206, 7250, 7278-7282, 7292-7299, 7323-7325, 7337-7392, 7395-7439, 7442-7527, 7530-7621, 7624-7710, 7713-7792, 9241, 9321-9323, 9336-9339, 9390-9391, 9412-9414, 9455-9470, 9483-9485, 9497-9511, 9598-9609, 9629-9635, 10488-10492, 10502, 10527-10544, 10549-10557, 10560-10635, 11175-11176) to a total of a minimum of 1,518 untranscribed pages.

Trial	Date	Time	Total time	ERN range	ERN pages	Total pages
Đorđević	19/05/2009	0900-0953 1032-1201 1232-1348	00:53:00 01:29:00 01:16:00	4675-4751	77	77
Đorđević	20/05/2009	0904-1030 1103-1228 1300-1347	01:26:00 01:25:00 00:47:00	4752-4827	76	76
Đorđević			**18:11:00**	**383**		**379**[394]
Šainović et al	14/07/2006	0858-1027 1050-1218 1241-1344	01:29:00 01:28:00 01:03:00	845-938	94	94
Šainović et al	28/01/2008	0859-1046 1115-1245 1345-1533	01:47:00 01:30:00 01:45:00	21140-21258	119	119
Šainović et al	27/02/2008	0900-1030 1051-1219 1251-1349	01:30:00 01:28:00 00:58:00	23265-23352	88	88
Šainović et al			**12:58:00**	**301**		**301**
Perišić	12/11/2008	0900-1015 1048-1206 1232-1341	01:15:00 01:18:00 01:09:00	1341-1436	96	96
Perišić	3/02/2009	1416-1529 1600-1724 1748-1750	01:13:00 01:24:00 00:02:00	3098-3163	66	66
Perišić	7/05/2009	0901-1017 1046-1202 1231-1348	01:16:00 01:16:00 01:17:00	5871-5957	87	87

394 This number includes: 1 blank page inserted to consolidate English and French transcript pagination (4674), and 3 full blank pages and 5 redacted ERN range pages (4524, 4547, 4567-4571) to a total of a minimum of 9 untranscribed pages.

Trial	Date	Time	Total time	ERN range	ERN pages	Total pages
Perišić	11/05/2009	1422-1530 1600-1716 1750-1909	01:08:00 01:16:00 01:19:00	5958-6050	93	93
Perišić			**13:53:00**	**342**		**342**[395]
Milošević	27/08/2002	0902-1031 1055-1217 1239-1342	01:29:00 01:22:00 01:03:00	8912-9011	100	100
Milošević	28/08/2002	0903-1033 1058-1208 1234-1345	01:30:00 01:10:00 01:09:00	9012-9113	102	96
Milošević	29/08/2002	0903-1035 1100-1212 1236-1349	01:32:00 01:12:00 01:13:00	9114-9219	106	99
Milošević	30/08/2002	0902-1030 1100-1208 1235-1337	01:28:00 01:08:00 01:02:00	9220-9312	93	85
Milošević	5/05/2003	0900-1216 1240-1349	03:16:00 01:09:00	20039-20160	122	77
Milošević	6/05/2003	0903-1033 1056-1218 1240-1347	01:30:00 01:22:00 01:07:00	20161-20283	123	123
Milošević	8/05/2003	0903-1031 1055-1336	01:28:00 02:41:00	20392-20499	108	97
Milošević	9/05/2003	0913-1046 1109-1230 1255-1405	01:33:00 01:21:00 01:10:00	20500-20625	126	126

395 This number includes: 1 blank page inserted to consolidate English and French transcript pagination (5957) and 1 blank redacted page (6011) to a total of a minimum of 2 untranscribed pages.

Trial	Date	Time	Total time	ERN range	ERN pages	Total pages
Milošević	8/07/2003	0902-1032 1057-1218 1243-1349	01:30:00 01:21:00 01:06:00	23785-23898	114	112
Milošević	25/08/2003	0902-1035 1100-1218 1244-1407 1424-1455	01:32:00 01:18:00 01:23:00 01:21:00	25118-25244	127	127
Milošević	15/10/2003	0903-1024 1048-1215 1240-1347	01:21:00 01:27:00 01:07:00	27525-27631	107	107
Milošević	16/10/2003	0904-1026 1051-1229 1252-1353	01:22:00 01:28:00 01:01:00	27632-27753	122	118
Milošević	24/11/2003	0904-1030 1055-1220 1243-1358	01:26:00 01:25:00 01:15:00	29454-29583	130	128
Milošević	26/11/2003	0904-1030 1053-1218 1240-1407	01:26:00 01:25:00 01:27:00	29584-29718	135	135
Milošević	27/11/2003	0910-0939 1009-1148 1224-1405	00:29:00 01:39:00 01:31:00	29719-29836	118	95
Milošević	22/03/2005	0903-1033 1102-1223 1245-1345	01:30:00 01:21:00 01:00:00	37605-37717	113	113
Milošević	23/03/2005	0903-1031 1056-1215 1240-1345	01:28:00 01:19:00 01:05:00	37718-37821	104	104

Trial	Date	Time	Total time	ERN range	ERN pages	Total pages
Milošević	24/03/2005	0906-1033 1058-1217 1244-1325	01:27:00 01:19:00 01:41:00	37822-37916	95	95
Milošević	6/04/2005	0904-1034 1058-1215 1240-1343	01:30:00 01:17:00 01:03:00	37917-38024	108	108
Milošević	7/04/2005	0906-1038 1106-1233 1258-1345	01:32:00 01:27:00 01:47:00	38025-38134	110	110
Milošević	27/04/2005	0904-1220 1242-1250	03:16:00 00:08:00	38853-38928	76	72
Milošević	4/05/2005	0908-1035 1059-1217 1243-1406	01:27:00 01:17:00 01:23:00	38929-39039	111	111
Milošević	5/05/2005	0907-1037 1103-1218 1244-1346	01:30:00 01:15:00 01:02:00	39040-39138	99	99
Milošević	6/05/2005	0903-1357	04:52:00	39139-39167	29	29
Milošević	9/05/2005	0904-1038 1102-1222 1245-1353	01:34:00 01:20:00 01:08:00	39168-39271	104	104
Milošević	10/05/2005	0904-1036 1100-1217 1244-1353	01:32:00 01:17:00 01:09:00	39272-39381	110	110
Milošević	11/05/2005	0904-1037 1104-1215[396] 1242-1345	01:33:00 01:09:00 01:03:00	39382-39486	105	105

[396] T. 39458 stating the start of court break has a typo: it says 15:15 hrs where it should be 12:15.

Trial	Date	Time	Total time	ERN range	ERN pages	Total pages
Milošević	17/05/2005	0903-1037 1100-1218 1244-1343	01:34:00 01:18:00 00:59:00	39487-39591	105	105
Milošević	18/05/2005	0905-1034 1100-1215 1240-1342	01:29:00 01:15:00 01:02:00	39592-39694	103	103
Milošević	19/05/2005	0904-0908 0915-1007 1056-1216 1240-1344	00:04:00 00:53:00 01:20:00 01:04:00	39695-39785	91	91
Milošević	25/05/2005	0901-1036 1057-1216 1239-1345	01:35:00 01:19:00 01:06:00	39786-39891	106	106
Milošević	26/05/2005	0904-1030 1054-1225 1249-1343	01:26:00 01:31:00 00:54:00	39892-39999	108	105
Milošević	27/05/2005	1419-1742 1803-1904	03:23:00 01:01:00	40000-40112	113	99
Milošević	31/05/2005	0908-1034 1100-1216 1239-1345	01:26:00 01:16:00 01:06:00	40113-40217	105	105
Milošević	1/06/2005	0903-1037 1058-1221 1245-1344	01:34:00 01:23:00 00:59:00	40218-40319	102	102
Milošević	2/06/2005	0904-1035 1100-1221 1243-1346	01:31:00 01:21:00 01:03:00	40320-40428	109	109
Milošević	6/06/2005	0902-1031 1054-1216 1240-1344	01:29:00 01:22:00 01:04:00	40429-40537	109	109

Trial	Date	Time	Total time	ERN range	ERN pages	Total pages
Milošević	7/06/2005	0913-1219 1244-1347	03:06:00 01:03:00	40538-40646	109	99
Milošević	8/06/2005	0955-1129 1205-1349	01:34:00 01:44:00	40647-40740	94	94
Milošević	15/06/2005	0902-1034 1058-1219 1245-1346	01:32:00 01:21:00 01:01:00	40741-40852	112	112
Milošević	9/11/2005	0905-1006 1026-1122 1139-1233 1251-1346	01:01:00 00:56:00 00:56:00 00:55:00	46257-46365	109	109
Milošević	10/11/2005	0903-1006 1028-1123 1145-1244 1307-1405	01:03:00 00:55:00 00:59:00 00:58:00	46366-46477	112	112
Milošević			**167:47:00**	**4,484**		**4,345**[397]

---

[397] This number includes: 329 blank pages and 40 blank ERN ranges inserted to consolidate English and French transcript pagination (8920, 8929, 8938, 8947, 8956, 8965, 8974, 8983, 8992, 9001, 9054-9060, 9152-9159, 9261-9269, 20092, 20101, 20110, 20120, 20130, 20139, 20148, 20157, 20171, 20182, 20193, 20204, 20215, 20226, 20238, 20248, 20259, 20270, 20281, 20404, 20418, 20431, 20444, 20457, 20485, 20497, 20511, 20522, 20533, 20544, 20555, 20566, 20577, 20589, 20601, 20612, 20623, 23811, 23840, 23868, 23893, 23832-23834, 23888, 25123, 25129, 25135, 25141, 25147, 25143, 25159, 25165, 25171, 25177, 25183, 25189, 25195, 25244, 27530, 27536, 27542, 27548, 27554, 27560, 27566, 27572, 27578, 27637, 27643, 27649, 27655, 27667, 27673, 27679, 27685, 29459, 29465, 29471, 29477, 29483, 29489, 29495, 29501, 29513, 29519, 29525, 29531, 29537, 29543, 29549, 29589, 29595, 29601, 29607, 29613, 29619, 29619, 29625, 29631, 29611, 29637, 29643, 29649, 29655, 29661, 29667, 29673, 29679, 29771-29784, 37617, 37630, 37643, 37656, 37669, 37682, 37695, 37708, 37729, 37741, 37753, 37765, 37777, 37789, 37801, 37813, 37832, 37843, 37854, 37865, 37876, 37887, 37898, 37929, 37942, 37955, 37968, 37981, 37994, 38007, 38040, 38056, 38072, 38088,

Trial	Date	Time	Total time	ERN range	ERN pages	Total pages
TOTAL			**2455:01:00**	**62,610**		**59,903**

38104, 38120, 38865, 38878, 38891, 38904, 38917, 38940, 38952, 38964, 38976, 38988, 39000, 39012, 39024, 39052, 39065, 39078, 39091, 39104, 39117, 39130, 39153, 39180, 39193, 39206, 39219, 39232, 39245, 39258, 39271, 39283, 39295, 39307, 39319, 39331, 39343, 39355, 39367, 39394, 39407, 39420, 39433, 39446, 39459, 39472, 39498, 39510, 39522, 39534, 39546, 39558, 39570, 39582, 39601, 39611, 39621, 39631, 39641, 39651, 39661, 39671, 39681, 39694, 39705, 39716, 39727, 39738, 39749, 39760, 39771, 39798, 39811, 39824, 39837, 39850, 39863, 39876, 39903, 39915, 39927, 39939, 39951, 39963, 39975, 39987, 40029, 40059, 40089, 40111, 40121, 40130, 40139, 40148, 40157, 40166, 40175, 40184, 40193, 40202, 40226, 40235, 40244, 40253, 40262, 40271, 40280, 40289, 40298, 40307, 40329, 40339, 40349, 40359, 40369, 40379, 40389, 40399, 40409, 40419, 40439, 40450, 40461, 40472, 40483, 40494, 40505, 40516, 40527, 40551, 40565, 40593, 40607, 40621, 40635, 40662, 40678, 40694, 40710, 40726, 40750, 40760, 40770, 40780, 40790, 40800, 40810, 40820, 40830, 40840, 46264, 46272, 46280, 46288, 46296, 46304, 46312, 46320, 46328, 46336, 46344, 46352, 46360, 46374, 46383, 46393, 46401, 46410, 46419, 46428, 46437, 46446, 46455, 46464), and 30 full blank pages and 116 redacted ERN range pages (9143, 20040-20085, 20393-20397, 20468-20475, 20480, 20481, 25228, 27619, 27658-27662, 29455, 29456, 29510, 29511, 29557-29559, 29582, 29724-29729, 29819-29820, 29824, 29828-29832, 37983, 38871-38875, 38887, 39993-39996, 40042-40053, 40101-40104, 40571-40581, 40785, 40803, 40804, 40805) to a total of a minimum of 115 untranscribed pages.

Appendix 6. The situation country and the ethnicity of testifying witnesses vs. language of interpreters and language of the transcript

Trial	Date	Situation country	Witness	Ethnicity of the witness	Language of interpreters	Language of the transcript
Blagojević and Jokić	21/07/2003	B&H	Mevludin Orić	B&H Muslim	BS *(ije)*	BS *(ije)*
Blagojević and Jokić	1/12/2003	B&H	Cvijetin Ristanović	B&H Serb	CRO *(ije)* SR *(e)*	BS *(ije)*
Blagojević and Jokić	1/12/2003	B&H	Nenad Đokić	B&H Serb	BS *(ije)*	BS *(ije)*
Blagojević and Jokić	19/01/2004	B&H	Miroslav Deronjić	B&H Serb	CRO *(ije)*	SR *(e)*
Blagojević and Jokić	20/01/2004	B&H	Miroslav Deronjić		CRO *(ije)* SR *(e)*	BS *(ije)*
Blagojević and Jokić	21/01/2004	B&H	Miroslav Deronjić		CRO *(ije)* SR *(e)*	BS *(ije)*
Blagojević and Jokić	22/01/2004	B&H	Miroslav Deronjić		BS *(ije)* CRO *(ije)*	BS *(ije)*
Blagojević and Jokić	8/06/2004	B&H	Petar Salapura	B&H Serb	BS *(ije)* CRO *(ije)*	BS *(ije)*
Blagojević and Jokić	9/06/2004	B&H	Petar Salapura		BS *(ije)* CRO *(ije)*	BS *(ije)*
Blagojević and Jokić	9/06/2004	B&H	Dragomir Keserović	B&H Serb	BS *(ije)* CRO *(ije)*	BS *(ije)*
Blagojević and Jokić	19/07/2004	B&H	Zoran Radosavljević	B&H Serb	BS *(ije)* CRO *(ije)*	BS *(ije)*
Blagojević and Jokić	19/07/2004	B&H	Mirko Rebić	B&H Serb	BS *(ije)* CRO *(ije)*	BS *(ije)*
Brđanin	25/04/2002	B&H	Adil Draganović	B&H Muslim	CRO *(ije)*	BS *(ije)*
Brđanin	26/04/2002	B&H	Adil Draganović		SR *(e)*	BS *(ije)*
Brđanin	15/05/2002	B&H	Adil Draganović		SR *(e)*	BS *(ije)*
Brđanin	9/12/2003	B&H	Radosava Džombić	B&H Serb	CRO *(ije)*	BS *(ije)*

Trial	Date	Situation country	Witness	Ethnicity of the witness	Language of interpreters	Language of the transcript
Brđanin	20/02/2004	B&H	Goran Nešković	B&H Serb	CRO (*ije*) SR (*e*)	BS (*ije*)
Brđanin	23/02/2004	B&H	Goran Nešković		CRO (*ije*) SR (*e*)	BS (*ije*)
Erdemović	19/11/1996	B&H	Dražen Erdemović	B&H Croat	CRO (*ije*) SR (*e*)	BS (*ije*)
Erdemović	20/11/1996	B&H	Dražen Erdemović		CRO (*ije*)	BS (*ije*)
Halilović	23/05/2005	B&H	Bakir Alispahić	B&H Muslim	SR (*e*)	BS (*ije*)
Halilović	24/05/2005	B&H	Bakir Alispahić		CRO (*ije*)	BS (*ije*)
Halilović	26/05/2005	B&H	Bakir Alispahić		CRO (*ije*)	BS (*ije*)
Halilović	27/05/2005	B&H	Bakir Alispahić		CRO (*ije*)	BS (*ije*)
Krajišnik	5/02/2004	B&H	Isak Gasi	B&H Muslim	BS (*ije*) CRO (*ije*)	BS (*ije*)
Krajišnik	11/02/2004	B&H	Suad Džafić	B&H Muslim	CRO (*ije*)	SR (*e*)
Krajišnik	11/02/2004	B&H	Nijaz Dubičić	B&H Muslim	CRO (*ije*)	SR (*e*)
Krajišnik	12/02/2004	B&H	Miroslav Deronjić	B&H Serb	CRO (*ije*)	SR (*e*)
Krajišnik	13/02/2004	B&H	Miroslav Deronjić		BS (*ije*)	SR (*e*)
Krajišnik	16/02/2004	B&H	Miroslav Deronjić		BS (*ije*)	SR (*e*)
Krajišnik	18/02/2004	B&H	Miroslav Deronjić		BS (*ije*)	SR (*e*)
Krajišnik	19/02/2004	B&H	Miroslav Deronjić		CRO (*ije*) SR (*e*)	SR (*e*)
Krajišnik	20/04/2004	B&H	Jasmin Fazlović	B&H Muslim	CRO (*ije*)	SR (*e*)
Krajišnik	21/04/2004	B&H	Rešid Hasanović	B&H Muslim	CRO (*ije*)	SR (*e*)
Krajišnik	23/04/2004	B&H	Midho Alić	B&H Muslim	SR (*e*)	SR (*e*)
Krajišnik	23/04/2004	B&H	Ahmet Hidić	B&H Muslim	CRO (*ije*)	SR (*e*)
Krajišnik	25/05/2004	B&H	Mirzet Karabeg	B&H Muslim	CRO (*ije*) SR (*e*)	SR (*e*)

Trial	Date	Situation country	Witness	Ethnicity of the witness	Language of interpreters	Language of the transcript
Krajišnik	26/05/2004	B&H	Mirzet Karabeg		CRO (*ije*) SR (*e*)	SR (*e*)
Krajišnik	26/05/2004	B&H	Rajif Begić	B&H Muslim	CRO (*ije*) SR (*e*)	SR (*e*)
Krajišnik	27/05/2004	B&H	Rajif Begić		BS (*ije*) CRO (*ije*)	SR (*e*)
Krajišnik	28/07/2004	B&H	Asim Egrlić	B&H Muslim	CRO (*ije*) SR (*e*)	SR (*e*)
Krajišnik	29/07/2004	B&H	Asim Egrlić		CRO (*ije*)	SR (*e*)
Krajišnik	30/08/2004	B&H	Izet Redžić	B&H Muslim	CRO (*ije*) SR (*e*)	SR (*e*)
Krajišnik	31/08/2004	B&H	Izet Redžić		SR (*e*)	SR (*e*)
Krajišnik	31/08/2004	B&H	Kadira Brković	B&H Muslim	CRO (*ije*)	SR (*e*)
Krajišnik	1/09/2004	B&H	Izet Redžić	B&H Muslim	CRO (*ije*) SR (*e*)	SR (*e*)
Krajišnik	1/09/2004	B&H	Ibro Osmanović	B&H Muslim	CRO (*ije*) SR (*e*)	SR (*e*)
Krajišnik	2/09/2004	B&H	Sulejman Crnčalo	B&H Muslim	SR (*e*)	SR (*e*)
Krajišnik	27/09/2004	B&H	Stjepan Kljuić	B&H Croat	CRO (*ije*) SR (*e*)	SR (*e*)
Krajišnik	28/09/2004	B&H	Stjepan Kljuić		CRO (*ije*)	SR (*e*)
Krajišnik	29/09/2004	B&H	Stjepan Kljuić		CRO (*ije*) SR (*e*)	SR (*e*)
Krajišnik	5/10/2004	B&H	Azim Medanović	B&H Muslim	CRO (*ije*) SR (*e*)	SR (*e*)
Krajišnik	26/10/2004	B&H	Predrag Radić	B&H Serb	BS (*ije*) CRO (*ije*)	SR (*e*)
Krajišnik	2/11/2004	B&H	Elvir Jahić	B&H Muslim	SR (*e*)	SR (*e*)

Trial	Date	Situation country	Witness	Ethnicity of the witness	Language of interpreters	Language of the transcript
Krajišnik	3/11/2004	B&H	Ramiz Mujkić	B&H Muslim	CRO (*ije*) SR (*e*)	SR (*e*)
Krajišnik	8/11/2004	B&H	Ismet Čengić	B&H Muslim	CRO (*ije*)	SR (*e*)
Krajišnik	9/11/2004	B&H	Ismet Čengić		CRO (*ije*) SR (*e*)	SR (*e*)
Krajišnik	9/11/2004	B&H	Boro Bjelobrk	B&H Serb	CRO (*ije*) SR (*e*)	SR (*e*)
Krajišnik	10/11/2004	B&H	Boro Bjelobrk		SR (*e*)	SR (*e*)
Krajišnik	22/11/2004	B&H	Mehmed Musić	B&H Muslim	CRO (*ije*)	SR (*e*)
Krajišnik	24/11/2004	B&H	Momčilo Mandić	B&H Serb	CRO (*ije*)	SR (*e*)
Krajišnik	25/11/2004	B&H	Momčilo Mandić		CRO (*ije*)	SR (*e*)
Krajišnik	29/11/2004	B&H	Momčilo Mandić		CRO (*ije*) SR (*e*)	SR (*e*)
Krajišnik	30/11/2004	B&H	Momčilo Mandić		CRO (*ije*) SR (*e*)	SR (*e*)
Krajišnik	6/12/2004	B&H	Ramiz Mujkić	B&H Muslim	BS (*ije*) CRO (*ije*)	SR (*e*)
Krajišnik	7/12/2004	B&H	Momčilo Mandić	B&H Serb	BS (*ije*) CRO (*ije*)	SR (*e*)
Krajišnik	9/12/2004	B&H	Momčilo Mandić		BS (*ije*) CRO (*ije*)	SR (*e*)
Krajišnik	10/12/2004	B&H	Momčilo Mandić		BS (*ije*) CRO (*ije*)	SR (*e*)
Krajišnik	14/03/2005	B&H	Dragan Đokanović	B&H Serb	CRO (*ije*) SR (*e*)	SR (*e*)
Krajišnik	15/03/2005	B&H	Dragan Đokanović		CRO (*ije*) SR (*e*)	SR (*e*)

Trial	Date	Situation country	Witness	Ethnicity of the witness	Language of interpreters	Language of the transcript
Krajišnik	17/03/2005	B&H	Dragan Đokanović		BS (*ije*) CRO (*ije*)	SR (*e*)
Krajišnik	22/03/2005	B&H	Bego Selimović	B&H Muslim	CRO (*ije*) SR (*e*)	SR (*e*)
Krajišnik	23/03/2005	B&H	Mevludin Sejmenović	B&H Muslim	BS (*ije*) CRO (*ije*)	SR (*e*)
Krajišnik	29/03/2005	B&H	Ramiz Alajbegović	B&H Muslim	BS (*ije*) CRO (*ije*)	SR (*e*)
Krajišnik	4/04/2005	B&H	Milan Trbojević	B&H Serb	CRO (*ije*) SR (*e*)	SR (*e*)
Krajišnik	5/04/2005	B&H	Milan Trbojević		CRO (*ije*) SR (*e*)	SR (*e*)
Krajišnik	6/04/2005	B&H	Milan Trbojević		CRO (*ije*) SR (*e*)	SR (*e*)
Krajišnik	7/04/2005	B&H	Milan Trbojević		SR (*e*)	SR (*e*)
Krajišnik	8/04/2005	B&H	Milan Trbojević		SR (*e*)	SR (*e*)
Krajišnik	11/04/2005	B&H	Stjepan Kljuić	B&H Croat	CRO (*ije*) SR (*e*)	SR (*e*)
Krajišnik	12/04/2005	B&H	Stjepan Kljuić		BS (*ije*) SR (*e*)	SR (*e*)
Krajišnik	12/04/2005	B&H	Sead Omeragić	B&H Muslim	BS (*ije*) SR (*e*)	SR (*e*)
Krajišnik	13/04/2005	B&H	Sead Omeragić		SR (*e*)	SR (*e*)
Krajišnik	15/04/2005	B&H	Milan Trbojević	B&H Serb	SR (*e*)	SR (*e*)
Krajišnik	25/04/2005	B&H	Mirsad Kuralić	B&H Muslim	BS (*ije*) CRO (*ije*)	SR (*e*)
Krajišnik	26/04/2005	B&H	Izet Mehinagić	B&H Muslim	BS (*ije*) CRO (*ije*)	SR (*e*)

Trial	Date	Situation country	Witness	Ethnicity of the witness	Language of interpreters	Language of the transcript
Krajišnik	24/05/2005	B&H	Osman Selak	B&H Muslim	CRO (*ije*) SR (*e*)	SR (*e*)
Krajišnik	1/06/2005	B&H	Berko Zečević	B&H Serb	CRO (*ije*)	SR (*e*)
Krajišnik	9/06/2005	B&H	Milorad Davidović	B&H Serb	CRO (*ije*) SR (*e*)	SR (*e*)
Krajišnik	10/06/2005	B&H	Milorad Davidović		CRO (*ije*) SR (*e*)	SR (*e*)
Krajišnik	15/06/2005	B&H	Nedjeljko Prstojević	B&H Serb	CRO (*ije*) SR (*e*)	SR (*e*)
Krajišnik	16/06/2005	B&H	Nedjeljko Prstojević		CRO (*ije*) SR (*e*)	SR (*e*)
Krajišnik	17/06/2005	B&H	Boro Bjelobrk	B&H Serb	CRO (*ije*) SR (*e*)	SR (*e*)
Krajišnik	17/06/2005	B&H	Nedjeljko Prstojević	B&H Serb	CRO (*ije*) SR (*e*)	SR (*e*)
Krajišnik	28/06/2005	B&H	Milan Tupajić	B&H Serb	CRO (*ije*) SR (*e*)	SR (*e*)
Krajišnik	29/06/2005	B&H	Milan Tupajić		CRO (*ije*) SR (*e*)	SR (*e*)
Krajišnik	30/06/2005	B&H	Milan Tupajić		CRO (*ije*)	SR (*e*)
Krajišnik	8/07/2005	B&H	Melika Malešević	B&H Muslim	CRO (*ije*) SR (*e*)	SR (*e*)
Krajišnik	19/07/2005	B&H	Radomir Nešković	B&H Serb	CRO (*ije*) SR (*e*)	SR (*e*)
Krajišnik	20/07/2005	B&H	Radomir Nešković		SR (*e*)	SR (*e*)
Krajišnik	11/10/2005	B&H	Nemanja Vasić	B&H Serb	BS (*ije*) SR (*e*)	SR (*e*)

Trial	Date	Situation country	Witness	Ethnicity of the witness	Language of interpreters	Language of the transcript
Krajišnik	27/10/2005	B&H	Aleksandar Divčić	B&H Serb	CRO (*ije*) SR (*e*)	SR (*e*)
Krajišnik	31/10/2005	B&H	Lazar Stavnjak	B&H Serb	CRO (*ije*) SR (*e*)	SR (*e*)
Krajišnik	2/11/2005	B&H	Slavko Đorđević	B&H Serb	CRO (*ije*) SR (*e*)	SR (*e*)
Krajišnik	7/11/2005	B&H	Božidar Antić	B&H Serb	CRO (*ije*)	SR (*e*)
Krajišnik	9/11/2005	B&H	Miloš Milinčić	B&H Serb	CRO (*ije*) SR (*e*)	SR (*e*)
Krajišnik	10/11/2005	B&H	Miloš Milinčić		CRO (*ije*) SR (*e*)	SR (*e*)
Krajišnik	16/11/2005	B&H	Rajko Kasagić	B&H Serb	CRO (*ije*) SR (*e*)	SR (*e*)
Krajišnik	17/11/2005	B&H	Vidomir Banduka	B&H Serb	SR (*e*)	SR (*e*)
Krajišnik	18/11/2005	B&H	Rajko Kasagić	B&H Serb	CRO (*ije*) SR (*e*)	SR (*e*)
Krajišnik	21/11/2005	B&H	Vidomir Banduka	B&H Serb	SR (*e*)	SR (*e*)
Krajišnik	5/12/2005	B&H	Slobodanka Hrvaćanin	B&H Serb	BS (*ije*)	SR (*e*)
Krajišnik	6/12/2005	B&H	Slobodanka Hrvaćanin		BS (*ije*) CRO (*ije*)	SR (*e*)
Krajišnik	8/12/2005	B&H	Slobodanka Hrvaćanin		BS (*ije*) SR (*e*)	SR (*e*)
Krajišnik	12/12/2005	B&H	Momčilo Mičić	B&H Serb	CRO (*ije*) SR (*e*)	SR (*e*)
Krajišnik	13/12/2005	B&H	Momčilo Mičić		CRO (*ije*) SR (*e*)	SR (*e*)
Krajišnik	17/01/2006	B&H	Dragan Kapetina	B&H Serb	CRO (*ije*) SR (*e*)	SR (*e*)

Trial	Date	Situation country	Witness	Ethnicity of the witness	Language of interpreters	Language of the transcript
Krajišnik	27/01/2006	B&H	Tomislav Savkić	B&H Serb	CRO (*ije*) SR (*e*)	SR (*e*)
Krajišnik	31/01/2006	B&H	Tomislav Savkić		BS (*ije*)	SR (*e*)
Krajišnik	8/03/2006	B&H	Nikola Poplašen	B&H Serb	SR (*e*)	SR (*e*)
Krajišnik	9/03/2006	B&H	Nikola Poplašen		SR (*e*)	SR (*e*)
Krajišnik	10/03/2006	B&H	Nikola Poplašen		BS (*ije*) SR (*e*)	SR (*e*)
Krajišnik	13/03/2006	B&H	Jovo Radojko	B&H Serb	BS (*ije*) SR (*e*)	SR (*e*)
Krajišnik	14/03/2006	B&H	Jovo Radojko		BS (*ije*) SR (*e*)	SR (*e*)
Krajišnik	17/03/2006	B&H	Nedeljko Lakić	B&H Serb	BS (*ije*)	SR (*e*)
Krajišnik	20/03/2006	B&H	Nedeljko Lakić		BS (*ije*) SR (*e*)	SR (*e*)
Krajišnik	21/03/2006	B&H	Boško Maričić	B&H Serb	CRO (*ije*) SR (*e*)	SR (*e*)
Krajišnik	22/03/2006	B&H	Boško Maričić		CRO (*ije*) SR (*e*)	SR (*e*)
Krajišnik	24/03/2006	B&H	Siniša Krsman	B&H Serb	BS (*ije*) SR (*e*)	SR (*e*)
Krajišnik	27/03/2006	B&H	Siniša Krsman		CRO (*ije*) SR (*e*)	SR (*e*)
Krajišnik	27/03/2006	B&H	Svetlana Čenić	B&H Serb	CRO (*ije*) SR (*e*)	SR (*e*)
Krajišnik	30/03/2006	B&H	Svetlana Čenić		B&C	SR (*e*)
Krajišnik	5/04/2006	B&H	Nenad Kecmanović	B&H Serb	CRO (*ije*) SR (*e*)	SR (*e*)

Trial	Date	Situation country	Witness	Ethnicity of the witness	Language of interpreters	Language of the transcript
Krajišnik	6/04/2006	B&H	Milovan Bjelica	B&H Serb	BS (*ije*) CRO (*ije*)	SR (*e*)
Krajišnik	7/04/2006	B&H	Milovan Bjelica		SR (*e*)	SR (*e*)
Krajišnik	25/04/2006	B&H	Momčilo Krajšnik	B&H Serb	BS (*ije*) CRO (*ije*)	SR (*e*)
Krajišnik	26/04/2006	B&H	Momčilo Krajšnik		CRO (*ije*) SR (*e*)	SR (*e*)
Krajišnik	27/04/2006	B&H	Momčilo Krajšnik		CRO (*ije*) SR (*e*)	SR (*e*)
Krajišnik	2/05/2006	B&H	Momčilo Krajšnik		BS (*ije*) SR (*e*)	SR (*e*)
Krajišnik	8/05/2006	B&H	Momčilo Krajšnik		BS (*ije*) CRO (*ije*)	SR (*e*)
Krajišnik	27/06/2006	B&H	Amir Delić	B&H Muslim	BS (*ije*) CRO (*ije*)	SR (*e*)
Krajišnik	6/07/2006	B&H	Biljana Plavšić	B&H Serb	BS (*ije*) CRO (*ije*)	SR (*e*)
Krajišnik	7/07/2006	B&H	Biljana Plavšić		BS (*ije*) CRO (*ije*)	SR (*e*)
Krajišnik	12/07/2006	B&H	Branko Đerić	B&H Serb	BS (*ije*) CRO (*ije*)	SR (*e*)
Krajišnik	13/07/2006	B&H	Branko Đerić		BS (*ije*) CRO (*ije*)	SR (*e*)
Krstić	22/05/2000	B&H	Dražen Erdemović	B&H Croat	CRO (*ije*) SR (*e*)	SR (*e*)
Krstić	21/11/2003	B&H	Miroslav Deronjić	B&H Serb	CRO (*ije*) SR (*e*)	SR (*e*)

Trial	Date	Situation country	Witness	Ethnicity of the witness	Language of interpreters	Language of the transcript
Krstić	21/11/2003	B&H	Dragan Obrenović	B&H Serb	CRO (*ije*) SR (*e*)	SR (*e*)
Krstić	21/11/2003	B&H	Momir Nikolić	B&H Serb	CRO (*ije*) SR (*e*)	SR (*e*)
Lukić	29/08/2008	B&H	Mirsada Kahriman	B&H Muslim	CRO (*ije*) SR (*e*)	BS (*ije*)
Lukić	19/09/2008	B&H	Nurko Dervišević	B&H Muslim	CRO (*ije*) SR (*e*)	BS (*ije*)
Lukić	23/09/2008	B&H	Mirsad Tokača	B&H Muslim	CRO (*ije*) SR (*e*)	BS (*ije*)
Lukić	23/09/2008	B&H	Islam Kustura	B&H Muslim	CRO (*ije*) SR (*e*)	BS (*ije*)
Lukić	24/09/2008	B&H	Islam Kustura		SR (*e*)	BS (*ije*)
Lukić	25/09/2008	B&H	Zehra Turjačanin	B&H Muslim	BS (*ije*) CRO (*ije*)	BS (*ije*)
Lukić	2/10/2008	B&H	Adem Berberović	B&H Muslim	BS (*ije*)	BS (*ije*)
Nikolić	10/10/1995	B&H	Ibro Osmanović	B&H Muslim	CRO (*ije*) SR (*e*)	BS (*ije*)
Nikolić	10/10/1995	B&H	Beđo Čakišić	B&H Muslim	CRO (*ije*) SR (*e*)	BS (*ije*)
Nikolić	10/10/1995	B&H	Amir Berbić	B&H Muslim	CRO (*ije*) SR (*e*)	BS (*ije*)
Nikolić	10/10/1995	B&H	Sead Ambešković	B&H Muslim	CRO (*ije*) SR (*e*)	BS (*ije*)
Popović	28/08/2006	B&H	Mevludin Orić	B&H Muslim	BS (*ije*) SR (*e*)	BS (*ije*)
Popović	29/08/2006	B&H	Mevludin Orić		BS (*ije*) SR (*e*)	BS (*ije*)

Trial	Date	Situation country	Witness	Ethnicity of the witness	Language of interpreters	Language of the transcript
Popović	30/08/2006	B&H	Mevludin Orić		BS (*ije*) SR (*e*)	BS (*ije*)
Popović	31/08/2006	B&H	Mevludin Orić		BS (*ije*) CRO (*ije*)	BS (*ije*)
Popović	6/09/2006	B&H	Ahmo Hasić	B&H Muslim	BS (*ije*) CRO (*ije*)	BS (*ije*)
Popović	7/09/2006	B&H	Ahmo Hasić		CRO (*ije*)	BS (*ije*)
Popović	31/01/2007	B&H	Zlatan Čelanović	B&H Serb	CRO (*ije*) SR (*e*)	BS (*ije*)
Popović	6/02/2007	B&H	Esma Palić	B&H Muslim	SR (*e*)	BS (*ije*)
Popović	30/03/2007	B&H	Hamdija Torlak	B&H Muslim	SR (*e*)	BS (*ije*)
Popović	2/04/2007	B&H	Hamdija Torlak		SR (*e*)	BS (*ije*)
Popović	16/04/2007	B&H	Lazar Listić	B&H Serb	BS (*ije*)	BS (*ije*)
Popović	17/04/2007	B&H	Lazar Listić		BS (*ije*) CRO (*ije*)	BS (*ije*)
Popović	18/04/2007	B&H	Lazar Listić		BS (*ije*)	BS (*ije*)
Popović	18/04/2007	B&H	Rajko Babić	B&H Serb	BS (*ije*)	BS (*ije*)
Popović	19/04/2007	B&H	Radivoje Lakić	B&H Serb	BS (*ije*) SR (*e*)	BS (*ije*)
Popović	24/04/2007	B&H	Tanasko Tanić	B&H Serb	SR (*e*)	BS (*ije*)
Popović	24/04/2007	B&H	Nebojša Jeremić	B&H Serb	SR (*e*)	BS (*ije*)
Popović	25/04/2007	B&H	Nebojša Galić	B&H Serb	BS (*ije*) SR (*e*)	BS (*ije*)
Popović	1/05/2007	B&H	Darko Gojković	B&H Serb	SR (*e*)	BS (*ije*)
Popović	1/05/2007	B&H	Stanoje Brićaković	B&H Serb	SR (*e*)	BS (*ije*)
Popović	1/05/2007	B&H	Mendeljev Đurić	B&H Serb	SR (*e*)	BS (*ije*)
Popović	2/05/2007	B&H	Mendeljev Đurić		CRO (*ije*) SR (*e*)	BS (*ije*)

Trial	Date	Situation country	Witness	Ethnicity of the witness	Language of interpreters	Language of the transcript
Popović	4/05/2007	B&H	Dražen Erdemović	B&H Croat	SR (*e*)	BS (*ije*)
Popović	7/05/2007	B&H	Dražen Erdemović		SR (*e*)	BS (*ije*)
Popović	7/05/2007	B&H	Milorad Birčaković	B&H Serb	SR (*e*)	BS (*ije*)
Popović	10/05/2007	B&H	Jevto Bogdanović	B&H Serb	SR (*e*)	BS (*ije*)
Popović	14/05/2007	B&H	Slavko Perić	B&H Serb	SR (*e*)	BS (*ije*)
Popović	14/05/2007	B&H	Milanko Jovičić	B&H Serb	SR (*e*)	BS (*ije*)
Popović	16/05/2007	B&H	Ostoja Stanišić	B&H Serb	SR (*e*)	BS (*ije*)
Popović	17/05/2007	B&H	Ostoja Stanišić		BS (*ije*) SR (*e*)	BS (*ije*)
Popović	18/05/2007	B&H	Miloš Đukanović	B&H Serb	BS (*ije*) SR (*e*)	BS (*ije*)
Popović	18/05/2007	B&H	Mirko Trivić	B&H Serb	BS (*ije*) SR (*e*)	BS (*ije*)
Popović	21/05/2007	B&H	Mirko Trivić		SR (*e*)	BS (*ije*)
Popović	23/05/2007	B&H	Mirko Trivić		SR (*e*)	BS (*ije*)
Popović	24/05/2007	B&H	Đuro Rodić	B&H Serb	BS (*ije*) SR (*e*)	BS (*ije*)
Popović	29/05/2007	B&H	Manojlo Milovanović	B&H Serb	SR (*e*)	BS (*ije*)
Popović	30/05/2007	B&H	Manojlo Milovanović		SR (*e*)	BS (*ije*)
Popović	31/05/2007	B&H	Manojlo Milovanović		CRO (*ije*) SR (*e*)	BS (*ije*)
Popović	12/06/2007	B&H	Đuro Rodić	B&H Serb	CRO (*ije*) SR (*e*)	BS (*ije*)
Popović	14/06/2007	B&H	Miodrag Dragutinović	B&H Serb	CRO (*ije*) SR (*e*)	BS (*ije*)
Popović	15/06/2007	B&H	Miodrag Dragutinović		CRO (*ije*) SR (*e*)	BS (*ije*)

Trial	Date	Situation country	Witness	Ethnicity of the witness	Language of interpreters	Language of the transcript
Popović	19/06/2007	B&H	Miodrag Dragutinović		CRO (*ije*) SR (*e*)	BS (*ije*)
Popović	19/06/2007	B&H	Dobrisav Stanojević	B&H Serb	CRO (*ije*) SR (*e*)	BS (*ije*)
Popović	20/06/2007	B&H	Dobrisav Stanojević		BS (*ije*)	BS (*ije*)
Popović	20/06/2007	B&H	Srećko Aćimović	B&H Serb	BS (*ije*)	BS (*ije*)
Popović	21/06/2007	B&H	Srećko Aćimović		BS (*ije*) SR (*e*)	BS (*ije*)
Popović	22/06/2007	B&H	Srećko Aćimović		CRO (*ije*) SR (*e*)	BS (*ije*)
Popović	26/06/2007	B&H	Marko Milošević	B&H Serb	CRO (*ije*) SR (*e*)	BS (*ije*)
Popović	26/06/2007	B&H	Mitar Lazarević	B&H Serb	CRO (*ije*) SR (*e*)	BS (*ije*)
Popović	28/06/2007	B&H	Predrag Čelić	B&H Serb	BS (*ije*) SR (*e*)	BS (*ije*)
Popović	9/07/2007	B&H	Milenko Pepić	B&H Serb	BS (*ije*) SR (*e*)	BS (*ije*)
Popović	21/08/2007	B&H	Dragan Todorović	B&H Serb	CRO (*ije*) SR (*e*)	BS (*ije*)
Popović	27/08/2007	B&H	Bogdan Sladojević	B&H Serb	CRO (*ije*) SR (*e*)	BS (*ije*)
Popović	30/08/2007	B&H	Damjan Lazarević	B&H Serb	CRO (*ije*)	BS (*ije*)
Popović	30/08/2007	B&H	Dragoje Ivanović	B&H Serb	CRO (*ije*)	BS (*ije*)
Popović	13/09/2007	B&H	Milomir Savčić	B&H Serb	CRO (*ije*) SR (*e*)	BS (*ije*)
Popović	17/09/2007	B&H	Petar Škrbić	B&H Serb	CRO (*ije*)	BS (*ije*)

Trial	Date	Situation country	Witness	Ethnicity of the witness	Language of interpreters	Language of the transcript
Popović	19/09/2007	B&H	Petar Škrbić		CRO (*ije*) SR (*e*)	BS (*ije*)
Popović	20/11/2007	B&H	Mile Janjić	B&H Serb	CRO (*ije*) SR (*e*)	BS (*ije*)
Popović	6/12/2007	B&H	Zoran Petrović	B&H Serb	CRO (*ije*) SR (*e*)	BS (*ije*)
Popović	3/06/2008	B&H	Momčilo Krajišnik	B&H Serb	CRO (*ije*) SR (*e*)	BS (*ije*)
Popović	5/06/2008	B&H	Milenko Lazić	B&H Serb	CRO (*ije*)	BS (*ije*)
Popović	9/06/2008	B&H	Pero Mijatović	B&H Serb	BS (*ije*) CRO (*ije*)	BS (*ije*)
Popović	9/06/2008	B&H	Dragan Stojkić	B&H Serb	BS (*ije*) CRO (*ije*)	BS (*ije*)
Popović	9/06/2008	B&H	Zoran Aćimović	B&H Serb	BS (*ije*) CRO (*ije*)	BS (*ije*)
Popović	10/06/2008	B&H	Zoran Aćimović		CRO (*ije*)	BS (*ije*)
Popović	10/06/2008	B&H	Gordan Bjelanović	B&H Serb	CRO (*ije*)	BS (*ije*)
Popović	11/06/2008	B&H	Gordan Bjelanović		BS (*ije*) CRO (*ije*)	BS (*ije*)
Popović	11/06/2008	B&H	Zoran Radosavljević	B&H Serb	BS (*ije*) CRO (*ije*)	BS (*ije*)
Popović	11/06/2008	B&H	Drago Ćvorić	B&H Serb	BS (*ije*) CRO (*ije*)	BS (*ije*)
Popović	17/06/2008	B&H	Nedo Blagojević	B&H Serb	CRO (*ije*)	BS (*ije*)
Popović	18/06/2008	B&H	Branko Bogićević	B&H Serb	BS (*ije*) CRO (*ije*)	BS (*ije*)
Popović	18/06/2008	B&H	Zoran Jovanović	B&H Serb	BS (*ije*) CRO (*ije*)	BS (*ije*)

Trial	Date	Situation country	Witness	Ethnicity of the witness	Language of interpreters	Language of the transcript
Popović	24/06/2008	B&H	Miladin Kovačević	B&H Serb	BS (*ije*) CRO (*ije*)	BS (*ije*)
Popović	25/06/2008	B&H	Dušan Dunjić	B&H Serb	BS (*ije*) CRO (*ije*)	BS (*ije*)
Popović	26/06/2008	B&H	Dušan Dunjić		BS (*ije*) CRO (*ije*)	BS (*ije*)
Popović	30/06/2008	B&H	Oliver Stojković	B&H Serb	BS (*ije*) CRO (*ije*)	BS (*ije*)
Popović	30/06/2008	B&H	Petar Vuga	B&H Serb	BS (*ije*) CRO (*ije*)	BS (*ije*)
Popović	1/07/2008	B&H	Petar Vuga		BS (*ije*) CRO (*ije*)	BS (*ije*)
Popović	3/07/2008	B&H	Petar Vuga		BS (*ije*) CRO (*ije*)	BS (*ije*)
Popović	7/07/2008	B&H	Petar Vuga		SR (*e*)	BS (*ije*)
Popović	10/07/2008	B&H	Spiridon Alačov	B&H Serb	BS (*ije*) CRO (*ije*)	BS (*ije*)
Popović	10/07/2008	B&H	Vojislav Medić	B&H Serb	BS (*ije*) CRO (*ije*)	BS (*ije*)
Popović	11/07/2008	B&H	Vojislav Medić		CRO (*ije*)	BS (*ije*)
Popović	11/07/2008	B&H	Ljubomir Mitrović	B&H Serb	CRO (*ije*)	BS (*ije*)
Popović	22/07/2008	B&H	Branimir Grulović	B&H Serb	BS (*ije*) CRO (*ije*)	BS (*ije*)
Popović	22/07/2008	B&H	Marinko Jevđević	B&H Serb	BS (*ije*) CRO (*ije*)	BS (*ije*)
Popović	23/07/2008	B&H	Marinko Jevđević		CRO (*ije*)	BS (*ije*)
Popović	25/07/2008	B&H	Željko Kerkez	B&H Serb	CRO (*ije*)	BS (*ije*)

Trial	Date	Situation country	Witness	Ethnicity of the witness	Language of interpreters	Language of the transcript
Popović	28/07/2008	B&H	Špiro Pereula	B&H Serb	BS (*ije*) SR (*e*)	BS (*ije*)
Popović	28/07/2008	B&H	Miladin Jovanović	B&H Serb	BS (*ije*) SR (*e*)	BS (*ije*)
Popović	28/07/2008	B&H	Perica Vasović	B&H Serb	BS (*ije*) SR (*e*)	BS (*ije*)
Popović	29/07/2008	B&H	Perica Vasović		CRO (*ije*) SR (*e*)	BS (*ije*)
Popović	29/07/2008	B&H	Ljuban Mrković	B&H Serb	CRO (*ije*) SR (*e*)	BS (*ije*)
Popović	29/07/2008	B&H	Svetlana Radovanović	B&H Serb	CRO (*ije*) SR (*e*)	BS (*ije*)
Popović	25/08/2008	B&H	Slobodan Remetić	B&H Serb	CRO (*ije*) SR (*e*)	BS (*ije*)
Popović	29/08/2008	B&H	Miroslava Čekić	B&H Serb	CRO (*ije*) SR (*e*)	BS (*ije*)
Popović	29/08/2008	B&H	Milan Kerkez	B&H Serb	CRO (*ije*) SR (*e*)	BS (*ije*)
Popović	1/09/2008	B&H	Bojan Subotić	B&H Serb	BS (*ije*) SR (*e*)	BS (*ije*)
Popović	10/09/2008	B&H	Ljubomir Gogić	B&H Serb	CRO (*ije*)	BS (*ije*)
Popović	17/09/2008	B&H	Mislislav Cvijetinović	B&H Serb	BS (*ije*) CRO (*ije*)	BS (*ije*)
Popović	17/09/2008	B&H	Milisav Nikolić	B&H Serb	BS (*ije*) CRO (*ije*)	BS (*ije*)
Popović	24/09/2008	B&H	Milan Radić	B&H Serb	BS (*ije*) CRO (*ije*)	BS (*ije*)

Trial	Date	Situation country	Witness	Ethnicity of the witness	Language of interpreters	Language of the transcript
Popović	24/09/2008	B&H	Petko Tomić	B&H Serb	BS (*ije*) CRO (*ije*)	BS (*ije*)
Popović	1/10/2008	B&H	Mićo Gavrić	B&H Serb	BS (*ije*) CRO (*ije*)	BS (*ije*)
Popović	6/10/2008	B&H	Mladen Bajagić	B&H Serb	BS (*ije*) SR (*e*)	BS (*ije*)
Popović	7/10/2008	B&H	Mladen Bajagić		SR (*e*)	BS (*ije*)
Popović	8/10/2008	B&H	Mladen Bajagić		BS (*ije*) SR (*e*)	BS (*ije*)
Popović	9/10/2008	B&H	Mladen Bajagić		BS (*ije*) CRO (*ije*)	BS (*ije*)
Popović	9/10/2008	B&H	Zarko Zarić	B&H Serb	BS (*ije*) CRO (*ije*)	BS (*ije*)
Popović	10/10/2008	B&H	Žarko Zarić		CRO (*ije*) SR (*e*)	BS (*ije*)
Popović	10/10/2008	B&H	Nenad Filipović	B&H Serb	CRO (*ije*) SR (*e*)	BS (*ije*)
Popović	20/10/2008	B&H	Dragoslav Trišić	B&H Serb	CRO (*ije*) SR (*e*)	BS (*ije*)
Popović	23/10/2008	B&H	Ljubisav Simić	B&H Serb	CRO (*ije*) SR (*e*)	BS (*ije*)
Popović	23/10/2008	B&H	Zoran Janković	B&H Serb	CRO (*ije*) SR (*e*)	BS (*ije*)
Popović	28/10/2008	B&H	Dragan Nešković	B&H Serb	CRO (*ije*) SR (*e*)	BS (*ije*)
Popović	28/10/2008	B&H	Slaviša Simić	B&H Serb	CRO (*ije*) SR (*e*)	BS (*ije*)
Popović	30/10/2008	B&H	Milan Stojčinović	B&H Serb	BS (*ije*)	BS (*ije*)

Trial	Date	Situation country	Witness	Ethnicity of the witness	Language of interpreters	Language of the transcript
Popović	30/10/2008	B&H	Jovo Marković	B&H Serb	BS (*ije*)	BS (*ije*)
Popović	31/10/2008	B&H	Jovo Marković		BS (*ije*) CRO (*ije*)	BS (*ije*)
Popović	7/11/2008	B&H	Branislav Ristivojević	B&H Serb	BS (*ije*) CRO (*ije*)	BS (*ije*)
Popović	12/11/2008	B&H	Branislav Ristivojević		BS (*ije*) SR (*e*)	BS (*ije*)
Popović	13/11/2008	B&H	Branislav Ristivojević		CRO (*ije*) SR (*e*)	BS (*ije*)
Popović	13/11/2008	B&H	Pero Mijatović	B&H Serb	CRO (*ije*) SR (*e*)	BS (*ije*)
Popović	13/11/2008	B&H	Ljubomir Obradović	B&H Serb	CRO (*ije*) SR (*e*)	BS (*ije*)
Popović	14/11/2008	B&H	Ljubomir Obradović		BS (*ije*) SR (*e*)	BS (*ije*)
Popović	17/11/2008	B&H	Ljubomir Obradović		BS (*ije*) SR (*e*)	BS (*ije*)
Popović	18/11/2008	B&H	Ljubomir Obradović		CRO (*ije*) SR (*e*)	BS (*ije*)
Popović	19/11/2008	B&H	Ljubomir Obradović		CRO (*ije*) SR (*e*)	BS (*ije*)
Popović	19/11/2008	B&H	Novica Simić	B&H Serb	CRO (*ije*) SR (*e*)	BS (*ije*)
Popović	20/11/2008	B&H	Novica Simić		CRO (*ije*) SR (*e*)	BS (*ije*)
Popović	21/11/2008	B&H	Novica Simić		CRO (*ije*) SR (*e*)	BS (*ije*)

Trial	Date	Situation country	Witness	Ethnicity of the witness	Language of interpreters	Language of the transcript
Popović	24/11/2008	B&H	Novica Simić		CRO (*ije*) SR (*e*)	BS (*ije*)
Popović	26/11/2008	B&H	Velo Pajić	B&H Serb	CRO (*ije*) SR (*e*)	BS (*ije*)
Popović	26/11/2008	B&H	Ratko Miljanović	B&H Serb	CRO (*ije*) SR (*e*)	BS (*ije*)
Popović	27/11/2008	B&H	Ratko Miljanović		CRO (*ije*) SR (*e*)	BS (*ije*)
Popović	28/11/2008	B&H	Ratko Miljanović		BS (*ije*) CRO (*ije*)	BS (*ije*)
Popović	1/12/2008	B&H	Dragiša Masal	B&H Serb	CRO (*ije*) SR (*e*)	BS (*ije*)
Popović	3/12/2008	B&H	Vojislav Babić	B&H Serb	CRO (*ije*) SR (*e*)	BS (*ije*)
Popović	3/12/2008	B&H	Slavko Kralj	B&H Serb	CRO (*ije*) SR (*e*)	BS (*ije*)
Popović	4/12/2008	B&H	Slavko Kralj		CRO (*ije*) SR (*e*)	BS (*ije*)
Popović	5/12/2008	B&H	Slavko Kralj		CRO (*ije*) SR (*e*)	BS (*ije*)
Popović	9/12/2008	B&H	Nedeljko Ilić	B&H Serb	CRO (*ije*) SR (*e*)	BS (*ije*)
Popović	9/12/2008	B&H	Maja Spiroski	B&H Serb	CRO (*ije*) SR (*e*)	BS (*ije*)
Popović	9/12/2008	B&H	Ranko Klačar	B&H Serb	CRO (*ije*) SR (*e*)	BS (*ije*)
Popović	11/12/2008	B&H	Milenko Jevđević	B&H Serb	CRO (*ije*) SR (*e*)	BS (*ije*)

Trial	Date	Situation country	Witness	Ethnicity of the witness	Language of interpreters	Language of the transcript
Popović	15/12/2008	B&H	Milenko Jevđević		CRO (*ije*) SR (*e*)	BS (*ije*)
Popović	12/01/2009	B&H	Slobodan Kosovac	B&H Serb	CRO (*ije*) SR (*e*)	BS (*ije*)
Popović	13/01/2009	B&H	Slobodan Kosovac		CRO (*ije*)	BS (*ije*)
Popović	14/01/2009	B&H	Slobodan Kosovac		BS (*ije*) CRO (*ije*)	BS (*ije*)
Popović	15/01/2009	B&H	Slobodan Kosovac		CRO (*ije*) SR (*e*)	BS (*ije*)
Popović	16/01/2009	B&H	Slobodan Kosovac		CRO (*ije*) SR (*e*)	BS (*ije*)
Popović	19/01/2009	B&H	Slobodan Kosovac		CRO (*ije*)	BS (*ije*)
Popović	20/01/2009	B&H	Slobodan Kosovac		CRO (*ije*) SR (*e*)	BS (*ije*)
Popović	21/01/2009	B&H	Slobodan Kosovac		CRO (*ije*) SR (*e*)	BS (*ije*)
Popović	22/01/2009	B&H	Slobodan Kosovac		SR (*e*)	BS (*ije*)
Popović	27/01/2009	B&H	Vinko Pandurević	B&H Serb	CRO (*ije*) SR (*e*)	BS (*ije*)
Popović	28/01/2009	B&H	Vinko Pandurević		CRO (*ije*) SR (*e*)	BS (*ije*)
Popović	29/01/2009	B&H	Vinko Pandurević		CRO (*ije*) SR (*e*)	BS (*ije*)
Popović	30/01/2009	B&H	Vinko Pandurević		CRO (*ije*) SR (*e*)	BS (*ije*)
Popović	2/02/2009	B&H	Vinko Pandurević		SR (*e*)	BS (*ije*)
Popović	3/02/2009	B&H	Vinko Pandurević		SR (*e*)	BS (*ije*)

Trial	Date	Situation country	Witness	Ethnicity of the witness	Language of interpreters	Language of the transcript
Popović	9/02/2009	B&H	Vinko Pandurević		BS (*ije*) CRO (*ije*)	BS (*ije*)
Popović	10/02/2009	B&H	Vinko Pandurević		CRO (*ije*) SR (*e*)	BS (*ije*)
Popović	11/02/2009	B&H	Vinko Pandurević		CRO (*ije*) SR (*e*)	BS (*ije*)
Popović	12/02/2009	B&H	Vinko Pandurević		BS (*ije*) CRO (*ije*)	BS (*ije*)
Popović	13/02/2009	B&H	Vinko Pandurević		BS (*ije*) CRO (*ije*)	BS (*ije*)
Popović	16/02/2009	B&H	Vinko Pandurević		SR (*e*)	BS (*ije*)
Popović	17/02/2009	B&H	Vinko Pandurević		SR (*e*)	BS (*ije*)
Popović	18/02/2009	B&H	Vinko Pandurević		CRO (*ije*) SR (*e*)	BS (*ije*)
Popović	19/02/2009	B&H	Vinko Pandurević		SR (*e*)	BS (*ije*)
Popović	20/02/2009	B&H	Vinko Pandurević		CRO (*ije*)	BS (*ije*)
Popović	23/02/2009	B&H	Vinko Pandurević		CRO (*ije*) SR (*e*)	BS (*ije*)
Popović	25/02/2009	B&H	Vinko Pandurević		CRO (*ije*) SR (*e*)	BS (*ije*)
Popović	26/02/2009	B&H	Vinko Pandurević		CRO (*ije*)	BS (*ije*)
Popović	27/02/2009	B&H	Vinko Pandurević		BS (*ije*) CRO (*ije*)	BS (*ije*)
Popović	2/03/2009	B&H	Vinko Pandurević		CRO (*ije*) SR (*e*)	BS (*ije*)
Popović	3/03/2009	B&H	Vinko Pandurević		CRO (*ije*) SR (*e*)	BS (*ije*)

Trial	Date	Situation country	Witness	Ethnicity of the witness	Language of interpreters	Language of the transcript
Popović	11/03/2009	B&H	Nikodin Jovičić	B&H Serb	SR (*e*)	BS (*ije*)
Popović	21/04/2009	B&H	Momir Nikolić	B&H Serb	CRO (*ije*)	BS (*ije*)
Popović	22/04/2009	B&H	Momir Nikolić		CRO (*ije*) SR (*e*)	BS (*ije*)
Popović	6/07/2009	B&H	Saša Jovanović	B&H Serb	CRO (*ije*)	BS (*ije*)
Popović	15/07/2009	B&H	Sreten Milošević	B&H Serb	CRO (*ije*) SR (*e*)	BS (*ije*)
Stanišić and Župljanin	6/10/2009	B&H	Mirzet Karabeg	B&H Muslim	CRO (*ije*) SR (*e*)	SR (*e*)
Stanišić and Župljanin	6/10/2009	B&H	Enis Šabanović	B&H Muslim	CRO (*ije*) SR (*e*)	SR (*e*)
Stanišić and Župljanin	7/10/2009	B&H	Nedeljko Đekanović	B&H Serb	CRO (*ije*) SR (*e*)	SR (*e*)
Stanišić and Župljanin	8/10/2009	B&H	Nedjeljko Đekanović		BS (*ije*) CRO (*ije*)	SR (*e*)
Stanišić and Župljanin	12/10/2009	B&H	Branko Basara	B&H Serb	CRO (*ije*) SR (*e*)	SR (*e*)
Stanišić and Župljanin	13/10/2009	B&H	Branko Basara (1302)		SR (*e*)	SR (*e*)
Stanišić and Župljanin	15/10/2009	B&H	Nedjeljko Đekanović	B&H Serb	CRO (*ije*) SR (*e*)	SR (*e*)
Stanišić and Župljanin	15/10/2009	B&H	Milenko Delić	B&H Serb	CRO (*ije*) SR (*e*)	SR (*e*)
Stanišić and Župljanin	19/10/2009	B&H	Milenko Delić (1557)		CRO (*ije*) SR (*e*)	SR (*e*)
Stanišić and Župljanin	20/10/2009	B&H	Milenko Delić		BS (*ije*) CRO (*ije*)	SR (*e*)
Stanišić and Župljanin	20/10/2009	B&H	Isak Gaši	B&H Muslim	BS (*ije*) CRO (*ije*)	SR (*e*)

Trial	Date	Situation country	Witness	Ethnicity of the witness	Language of interpreters	Language of the transcript
Stanišić and Župljanin	21/10/2009	B&H	Isak Gaši		BS (*ije*) SR (*e*)	SR (*e*)
Stanišić and Župljanin	21/10/2009	B&H	Cvjetko Ignjić	B&H Serb	BS (*ije*) SR (*e*)	SR (*e*)
Stanišić and Župljanin	26/10/2009	B&H	Aleksandar Krulj	B&H Serb	CRO (*ije*) SR (*e*)	SR (*e*)
Stanišić and Župljanin	27/10/2009	B&H	Aleksandar Krulj		CRO (*ije*) SR (*e*)	SR (*e*)
Stanišić and Župljanin	28/10/2009	B&H	Aleksandar Krulj		CRO (*ije*) SR (*e*)	SR (*e*)
Stanišić and Župljanin	30/10/2009	B&H	Branko Đerić	B&H Serb	BS (*ije*) SR (*e*)	SR (*e*)
Stanišić and Župljanin	3/11/2009	B&H	Branko Đerić		CRO (*ije*) SR (*e*)	SR (*e*)
Stanišić and Župljanin	11/11/2009	B&H	Petko Panić	B&H Serb	CRO (*ije*) SR (*e*)	SR (*e*)
Stanišić and Župljanin	12/11/2009	B&H	Petko Panić		SR (*e*)	SR (*e*)
Stanišić and Župljanin	13/11/2009	B&H	Petko Panić		CRO (*ije*) SR (*e*)	SR (*e*)
Stanišić and Župljanin	16/11/2009	B&H	Dragan Majkić	B&H Serb	SR (*e*)	SR (*e*)
Stanišić and Župljanin	2/12/2009	B&H	Adil Draganović	B&H Muslim	CRO (*ije*) SR (*e*)	SR (*e*)
Stanišić and Župljanin	2/12/2009	B&H	Milan Trbojević	B&H Serb	CRO (*ije*) SR (*e*)	SR (*e*)
Stanišić and Župljanin	1/02/2010	B&H	Vitomir Žepinić	B&H Serb	BS (*ije*) CRO (*ije*)	SR (*e*)
Stanišić and Župljanin	2/02/2010	B&H	Asim Bašić	B&H Muslim	CRO (*ije*) SR (*e*)	SR (*e*)

Trial	Date	Situation country	Witness	Ethnicity of the witness	Language of interpreters	Language of the transcript
Stanišić and Župljanin	3/02/2010	B&H	Asim Egrlić	B&H Muslim	BS (*ije*) SR (*e*)	SR (*e*)
Stanišić and Župljanin	5/02/2010	B&H	Atif Džafić	B&H Muslim	BS (*ije*) CRO (*ije*)	SR (*e*)
Stanišić and Župljanin	15/02/2010	B&H	Neđo Vlaški	B&H Serb	BS (*ije*) SR (*e*)	SR (*e*)
Stanišić and Župljanin	17/02/2010	B&H	Neđo Vlaški		CRO (*ije*) SR (*e*)	SR (*e*)
Stanišić and Župljanin	18/02/2010	B&H	Milan Šćekić	B&H Serb	BS (*ije*) CRO (*ije*)	SR (*e*)
Stanišić and Župljanin	19/02/2010	B&H	Milan Šćekić		BS (*ije*) CRO (*ije*)	SR (*e*)
Stanišić and Župljanin	23/02/2010	B&H	Drago Borovčanin	B&H Serb	CRO (*ije*) SR (*e*)	SR (*e*)
Stanišić and Župljanin	24/02/2010	B&H	Drago Borovčanin		CRO (*ije*) SR (*e*)	SR (*e*)
Stanišić and Župljanin	25/02/2010	B&H	Drago Raković	B&H Serb	CRO (*ije*) SR (*e*)	SR (*e*)
Stanišić and Župljanin	8/03/2010	B&H	Ibro Osmanović	B&H Muslim	CRO (*ije*)	SR (*e*)
Stanišić and Župljanin	15/03/2010	B&H	Vladimir Tutuš	B&H Serb	CRO (*ije*)	SR (*e*)
Stanišić and Župljanin	18/03/2010	B&H	Vladimir Tutuš		CRO (*ije*)	SR (*e*)
Stanišić and Župljanin	19/03/2010	B&H	Vladimir Tutuš		CRO (*ije*)	SR (*e*)
Stanišić and Župljanin	30/03/2010	B&H	Slobodan Škipina	B&H Serb	CRO (*ije*)	SR (*e*)
Stanišić and Župljanin	31/03/2010	B&H	Slobodan Škipina		CRO (*ije*) SR (*e*)	SR (*e*)
Stanišić and Župljanin	16/04/2010	B&H	Radomir Rodić	B&H Serb	BS (*ije*) SR (*e*)	SR (*e*)
Stanišić and Župljanin	26/04/2010	B&H	Edin Hadžović	B&H Muslim	CRO (*ije*)	SR (*e*)

Trial	Date	Situation country	Witness	Ethnicity of the witness	Language of interpreters	Language of the transcript
Stanišić and Župljanin	27/04/2010	B&H	Miroslav Vidić	B&H Serb	BS (*ije*) CRO (*ije*)	SR (*e*)
Stanišić and Župljanin	28/04/2010	B&H	Miroslav Vidić		CRO (*ije*)	SR (*e*)
Stanišić and Župljanin	4/05/2010	B&H	Momčilo Mandić	B&H Serb	BS (*ije*) CRO (*ije*)	SR (*e*)
Stanišić and Župljanin	5/05/2010	B&H	Momčilo Mandić		BS (*ije*) CRO (*ije*)	SR (*e*)
Stanišić and Župljanin	6/05/2010	B&H	Momčilo Mandić		BS (*ije*)	SR (*e*)
Stanišić and Župljanin	7/05/2010	B&H	Momčilo Mandić		CRO (*ije*) SR (*e*)	SR (*e*)
Stanišić and Župljanin	10/05/2010	B&H	Obren Petrović	B&H Serb	CRO (*ije*)	SR (*e*)
Stanišić and Župljanin	11/05/2010	B&H	Obren Petrović		CRO (*ije*)	SR (*e*)
Stanišić and Župljanin	12/05/2010	B&H	Obren Petrović		CRO (*ije*)	SR (*e*)
Stanišić and Župljanin	19/05/2010	B&H	Branko Perić	B&H Serb	CRO (*ije*) SR (*e*)	SR (*e*)
Stanišić and Župljanin	20/05/2010	B&H	Branko Perić		CRO (*ije*)	SR (*e*)
Stanišić and Župljanin	21/05/2010	B&H	Branko Perić		CRO (*ije*)	SR (*e*)
Stanišić and Župljanin	25/05/2010	B&H	Predrag Radulović	B&H Serb	BS (*ije*) CRO (*ije*)	SR (*e*)
Stanišić and Župljanin	26/05/2010	B&H	Predrag Radulović		BS (*ije*) CRO (*ije*)	SR (*e*)
Stanišić and Župljanin	27/05/2010	B&H	Predrag Radulović		CRO (*ije*)	SR (*e*)
Stanišić and Župljanin	28/05/2010	B&H	Predrag Radulović		BS (*ije*) SR (*e*)	SR (*e*)
Stanišić and Župljanin	31/05/2010	B&H	Predrag Radulović		CRO (*ije*)	SR (*e*)
Stanišić and Župljanin	1/06/2010	B&H	Predrag Radulović		BS (*ije*) SR (*e*)	SR (*e*)

Trial	Date	Situation country	Witness	Ethnicity of the witness	Language of interpreters	Language of the transcript
Stanišić and Župljanin	2/06/2010	B&H	Predrag Radulović		CRO (*ije*) SR (*e*)	SR (*e*)
Stanišić and Župljanin	8/06/2010	B&H	Radomir Njeguš	B&H Serb	CRO (*ije*) SR (*e*)	SR (*e*)
Stanišić and Župljanin	10/06/2010	B&H	Dragan Kezunović	B&H Serb	CRO (*ije*) SR (*e*)	SR (*e*)
Stanišić and Župljanin	11/06/2010	B&H	Dragan Kezunović		BS (*ije*) SR (*e*)	SR (*e*)
Stanišić and Župljanin	14/06/2010	B&H	Dragan Kezunović		BS (*ije*) SR (*e*)	SR (*e*)
Stanišić and Župljanin	21/06/2010	B&H	Sulejman Crnčalo	B&H Muslim	CRO (*ije*) SR (*e*)	SR (*e*)
Stanišić and Župljanin	22/06/2010	B&H	Sulejman Crnčalo		BS (*ije*) SR (*e*)	SR (*e*)
Stanišić and Župljanin	22/06/2010	B&H	Radomir Kezunović	B&H Serb	BS (*ije*) SR (*e*)	SR (*e*)
Stanišić and Župljanin	16/07/2010	B&H	Sreto Gajić	B&H Serb	CRO (*ije*) SR (*e*)	SR (*e*)
Stanišić and Župljanin	16/08/2010	B&H	Nusret Sivac	B&H Muslim	CRO (*ije*) SR (*e*)	SR (*e*)
Stanišić and Župljanin	17/08/2010	B&H	Nusret Sivac		CRO (*ije*) SR (*e*)	SR (*e*)
Stanišić and Župljanin	17/08/2010	B&H	Biljana Simeunović	B&H Serb	CRO (*ije*) SR (*e*)	SR (*e*)
Stanišić and Župljanin	19/08/2010	B&H	Sulejman Tihić	B&H Muslim	CRO (*ije*) SR (*e*)	SR (*e*)
Stanišić and Župljanin	20/08/2010	B&H	Sulejman Tihić		CRO (*ije*)	SR (*e*)

Trial	Date	Situation country	Witness	Ethnicity of the witness	Language of interpreters	Language of the transcript
Stanišić and Župljanin	24/08/2010	B&H	Milorad Davidović	B&H Serb	BS (*ije*) CRO (*ije*)	SR (*e*)
Stanišić and Župljanin	25/08/2010	B&H	Gojko Vasić	B&H Serb	CRO (*ije*) SR (*e*)	SR (*e*)
Stanišić and Župljanin	1/09/2010	B&H	Nenad Krejić	B&H Serb	BS (*ije*) SR (*e*)	SR (*e*)
Stanišić and Župljanin	2/09/2010	B&H	Nenad Krejić		BS (*ije*) SR (*e*)	SR (*e*)
Stanišić and Župljanin	2/09/2010	B&H	Marinko Kovačević	B&H Serb	BS (*ije*) SR (*e*)	SR (*e*)
Stanišić and Župljanin	3/09/2010	B&H	Marinko Kovačević (14155)		BS (*ije*) CRO (*ije*)	SR (*e*)
Stanišić and Župljanin	6/09/2010	B&H	Marinko Kovačević		CRO (*ije*)	SR (*e*)
Stanišić and Župljanin	29/09/2010	B&H	Slobodanka Gačinović	B&H Serb	BS (*ije*) CRO (*ije*)	SR (*e*)
Stanišić and Župljanin	30/09/2010	B&H	Slobodanka Gačinović		CRO (*ije*)	SR (*e*)
Stanišić and Župljanin	30/09/2010	B&H	Simo Mišković	B&H Serb	CRO (*ije*)	SR (*e*)
Stanišić and Župljanin	1/10/2010	B&H	Simo Mišković		CRO (*ije*)	SR (*e*)
Stanišić and Župljanin	4/10/2010	B&H	Simo Mišković		CRO (*ije*) SR (*e*)	SR (*e*)
Stanišić and Župljanin	7/10/2010	B&H	Slobodan Avlijaš	B&H Serb	CRO (*ije*) SR (*e*)	SR (*e*)
Stanišić and Župljanin	8/10/2010	B&H	Slobodan Avlijaš		CRO (*ije*)	SR (*e*)
Stanišić and Župljanin	12/04/2011	B&H	Andrija Bjelošević	B&H Serb	BS (*ije*)	SR (*e*)
Stanišić and Župljanin	13/04/2011	B&H	Andrija Bjelošević		CRO (*ije*)	SR (*e*)
Stanišić and Župljanin	14/04/2011	B&H	Andrija Bjelošević		BS (*ije*) CRO (*ije*)	SR (*e*)
Stanišić and Župljanin	15/04/2011	B&H	Andrija Bjelošević		CRO (*ije*)	SR (*e*)

Trial	Date	Situation country	Witness	Ethnicity of the witness	Language of interpreters	Language of the transcript
Stanišić and Župljanin	18/04/2011	B&H	Andrija Bjelošević		CRO (*ije*)	SR (*e*)
Stanišić and Župljanin	19/04/2011	B&H	Andrija Bjelošević		CRO (*ije*)	SR (*e*)
Stanišić and Župljanin	20/04/2011	B&H	Andrija Bjelošević		CRO (*ije*) SR (*e*)	SR (*e*)
Stanišić and Župljanin	21/04/2011	B&H	Andrija Bjelošević		CRO (*ije*)	SR (*e*)
Stanišić and Župljanin	17/05/2011	B&H	Andrija Bjelošević		CRO (*ije*) SR (*e*)	SR (*e*)
Stanišić and Župljanin	18/05/2011	B&H	Andrija Bjelošević		CRO (*ije*) SR (*e*)	SR (*e*)
Stanišić and Župljanin	19/05/2011	B&H	Andrija Bjelošević		CRO (*ije*) SR (*e*)	SR (*e*)
Stanišić and Župljanin	20/05/2011	B&H	Andrija Bjelošević		CRO (*ije*) SR (*e*)	SR (*e*)
Stanišić and Župljanin	23/05/2011	B&H	Andrija Bjelošević		SR (*e*)	SR (*e*)
Stanišić and Župljanin	24/05/2011	B&H	Andrija Bjelošević		BS (*ije*) SR (*e*)	SR (*e*)
Stanišić and Župljanin	25/05/2011	B&H	Andrija Bjelošević		BS (*ije*) SR (*e*)	SR (*e*)
Stanišić and Župljanin	27/05/2011	B&H	Dragomir Andan	B&H Serb	BS (*ije*) CRO (*ije*)	SR (*e*)
Stanišić and Župljanin	30/05/2011	B&H	Dragomir Andan		BS (*ije*)	SR (*e*)
Stanišić and Župljanin	31/05/2011	B&H	Dragomir Andan		CRO (*ije*) SR (*e*)	SR (*e*)
Stanišić and Župljanin	1/06/2011	B&H	Dragomir Andan		BS (*ije*) CRO (*ije*)	SR (*e*)
Stanišić and Župljanin	2/06/2011	B&H	Dragomir Andan		CRO (*ije*) SR (*e*)	SR (*e*)

Trial	Date	Situation country	Witness	Ethnicity of the witness	Language of interpreters	Language of the transcript
Stanišić and Župljanin	3/06/2011	B&H	Dragomir Andan		CRO (*ije*) SR (*e*)	SR (*e*)
Tolimir	17/05/2010	B&H	Dražen Erdemović	B&H Croat	CRO (*ije*) SR (*e*)	SR (*e*)
Tolimir	17/05/2011	B&H	Manojlo Milovanović	B&H Serb	BS (*ije*) SR (*e*)	SR (*e*)
Tolimir	18/05/2011	B&H	Manojlo Milovanović		BS (*ije*) SR (*e*)	SR (*e*)
Vasiljević	18/09/2001	B&H	Mevsud Poljo	B&H Muslim	CRO (*ije*) SR (*e*)	SR (*e*)
Martić	16/01/2006	CRO	Veljko Džakula	CRO Serb	CRO (*ije*) SR (*e*)	CRO (*ije*)
Martić	17/01/2006	CRO	Veljko Džakula		CRO (*ije*) SR (*e*)	CRO (*ije*)
Martić	18/01/2006	CRO	Veljko Džakula		CRO (*ije*) SR (*e*)	CRO (*ije*)
Martić	19/01/2006	CRO	Veljko Džakula		CRO (*ije*) SR (*e*)	CRO (*ije*)
Martić	06/02/2006	CRO	Radosav Maksić	CRO Serb	CRO (*ije*) SR (*e*)	CRO (*ije*)
Martić	07/02/2006	CRO	Radosav Maksić		CRO (*ije*) SR (*e*)	CRO (*ije*)
Martić	09/02/2006	CRO	Jasna Denona	CRO Croat	SR (*e*)	CRO (*ije*)
Martić	15/02/2006	CRO	Milan Babić	CRO Serb	BS (*ije*) CRO (*ije*)	CRO (*ije*)
Martić	16/02/2006	CRO	Milan Babić		BS (*ije*) CRO (*ije*)	CRO (*ije*)

Trial	Date	Situation country	Witness	Ethnicity of the witness	Language of interpreters	Language of the transcript
Martić	17/02/2006	CRO	Milan Babić		CRO (*ije*) SR (*e*)	CRO (*ije*)
Martić	20/02/2006	CRO	Milan Babić		CRO (*ije*) SR (*e*)	CRO (*ije*)
Martić	21/02/2006	CRO	Milan Babić		CRO (*ije*)	CRO (*ije*)
Martić	2/03/2006	CRO	Milan Babić		CRO (*ije*)	CRO (*ije*)
Martić	3/03/2006	CRO	Milan Babić		CRO (*ije*)	CRO (*ije*)
Martić	21/03/2006	CRO	Ana Kesić	CRO Croat	CRO (*ije*) SR (*e*)	CRO (*ije*)
Martić	22/03/2006	CRO	Marica Vuković	CRO Croat	BS (*ije*) SR (*e*)	CRO (*ije*)
Martić	23/03/2006	CRO	Ante Marinović	CRO Croat	SR (*e*)	CRO (*ije*)
Martić	24/03/2006	CRO	Marko Vuković	CRO Croat	SR (*e*)	CRO (*ije*)
Martić	27/03/2006	CRO	Vlado Vuković	CRO Croat	BS (*ije*) SR (*e*)	CRO (*ije*)
Martić	28/03/2006	CRO	Vlado Vuković		BS (*ije*)	CRO (*ije*)
Martić	29/03/2006	CRO	Neven Šegarić	CRO Croat	CRO (*ije*) SR (*e*)	CRO (*ije*)
Martić	29/03/2006	CRO	Marko Miljanić	CRO Croat	CRO (*ije*) SR (*e*)	CRO (*ije*)
Martić	30/03/2006	CRO	Marko Miljanić		CRO (*ije*) SR (*e*)	CRO (*ije*)
Martić	30/03/2006	CRO	Hamdija Krupić	CRO Muslim	CRO (*ije*) SR (*e*)	CRO (*ije*)
Martić	31/03/2006	CRO	Hamdija Krupić		CRO (*ije*) SR (*e*)	CRO (*ije*)
Martić	5/04/2006	CRO	Luka Brkić	CRO Croat	BS (*ije*) CRO (*ije*)	CRO (*ije*)

Trial	Date	Situation country	Witness	Ethnicity of the witness	Language of interpreters	Language of the transcript
Martić	6/04/2006	CRO	Josip Josipović	CRO Croat	CRO (*ije*)	CRO (*ije*)
Martić	7/04/2006	CRO	Josip Josipović		CRO (*ije*)	CRO (*ije*)
Martić	7/04/2006	CRO	Luka Brkić	CRO Croat	CRO (*ije*)	CRO (*ije*)
Martić	11/04/2006	CRO	Ivan Grujić	CRO Croat	CRO (*ije*) SR (*e*)	CRO (*ije*)
Martić	12/04/2006	CRO	Davor Strinović	CRO Croat	SR (*e*)	CRO (*ije*)
Martić	13/04/2006	CRO	Davor Strinović		CRO (*ije*)	CRO (*ije*)
Martić	26/04/2006	CRO	Stanko Erstić	CRO Croat	CRO (*ije*) SR (*e*)	CRO (*ije*)
Martić	2/05/2006	CRO	Rade Rašeta	CRO Croat	CRO (*ije*) SR (*e*)	CRO (*ije*)
Martić	3/05/2006	CRO	Rade Rašeta	CRO Croat	SR (*e*)	CRO (*ije*)
Martić	12/06/2006	CRO	Mladen Lončar	CRO Croat	BS (*ije*)	CRO (*ije*)
Martić	13/06/2006	CRO	Mladen Lončar		BS (*ije*) CRO (*ije*)	CRO (*ije*)
Martić	15/06/2006	CRO	Branko Lazarević	CRO Croat	BS (*ije*) SR (*e*)	CRO (*ije*)
Martić	19/06/2006	CRO	Sanja Buntić	CRO Croat	BS (*ije*) CRO (*ije*)	CRO (*ije*)
Martić	19/06/2006	CRO	Rašeljka Grmoja	CRO Croat	BS (*ije*) CRO (*ije*)	CRO (*ije*)
Martić	20/06/2006	CRO	Mina Žunac	CRO Croat	BS (*ije*)	CRO (*ije*)
Martić	12/07/2006	CRO	Slobodan Jarčević	CRO Serb	BS (*ije*) CRO (*ije*)	CRO (*ije*)
Martić	13/07/2006	CRO	Slobodan Jarčević		BS (*ije*) CRO (*ije*)	CRO (*ije*)
Martić	14/07/2006	CRO	Slobodan Jarčević		BS (*ije*)	CRO (*ije*)

Trial	Date	Situation country	Witness	Ethnicity of the witness	Language of interpreters	Language of the transcript
Martić	14/08/2006	CRO	Ratko Lićina (6365)	CRO Serb	BS (*ije*) CRO (*ije*)	CRO (*ije*)
Martić	15/08/2006	CRO	Ratko Lićina		BS (*ije*)	CRO (*ije*)
Martić	16/08/2006	CRO	Ratko Lićina		BS (*ije*)	CRO (*ije*)
Martić	18/08/2006	CRO	Ratko Lićina		CRO (*ije*)	CRO (*ije*)
Martić	17/08/2006	CRO	Ratko Lićina		BS (*ije*) CRO (*ije*)	CRO (*ije*)
Martić	6/09/2006	CRO	Slobodan Perić	CRO Serb	BS (*ije*)	CRO (*ije*)
Martić	7/09/2006	CRO	Slobodan Perić		BS (*ije*)	CRO (*ije*)
Martić	8/09/2006	CRO	Slobodan Perić		BS (*ije*)	CRO (*ije*)
Martić	11/09/2006	CRO	Branko Popović	CRO Serb	CRO (*ije*) SR (*e*)	CRO (*ije*)
Martić	12/09/2006	CRO	Lazar Macura	CRO Serb	BS (*ije*)	CRO (*ije*)
Martić	13/09/2006	CRO	Lazar Macura		BS (*ije*) CRO (*ije*)	CRO (*ije*)
Martić	14/09/2006	CRO	Lazar Macura		BS (*ije*) SR (*e*)	CRO (*ije*)
Martić	15/09/2006	CRO	Lazar Macura		BS (*ije*) SR (*e*)	CRO (*ije*)
Martić	15/09/2006	CRO	Ljubica Vujanić	CRO Serb	BS (*ije*) SR (*e*)	CRO (*ije*)
Martić	18/09/2006	CRO	Ljubica Vujanić		BS (*ije*) SR (*e*)	CRO (*ije*)
Martić	18/09/2006	CRO	Milan Dragišić	CRO Serb	BS (*ije*) SR (*e*)	CRO (*ije*)
Martić	19/09/2006	CRO	Milan Dragišić		BS (*ije*) SR (*e*)	CRO (*ije*)

Trial	Date	Situation country	Witness	Ethnicity of the witness	Language of interpreters	Language of the transcript
Martić	20/09/2006	CRO	Milan Dragišić		BS (*ije*) SR (*e*)	CRO (*ije*)
Martić	20/09/2006	CRO	Stevo Plejo	CRO Serb	BS (*ije*) SR (*e*)	CRO (*ije*)
Martić	21/09/2006	CRO	Stevo Plejo		BS (*ije*) CRO (*ije*)	CRO (*ije*)
Martić	22/09/2006	CRO	Stevo Plejo		CRO (*ije*) SR (*e*)	CRO (*ije*)
Martić	9/10/2006	CRO	Nikola Medaković	CRO Serb	CRO (*ije*)	SR (*e*)
Martić	10/10/2006	CRO	Nikola Medaković		BS (*ije*) CRO (*ije*)	SR (*e*)
Martić	11/10/2006	CRO	Nikola Medaković		BS (*ije*) CRO (*ije*)	SR (*e*)
Martić	12/10/2006	CRO	Nikola Medaković		BS (*ije*) CRO (*ije*)	SR (*e*)
Martić	18/10/2006	CRO	Borislav Đukić	CRO Serb	CRO (*ije*) SR (*e*)	SR (*e*)
Martić	19/10/2006	CRO	Borislav Đukić		CRO (*ije*) SR (*e*)	SR (*e*)
Martić	20/10/2006	CRO	Borislav Đukić		BS (*ije*) CRO (*ije*)	SR (*e*)
Martić	23/10/2006	CRO	Borislav Đukić		BS (*ije*) CRO (*ije*)	SR (*e*)
Martić	23/10/2006	CRO	Mile Dakić	CRO Serb	BS (*ije*) CRO (*ije*)	SR (*e*)
Martić	25/10/2006	CRO	Mile Dakić		CRO (*ije*) SR (*e*)	SR (*e*)

Trial	**Date**	**Situation country**	**Witness**	**Ethnicity of the witness**	**Language of interpreters**	**Language of the transcript**
Martić	26/10/2006	CRO	Mile Dakić		CRO (*ije*) SR (*e*)	SR (*e*)
Martić	26/10/2006	CRO	Zoran Lakić	CRO Serb	CRO (*ije*) SR (*e*)	SR (*e*)
Martić	27/10/2006	CRO	Zoran Lakić		BS (*ije*) SR (*e*)	SR (*e*)
Martić	30/10/2006	CRO	Zoran Lakić		SR (*e*)	CRO (*ije*)
Martić	30/10/2006	CRO	Nada Pupovac	CRO Serb	SR (*e*)	CRO (*ije*)
Martić	31/10/2006	CRO	Nada Pupovac		SR (*e*)	CRO (*ije*)
Martić	1/11/2006	CRO	Nada Pupovac		SR (*e*)	CRO (*ije*)
Martić	3/11/2006	CRO	Dragan Knežević	CRO Serb	CRO (*ije*) SR (*e*)	CRO (*ije*)
Martić	10/11/2006	CRO	Nikola Dobrijević	CRO Serb	CRO (*ije*)	CRO (*ije*)
Martić	13/11/2006	CRO	Nikola Dobrijević		CRO (*ije*) SR (*e*)	CRO (*ije*)
Martić	14/11/2006	CRO	Smilja Avramov	CRO Serb	CRO (*ije*)	CRO (*ije*)
Martić	15/11/2006	CRO	Smilja Avramov		CRO (*ije*)	CRO (*ije*)
Šainović et al	28/01/2008	KS	Saša Antić	SR Serb	CRO (*ije*) SR (*e*)	SR (*e*)
Šainović et al	28/01/2008	KS	Pavle Gavrilović	SR Serb	CRO (*ije*) SR (*e*)	SR (*e*)
Šainović et al	28/01/2008	KS	Radomir Mladenović	SR Serb	CRO (*ije*) SR (*e*)	SR (*e*)
Šainović et al	27/02/2008	KS	Radojica Nikčević	SR Serb	CRO (*ije*) SR (*e*)	SR (*e*)
Šainović et al	27/02/2008	KS	Petar Dujković	SR Serb	CRO (*ije*) SR (*e*)	SR (*e*)
Perišić	12/11/2008	All	Branko Bubenik	CRO Croat	SR (*e*)	CRO (*ije*)

Trial	Date	Situation country	Witness	Ethnicity of the witness	Language of interpreters	Language of the transcript
Perišić	3/02/2009	All	Vekaz Turković	B&H Muslim	BS (*ije*) CRO (*ije*)	CRO (*ije*)
Perišić	7/05/2009	All	Rade Rašeta	B&H Serb	BS (*ije*) SR (*e*)	CRO (*ije*)
Perišić	11/05/2009	All	Rade Rašeta		BS (*ije*) SR (*e*)	CRO (*ije*)
Milošević	5/05/2003	All	Dževad Gušić	B&H Muslim	BS (*ije*) CRO (*ije*)	CRO (*ije*)
Milošević	6/05/2003	All	Dževad Gušić		BS (*ije*) CRO (*ije*)	CRO (*ije*)
Milošević	9/05/2003	All	Džemal Bećirević	B&H Muslim	CRO (*ije*) SR (*e*)	CRO (*ije*)
Milošević	9/05/2003	All	Fadil Banjanović	B&H Muslim	CRO (*ije*) SR (*e*)	CRO (*ije*)
Milošević	8/07/2003	All	Edhem Pašić	B&H Muslim	BS (*ije*) CRO (*ije*)	CRO (*ije*)
Milošević	25/08/2003	All	Dražen Erdemović	B&H Croat	BS (*ije*) CRO (*ije*)	CRO (*ije*)
Milošević	15/10/2003	All	Milan Milanović	B&H Serb	BS (*ije*) CRO (*ije*)	CRO (*ije*)
Milošević	16/10/2003	All	Sead Omeragić	B&H Muslim	CRO (*ije*)	CRO (*ije*)
Milošević	24/11/2003	All	Ibro Osmanović	B&H Muslim	CRO (*ije*) SR (*e*)	CRO (*ije*)
Milošević	24/11/2003	All	Esad Velić	B&H Muslim	CRO (*ije*) SR (*e*)	CRO (*ije*)
Milošević	26/11/2003	All	Esad Velić		SR (*e*)	CRO (*ije*)
Milošević	26/11/2003	All	Miroslav Deronjić	B&H Serb	SR (*e*)	CRO (*ije*)
Milošević	27/11/2003	All	Miroslav Deronjić		BS (*ije*)	CRO (*ije*)

Trial	Date	Situation country	Witness	Ethnicity of the witness	Language of interpreters	Language of the transcript
Milošević	22/03/2005	All	Radomir Gojović	B&H Serb	CRO (*ije*) SR (*e*)	CRO (*ije*)
Milošević	22/03/2005	All	Danica Marinković	B&H Serb	CRO (*ije*) SR (*e*)	CRO (*ije*)
Milošević	23/03/2005	All	Danica Marinković		SR (*e*)	CRO (*ije*)
Milošević	24/03/2005	All	Danica Marinković		CRO (*ije*)	CRO (*ije*)
Milošević	6/04/2005	All	Danica Marinković		BS (*ije*) CRO (*ije*)	CRO (*ije*)
Milošević	7/04/2005	All	Danica Marinković		CRO (*ije*) SR (*e*)	CRO (*ije*)
Milošević	7/04/2005	All	Slaviša Dobrićanin	SR Serb	CRO (*ije*) SR (*e*)	CRO (*ije*)
Milošević	27/04/2005	All	Dragan Jašović	SR Serb	CRO (*ije*)	CRO (*ije*)
Milošević	27/04/2005	All	Zvonko Gvozdenović	SR Serb	CRO (*ije*)	CRO (*ije*)
Milošević	4/05/2005	All	Radovan Paponjak	SR Serb	BS (*ije*) SR (*e*)	SR (*e*)
Milošević	5/05/2005	All	Radovan Paponjak		CRO (*ije*)	SR (*e*)
Milošević	6/05/2005	All	Radovan Paponjak		CRO (*ije*) SR (*e*)	SR (*e*)
Milošević	9/05/2005	All	Radovan Paponjak		BS (*ije*) SR (*e*)	SR (*e*)
Milošević	10/05/2005	All	Radovan Paponjak		CRO (*ije*) SR (*e*)	SR (*e*)
Milošević	11/05/2005	All	Obrad Stevanović	SR Serb	CRO (*ije*) SR (*e*)	SR (*e*)
Milošević	17/05/2005	All	Obrad Stevanović		CRO (*ije*) SR (*e*)	SR (*e*)

Trial	Date	Situation country	Witness	Ethnicity of the witness	Language of interpreters	Language of the transcript
Milošević	18/05/2005	All	Obrad Stevanović		CRO (*ije*) SR (*e*)	SR (*e*)
Milošević	19/05/2005	All	Obrad Stevanović		CRO (*ije*) SR (*e*)	SR (*e*)
Milošević	25/05/2005	All	Obrad Stevanović		CRO (*ije*) SR (*e*)	SR (*e*)
Milošević	26/05/2005	All	Obrad Stevanović		CRO (*ije*) SR (*e*)	SR (*e*)
Milošević	27/05/2005	All	Obrad Stevanović		CRO (*ije*) SR (*e*)	SR (*e*)
Milošević	31/05/2005	All	Obrad Stevanović		CRO (*ije*) SR (*e*)	SR (*e*)
Milošević	1/06/2005	All	Obrad Stevanović		CRO (*ije*) SR (*e*)	SR (*e*)
Milošević	2/06/2005	All	Obrad Stevanović		BS (*ije*) CRO (*ije*)	SR (*e*)
Milošević	6/06/2005	All	Obrad Stevanović		BS (*ije*) CRO (*ije*)	SR (*e*)
Milošević	7/06/2005	All	Obrad Stevanović		CRO (*ije*) SR (*e*)	SR (*e*)
Milošević	8/06/2005	All	Obrad Stevanović		BS (*ije*) CRO (*ije*)	SR (*e*)
Milošević	15/06/2005	All	Obrad Stevanović		BS (*ije*) CRO (*ije*)	SR (*e*)
Milošević	15/06/2005	All	Dragan Jašović	B&H Serb	BS (*ije*) CRO (*ije*)	SR (*e*)

References and Bibliography

Books and journal articles

Alexovičková, Iveta (2012), From hiring to firing: a comparative study on selected legal safeguards for the independence and impartiality of international civil servants serving in the United Nations Secretariat and in the European Commission. Wolf Legal Publishers: Nijmegen.

Andrić, Ivo (2004), The bridge on the Drina. Bosanska riječ: Sarajevo.

Baker, M. (2011), In other words: a coursebook on translation (second edition), Routledge: London and New York.

Bassiouni, Cherif (1994), Former Yugoslavia: Investigating Violations of International Humanitarian Law and Establishing an International Criminal Tribunal. Fordham International Law Journal, 18/4.

Bassiouni, Cherif (2011), Crimes against humanity: historical evolution and contemporary application. Cambridge University Press: Cambridge.

Blažević, Robert and Alijagić, Amina (2010), Antižidovsko i rasno zakonodavstvo u Fašističkoj Italiji, Nacističkoj Njemačkoj i Ustaškoj NDH. Zbornik Pravnog fakulteta: Zagreb.

Brammertz, Serge and Jarvis, Michelle (eds.) (2016), Prosecuting conflict-related sexual violence. Oxford University Press: Oxford.

Cao, D. (2007), Translating law. Multilingual Matters: Bristol.

Carrier, Peter (2006), Holocaust monuments and national memory cultures in France and Germany since 1989. Berghahn Books: New York.

Čulinović, Ferdo (1961), Jugoslavija između dva rata. Jugoslavenska akademija znanosti i umjetnosti: Zagreb.

Dadrian, Vahakn and Akçam, Taner (2012), Judgment at Istanbul: the Armenian genocide trials. Berghahn Books: New York.

Dedijer, Vladimir (1987), Vatikan i Jasenovac: dokumenti. Izdavačka radna organizacija Rad: Beograd.

Draženović-Carrieri, Maja (2002), B/C/S A practical approach. Lexicography and language policy in South-Slavic languages after 1989. Verlag Otto Sagner: Munich.

Elias-Bursać, Ellen (2015), Translating evidence and interpreting testimony at a war crimes tribunal. Palgrave Macmillan: London.

Fine, John V. A. (1985), The Bosnian Church: A new interpretation: A study of the Bosnian Church and its place in state and society from the 13th to the 15th centuries. East European quarterly.

Gaiba, Francesca (1998), The origins of simultaneous interpreting: the Nuremberg trial. University of Ottawa Press: Ottawa.

Garašanin, Ilija (1844), Načertanije. Institut za istraživanje genocida, Univerzitet u Sarajevu: Sarajevo.

Gordon, Gregory S. (2017), Speech atrocity crimes: foundation, fragmentation, fruition. Oxford University Press: Oxford.

Hadžijahić, Muhamed (1985), Građa o posljednjim ostacima bosančice u nas. Anali Gazi Husrev-begove biblioteke, Sarajevo.

Hajdarpašić, Edin (2015), Whose Bosnia? Nationalism and political imagination in the Balkans 1840-1914. Cornell University Press: Ithaca and London.

Hajdu, Nata (undated), The kindapper and the kidnapped: interpreting at the ICTY: https://bit.ly/2REGUBn.

Hepburn, Phillip (2012), The Translation of Evidence at the ICTY: A Groundbreaking Institution. Translation and Interpreting Studies, 7/1: 54-71.

Imamović, Mustafa (2014), Historija države i prava Bosne i Hercegovine. University Press: Sarajevo.

Imber, Colin (2002), The Ottoman Empire, 1300-1650: the structure of power. Palgrave Macmillan: London.

Isaković, Alija (2001), Vid bosanskog jezika. Anali Gazi Husrev-begove biblioteke XIX-XX, Sarajevo.

Judah, Tim (1997), The Serbs: the sweet and rotten smell of history. Daedalus, 126.

Kamusella, Tomasz (2009), The politics of language and nationalism in modern Central Europe. Palgrave Macmillan: London.

Kasumović, Ahmet (2001), Bosanskohercegovački muslimani i njihov jezik. Anali Gazi Husrev-begove biblioteke XIX-XX, Sarajevo.

Klaić, Vjekoslav (1899), Povijest Hrvata. Knjižara Lav Hartmana (Kugli i Deutsch): Zagreb.

Knežević, fra Antun (2012) Bosanski prijatelj. Duh Bosne, Svezak 07, Br. 1, Januar. https://bit.ly/2VtiNq5.

Lunt, Horace (1974), Old Church Slavonic grammar. Mouton: The Hague.

Meron, Theodore (2011), The making of international criminal justice, a view from the bench: selected speeches. Oxford University Press: Oxford.

Mowbray, Jacqueline (2012), Linguistic justice: international law and language policy. Oxford University Press: Oxford.

Mulayim, Sedat and Lai, Miranda (2016), Ethics for police translators and interpreters. CRC Press: Boca Raton.

Nikolić, Marijana (2005), Interpreting after Nuremberg: international war crimes trials. Proteus 14.

Pavetić, Janja (2012), Interview with Greiss lecturer Marijana Nikolić. SlavFile: Newsletter of the Slavic Languages Division.

Pešikan, Mitar, Jerković, Jovan, Pižurica, Mato (2010), Pravopis srpskoga jezika (izmenjeno i dopunjeno izdanje). Matica Srpska: Novi Sad.

Petrović, Petar II Njegoš (2012), The mountain wreath. Nova knjiga: Beograd.

Rizvić, Muhsin (1995), Bosanski muslimani u Andrićevom svijetu. Ljiljan: Sarajevo.

Starr, Sonia B. (2009), Ensuring Defense Counsel Competence at International Criminal Tribunals. UCLA Journal of International Law and Foreign Affairs, 14/1: 169-206.

Šarčević, Susan (1997), New approach to legal translation. Kluwer Law International: The Hague.

Šarčević, Susan (2000), Legal Translation and Translation Theory: a Receiver-oriented Approach. Legal Translation: History, Theory/ies, Practice.

Šipka, Milan (1999), Standardni jezik u Bosni i Hercegovini u dokumentima jezičke politike. Open Society Institute: Budapest.

Škegro, Ante (2005), Bilino polje: primjer jedne historiografske kontroverze in Fenomen 'krstjani' u srednjovjekovnoj Bosni i Humu. Institut za istoriju, Sarajevo, and Hrvatski institut za povijest, Zagreb.

Tabeau, Ewa (ed.) (2009), Conflict in numbers: casualties of the 1990s wars in the former Yugoslavia (1991–1999). Helsinki Committee for Human Rights in Serbia: Belgrade.

University of Texas and ICTY Victims and Witnesses Unit (2016), Echoes of testimonies: a pilot study into the long-term impact of bearing witness before the ICTY: https://bit.ly/3acryu9.

Van Parijs, Phillipe (2011), Linguistic justice for Europe and for the world. Oxford University Press: Oxford.

Various authors (1986), Draft Memorandum of the Serbian Academy of Arts and Sciences. Serbian Academy of Arts and

Sciences.
Warah, Rasna (2016), UNsilenced: unmasking the United Nations' culture of cover-ups, corruption and impunity. AuthorHouse: UK.
Weiss, Thomas G. (2012), What's wrong with the UN and how to fix it. Polity Press: Cambridge.
Žeželj, Mirko (1967), Prošlost u slikama. Školska Knjiga: Zagreb.

International treaties and the laws from the situation country

Basic Principles on the Independence of the Judiciary (1985).
Constitution of the FB&H (1994).
Constitution of the Kingdom of the Serbs, Croats, and Slovenes (1921).
Constitution of the Republika Srpska (2005).
Constitution of the SFRY (1974).
Guidelines on the Role of Prosecutors (1990).
Human Rights Standards and Practice for the Police: Expanded Pocket Book on Human Rights for the Police (2004).
International Covenant on Civil and Political Rights (1966).
International Prosecutors Association, Standards of Professional Responsibility and Statement of the Essential Duties and Rights of Prosecutors (1999).
Joint Ministry of Finance, Decree 168539 (1907), Arhiv Bosne i Hercegovine: Sarajevo.
Joint Ministry of Finance, Decree 6687 (1880), Arhiv Bosne i Hercegovine: Sarajevo.
Republic of B&H, Institute for Statistics of the Republic of B&H, Statistical Bulletin 233, The 1991 Census of population, households, dwellings and agricultural lands, Ethnic characteristics of the population, The 1991 results on the level of the Republic and on the municipal level, Sarajevo, October 1993.
Republic of Serbia, Higher Court in Belgrade, About rehabilitation.
Republic of Serbia, Official Gazette of the Republic of Serbia 92/2011 (2011), Law on Rehabilitation.
The Kingdom of the Serbs, the Croats and the Slovenes, Official Gazette LXXXI/204 (1929), Orthographic Instructions for all elementary, high, and professional schools.
The Kingdom of Yugoslavia, Official Gazette CXIX/289 (1929), The Law on People's Schools.

The Kingdom of Yugoslavia, Official Gazette LXIII/167 (1930), Constitution of the Islamic Religious Community of the Kingdom of Yugoslavia.
The Kingdom of Yugoslavia, Official Gazette LXVI/207 (1931), Constitution of the Kingdom of Yugoslavia.
The Serbian Gazette LXXX/257 (1913), Decision to enact the following provisions of the Constitution of the Kingdom of Serbia of 5 June 1903 in the annexed Old Serbia.
Treaty of Berlin (1878).
Universal Declaration of Human Rights (1948).

UN documents

UN vacancies, AFRO/WHO, Interpreters (English, French, Portuguese): https://bit.ly/3bcrBHN.
UN vacancies, ICRC (grade not defied), Senior Arabic Translator/Reviser: https://bit.ly/2V8X9sf.
UN vacancies, ICTY, G-5 Language Assistant: https://bit.ly/2yehXpm.
UN vacancies, ICTY, G-5 UNDU Language Assistant (Albanian, B/C/S and English): https://bit.ly/2z2kgwc.
UN vacancies, ICTY, G-5 UNDU Language Assistant (B/C/S and English): https://bit.ly/2V7I4Y1.
UN vacancies, ICTY, G-5 VWU Administrative Assistant (Dutch, B/C/S and English): https://bit.ly/3bcHbD1.
UN vacancies, ICTY, G-5 VWU Witness Assistant (Dutch, B/C/S and English): https://bit.ly/2Vw245v.
UN vacancies, ICTY, Intelligence Analyst (Criminal): https://bit.ly/3chltOs.
UN vacancies, ICTY, Intelligence Analyst (Military): https://bit.ly/3enah4O,
UN vacancies, ICTY, P-2 Associate Translator (B/C/S): https://bit.ly/3elN3fi.
UN vacancies, ICTY, P-3 Translator (B/C/S): https://bit.ly/2RHuJ6O.
UN vacancies, ICTY, P-4 Translator/Reviser (English): https://bit.ly/2yjokYl.
UN vacancies, IMF Editor (External relations officer): https://bit.ly/34AD6Gi.
UN vacancies, OPCW, P-3 Linguist (Chinese): https://bit.ly/2wL2Ao8).

UN vacancies, Secretariat of the Pacific Community, Interpreter/Translator: https://bit.ly/2wFbmns).
UN vacancies, UNDP P-3 Interpreter/Translation Specialist: https://bit.ly/2yfesz6).
UN vacancies, UNOPS, IICA-2 Bilingual Communications Consultant/Translator (English and Somali): https://bit.ly/2RE5kLa.
UN, Administrative Instruction: Language Allowance and Language Incentives (ST/AI/1999/2) (1999).
UN, Board of Auditors, Financial report and audited financial statements for biennium 2002-2003 ended 31 December 2003 (A/59/5/Add.12) (2004).
UN, Competitive examinations for recruitment and placement in posts requiring specific language skills in the professional category (ST/AI/1998/7) (1998).
UN, Competitive examinations for recruitment and placement in posts requiring specific language skills in the professional category (ST/AI/1998/7/Amend.1) (2012).
UN, Details of UN Salaries, Hazard Pay, Rental Subsidy, Mobility and Hardship Scheme, and other Allowances, Benefits: https://bit.ly/3enl7rC.
UN, Final report of Commission of Experts established pursuant to the UN Security Council Resolution 771 (S/1994/673) (1994).
UN, General Assembly Resolution 152(II) on simultaneous interpreting (1947).
UN, Human resources management (A/RES/49/222) (1995).
UN, Human resources management (A/RES/51/226) (1996).
UN, Human resources management (A/RES/53/221) (1999).
UN, Human resources management reform (A/55/253) (2000), Appendix III.
UN, ICSC Compendium (1980).
UN, ICSC Standards for Translators and Revisers (1981).
UN, ICSC Standards of Conduct for the International Civil Service (2013).
UN, ICSC Statute and Rules of Procedure and Evidence (1987).
UN, Improving the performance of the DGACM (A/57/289) (2002).
UN, Information sensitivity, classification and handling (ST/SGB/2007/6) (2007).
UN, JIU, Multilingualism in the UN System organizations: status of implementation (JIU/REP/2011/4) (2011).
UN, Language Proficiency Tests (2016): https://bit.ly/2RzJ05g.
UN, LCEs: sample examinations: https://bit.ly/2VxDT6H.

UN, Managed Reassignment Programme (ST/AI/2007/2) (2007).
UN, Mobility framework (A/68/265) (2014).
UN, OIOS Internal Audit Division, Audit of Language Services at ICTY (2009).
UN, OIOS Report on the audit and investigation of the ICTY (A/54/120) (1999).
UN, Peacekeeping, UNPROFOR: https://bit.ly/3bafD1b.
UN, Policies for Obtaining the Services of Individuals on Behalf of the Organization (ST/SGB/177) (1982).
UN, Report of the ICTY (A/49/342) (1994).
UN, Report of the ICTY (A/50/365) (1995).
UN, Report of the ICTY (A/51/292) (1996).
UN, Report of the ICTY (A/52/375) (1997).
UN, Report of the ICTY (A/53/219) (1998).
UN, Report of the ICTY (A/54/187) (1999).
UN, Report of the ICTY (A/55/273) (2000).
UN, Report of the ICTY (A/56/352) (2001).
UN, Report of the ICTY (A/57/379) (2002).
UN, Report of the ICTY (A/58/297) (2003).
UN, Report of the ICTY (A/59/215) (2004).
UN, Report of the ICTY (A/60/267) (2005).
UN, Report of the ICTY (A/61/271) (2006).
UN, Report of the ICTY (A/62/172) (2007).
UN, Report of the ICTY (A/63/210) (2008).
UN, Report of the ICTY (A/64/205) (2009).
UN, Report of the ICTY (A/65/205) (2010).
UN, Report of the ICTY (A/66/210) (2011).
UN, Report of the ICTY (A/67/214) (2012).
UN, Report of the ICTY (A/68/255) (2013).
UN, Report of the ICTY (A/69/225) (2014).
UN, Report of the ICTY (A/70/226) (2015).
UN, Report of the ICTY (A/71/263) (2016).
UN, Report of the ICTY (A/72/266) (2017).
UN, Secretary-Generals' Bulletin: Building the future (ST/SGB/1998/6) (1998).
UN, Security Council Resolution 780 Establishing a Commission of Experts to Examine and Analyze Information Submitted Pursuant to Resolution 771 (S/RES/780) (1992).
UN, Security Council veto list: https://bit.ly/2xC8jNo.
UN, Special conditions for recruitment or placement of candidates successful in a competitive examination for posts requiring special language skills (ST/AI/2000/1) (2000).

UN, Special conditions for recruitment or placement of candidates successful in a competitive examination for posts requiring special language skills (ST/AI/2003/1) (2003).
UN, Staff Regulations (ST/SGB/2014/2) (2014).
UN, Staff Rules and Staff Regulations (ST/SGB/2014/1) (2015).
UN, Travel Allowance: https://bit.ly/2wCOQvo.
UN, Verbatim Reporters: https://bit.ly/3chon5R.

ICTY documents

ICTY, About, Tribunal, Organizational chart: https://bit.ly/2wDMpc1.
ICTY, Cases, *Aleksovski*: https://bit.ly/3a6zc9l.
ICTY, Cases, *Babić*: https://bit.ly/2xu5nlK.
ICTY, Cases, *Blagojević & Jokić*: https://bit.ly/2xvikfd.
ICTY, Cases, *Blaškić*: https://bit.ly/34HeFqL.
ICTY, Cases, *Boškoski & Tarčulovski*: https://bit.ly/2Katjxa.
ICTY, Cases, *Bralo*: https://bit.ly/3exZx3I.
ICTY, Cases, *Brđanin*, Decision on motion to set aside confidential subpoena to give evidence (2002): https://bit.ly/3b9NozM.
ICTY, Cases, *Češić*: https://bit.ly/2REgnUC.
ICTY, Cases, *Ćorić*, Decision on motions related to Valentin Ćorić's request for variation of early release conditions: https://bit.ly/2wZGfDo.
ICTY, Cases, *Delić*, Response to urgent defence motion concerning failure of prosecution to comply with Rule 68 (2008): https://bit.ly/2VqCteh.
ICTY, Cases, *Deronjić*: https://bit.ly/34FhWXv.
ICTY, Cases, *Dokmanović*: https://bit.ly/3b8CqdR.
ICTY, Cases, *Đorđević*, Decision on Prosecution's renewed motion for admission of evidence of [witness] pursuant to Rule 92*quater* (2009): https://bit.ly/3a9E9hM.
ICTY, Cases, *Dragomir Milošević*: https://bit.ly/3elDNI5.
ICTY, Cases, *Furundžija*: https://bit.ly/2Vti6gx.
ICTY, Cases, *Galić*: https://bit.ly/34C1esd.
ICTY, Cases, *Gotovina et al.*: https://bit.ly/2XCSyAc.
ICTY, Cases, *Hadžić*: Decision on matters relating to certain documents and transcripts (2014).
ICTY, Cases, *Hadžić*: https://bit.ly/2VhBWg3.
ICTY, Cases, *Hadžihasanović & Kubura*: https://bit.ly/2xn79Fz.
ICTY, Cases, *Halilović*, Decision on motion for exclusion of statement of accused (2005): https://bit.ly/2XyYJ8D.

ICTY, Cases, *Jelisić*: https://bit.ly/2xzee5R.
ICTY, Cases, *Jokić*: https://bit.ly/3erVyFU.
ICTY, Cases, *Karadžić*, B/C/S translation of the Statement of the OTP on the Conviction of Radovan Karadžić (2016).
ICTY, Cases, *Karadžić*, Decision on Prosecution motion seeking determination that the Accused understands English for the purposes of the [ICTY-S] and [ICTY-RPE] (2009).
ICTY, Cases, *Karadžić*, Decision on the Accused's request that all materials, including transcripts, be disclosed to him in Serbian and Cyrillic script (2008).
ICTY, Cases, *Karadžić*: https://bit.ly/3emv88r.
ICTY, Cases, *Kordić and Čerkez*, Decision on appeal regarding statement of a deceased witness (2000): https://bit.ly/2XyXOAb.
ICTY, Cases, *Kovačević*: https://bit.ly/2yiLrSU.
ICTY, Cases, *Krajišnik*: https://bit.ly/2V8G0is.
ICTY, Cases, *Krnojelac*: https://bit.ly/2RCPksS.
ICTY, Cases, *Krstić*: https://bit.ly/3ci7Pe0.
ICTY, Cases, *Kunarac et al.*: https://bit.ly/2V7DeKi.
ICTY, Cases, *Kupreškić et al.*: https://bit.ly/2xr3c2k.
ICTY, Cases, *Kvočka et al.*: https://bit.ly/2Vt3tdi.
ICTY, Cases, *Limaj et al.*, Decision on the Defense motion on Prosecution practice of "proofing" witnesses (2004): https://bit.ly/3elhIJF.
ICTY, Cases, *Lukić*, Judgment on Appeals (2012).
ICTY, Cases, *Lukić*: https://bit.ly/2VvYmJa.
ICTY, Cases, *Martić*: https://bit.ly/2Vwd2bq.
ICTY, Cases, *Milošević*: https://bit.ly/2V8d9uB.
ICTY, Cases, *Mladić*, Decision on Prosecution Rule 92quater motion (2013).
ICTY, Cases, *Mladić*: https://bit.ly/2ybPeBy.
ICTY, Cases, *Mrđa*: https://bit.ly/3bbuyIB.
ICTY, Cases, *Mrkšić et al.*: https://bit.ly/3baYqF5.
ICTY, Cases, *Mucić et al.*, Decision on Defense application for forwarding the documents in the language of the accused (1996).
ICTY, Cases, *Mucić et al.*, Decision on motion of Esad Landžo pursuant to Rule 73 (1997).
ICTY, Cases, *Mucić et al.*, Decision on the motion ex parte by the defence of Zdravko Mucić concerning the issue of subpoena to an interpreter (1997).
ICTY, Cases, *Mucić et al.*, Order on Zdravko Mucić's oral request for Serbo-Croatian interpreting (1997): https://bit.ly/3civnPX.

ICTY, Cases, *Mucić et al.*, Order on Zdravko Mucić's oral request for Serbo-Croatian interpreting (1997).
ICTY, Cases, *Naletilić & Martinović*: https://bit.ly/2yXyqyt.
ICTY, Cases, *Nenad Banović and Predrag Banović*: https://bit.ly/2VvW1Or.
ICTY, Cases, *Nikolić, M.*: https://bit.ly/2VcaKPH.
ICTY, Cases, *Nikolić*: https://bit.ly/3chElNl.
ICTY, Cases, *Obrenović*: https://bit.ly/3bfQt1e.
ICTY, Cases, *Orić*: https://bit.ly/3aejWro.
ICTY, Cases, *Perišić*: https://bit.ly/3ckOLvD.
ICTY, Cases, *Plavšić*: https://bit.ly/2yiieaG.
ICTY, Cases, *Popović et al.*, Public redacted version of 30 November 2012 decision on request to terminate appellate proceedings in relation to Milan Gvero (2013): https://bit.ly/2xjN4zW.
ICTY, Cases, *Prlić et al.*: https://bit.ly/2wFoMQm.
ICTY, Cases, *Rajić*: https://bit.ly/2XyM1Xv.
ICTY, Cases, *Šainović et al.*, Decision on Prosecution request for extension of time to submit corrected translation of exhibit P942 (2007).
ICTY, Cases, *Šainović et al.*, Order RE exhibit P1999 (2007).
ICTY, Cases, *Šainović et al.*, Order RE exhibits 6D132 and 6D1496 (2008).
ICTY, Cases, *Šainović et al.*, Order RE exhibits 6D202 (2008): https://bit.ly/3acmkOS.
ICTY, Cases, *Šainović et al.*, Order RE exhibits P2166 and P1506 (2008).
ICTY, Cases, *Šainović et al.*, Second order on exhibits P2885, 1D279, 1D671, 4D3, 4D95, 4D106, and 5D272 (2008).
ICTY, Cases, *Šešelj*, B/C/S translation of the Information on the Partially Dissenting Opinion of Judge Lattanzi in Judgement in the case of Vojislav Šešelj (2016).
ICTY, Cases, *Šešelj*, B/C/S translation of the Statement of the OTP on the Judgement of Vojislav Šešelj (2016).
ICTY, Cases, *Šešelj*, Decision on defendant's motions concerning the quality of interpreting (2008).
ICTY, Cases, *Šešelj*, Decision on motion for admission of [witness] testimony pursuant to Rule 92*quater* (2009).
ICTY, Cases, *Šešelj*, Judgment Summary (31 March 2016): https://bit.ly/3emZqrx.
ICTY, Cases, *Šešelj*: https://bit.ly/2z0oRir.
ICTY, Cases, *Sikirica et al.*: https://bit.ly/2K84Cl6.
ICTY, Cases, *Simić et al.,* Ex parte confidential: Decision on the

Prosecution motion under Rule 73 for a ruling concerning the testimony of a witness (1999): https://bit.ly/2XGmmvM.
ICTY, Cases, *Stakić*: https://bit.ly/3ciqMNG.
ICTY, Cases, *Stanišić and Simatović*: https://bit.ly/3acGxUK.
ICTY, Cases, *Stanišić and Župljanin*: https://bit.ly/2V5HCte.
ICTY, Cases, *Strugar*: https://bit.ly/2xy7zIZ.
ICTY, Cases, *Todorović*: https://bit.ly/3ckVhCw.
ICTY, Cases, *Tolimir*: https://bit.ly/3bkrzxi.
ICTY, Cases, *Vasiljević*: https://bit.ly/3b9CZEe.
ICTY, Cases, *Zelenović*: https://bit.ly/3acIdho.
ICTY, Cases: https://bit.ly/2xBEH2E.
ICTY, Documents, Defence: Defense Counsel: Pre-Trial Legal Aid Policy (2006).
ICTY, Documents, Defence: Defense Counsel: Trial Legal Aid Policy (2009).
ICTY, Documents, Defence: Directive on the assignment of defense counsel (2006).
ICTY, Documents, Defence: Directive on the assignment of defense counsel (undated), Appendix I.
ICTY, Documents, Defence: Directive on the assignment of defense counsel (undated).
ICTY, Documents, Defence: Frequently asked questions on Translation Requests.
ICTY, Documents, Defence: Remuneration scheme for persons assisting indigent self-represented accused (2010).
ICTY, Documents, Miscellaneous: Code of Professional Conduct for Counsel Appearing Before the International Tribunal (2009).
ICTY, Documents, Miscellaneous: Code of Professional Conduct for Defense Counsel Appearing Before the International Tribunal (2009).
ICTY, Documents, Miscellaneous: Code of professional conduct for the judges of the Tribunal (2016): https://bit.ly/3cu7V2q.
ICTY, Documents, Miscellaneous: Standard of Professional Conduct for Prosecution Counsel (1999).
ICTY, Documents, Miscellaneous: The Code of Ethics for Interpreters and Translators Employed by the Tribunal (1999).
ICTY, Documents, Practice directions: Practice direction on the length of briefs and motions (2001, 2002, 2005).
ICTY, Documents, Practice directions: Procedure for the Proposal, Consideration of and Publication of Amendments to the [RPE] of the International Tribunal (2002).
ICTY, Former judges: https://bit.ly/2VsVpsT.

ICTY, Press, Publications: ADC-ICTY Developed Practices: Manual of International Criminal Defense (2011), UNICRI Publisher: https://bit.ly/2xC2784.
ICTY, Press, Publications: Manual on Developed Practices (2009), UNICRI Publisher: https://bit.ly/2xC2784.
ICTY, Translation and interpreting: https://bit.ly/2XDgtj2.

Newspaper articles and blogs

Brittain, Chloe (undated). Transcription time per audio hour: how long should transcribing actually make? Opal Transcription Services: https://bit.ly/3emrMCj.
Faktor.ba (2016), Podsjećanje na stradanje pjesnikinje Mubere Mujagić: Profesorica kojoj su dohakali Njegoš i Ivan Mažuranić: https://bit.ly/3b7Uxkf.
NPR book reviews (2014), The secret operation to bring Nazi scientists to America: https://bit.ly/2RMGAjR.

Miscellaneous

B&H Court Criminal Defense Section, OKO Reporter: https://bit.ly/2VrjKiS.
Council for Defense of Radovan Karadžić: https://bit.ly/3clS99p.
Defending Milošević! Defending Serbia!: https://bit.ly/3aa6cxm.
EU, Official Journal of the European Union L 280/1 (2010), Directive of the European Parliament and of the Council on the right to interpreting and translation in criminal proceedings.
FIT, Translator's Charter (1963-1994).
ICTR, Cases, *Nahimana et al.*: https://bit.ly/2XzT1Dx.
LinkedIN, Ellen Elias-Bursać: https://bit.ly/2RF8DBF.
LinkedIN, Phillip Hepburn: https://bit.ly/3a5nJa4.
Om3ga solutions, Daktilograf: https://bit.ly/2wEZMbW.
OSCE, Supporting the Transition Process: Lessons Learned and Best Practices in Knowledge Transfer: Final Report (2009): https://bit.ly/3cj6Dab.
OSCE, War Crimes Justice Project (undated): https://bit.ly/2VfRuj2.
SixPack design studio: https://bit.ly/3btol7P.
Statement on release, Zoran Kupreškić, Mirjan Kupreškić, and Vlatko Kupreškić: https://bit.ly/3abF94U.
Statement on release, Biljana Plavšić: https://bit.ly/3cnL6NC.

Statement on release, Dario Kordić: https://bit.ly/2z3Mbf3.
Statement on release, Duško Tadić: https://bit.ly/2xqGXd7.
Statement on release, Ljubomir Borovčanin: https://bit.ly/3biO4mp.
Statement on release, Momčilo Krajišnik: https://bit.ly/3anbBBC.
Statement on release, Radovan Karadžić: https://bit.ly/3ev81bK.
Statement on release: Vojislav Šešelj: https://bit.ly/2K94H8a.
UK, Ministry of Justice (2017), Criminal court statistics quarterly, England and Wales, January to March 2017 https://bit.ly/3cMaUmZ.
UNESCO, Recommendation on the Legal Protection of Translators and Translations and the Practical Means to improve the Status of Translators (1976).